Ceremony Men

SUNY series, Tribal Worlds:
Critical Studies in American Indian Nation Building
———————
Brian Hosmer and Larry Nesper, editors

Ceremony Men

Making Ethnography and the
Return of the Strehlow Collection

JASON M. GIBSON

Front Cover Image: Tim Leura Tjapaltjarri/Peltharr (1972) Emu Ceremonial Dreaming. Powder pigment on composition board, 91.5 × 60.5 cm. Private Collection. © Estate of the artist licensed by Aboriginal Artists Agency Ltd.

Published by State University of New York Press, Albany

© 2020 State University of New York

All rights reserved

No part of this book may be used or reproduced in any manner without written permission. No part of this book may be stored in a retrieval system or transmitted in any form or by any means including electronic, electrostatic, magnetic tape, mechanical, photocopying, recording, or otherwise without the prior permission in writing of the publisher.

For information, contact State University of New York Press, Albany, NY
www.sunypress.edu

Library of Congress Cataloging-in-Publication Data

Names: Gibson, Jason M., author.
Title: Ceremony men : making ethnography and the return of the Strehlow collection / Jason M. Gibson.
Description: Albany : State University of New York Press, 2020. | Series: SUNY series, tribal worlds: critical studies in American Indian nation building | Includes bibliographical references and index.
Identifiers: LCCN 2019036180 | ISBN 9781438478555 (hardcover : alk. paper) | ISBN 9781438478548 (pbk. : alk. paper) | ISBN 9781438478562 (ebook)
Subjects: LCSH: Aboriginal Australians—Antiquities—Collection and preservation. | Australia—Antiquities—Collection and preservation. | Archaeology—Moral and ethical aspects—Australia. | Ethnology—Australia. | Strehlow, T. G. H. (Theodor George Henry), 1908–1978. | Strehlow Research Centre.
Classification: LCC GN666 .G57 2020 | DDC 305.800994—dc23
LC record available at https://lccn.loc.gov/2019036180

10 9 8 7 6 5 4 3 2 1

In honor of
all of the "ceremony men"

Contents

List of Illustrations	ix
Acknowledgments	xi
Language and Orthography	xv
Introduction	1
Chapter 1 Archive and Field	23
Chapter 2 Early *Alhernter* Encounters	47
Chapter 3 Strehlow's Scope	73
Chapter 4 A Balancing Act	97
Chapter 5 *Urrempel* Man	129
Chapter 6 Declarations of Relatedness	155
Chapter 7 The Intermingling of Intimate Narratives	183
Chapter 8 "You're my *Kwertengerl*"	211
Conclusion	239
References	255
Index	293

Illustrations

Maps

0.1	Some of the key places in Anmatyerr country.	xvii
I.1	Approximate distribution of Arandic languages of central Australia.	6
1.1	The Anmatyerr communities.	35
4.1	Ceremonial Festival Sites near Alice Springs. Grayed-out area represents Alice Springs township area.	110
6.1	Approximate location of a number of Anmatyerr sites and estates.	159
7.1	Map of Ingkaparleparl's burial site on the Hanson Creek, south of Ti Tree.	196

Figures

1.1	At Arrarngkerlk hills with Jimmy Haines and Paddy Kemarr.	27
2.1	Ernest Kramer's photograph of some of the men who worked for Thomas Moar at the Woodforde Crossing.	56
2.2	Jack Arlpalywerrng Pwerrerl wearing the hat made for him by F. R. Scott.	59
2.3	Anmatyerr men decorated for althart (a public ceremony) at Tea Tree Well in August 1927.	63

2.4	Urabuta, one of Tindale's Anmatyerr informants.	67
3.1	Arawe-irreke (Raueruka) or "Nathanael."	77
3.2	Mickey Dow Dow gathering *alangkwe* (bush bananas) at Apwerte Irretyepe to the northwest of Alice Springs.	94
4.1	Strehlow's recreation of Aremelareny and Lywenge's drawings of the *ahakey* story (Strehlow Field Diary 1932).	107
4.2	One of the informants at Werlatyatherre (possibly Bob Rubuntja) and T.G.H. Strehlow, the "denizen of the ceremonial ground," in conversation.	113
4.3	"Last views of my Wolatjatara (Werlatyatherre) camp, 6th Oct 1955."	117
4.4	Aileron informants September 6, 1968.	119
4.5	Kenny Penangk Tilmouth at Alcoota Station in 1965.	121
4.6	Alcoota men recording songs to tape in 1965.	123
5.1	With Mark Inkamala at Mpaltyartakerte where some of Ted Strehlow's ashes were laid to rest.	139
5.2	Harold Payne in 1971.	142
5.3	With Harold Payne Mpetyan at Ahalper, April 2015.	143
6.1	Paddy Kemarr at Ti Tree creek camp.	161
6.2	Singing Anmanty at Altywepe keretek, November 2016.	179
7.1	Malcolm Heffernan at Artwertakert, in the vicinity of where his grandfather was buried in 1937.	199
7.2	Paddy Kemarr at the "seed" tree of Ntapwet Ngal.	207

Acknowledgments

This book is the culmination of a decade of my life, and I am indebted to many people who helped me along the way. Naturally, I lay claim to all the weaknesses (as well as the strengths!) remaining in the work but must thank all those who provided me with important intellectual, emotional, and material support.

I am, of course, forever indebted to the many Anmatyerr and Arrernte people who have spoken with me over the years. There have been so many that it would be very hard to name them all, but my closest friends and acquaintances and those who agreed to be recorded deserve special mention: Eric Penangk, Ken Tilmouth Penangk, Jimmy Haines Ngwarray, Paddy Kemarr Willis, Laurie Arwengalker Ngal, Harold "Papelaw" Payne, Andrew Glenn, James Glenn, Rodney Cook Mpetyan, Ronnie McNamara, Huckitta Lynch, Lesley Stafford, Ray Nelson Penangk, Clem Peltharr, Mick Turner Ngal, Tony Scrutton Ngwarray, Sebastian Walker Jupurrula, Bentley Brown, Bruce Brown, Kieran Haines, Alyepe Martin McMillan Kemarr, Tywelam, Ronnie Ross Arempeyareny Penangk, Stuart Petersen, Nathaniel Dixon Ngwarray, Johnny Dixon Peltharr, Martin Hagan, Cindy Presley Penangk, Samantha Greenwood Ngwarray, and April Campbell Pengart. Many of you are friends, and I hope this book can do something to convey my respect. Malcolm Heffernan Pengart was particularly important to the making of this book. I cannot thank him enough for his patient tuition in Anmatyerr language and his gentle instruction in Anmatyerr and Arrernte lifeworlds. Malcolm participated in this research more than anyone else, joining me on fieldwork trips, engaging in archival work, and introducing me to new people across the region.

I am also thankful to many of the staff who have worked at the Strehlow Research Centre over the past ten years, in particular, Adam

Macfie, Michael Cawthorn, Graeme Shaughnessy, Felicity Green, and Mark Inkamala. I also acknowledge the trust placed in me by the Strehlow Board to conduct this work responsibly and with respect to the cultural restrictions placed on much of the material. Shaun Angeles, the present-day Arrernte researcher at the Centre, joined me one some of my journeys to Anmatyerr country, but our conversations began many years earlier during a hunting trip to Arewengkwerte (Yambah Station). Back then we had absolutely no idea that we would one day share a deep passion for the Strehlow collection. He has been an important sounding board over the years.

This research has also benefitted from invaluable linguistic advice from a number of Arandic language specialists. Jennifer Green was extraordinarily generous with her time, and her long association with Anmatyerr people and her knowledge of the language was extremely helpful along the way. David Moore, Mary Flynn, David Strickland, Gavan Breen, Barry McDonald, and Myfany Turpin also fielded my various enquiries, and Paul Albrecht and Gary Stoll, too, each in his own way, gave useful insights and important historical background.

This book has been enriched through a rigorous process of peer review. John Bradley, Rachel Standfield, and Liam Brady at Monash University's Indigenous Studies Centre first guided me through this work during its dissertation stage, whereas Fred Myers and Howard Morphy offered tremendous support in getting this work into publication. I also feel particularly fortunate to have benefitted from correspondence with a range of scholars, including Anna Kenny, Luise Hercus, Charley Ward, Dianne Austin-Broos, and Philip Batty. Richard Gillespie at Museum Victoria, Helen Gardner at Deakin University, and Jane Lydon at the University of Western Australia also offered crucial support and inspiration at various stages. Special thanks are also due to John Kean and Lucas Jordan for their camaraderie in the trials of fieldwork, adventuring, and writing. Lucas was a particularly important companion during my early years on Anmatyerr country, and John not only shared his memories of the Anmatyerr men he knew in the 1970s and 1980s but endured earlier drafts.

Writing and research can be a lonely process, and I am fortunate to have had the support of a wide circle of friends and family. Catherine Nano made her home in Alice Springs open to me whenever I visited central Australia, and Therese Smith was an important reader and editor of the manuscript in its penultimate stage. Most of all, though, Ada Nano, gave her unconditional support over many years. I am forever grateful for her patience with me and my very particular research obsessions. Our son, Arthur Gibson, was also very understanding of his father's seemingly endless work on "chapters" during the early years of his life. Finally, without the wonderful parenting of Peter and Maree Gibson, who taught me the value of listening and learning from others, I would never have had the opportunity or self-belief to venture into the world of scholarly writing.

I thank you all.

Note on Cover Art

The cover of this book features *Emu Ceremonial Dreaming* (1972), an acrylic painting by the Anmatyerr artist Tim Leura Peltharr. The painting was chosen after consultation with Anmatyerr men who agreed the image represented the key themes of the book. At the center of the image is a ceremonial performer representing an Emu "father" who assists male initiates into manhood. On his chest is a black circle denoting the place from which the emu's distinctive, deep drumming sound is made; the black mark on his forehead represents the emu's beak. The shield carried across the back of the performer would normally carry a personal totemic design, while the surrounding painted boards represent groups of "ceremony men" coming together to share their ceremonial knowledge.

Language and Orthography

The orthography favored in this book is the one devised by the Institute for Aboriginal Development (IAD) in Alice Springs and currently in use amongst Anmatyerr and Northern Arrernte communities. This orthography has been developed over a number of years, in close consultation with people across the Arandic-speaking region. Although it is admittedly difficult for the untrained reader to use, once understood this orthography is an invaluable tool for attempting to interpret and pronounce Arandic words. Those interested in understanding why the Arandic languages are spelt using this orthography should read Turpin's *Have you ever wondered why Arrernte is spelt the way it is?* (Turpin, n.d.).

When directly quoting from Strehlow's work, I have included his original Arrernte spelling followed by the current orthographic spelling in brackets or parentheses (e.g., *njinanga* [*anyenhenge*]). Aboriginal language words or phrases have been italicized in the text with the exception of place names, which are capitalized and followed by, where possible, the more commonly known English name in parentheses.

My own translations of Anmatyerr or Arrernte words or phrases are presented in brackets, and at times additional explanatory information may be provided in notes. In some cases, I have had to translate Arrernte or Anmatyerr text that Strehlow left untranslated in his diaries. On these occasions, I have transferred his original rendering of the quote into the accepted contemporary orthography before additionally translating them into English and providing the original Strehlow text in a note. Anmatyerr material is rendered according to the *Central and Eastern Anmatyerr to English Dictionary* (Green, 2010) and the Arrernte material as per the *Eastern and Central Arrernte to English Dictionary* (Dobson and Henderson, 1994). I chose not to use the varied spelling systems currently in use for

Western Arrernte (see Roennfeldt and Western Arrarnta Communities, 2006; Breen et al., 2000).

It should be noted that the Anmatyerr orthography omits word-final "e" vowels that are used in the Eastern and Central Arrernte orthography. For example, *urrempel* (Anmatyerr) and *urrempele* (Arrernte) sound the same although the spellings vary. My spelling choices vary between Arrernte and Anmatyerr depending on context.

A Note on Sources

Strehlow's field diaries are cited throughout the text as manuscripts rather than as archival sources and are listed in the References at the end of the book. These references refer to the typed version of each diary unless handwritten versions only are available. These diaries are kept at the Strehlow Research Centre in Alice Springs and can be accessed via application to the Centre.

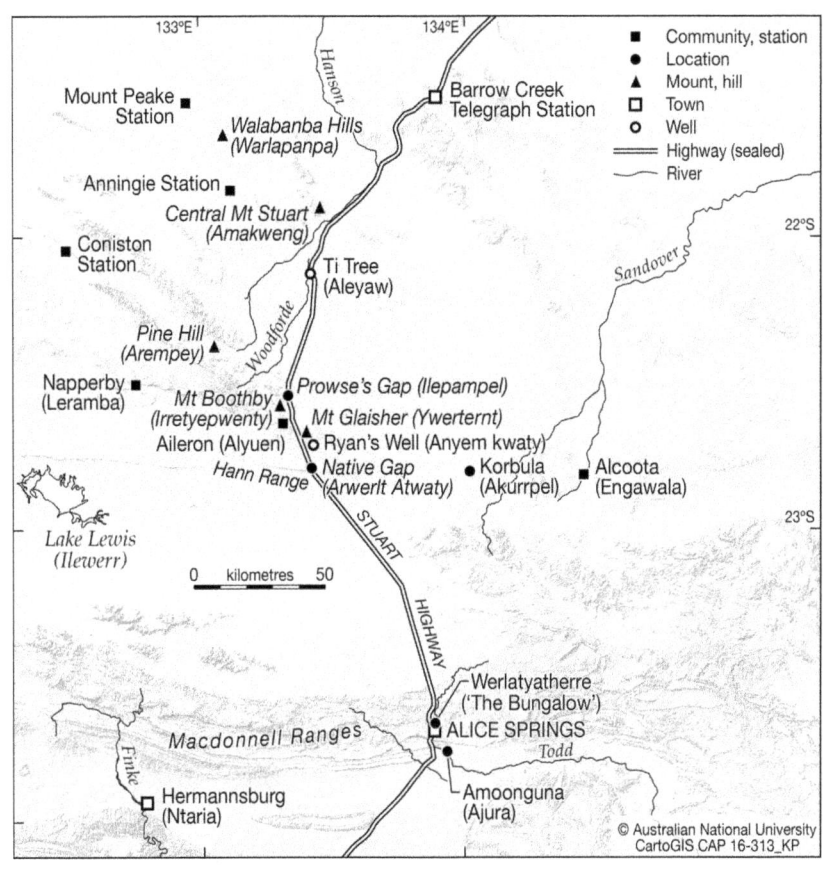

Map I.1. Some of the key places in Anmatyerr country.

Introduction

> The subjects of ethnographies, it should never be forgotten, are always more interesting than their authors.
>
> —R.J. Smith (1990)

In the autumn of 2016, I met with two Arrernte men, Shaun and Martin, who had flown from the remote township of Alice Springs, in the center of Australia, to meet with me at my office in the Melbourne Museum. The purpose of their visit was to discuss the potential return of sacred ritual objects to central Australia. I had known both of these men for a number of years, but Shaun and I had a particularly long association. We had worked together at an Aboriginal youth service in Alice Springs over a decade earlier, and as we struck up a friendship he had taken me on a hunting trip for kangaroo on his homelands at Arewengkwerte. Our paths had diverged over the years, but we had once again come together as professionals in the Indigenous museum and heritage sector. Shaun now worked as a researcher at the Strehlow Research Centre in Alice Springs, and I had returned to my home city of Melbourne where I worked in the museum's Indigenous Cultures Department.

Over a number of days, Shaun and I looked into the history of these sacred objects, with Shaun's uncle Martin providing prudent counsel, pondering how they came to be in the possession of a museum 2,300 kilometers from their place of origin. Our research and discussions meandered along a path that eventually led us back to questions about the degree of agency exhibited by central Australian men in the production of collections such as this. The assumption that collectors and anthropologists had dragooned or tricked these men into handing over their treasured possessions and knowledge proved to be a far too simplistic explanation.

I believed, like so many of the Arrernte and Anmatyerr men with whom I have discussed this history over the past decade, that things were rather different. The Aboriginal informants to Australian ethnographers had not been supplicants or dupes, but rather extraordinary figures who were integral to the story of how ethnographic collections were made. Some even saw their ancestors as visionaries who, knowing the rapid pace of cultural change, had enabled anthropologists to film and record their most secretive ceremonial performances with future generations in mind (Angeles, 2016). Although the reasoning and motivations of these past generations were often unexplained in official histories and anthropological monographs, it was the unearthing of *their* stories that mattered to most central Australian Aboriginal men. What was the nature of their relationship with ethnographers? Why did so many share their most treasured and secretive ritual content? What were they hoping to achieve from these interactions? I also wondered, if we accept the agency and intent of these informants, how does it change the way we understand these collections, and what would it mean for their ongoing and future relevancy?

It is via the collection of one of Australia's most well-known and controversial ethnographers, Theodor George Henry (T.G.H.) Strehlow (1908–1978), and the agency of his predominantly Arrernte and Anmatyerr informants, that these and other questions are addressed in *Ceremony Men*. Although T.G.H. Strehlow's personal biography and his work on Arrernte men's sacred traditions have been well canvassed in the literature, exactly how the interests and motivations of his informants shaped his ethnographic practice, and what these men and their descendants make of his work today, has not been adequately considered. Having spoken with some of the men who performed in front of Strehlow's recording devices or saw him at work, I knew that their side of the story could be told. These men not only had their own particular take on this history but had strong views about the relevancy and value of ethnographic collections.

Almost all research on Strehlow has focused on his relationships with the Arrernte, the group of central Australian Aboriginal people with whom he spent most of his time, but this research had failed to explore his larger presence across the region. My discussions with various Anmatyerr people over the years had alerted me to Strehlow's little-known work with the northern neighbors to the Arrernte, the Anmatyerr. In fact, the richness of Strehlow's ethnography became apparent to me only after I was prompted by Anmatyerr people to look more closely at his collection. As a cultural and linguistic group with deep affinities with the Arrernte, but possessing a distinct identity of their own, the Anmatyerr bring a new perspective to a well-worn historical narrative. For the Anmatyerr, Strehlow and the men he worked with were all *"Urrempel men" or "Ceremony men,"* a cohort of men actively pursuing, demonstrating, and sharing in ritual knowledge. It is the Anmatyerr views on the Strehlow collection and their attitudes toward his collection that fundamentally concerns this thesis.

Anmatyerr men told me many of the same *Anengkerr* (Dreaming) stories that they had revealed to Strehlow. Defined as the narratives of eternal beings that originated at the beginning of creation, the *Anengkerr* concept (like its Arrernte equivalent, *Altyerre*) occupies a central place in Anmatyerr ontologies. These ancestors formed and persist in the landscape, and knowledge of their presence and their actions is expressed in song, storytelling, ritual dance, and artistic design. Although the suitability of "Dreaming" to refer to this concept has been contested because it is seen to diminish and reduce complex Aboriginal belief to something "unreal" (Wolfe, 1991; 1997) the glossing of *Anengkerr* as "Dreamtime" or "Dreaming" does have a salience to contemporary speakers and a firm basis in the semantics of the language (Morphy, 1996; Green, 2012). In time, I came to realize that Strehlow had recorded many of the same songs and stories that people had explained to me, and that I had been taken to many of the same Anengkerr sites shown to Strehlow decades earlier.

This inadvertent "shadowing" of Strehlow and his interlocutors became what anthropologist Michael Jackson (2006) has described as a useful "mode of discovery" in the course of bridging historical events and contemporary interpretations. This process was further aided by the fact that I could take digital copies of the audio recordings made of these songs and the films of their associated ceremonial performances into the field with me. This was the first time that this highly restricted body of knowledge had left the confines of archives and museums and had been allowed to be shared with people in remote Aboriginal communities. Collaboratively unpacking Strehlow's corpus, Anmatyerr perspectives have helped me produce an *historical* and *ethnographic* critique that decouples its contents from the confines of T.G.H. Strehlow's biography.

The Ethnographer T.G.H. Strehlow

To write about T.G.H. or "Ted" Strehlow is in many respects to go over old ground. Subject to two biographies (Hill, 2003; McNally, 1981), often referenced in the history of Australian anthropology and linguistics (Morton, 1995; 2004; Moore, 2008), cited in works of literary and cultural studies (Morrison, 2017; Watson, 2017), and noted in the broader history of "race relations" in Australia (Rowse, 1999; Inglis, 2002), Strehlow's story is relatively well known. Born to German parents at the remote Lutheran mission of Hermannsburg in the Northern Territory in 1908, he was raised learning the language of the predominant Western Arrernte population. His father, the Lutheran Reverend Carl Strehlow, had been stationed at the mission since 1894 and had become an excellent ethnographer and linguist (see Kenny, 2013; Veit, 2004). Strehlow's mother, Frieda, also spoke Arrernte and dedicated herself to the welfare of the mission inhabitants (Strehlow, 2011). In addition to learning the Arrernte language, T.G.H. was also schooled in German and English and came to possess an admirable ability with languages, later completing studies in English Literature, Latin, Greek, and classical studies.

Although young Ted's feet were firmly planted in the traditions of the Old World, in the eyes of his academic mentors it was his fluency in an Aboriginal language that offered him most potential as a scholar (Jones, 2004). He was encouraged to return to central Australia where he, first, put his language skills to use in order to survey the extent and variety of the Arandic languages (of which Anmatyerr was one) (see map 2) and, second, began recording the mythological traditions of the people in this region. To some extent building on his father's earlier work on the Arrernte and Luritja, Strehlow spent close to four decades recording place names, songs, myths, genealogies, and closed men's ceremonies (Strehlow, 1907a). The collection he amassed is not only voluminous but visually and aurally compelling. It contains over twenty-six hours of raw 16mm film footage, depicting over eight hundred unique ceremonies, approximately 150 hours of song recordings, and over eight thousand still photographs of ceremony and landscape. Forty-four meticulously kept and extremely detailed field diaries, as well as over twelve hundred artifacts (mostly sacred objects and ritual paraphernalia), make this the most complete collection of cultural material of any Indigenous people in Australia, and perhaps the world.

Strehlow's approach to ethnography was largely empirical, and he possessed a general distrust of overly theoretical agendas (Gibson, 2017; Austin-Broos, 1997). Although he never read their works, his style resembled the type of linguistically minded, salvage anthropology pioneered by seminal ethnographers in the American tradition, Franz Boas and

Edward Sapir (see Adams, 2016; Hester, 1968; Gruber, 1970). The practice of salvage ethnography had begun in earnest in Australia with the arrival of the Cambridge Anthropological Expedition team, led by Alfred Cort Haddon to the Torres Strait in 1898 and was extended by Walter Baldwin Spencer and Francis James Gillen's during their expedition across Central Australia in 1901 (Haddon et al., 1901; Spencer and Gillen, 1904). Premised on the widely held idea that Indigenous Australians were set to decline upon contact with European society, these expeditions pioneered the use of audio and filmic documentation to record as best they could the unique cultural practices of the people. Strehlow took up the mantle of salvage ethnographer with gusto and, like most of his contemporaries, persistently made the case that urgent research was required before the languages and cultures of Australia completely perished in the face of colonization. In his view, central Australia was becoming increasingly "empty and silent" of song and ritual, and it was his role to save "the last scraps of the local traditions before complete oblivion settled down upon them" (1968a, p. 92).

Strehlow's personal commitment to this project was remarkable. His published outputs revealed a poetic and "literary" quality to Aboriginal culture that had hitherto been imperceptible to the wider public. In the later stages of his career, however, he became ruthlessly proprietorial over his collection and was blinkered to the rights and wishes of contemporary central Australian Aboriginal men. Unlike his counterpart in Australian anthropology, Ronald Berndt, who could see the potential of rich ethnographic collections like this as a source of "social meaning and emotional stability" for Arandic peoples, Strehlow regarded the material as his personal inheritance (Berndt, 1979a, p. 88). The inadvertent publication of a selection of his photographs of secret-sacred ceremonies in a popular Australian magazine and his repeated claims to being the only appropriate heir to Arandic ceremonial traditions almost completely overshadowed his decades of work. Strehlow's collection, as others have noted, became well known "for all the wrong reasons" (Peterson, Allen, and Hamby, 2008a, p. 6).

After Strehlow's death in 1978, the controversies around his collection continued. The extensive compendium of artifacts, recordings, and manuscripts were passed on to his second wife, Kathleen, and their young son Carl. But the great cultural wealth of the material meant that it became the subject of numerous disputes of ownership involving government agencies and Aboriginal organizations (Smith, 2009;

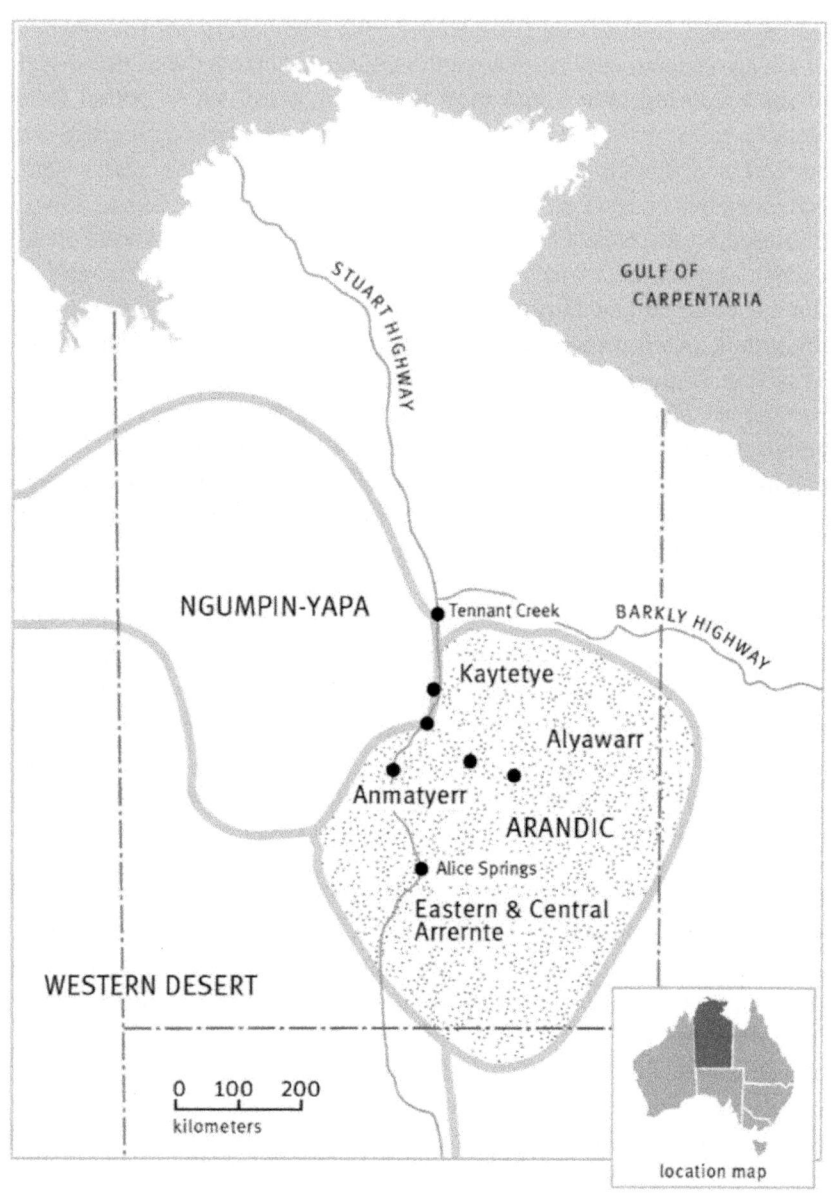

Map I.1. Approximate distribution of Arandic languages of central Australia.

Hugo, 1997). Kathleen covetously guarded the collection as her own and planned to move it overseas. After protracted negotiations, the Northern Territory Government eventually managed to purchase the collection for an undisclosed sum and established a new home for the corpus, back in central Australia, at the purpose-built Strehlow Research Centre in Alice Springs. Since that time, Aboriginal and non-Aboriginal researchers and community members have been able to access the collection, though far more needs to be done in terms of engaging with Aboriginal expertise and understanding the untold story of Aboriginal participation in its creation.

Agency in the Archive

Remarkably few serious attempts have been made to record the perspectives of Aboriginal informants in the making of this ethnographic corpus. Those who have chosen to investigate the degree of Aboriginal agency in this history have tended to look back through Strehlow's accounts for snippets of evidence, while others have simply concluded that it is simply too difficult to fathom their "original intentions" (Kimber, 2004; Morton, 1995, p. 56). None had attempted to significantly reshape their analysis of either the history or the content of the collection via the interpretations and evaluations of contemporary Aboriginal people. Bringing these perspectives to the fore, I take Ann Stoler's advice and cast the Strehlow corpus not as a receptacle of objective knowledge or anthropological fact, but as a site where ethnographic knowledge was, and continues to be, produced (2010). And while I have permitted the *non-archived* evidence of ethnographic experience to inform my analyses, I have constantly returned to Strehlow's collection looking for balance and contrast. As Stoler contends, it is important that we do not move too "quickly and confidently" to readings "against the grain" without moving first *along the grain* and becoming familiar with the archival evidence (2006, p. 100).

The archive offers multiple possibilities for inquiry: for biographical study, for understanding the development of anthropological theorization and methodological practice, and for a critical analysis of the formation of the archive itself. Strehlow's archive is thus treated as a critical starting point to the analysis. Other analyses of colonial archives have demonstrated the process by which the native voices, meanings, and histories were appropriated or erased by "colonial forms and logics of knowledge," and these silences, or omissions, are now widely recognized as a significant evidential source in the making of histories and epistemes (Dirks, 1993, p. 310; see also Sider and Smith, 1997; Trouillot, 1995). These silences occur for a number of reasons. There may simply be a gap in the knowledge being conveyed, a deliberate act of concealment may have occurred, or even more interesting, these silences might involve a strategic concealment by the less powerful hoping to avoid detection or scrutiny (Scott, 1990). Reading the interrelationships of "native informants" and settler-colonial ethnographers back into these histories requires a deeper appreciation of the archive—not so much as a source of anthropological fact, but—as an assemblage of traces waiting for the right question to be put to them.

In this case, where Anmatyerr and Arrernte perspectives on the Strehlow legacy are possible, I tack between the archival/historical and the ethnographic/contemporary to draw out a deeper appreciation of both. Finding evidence of Indigenous agency amongst the archives of colonialism is now a growing area of study. Older ethnographic auction catalogues, explorer's journals, museum and archival sources, as well as early anthropological works are being scoured by scholars looking for evidence of Indigenous accomplishment, presence, or motivation (Torrence and Clarke, 2011; Konishi, Nugent, and Shellam, 2015; Malaurie, 2003; Driver and Jones, 2009; Harrison, Byrne, and Clarke, 2013). Seeking to uncover similar creative responses from Indigenous people to colonial interests and agendas, this work too develops evidence to counter conventional emphases on the achievements of a singular, "heroic," "white" protagonist. By acknowledging the activity of *all* of the participants, I regard ethnographic collections such as Strehlow's as fundamentally co-productions. These assemblages are not simply *found* in the field, but are *made* by agents (Kirshenblatt-Gimblett, 1998, p. 2). Scholarly disciplines and regimes of "collecting, ordering, governing" certainly shape these collections at a structural level (Bennett et al., 2017), but I contend that they are equally representative of the *individuals* and the *relationships* that made them.

The significance of this researcher/researched interrelationships has been of particular concern to anthropology for some time now (Hymes, 1972; Tedlock, 1979; Fabian, 1983), although few have used this dynamic to examine the history and interpretation of an anthropological collection. Beginning with Tedlock and Mannheim's assertion that all ethnography (including Strehlow's and indeed my own) ought to be recognized as an "intercultural phenomenon, produced, reproduced and revised in dialogues between fieldworkers and their subjects" (1995, p. 1), I go further in insisting that the knowledge produced is fundamentally a product of the differential relations *between* the perceiver (anthropologist) and the perceived (informant). Neither are separate entities at all, but "*relations between two coordinates* . . . each serving to differentiate the other" (Holquist, 2000, p. 26). The knowledge produced in the archive or the museum collection, then, cannot be embodied exclusively in either of these categories—researcher or researched—but is a property of their relation.

Introducing Anmatyerr People

In teasing out these relationships I have tried to balance an appreciation of "the archive" against the recollections, commentaries, opinions, memories, and critiques of Anmatyerr people. This involved fieldwork across seven Anmatyerr communities and discussions with over forty men spanning three generations. The majority of these men had neither seen, heard, or read any of the Strehlow materials before, though two of them, Harold Payne and Ken Tilmouth, had acted as informants to Strehlow in the late 1960s and 1970s. Like many of the other men from across the region, they generously offered their explanations of the ceremonies and songs that had been recorded and their views of the present and future value of this material.

The process of eliciting Anmatyerr and Arrernte testimony, as well as documenting the manner in which these people understood and utilized this collection, marks a significant intervention into the narrative of cultural decline propagated by Strehlow and others. In the absence of any ethnographic evidence, most have either assumed that there were "not many senior men" with authoritative knowledge of material collected by Strehlow to provide useful commentary or that the collection is now so "*mysterious*" to Aboriginal people that they "themselves are *unsure* of *who* may see *what*" (Cohen, 2001a, p. 133; Smith, 2009, pp. 85–86, my emphasis). The Anmatyerr and Arrernte responses to the elements of the collection examined in *Ceremony Men* demonstrate just how inaccurate this view is.

While attenuation of ritual knowledge is certainly evident, these presumptions are far too fatalistic and fail to appreciate the different ways that *Anengkerr* (Dreaming), song, ceremony, and place continue to animate the lifeworlds of Anmatyerr people. Senior men, albeit in small numbers, have considerable confidence in song and ritual knowledge, and when given the opportunity, they and others across the generations have been able to illuminate this collection with surprising adroitness. As well as this continuity, though, there are also important sociocultural changes and ontological shifts that have occurred since the mid–twentieth century (chapter 8) that need to be understood not simply as deficiencies but as creative adjustments made during the tumultuous times of colonial Australia in the twentieth century.

It is important to point out, however, that these Anmatyerr perspectives and experiences are not necessarily shared by the Arrernte. The distinctive histories and experiences of the two groups make their interpretations and interests in the collection quite distinct from one another. Unlike Arrernte populations who have had to grapple with two competing Christian missions (Catholic in the east and Lutheran in the west) and the expanding township of Alice Springs (in the center of Arrernte territory), the Anmatyerr have suffered comparatively less settler intervention in their region. Anmatyerr traditional lands have never hosted a sizeable township, mission, or government settlement, and their interactions with *alhernter* (Europeans) have been shaped almost solely by a long-term engagement with pastoralism. The Anmatyerr have also received far less attention from ethnographers than have the Arrernte, who are recognized as one of the most closely studied Aboriginal groups in Australia. They would later feature in Emile Durkheim's *The Elementary Forms of Religious Life* (1915) and to a lesser extent in Freud's *Totem and Taboo* (1913).

Given these links and the geographical proximity of the Anmatyerr to the Arrernte, as well as their significant ties in ritual, language, and kin, it is unsurprising that Strehlow was drawn into their territory. As a result, he filmed seventy-two separate ceremonial performances (what he labeled as "acts") between 1953 and 1965 and recorded thirty Anmatyerr songs. He traveled across the length and breadth of their traditional lands twice (first in 1932 and again in 1968), and also made a number of brief forays into their region over the years, mapping a large number of significant sites associated with the songs and mythologies. There are also a number of Anmatyerr-specific "family trees" detailing the names and totemic affiliations of 370 individuals. Over fifty Anmatyerr men helped Strehlow compile this material, and it now stands as the most extensive ethnography of the Anmatyerr people produced prior to introduction of land rights anthropology in the late 1970s (which was used to establish Aboriginal rights to land under Australian law).

This concentration on Anmatyerr experiences should not, however, suggest that I have altogether disregarded the perspectives of Arrernte people. Senior men like Ken Tilmouth Penangk and Paddy Kemarr repeatedly told me that "Arrernte and Anmatyerr are the same" and that the linguistic, kin, and cultural connections between the two groups was extensive. Tired of these orthodox categories, which position individuals as representatives of a particular "tribe" or "language group," some people looked for alternatives. When pressed on the issue, Paddy, for example, would describe himself as being *Kal ntheyelkwer*, making reference to the "old language" spoken by people from the western Anmatyerr region, while others used "*Artety unanth*," an ethnonym referring to the "mulga scrub" environment of the central and northern Anmatyerr area. Leaving the limitations of classification to one side, contemporary speakers of Anmatyerr nonetheless agree that they do have a distinct identity.

There are now well-entrenched attitudes and opinions about the Strehlow collection among the Arrernte community. Some Arrernte people argue that Strehlow was a duplicitous or even corrupt character that dispossessed them of their cultural heritage. Others speak of him with great fondness. Regardless, most will admit that the Strehlow collection is an important cultural resource for future generations as they rediscover details about their traditions and family histories and use the material as evidence in land claims (see Malbunka, 2004; Wilmot and Morgan, 2010; Kenny, 2013, pp. 187–193). To the Anmatyerr, though, Strehlow is a marginal historical figure of little significance to their cultural history or future. As their communities are located hundreds of kilometers from Alice Springs, where the Strehlow Research Centre is located, and their interactions with Strehlow were far fewer to begin with, their utilization of this collection has been much less frequent and far less political. Their distance from the controversial, and at times politicized, discourse surrounding this material gives Anmatyerr perspectives a distinctive freshness and invites innovative thinking about the value of such a collection.

Belonging to Men

There is an obvious absence of female perspectives in this research, but this omission is not accidental. Strehlow's collection is almost exclusively focused on the song and ritual practices of men and is commonly understood as being utterly forbidden to women. One of the hallmarks of Central Australian Aboriginal society is the particularly strong divisions between male and female roles and responsibilities (Collmann, 1988). These gendered domains are evident in everyday interactions, but are particularly strong when it comes to the ritual sphere, where men and women generally have their own songs, dances, rituals, and mythological descriptions (Spencer and Gillen, 1899; Elkin, 1935; Berndt, 1974). While these gendered domains share a great deal and will at times intermingle, men's ritual in Central Australia is generally demarcated as "men's business," or in Anmatyerr as "*artwekenh*," literally "belonging to men." This male sphere is highly secretive and its contents closely guarded by men with the requisite ritual knowledge and social standing (Myers, 2014; Jones, 1995a).

The lives of Central Australian Aboriginal women, children, and the uninitiated were largely cordoned off in Strehlow's ethnography, as were the everyday, mundane aspects of social life. His ethnography was in no way expansive and never attempted to describe the heterogeneous nature of Arandic being or domestic community life. Myopically focused on male ritual and myth, women barely figure in his broader ethnographic scheme and are only cursorily noted (1971a, pp. 650–653). Like most of his contemporaries, Strehlow accepted that female song and ceremony was secondary in a religious domain seemingly controlled by men (Bell, 1984; Elkin, 1935, p. 197). Subsequent research has of course shown just how much women participate in ceremonial life, how they maintain their own song and ceremonial traditions, and how they may also be privy to some of the song and ceremonial traditions of men (Moyle, 1986, pp. 76–127; Bell, 1985; Bradley and Yanyuwa Families, 2010, pp. 173–177). But for Strehlow these concerns lay far beyond his interests.

Strehlow's close proximity and involvement in the secretive male ritual world has made it very difficult for him to cross over into the female domain. To do so would have almost certainly caused suspicion among his male informants and raised anxieties about what he might inadvertently reveal to women. Mick Werlaty Pengart, one of Strehlow's most important Anmatyerr informants in the 1960s, for example, explained that Strehlow's Land Rover "was known everywhere as a sort of travelling 'sacred cave' (*maka maka*) and that no women could normally approach it or even look in its direction" (T.G.H. Strehlow, 1964a, p. xx). Arrernte men today similarly recall that when they saw Strehlow's car arrive in their communities, women and children knew to keep well clear. Martin

McMillan Kemarr was a young boy when he remembered seeing Strehlow arrive at the Santa Teresa Mission:

> I saw it from a long way . . . Didn't interfere or anything . . . That's when all the kids were running around everywhere. And we said "Hey, there is a stranger over there!" . . . I was hiding you know. I didn't know what was going on. I thought that must be *akiw* (men's ceremony camp) or something. So, we sneaked away and hid ourself . . . didn't say anything after that, nothing.

The secrecy and restrictions associated with men's ceremonial matters continue to be taken extremely seriously by Arrernte and Anmatyerr people. The Strehlow Research Centre building, widely understood by the local Aboriginal populace of Alice Springs as a place of "men's business," is often described as being "*amek-amek*" (restricted or off-limits) (see chapter 9). Only the "family trees" (genealogies) and a small number of nonceremonial photographs are ever accessed by women, and even in these cases some women approach the building with a degree of caution and will often send in other researchers or friends to collect information on their behalf. Female perspectives and analyses of this collection—while not impossible as the work of both Anna Kenny (2014) and Dianne Austin-Broos (2009) have shown—is nonetheless incredibly difficult when the ceremonial content of the collection is being considered.

While it is conceivable that some senior women will have knowledge of aspects of these songs and ceremonies, this cannot, as Eric Michaels has observed, be confused with the right to speak publicly about these matters (1985, p. 508). I was therefore careful not to elicit or invite the views of women during the course of this research out of respect for their responsibilities in this predicament. Moreover, I wanted to ensure that my own reputation among the male Arrernte and Anmatyerr community was not jeopardized. As the ceremonies and songs discussed herein continue to be treated with extreme sensitivity and secretiveness, serious limitations have been placed on how I present and discuss this material. Strehlow's methodical explanations and translations of song texts, and his detailed descriptions of ceremonies as well as visual evidence of the ceremonies, cannot be reproduced here. Accordingly, the deeper clarifications and explanations of the ritual or mythological proffered by the men I spoke with have been deliberately truncated, rendered with intentional ambiguity, or excluded. To be doubly sure of the acceptability of the information presented in this book, an iterative process of writing was also adopted whereby interview transcripts and extracts were discussed with the relevant people prior to submission.

The Relational, History, and Ethnography

In devising an analytical framework, *Ceremony Men* draws on several disciplines, including sociocultural anthropology, history, and museum studies. Ultimately an empirically driven study, unbound by any specific theoretical model/s, I have sought to understand the making of this archive and its interpretation today through a conceptual approach that resonates with strands of thinking associated with dialogical, phenomenological, and existentialist anthropology (Jackson, 1996; Desjarlais and Throop, 2011; Dastur, 2010; Ram and Houston, 2015; Jackson and Piette, 2015; Jackson, 2005; 2013). At the heart of this approach is an emphasis on the relationships between informants and ethnographers and the production of ethnographic knowledge. Michael Jackson's prioritizing of "radically empirical" research that honors the sites of lived social experience where "meanings are made, will is exercised, and reflection takes place" has been particularly influential (1996, p. 22).

Understanding the social world in this way means that if we are to appreciate what the Strehlow collection means to people today, as well as appreciate its history, we can best deliver this via fieldwork and shared practical activity. Expressed in another way, I have written this book in a manner that stresses the perceptions and experiences of people and their social contexts first and foremost, even where historical material is the original impetus. Interpretation of the collection and its history is conducted from this vantage point rather than via recourse to conceptual abstractions like the "Indigenous" and "non-Indigenous" binaries or through the lens of historically determined and structural relationships. Chris Anderson, a museum anthropologist with wide-ranging experience in the repatriation of culturally significant objects across Australia, has called for similar particularistic and local analyses:

> The focus on gross structural relations in Australian history has precluded or ignored micro-ethnographic and historical accounts of what actually happened on the ground. Also in

> the re-telling (reinvention?) of colonial encounter, social action has been all but left out. The battle lines have been too sharply drawn. (Anderson, 1995a, p. 1)

I have therefore tried to write close to the contents of local history and experience in a way that potentially unsettles some of the binaries that now commonly circulate these politicized histories. Even though I adopt a decidedly less politicized language than the "subaltern studies" of postcolonial theory, I do nevertheless share their deep concern with non-Western, subjective experiences, memories, and personal journeys (Gandhi, 1998; Spivak, 1988; Chandra, 2015). Challenging the well-established epistemological divisions in Western scholarship that mark off the world of the "objective" European intellect from the world of the "irrational" or "authentic" Indigene, I try to gain a better appreciation of ethnographies as being sites of encounter and exchange (Sahlins, 1995; Povinelli, 2002; Merlan, 2006; Hinkson, 2005). Accepting that such categories are mutually constituting, historically contingent, and ultimately too porous to be definitively bounded, I use the term "intercultural" to again draw attention to this relationality (Myers, 2002; Merlan, 2005; 2013; Smith and Hinkson, 2005; Sullivan, 2006; Abercrombie, 1998; Ottosson, 2016). Rather than developing a narrative that pits Strehlow, the "non-Indigenous" linguist-ethnographer, against the "Indigenous" Anmatyerr and Arrernte, I chose to look for the ways in which cultural differences are mediated, intermingled, and interrelated.

The theme of relationality is further explored as I investigate the relationship between historical material and contemporary lives. Here I have tried, as Austin-Broos (2009) does in her exploration of Arrernte cultural identity and its connections with the past, to use my own experience as means of developing an interpretive understanding. Away from the Australia deserts, anthropological explorations of Indigenous people's reactions and interpretations of archival and museum objects have also proven equally motivating. Haidy Geismar's (2009) collaborative return of early twentieth-century photography to the Indigenous people of Vanuatu and Orin Starn's (2004) collaborative research with the Indigenous peoples in northern California into the fate of Ishi, the so-called "last" of the Yahi people, each highlight the value of shared discovery. The chapters in this book expose my interactions with people to varying degrees. These are woven into the narrative so as to illustrate how ethnographic understanding is never arrived at in a neutral or disengaged manner but is negotiated and tested in relationship with others.

Though not losing sight of the historically conditioned inequalities that underpin the physical, political, and legal structures in settler colonial states such as Australia, I use descriptions of the relational, experiential, and local to guide my analysis. Structural issues are not discarded in discussions of historical or present interactions, but neither do they take on a primacy. Jackson puts it this way:

> What is critical about experience is that it is at once determined by historically located or socially constituted pre-understandings and at the same time never entirely reducible to such pre-givens. (Jackson, 2015, p. 294)

As chapters 3, 4, and 5 in this book demonstrate, changing historical, colonial, and economic contexts, including the early period of colonial violence in the Northern Territory of Australia, undoubtedly set the tone of relationships with ethnographers and settlers more generally. Many Central Australian Aboriginal people also came to know T.G.H. Strehlow either via his work with colonial authorities in "Native Affairs" or through his scholarly research, which was generally enabled by significant university and government funding and aided by local pastoralists. In chapters 6 and 7, Anmatyerr men explain the interactions with Strehlow with reference to some of these larger historical, socioeconomic considerations. These descriptions allow for issues of power to enter the analysis, as they are constituted in personal or group experiences, rather than emanating from theoretical models.

As such, I have tried to avoid reducing these complex interactions between people and groups to an interplay between powerful colonial apparatuses and "anticolonial responses" (Veracini. 2011, p. 3). To do so would leave little space for the somewhat "unexpected" political, social, or religious ensembles that emerge during "moments of colonial stress" (Clifford, 2001, p. 478). As Gardener and McConvell (2015) have shown in their analysis of some of the earliest anthropological investigations, colonial expectations often struggle to "contain" the interdependent and personal relationships that arise amid ethnographic work. Strehlow's regular participation and inclusion in ceremonial events (chapter 5 and 6) and the way in which Anmatyerr people now encourage institutions like museums to adopt their own systems of managing this collection (chapter 9) speak to the type of interrelation that has been a characteristic of collections as "contact zones" (Clifford, 1997, pp. 188–219). Contrary to the view that ethnographies and their collections are simply powerful instruments of Western dominance, these collections can become important arenas where "different cultures intersect, interact and are mutually influenced by the encounter" (Clifford, quoted in McCarthy, 2016, p. 5).

Working at the intersection between ethnographic and historical methodologies, I embrace a view of the past that incorporates and welcomes social memory and orality. While some of the more "historical" chapters presented early on (chapters 3, 4, and 5) are based on archival sources, they are too at times mingled with insights derived from my fieldwork. The more "ethnographic" chapters that follow (chapters 6, 7, 8, and 9) are similarly balanced by responding to the contents of the historical archive, although they emphasize Anmatyerr remembrances and versions of events.

Like so many other minority and colonized peoples, the local histories of the Anmatyerr have never been well documented, and their "reserves of memory" have been granted "little or no historical capital" (Nora, 1989, pp. 7–8). Listening to Anmatyerr oral memories was, however, crucial to not only permitting more actors, and more stories, upon the stage of this history, but allowed for my ethnographic experience to function as an interpretive guide to the overall research. I took the phenomenological view that "History" can only ever be understood in response to the changing social contexts of those that interpret and remember it and is thus produced in a dialectical relationship with the present (Jones and Russell, 2012, pp. 270–271; Ram and Houston 2015, p. 18). As such, neither *speaking* nor *writing* is held up here as being a lone purveyor of "historical truth" (Platt and Quisbert, 2007, p. 123). It was through the weighing-up of orally transmitted "Indigenous histories" in the "present" and the histories of Indigenous people written from a "European point of view" that insights were gained.

Despite the sincere efforts of some historians who have striven for a more anthropological understanding of colonial encounter (e.g., Dening, 1980; 2004; Clendinnen, 2005), the discipline of history has rarely consulted ethnographies as a path to interpreting the experiences of Indigenous peoples. Fewer historians still have actually carried out fieldwork of their own among these communities to write in a way that reflects the different epistemologies and ontologies of non-Western peoples. Minoru Hokari's work stands out as one of few attempts to delineate a specific "mode of historical practice" of an Indigenous group, although this has been a concern in anthropology for some time (Hokari, 2005; for previous anthropological exlporation on this topic, see Sutton, 1988; Kolig, 2000). In a similar vein, this book emphasizes the manner in which Anmatyerr people's sense of the past is a lived experience, created and maintained through a complex web of relationships between people and Ancestral beings and significant places. These "histories" are often produced via performative acts such as storytelling, singing, and traveling, and are almost always contextualized in terms of specific local experiences and worldviews.

Among the *artety nwanth* (mulga expanse) of Anmatyerr country and the hubbub of life in remote Aboriginal communities, the history of Strehlow's archive really came to life. The songs and ceremonies, recorded long ago with men who are now deceased, produced keen demonstrations of present personal relationships (chapter 7) and evoked the eternal and unchanging presence of *Anengkerr* ancestor beings and their associated stories and places. Field-diary extracts and genealogies likewise invited in-depth discussions of local histories (chapter 6) and led to investigations into the intermingling forces of literacy and orality in these communities, as well as the apparently shifting ontologies of Anmatyerr people (chapter 8). These fuller explications of the collection were not simply "historical" but referred to a present and ongoing value for people across time and space.

Chapter Overview

This book is structured in such a way that explanations of the ethnographic and historical context are first examined, followed by an in-depth, collaborative examination of the different facets of the Strehlow collection. Mindful that all social research is inherently implicated in subjective and intersubjective concerns, chapter 1 begins by laying bare the foundations to my own research endeavor before venturing into a critique of someone else's. This reflexive account addresses some of the issues I encountered as a person of urban-Australian, Scottish-English heritage conducting research with Aboriginal people today. Deeply aware of my own position as someone granted a relatively rare opportunity to work in the often-closed world of central Australian ceremonial content, I focus on some of the issues confronted.

The various archival challenges of working with Strehlow's complex collection are also explained in this chapter. The unpublished field diaries that form the foundation of Strehlow's collection brim with extraordinary detail, but in order to understand their full significance they must be read with reference to his extensive collection of audio, film, map, and artifacts.

Readers must also possess a degree of linguistic and cultural familiarity. One of the primary arguments made here is that collections such as this are almost always best examined in a collaborative manner, by those who possess expertise in the relevant languages, cultural practices, and local histories.

The historical context of Anmatyerr engagements with settler society, and specifically their interactions with ethnographers, is canvassed in chapter 2. In this chapter, the history of these relationships, from the arrival of colonial settlers in the region in the 1870s to the period when Strehlow began his research in the early 1930s, is sketched out. These historical intricacies, where Anmatyerr and *alhernter* people would meet, grapple with each other's worldviews, and enter into zones of cultural translation, were nonetheless carried out within asymmetrical relations of socioeconomic power. Understanding these past engagements (particularly those between ethnographers and Anmatyerr people in the early twentieth century) provides important background to the manner in which people later interacted with Strehlow.

Chapter 3 follows on from this by providing a detailed examination of Strehlow's contributions in the field of ethnography. As the bulk of the literature on Strehlow to date has concentrated on his life story, this chapter instead places far greater emphasis on the substance of his ethnography. Bringing an interest in the classics, literature, and the universality of the human condition with him into the field, Strehlow assumed a unique place among his contemporaries. Beginning with an epistemological critique of Strehlow's rhetoric, this chapter serves as a starting point from which we can better appreciate the way in which he portrayed Indigenous agency in his field diaries and publications.

The relatively unexplored career of Strehlow as a fieldworker is interrogated in chapter 4. Zeroing in on his work with the Anmatyerr, this chapter reveals how methodologies in ethnographic practice underwent considerable changes during the mid- to late twentieth century. Strehlow's fieldwork methods changed considerably over the years, from conducting surveys of language and myth early on, to hosting "ceremonial festivals" for the purposes of documentation, through to intensive mapping of sites in the later period. Using Strehlow's diarized accounts of this history, we examine the intense relationship that developed between a large community of Aboriginal men and this singular character. His frequent presence at ceremonies afforded him the fitting epithet of *Akiwarenye* (a denizen of the ceremonial ground), but as his informants gained greater social and economic freedoms during the social changes of the 1960s, the ageing ethnographer came to feel "disowned."

Anmatyerr remembrances and evaluations of Strehlow are presented in chapter 5. Here, Anmatyerr men reveal their memories of what these exchanges signified and some of the reasons they and their forefathers decided to share their ceremonial patrimony. As in the previous chapter, the narrative of the "extraordinary" anthropologist/ethnographer is challenged and greater emphasis placed on the many Aboriginal men who planned recording events and chose to permit the documentation of their cultural inheritance. These men reworked their own cultural categories to facilitate their sharing with Strehlow and saw his obsessive "following" of mythological narratives ("songlines") as analogous to their own "*urrempel*" or "ceremony" men. In this respect, Strehlow was not unique. He resembled an existing cohort of men who actively sought out an expansive knowledge of song and ceremony.

The impressive collection of ceremonial films and song recordings are closely examined by Anmatyerr men in chapter 6. Seen as not only substantiations of the past but also confirmations of the present, these recordings are shown to be immediately relevant to the lives of present-day Anmatyerr people. Severely disrupting the assumption that loss of ritual knowledge has reduced people's capacity to speak authoritatively for this material, these discussions often reveal an intimate degree of understanding. Despite a noted reduction in a deeper, more involved ceremonial patrimony, the ongoing utilization of song and ceremony, particularly in initiation contexts, has facilitated the retention of much of this knowledge among a handful of senior central Australian Aboriginal ritual experts. Younger generations, too, although less skilled in singing or performing these rites, demonstrate knowledge of the way in which places, mythologies, and people interrelate with the material and make it meaningful.

Contemporary interpretations of the collection are further explored in chapter 7, where particular attention is paid to the collection's manuscript materials. Strehlow's field diaries, maps, and genealogical materials are closely scrutinized via a number of case studies that focus on individual life stories. The analysis is framed by the intersection between social memory in a predominantly oral society and the influences of the written archive. Despite slightly differing opinions among generations on the value of the "written down story," people generally read and decipher this material with direct reference (and deference) to the social memory held by elders. For some middle-aged and younger men, however, the gap between the lived experience of senior people and the "official" historical record now requires an intellectual feat of interpretation. Malcolm Heffernan Pengart's journey through the archives and across the country in search of the story of his grandfather's death demonstrates the manner in which archives can work to help Indigenous peoples better understand the colonial past, but also how orality and place interrelate with this evidence.

In chapter 8 I chart the prospects for the future of the Strehlow collection as a whole. While the logic of repatriation remains the primary rhetorical device through which Indigenous collections are often discussed (at least in academic and institutional circles), the Anmatyerr clearly think about these materials in diverse ways. People's sentiments about current and future relationships to the collection are always made with reference to the centrality of their own ongoing religious and ceremonial practices. Where expert ritual knowledge is faltering, however, the collection is increasingly being used as a site of potential cultural revitalization. In light of this, I contend that the Strehlow Research Centre and museums in general need to shift emphasis toward better embedding Indigenous epistemologies and responding to the mutable research and cultural resource needs of Aboriginal people.

In the concluding chapter I reflect on the ramifications of this study for the historical and anthropological issues raised. I draw together key issues and outline how museums, collections, and the writings produced by anthropologists "return" to ongoing social and cultural processes. Engaging with ethnographic resources can be a fruitful avenue through which we arrive at a better understanding of the human engagements that took place across—and within—the varying colonial relations of the past.

Chapter 1

Archive and Field

> He who stands aloof runs the risk of believing himself better than others and misusing his critique of society as an ideology for his private interest . . . The detached observer is as much entangled as the active participant.
>
> —Theodor Adorno, *Minima Moralia* (1951)

It was with Anmatyerr people that I shared in the excitement of finding song recordings, films, and genealogies in the Strehlow archive. It was via their generous guidance and explanations that I came to appreciate what the archive meant for them. Our relationships deepened over the course of this exploration, but in many cases they did not begin there. Beyond this scholarly quest were times where we came together over the years to share in life's larger joys and struggles; we celebrated births, mourned deaths, grappled with sickness and stress, and shared in new discoveries. But it was the very act of ethnography itself that created the bonds of connection, the "matrix of significant relationships" that otherwise may not have formed (Gergen and Gergen, 2002, p. 12).

In "the field" I did not simply encounter "a culture" and its representatives, but met with "the presence, personality and character" of individuals (Tamisari, 2014, p. 7). These acquaintances undoubtedly affected my comprehension of Anmatyerr social life, but it must be noted that they also influenced my handling of the historical sources. Although certainly informed by a rigorous reading of every element of Strehlow's collection, my readings of this archive were always negotiated and tested within a field of interpersonal relationships. Field diaries, song recordings, films, and genealogies, for example, were read in ways that connected them to contemporary people, and as I discovered new items, I would quickly ensure that materials were shared with the relevant individuals or families. These affective qualities of research, whilst almost always present but seldom acknowledged by scholars (see Robinson 2010), motivated my pursuit of further knowledge. I enjoyed the frisson of knowledge and experience co-joined.

While the relationships ethnographers establish with their informants is now recognized as fundamental to most anthropological projects (Jackson, 1998; Behar, 2008; Madison, 2012), opinions vary about how critical they are to epistemological questions. Given that in many ways this book hinges on a critique and interpretation of another anthropologist's work, it is important that my own motivations and influences are laid bare. All studies of people are, as Johannes Fabian reminds us, "questionable representations unless they show their own genesis" (1990, pp. xiv–xv). Having had a connection with Anmatyerr and Arrernte people for more than a decade, my experiences with them have provided important "headnotes" and given me reasons to delve into the details of Strehlow's collection. Including this subjective and intersubjective dimension does not necessarily erode objectivity but stands as a "commitment to methodological description" (Watson, 1987, p. 31) and may in fact be regarded as "a key instrument for the establishment of objective knowledge" (Kapferer, 2007, p. 82). As the following chapters reveal, my active participation in the return of Strehlow's collection in collaboration with numerous Arrernte and Anmatyerr men ultimately led to the type of "knowledge" that I have been able to produce about it.

Prior Interactions

I had known most of the men who agreed to work with me in this research for close to a decade or more. I first began working with Anmatyerr people in 2005 when I was employed by the Northern Territory Library to establish a digital archive of cultural and historical materials in the township of Ti Tree (see Gibson, 2007; 2009; Nakata et al., 2008; Gibson, 2008). Located almost at the center of the Australian continent and approximately two hundred kilometers from the nearest township of Alice Springs, Ti Tree is little more than a roadside stop on a remote stretch of the Stuart Highway. Positioned in the heartland of the Anmatyerr people's traditional territory, though, it serves as an important service center for the Anmatyerr people living in a number of remote communities and outstations (family "homelands") dotted across the region.

At Ti Tree, I came to know not just the Anmatyerr people who lived in the township or in the nearby communities of 6 Mile (Pmara Jutunta) and Nthwerrey (Nturiya), but also other Anmatyerr people who would pass by Ti Tree to pick up supplies or access services. I also came to know many of the older people who lived on the western fringe of the Ti Tree at "Creek Camp," an unofficial camp consisting of makeshift *iltha* (humpies) made of mulga branches, corrugated iron, and other found objects. I spent four years working for the Northern Territory Library in a hands-on support role to the Anmatjere Regional Council's establishment of its Anmatjere Library and Knowledge Centre at Ti Tree. Put simply, my task was to support the community at Ti Tree, but also the Arrernte community at Santa Teresa (Ltyentye Apurte), in the establishment of what the then Minister for Local Government, John Ah Kit, described as an "Indigenous Knowledge Centre." Originally conceived as a service that combined museum, library, and archival functions, the centerpiece of the Knowledge Centre service eventually became a digital collection of historical and cultural materials relevant to the local community.

As I was engaged in the training of Anmatyerr men and women in the management of their collections, I reflected on the various practical and theoretical issues that arose (Nakata et al., 2008; Gibson, Lloyd, and Richmond, 2011; Gibson 2007; 2009). Developing these local compilations required not only extensive research into the history of the region but meant working with people to record their own stories. This led to the recording of oral histories, the mapping of key cultural and social historical sites and people's commentaries on various archival materials: objects, audio recordings, photographs, and more. Given this focus on Central Australian Aboriginal history, my employers placed me in a spare office at the Strehlow Research Centre, one of the few research institutions in the Northern Territory and the place where the Strehlow collection was housed. This decision, though based purely on the best allocation of government resources, had long-lasting repercussions for me. Having an office here, whilst not being employed by the Centre, meant that I had a unique opportunity to observe how the collection was being used on a daily basis without being drawn into internal organizational affairs or local politics. I also worked closely with the Strehlow Research Centre staff in producing digital copies of some of the Strehlow collection materials for people at Santa Teresa and Ti Tree.

Knowing that the bulk of Strehlow's collection consisted of ceremonial, and thus secret-sacred material, my research began with those parts of the collection that were classified as "open" or "nonrestricted." In the main, this consisted of historical photographs and genealogies. The content aroused great interest from the Anmatyerr men and women that I knew in Aleyaw (Ti Tree), but in the predominantly Catholic community of Santa Teresa the Arrernte people associated with the library were far more guarded. For them, Strehlow was generally regarded as having exploited the trust of the old men, and thus anyone affiliated with the Strehlow Research Centre, or even anthropology generally, was to be treated with caution. In Ti Tree, though, Strehlow was remembered and discussed without fear or anxiety, partly due to his association with the Lutheran church that has been active in the Anmatyerr communities for over fifty years.

My keen interest in the collection deepened as Anmatyerr people helped me understand Strehlow's anthropology and I became more adept at reading Strehlow's orthography of the Arrernte language. Recognizing how fully engrossed I had become in the material, the Strehlow Research then asked for my assistance with producing detailed indexes for Strehlow's field diaries. At the same time, I would occasionally travel with Anmatyerr people on hunting trips and visit important sites associated with the *Anengkerr*, and I spent my weekends learning about the Arrernte and Anmatyerr languages with my language tutor and mentor Malcolm Heffernan Pengart. I began to delve into Strehlow's field diaries as part of my work and was often surprised by the similarities between Strehlow's experiences with Anmatyerr people and my own. The language, the concepts, the people, and the places that I read about in the Strehlow collection and discussed with Anmatyerr and Arrernte people were not reified in the historical past—they were still existing in the lives and the landscape of the region. This perspective jarred with the oft-heard lament of historians and anthropologists in Alice Springs that knowledge of place names, songs, and stories among the younger generations was deficient, or perhaps even absent.

At the request of the then Chairman of the Anmatyerr Regional Council, Tony Scrutton Ngwarray, I began researching the restricted contents of Strehlow's work. Initially, the Strehlow Research Centre staff seemed unsure as to whether the collection contained much Anmatyerr material at all, and we began searching the archives. The search nearly came to a stop when it was discovered that a researcher had annotated the so-called "Tjurunga Register," Strehlow's inventory of sacred objects, with the note "no Unmatjera material." Yet it was evident from Strehlow's published works that the Centre had to contain at least a small amount of audio, visual, and manuscript material of relevance to Anmatyerr people. Tony was particularly interested in discovering if Strehlow had collected any songs or stories that might be of relevance to him and his immediate family.

Continuing with my research in the archive, I soon came across an hour-long ceremonial film from 1965 featuring a large group of Anmatyerr performers at Alcoota Station. Thrilled by the discovery, I called Tony and invited him in to visit me at the Centre. As we read through the documentation, Tony quickly recognized the name of one the informants listed by Strehlow, "Kenny Ebmalamaraka" Penangk (Strehlow, 1965a, p. 157). Ken was now an elderly man, Tony explained, and regarded as one of the most senior and knowledgeable Anmatyerr men alive. His

Figure 1.1. At Arrarngkerlk hills with Jimmy Haines, Paddy Kemarr (hidden behind Jimmy), and Davey Presley (in background). August 2, 2008. Photo: L. Jordan.

traditional country lay to the northeast of Alice Springs, an area on the Arrernte and Anmatyerr "border," known as Atwel. Tony's adoptive grandfather, Eric Penangk, came from this area, and Tony was obviously excited about alerting Ken to this archival discovery. Within hours Tony had returned with Ken and Ken's son, Kevin, in tow.

For the first time, Ken watched all of the twenty-three film reels of silent color film without interruption. The films depicted a group of men proudly displayed with ceremonial prowess as they made highly complex ceremonial objects from all-natural materials. Leading proceedings was Ken's father, Mick Werlaty, and a young Ken could often be seen on the film assisting his *angey* (father) and busily preparing ceremonies for the sacred place of Akwerrperl (Korbula). Muttering only the occasional commentary throughout the screening, Ken was transfixed. At times he lifted a hand to interrupt the viewing and instruct others in the room about the particular *Anengkerr* (Dreaming) ancestors being represented in the ceremonies, or to explain their connections to particular places, but mostly he remained silent. At the conclusion of the eighty-minute screening, Ken stood up, shook his head in disbelief, and thanked me for instigating the event. He left the building with Kevin and Tony, saying little else. From my office window, though, I could see the three men outside in the car park excitedly discussing the film, and I knew much more could be done with the Strehlow collection.

Ken returned intermittently to the Strehlow Research Centre over the next few years to work with the Centre's anthropologist, Adam Macfie, on matching the silent, color film reels with the tape recordings made of the associated songs. Being able to identify the particular segments of song from the separate audio recordings, Ken helped Adam overlay excerpts from Strehlow's recordings of the Akwerrperl songs to their relevant ritual sequences using digital editing software. Under Ken's instruction, the silent singers on the film (including himself) were finally given a voice. This was the first time in the collection's history that an Arrernte or Anmatyerr person had actively worked on piecing together Strehlow's recordings. The potential for collaborative research into this collection was obvious.

Positioning

These early conversations and experiences fundamentally shaped the way I came to understand Strehlow's work. But finding the best academic framework from which I could explore this collection and its import for people today was never an easy task. When discussing this material with Anmatyerr and Arrernte people, I was at times asked if I was an anthropologist. The question was never easy for me to answer. In addition to being acutely aware of the vexed history of anthropology and its associations with colonialism (see Starn, 2011; Wolfe, 1999), as well as its tendency to fetishize tradition and objectify people, I was also mindful of the fact that most anthropologists in Central Australia were engaged in far more pragmatic tasks. These anthropologists were usually employed by the Central Land Council, a large and bureaucratic representative body for Aboriginal people in this part of Australia, and needed to attend to pressing material and political issues, usually associated with people's rights in land. These overworked employees usually had little opportunity to consider people's engagements with historical collections or delve into the minutia of song or ceremonial traditions.

I mostly baulked at the "anthropologist" label and preferred instead to straddle the disciplinary boundaries of ethnography and history. I was thus pleased when senior Anmatyerr elder Paddy Kemarr would introduce me using the ambiguous category of a "culture man" or someone "belonging to *tywerreng-thayt*," which I interpreted as meaning someone privy to aspects of men's ceremonial content but also being beholden to the limits and parameters of this knowledge. His ascription allowed a skirting of professional boundaries and scholarly definitions and permitted for fairly free-flowing exchanges. The alternate label of "historian" also felt similarly ill-fitting given the potential value of this material to present and future generations. My experience with "historical archives" suggested to me that the clearly demarcated discipline of "history" never really gained much currency in these communities anyway. As anthropologist Fred Myers noted following his time with the Pintupi of the Western Desert, the dividing lines between the phenomenal and the noumenal were fundamentally blurred in these societies as the fundamental ontology of the Dreaming ensured that the provinces of "past" and "present" were not always clear cut (1991, pp. 48–54). The "Dreaming," derived from a translation of the Arrernte word *altyerrenge*, referred to the concept of an eternal presence. The Ancestors of the Dreaming were eternally present in land, embodied in people, and reaffirmed in songs and ceremonies. Although Aboriginal people in Central Australia had certainly come to acquire a "history-consciousness" (Kolig, 2000, p. 27) and would engage with history-bearing media such as books, television documentaries, and the like, the localized narratives that explained links between people, land, and Dreaming remained critical.

The Strehlow materials had been recorded within recent lifetimes (between 1932 and 1971) and resonated deeply with people's living memories, as well as their present-day interpretations. As Tony Ngwarray put it to me one day, "We still have our ceremony you know . . . we could do a 'Strehlow part two'"—meaning that we could record and document Anmatyerr song and ritual, just as Tony's relatives had done with Strehlow in the past. Tony's rhetorical invitation rejected the purely historical purview and spoke to a desire among Anmatyerr people generally, to declare, communicate, and demonstrate the import of their ceremonial knowledge practices today. As I came to realize, these were also often the motivations of Strehlow's informants.

My work over the years had focused on the practical issues of improving access to cultural and historical materials, and it was clear to me just how cherished these items were. Historical and cultural resources such as photographs, song recordings, films, and genealogies were prized and rare documents in communities where heritage services such as museums, libraries, and archives were nonexistent. Only Ti Tree had a library facility; every other Anmatyerr community lacked local historical or cultural services. In return for providing access to this type of material, people would often encourage me to sit and listen to their interpretations and make a record of their rejoinders to the archive. These experiences greatly expanded my knowledge of Anmatyerr worldviews.

The cumulative effect of these exchanges was not lost on the people I worked with, who at times would comment that making an *alhernter* (white person) knowledgeable in these matters often worked in their favor by building sympathies or strategic alliances. As one younger man in his thirties noted during a discussion concerning people from another cultural group who were struggling to find evidence of their history in museum collections: "We're all right, though. We've got you. You work with us, together." Others would be more forthright in offering, "*Unta Anmatyerr-akin*" (you are also Anmatyerr), a generous indication of my attempts to achieve a better understanding of Anmatyerr social lives.

Those less familiar, though, would occasionally refer to me with the generic appellation of "*warlpal*" (white person) or "*alhernter*" (lit. pink/red nose). With all its connotations of personal anonymity and cultural boundedness, the use of such a generic, racial description inferred a long history of interactions with a seemingly endless flow of transient "whitefellas" through Aboriginal communities. Working relationships like this have emerged as significant sites of cultural mediation between Aboriginal and non-Aboriginal throughout Australia (see Batty, 2005) as a constant stream of "white" contract workers, anthropologists, lawyers, and "service providers" has meant that people often come to know each other only via their "institutionalized positions" (Tamisari, 2006, p. 21). The "anonymous power" of these institutions as well as the often closely associated Western categories of scholarship or professionalism that frame research with Aboriginal people have little currency in these remote Aboriginal communities. As much as institutional or disciplinary positions might create the initial conditions of interrelation, in these contexts it is the "*social*, rather than *bureaucratic* processes" that bind people together in meaningful ways (Eickelkamp, 2014, p. 417). Neatly divided professional domains do little to explain behaviors or establish expectations of one another.

According to anthropologist and linguist John von Sturmer, anyone conducting successful research with people belonging to cultures markedly different from their own "must be accorded a degree of insider status" (1981). But the very notion of an insider/outsider binary has come under significant critique in recent years (Voloder, 2008; Halstead, 2001; Webster and John, 2010; Ramsland and Mooney, 2012, pp. xiv–xv). In her account of working amongst Bosnian migrants in Australia, for example, Lelja Voloder (2008) has suggested that it is a researcher's *liminality*, rather than the degree of *insider* or *outsider* status, that ought to be recognized as giving rise to important insights. The discernments gleaned from ethnographic work therefore:

> need not rely on assumptions of shared experiences and identifications between oneself and participants, but rather that it is in the exploration of the convergences and divergences in these experiences and identifications that the researcher's experiential self can be used as a key heuristic resource. (Voloder, 2008, p. 28)

As much as fieldwork and personal connections might build important rapport and familiarity, the insider/outsider dichotomy does not adequately describe these experiences. Narmala Halstead, an anthropologist with experience in Guyana, has made similar observations; ethnographic researchers when working in these liminal zones will often find themselves occupying a range of positions, and not just one. These positions and relationships are neither wholly "inside" nor "outside," but always being negotiated and renegotiated with participants (Halstead, 2001; see also Marcus, 1998). Once brought into the fold, researchers are often "positioned" as someone whose "role" it is to help "promote" the particular cultural lives being studied (2001, p. 319). Halstead's experiences resonate with the way my own shifting roles were often explained as a "worker" for "Anmatyerr culture."

This expectation was explained to me in no uncertain terms whilst traveling with a small group of Anmatyerr men on our way to Ngukurr (an Aboriginal community to the north on the Roper River) in 2006. We had stopped for fuel at a roadhouse where a large tourist information sign featured archival black-and-white photographs of two Jingulu men decorated for a ceremonial performance. The pictured men were holding what appeared to me to be objects very similar to the restricted *tywerreng* (sacred objects of stone and wood that embody ancestral beings) of the Anmatyerr and Arrernte. I called Tony Ngwarray over to elicit his opinion of what I presumed to be an offensive image. Expecting to hear Tony rail over the public display of sacred imagery, I was surprised by his reply. Tony responded by chiding me for prying into the cultural politics of another group and reminded me to stay within my "own boundary," to focus on Anmatyerr concerns. Tony made it clear that my inclination toward "portable" or universal Aboriginal rights (Sutton, 2010, p. 81) was secondary to his localism and particularism.

I too was encouraged to put my knowledge, experience, and connections, particularly with museums, to the service of Anmatyerr interests. There have been occasions where I have been pulled aside and spoken to in hushed tones and asked to search the museums and archives "down south" (meaning in the metropolitan cities of Adelaide and Melbourne) for sacred objects removed from Anmatyerr country (see chapter 9). In this light, I was acutely aware of how my research interests were always entwined with the concerns of those being studied. Though anthropology as a discipline can be viewed as an exploration of *difference* via modes of cultural and temporal distancing (Fabian, 1983), it is evident that establishing knowledge of each other is primarily a matter of sociality. Interrelations are neatly summarized by Jackson:

> when the other recognises my humanity, and on the strength of this recognition incorporates me into his world . . . I am literally incorporated into his world, and it is on the basis of this incorporation and my reciprocal response to it that I begin to gain a knowledge of that world. Anthropology should never

forget that its project unfolds within the universal constraints of hospitality. (Jackson 1995, p. 119)

While fieldworkers might strive to assume a specific standpoint in relation to their participants, they too are often being actively positioned by their subjects. In Central and Northern Australia this positioning is most easily observed when "outsiders" are located within a local kinship system (Bradley and Yanyuwa Families, 2010; Turner, 2010; Kenny, 2008, p. 52; Gibson, 2013, p. 66). Peter Sutton, an anthropologist and linguist with decades of experience in Australia, has noted that where people have maintained a system of classificatory kinship, the concept of a "friendship" outside of kinship is nonexistent. Most researchers, then, being mostly newcomers and thus exterior to the local family relationship network, are typically reinterpreted as familial relations understood via what Sutton calls "fictive" or "adoptive" kinship arrangements (see Sutton, 2002; 2009a). By alluding to the local rubrics of interaction, this kind of "kin incorporation" renders the researcher socially real, or at least socially present.

The Anmatyerr, and many Arrernte, continue to use their system of classificatory kinship, known as *anpernerrenty*, as the cornerstone of their interactions. Paddy Kemarr's readiness to make an important point regarding the extreme restrictions around some of the ritual material, for example, would often remind me of his "fatherly" status to me. *Anpernerrenty* does not just concern relations between people but is inclusive of the connections between all living and nonliving things (Walsh, Dobson, and Douglas, 2013). As such, it is used to draw connections among people, places, animals, plants, and other nonhuman entities. As Arrernte elder Margaret Kemarr Turner (2010, pp. 80–81) has explained, *anpernerrenty* is a "relationship network" like "fine branching root threads" that "run onwards from us," and is all expansive. If I was going to attempt to see Strehlow's work from an Anmatyerr perspective, I needed to consider how his work, and my own, might be seen through these various skeins of interwoven relationships. Embarking on fieldwork, traveling between communities and important sites and talking with men, brought the expansive presence of *anpernerrenty* to the fore.

Anmatyerr Country

You know you have arrived in Anmatyerr territory when you pass through a gap in the Hann Range, known as Native Gap. For the Anmatyerr and

Arrernte, Native Gap is known as Arwerlt Atwaty, a site marking the gap between the shoulder blades of an *antwerrkenh* (black-headed python) Ancestor. From here, the highway takes you northward past the Aileron Roadhouse, where many Anmatyerr people will often come together to buy supplies, drink, and socialize. The Anmatyerr region is distinct from other parts of Central Australia, as the Aboriginal communities here live in close proximity to the flow of tourists driving between Alice Springs and Darwin, as well as having a somewhat marginal local horticultural and pastoral economy. Unlike many other Aboriginal populations in Central Australia that live mostly far away down dirt roads and surrounded by bushland now under Aboriginal Freehold Title, the Anmatyerr rub shoulders with wider settler society on a daily basis. Most Anmatyerr communities are located on small "excisions" within cattle stations and exist in marginal spaces on the edges of white expansion.

Although I have spent most of my time with people at Tree, I also came to visit and meet people in seven other Anmatyerr communities spread out across the region. These include Alyuen, a small family outstation located very close to the Aileron Roadhouse on the Stuart Highway; Engawala, a community of Anmatyerr and Eastern Arrernte people located within the Alcoota pastoral lease; the small family outstation of Mulga Bore (Akay) located on the Sandover Highway; Ahalper (New Store) on the eastern extent of Anmatyerr lands; the community of Laramba (Alherramp) located within the Napperby Station pastoral lease; Ti Tree township and the surrounding area with a long-term population living in a makeshift dwelling called "Creek Camp"; Six Mile (Pmara Jutunta), also known as "Ti Tree Six Mile"; and last, the community of Nturiya (Nthwerey), situated at the site of the old Ti Tree Station homestead (see map 1.1). Anmatyerr people will often refer to these communities also by the name of the pastoral lease on which they reside. Engawala, for example, is often simply referred to as Alcoota, and Laramba is often discussed as Napperby.

The majority of these communities have predominantly Aboriginal populations who speak Anmatyerr as a first language but often are also proficient in the related Arandic languages spoken by their neighbors, such as Kaytetye, Arrernte, and Alyawarr, and the non-Arandic language Warlpiri. Linguists suggest that although Anmatyerr continues to be spoken by approximately one thousand people, the language is under threat not just from English but an increasing use of Warlpiri (Marmion, Obata, and Troy, 2014, pp. 8–9). People will often alternate between using their own language, other Central Australian languages, and English with rela-

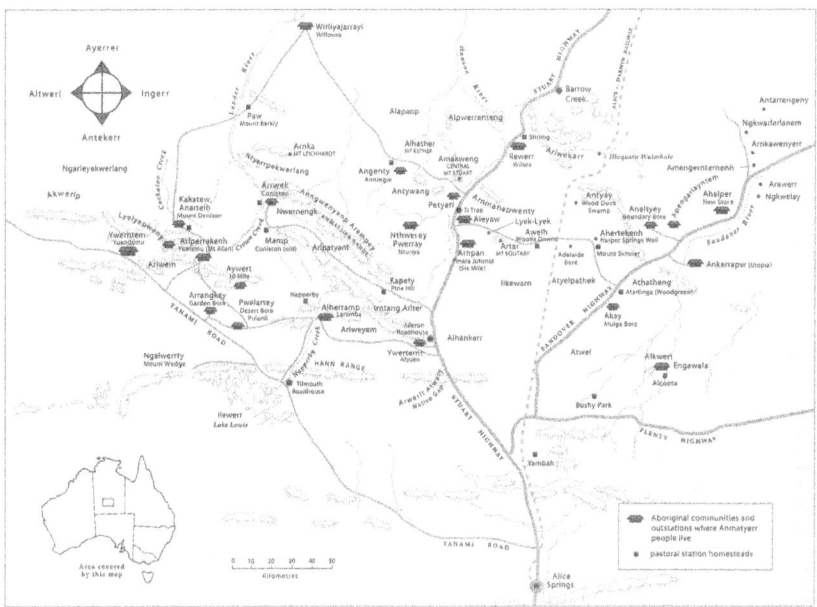

Map 1.1. The Anmatyerr communities (from Green, 2010).

tive ease. Older men and women often use a type of "Pidgin" or "Aboriginal English" they learned during their time working on the cattle stations that now cover the majority of their traditional lands.

As the significance of Anmatyerr associations with pastoralism are discussed in the following chapter, it should suffice here to say that most of the older and middle-aged generations of Anmatyerr people grew up living and working on these cattle stations. Like many other Aboriginal groups who have coexisted with pastoralism, "born in the cattle" (McGrath, 1987), Anmatyerr culture and language has been in part influenced by this history. Older men continue to wear "cowboy" style clothing and hats, and country-and-western music remains popular across generational and gender divides. Anmatyerr people will also commonly refer to their traditional *anyenheng* (patrilineal estates) as "blocks" marked by "boundary lines" or "fences," and use English terms such as "boss," "manager," and "worker" as ways of describing cultural responsibilities (see Austin-Broos, 2009, p. 125). Anmatyerr lands continue to be predominately covered by pastoral leases, and most communities and outstations exist as relatively small "excisions" surrounded by large tracts of pastoral land.

As with most remote Central and Northern Australian Aboriginal communities, unemployment is a significant issue across the Anmatyerr region. Small numbers of people do find seasonal employment with either local horticultural enterprises or cattle stations, but government-funded initiatives and welfare programs provide the primary economic stimulus in the region (Wirf, Campbell, and Rea, 2008; Hunt, 2008; Sanders and Holcombe, 2005). Education for children in these remote areas is extremely limited, and because there are currently no secondary schools in any of the Anmatyerr communities, opportunities to develop skills that might lead to new vocations are extremely narrow. In place of advanced schooling or immersion in long-term employment, Anmatyerr people express a strong desire to engage in activities that have greater local, cultural significance. According to a study looking into ways of "improving livelihood options" in these communities (Davies and Maru, 2011), it was discovered that "hunting" and "family life" were generally considered equally valuable, if not more so, to attaining Western-style education and employment.

A sizeable number of Anmatyerr people now live on the traditional lands of the Arrernte in the somewhat cosmopolitan township of Alice Springs, located over one hundred kilometers to the south of Anmatyerr territory. As this is also where the Strehlow Research Centre is located, I would often meet with people here to explore the collection's contents as we perused the storeroom or poured over Strehlow's diaries. Outside of the archive we also visited some of the sites where Strehlow's "festivals" (documentation events) were held close to Alice Springs and discuss the history of how Arrernte people and their visitors would hold ceremonies on the outskirts of town.

The restricted nature of the Strehlow collection meant that our discussions had to be conducted with great discretion. While it was generally assumed that I would be able to recognize information that was too sensitive or restricted for inclusion in this study, on a few occasions I was instructed to cease recording or refrain from taking notes. This generally occurred when our discussions ventured into the realm of the highly secretive men's initiation ceremonies or when discussing politically contentious matters such as disputes over rights in land. In most cases, though, people felt comfortable putting their names to the information they offered. Extremely aware of the growing significance of "the written-down story" for proving associations to land (for example in land rights and native title cases) and preserving information for future generations (see chapter 8), people generally wanted their commentaries documented with personal details intact.

When being asked to "*ingkwernem-ilem*" (put it in writing or make a record) or "*pwetewem-ilem*" (take a photo), it was clear they wanted their position in relation to other people, stories, and places documented. People understood that contextual *anpernerrenty* information—where someone was from, their relationships to land, their kin, and so on—would make all the difference for future generations trying to make sense of the material. As an ethnographer, I too wanted the results of my research to be useful to future generations and understood that the use of pseudonyms could hinder future reuse and reinterpretation of our discussions (Geest, 2003). This is in fact what made Strehlow's work so useful to contemporary generations, as personal connections could easily be made with his named informants and their genealogies and histories.

Reading Alongside People

My past experience of working on historical material in the region suggested to me that the most suitable means of achieving greater insights into the production of Strehlow's collection would be to allow Anmatyerr and Arrernte people the time and space to follow their own interests in the material. The content itself, being so visually and aurally stimulating, easily inspired and elicited conversations and I could join in by either supplying additional information or asking questions. This collaborative examination could, as anthropologist Luke Lassiter has described it, enable one to "read alongside with natives" rather than simply observe or "read over their shoulders" (2001). As we watched films or discussed song recordings in groups of up to eight men, I would often be asked to retrieve further information from my laptop, jot down pertinent information, or just sit patiently, be quiet, and listen to explanations.

So eager were most men to examine the material that I was usually instructed to start screening or playing recordings almost immediately. Having already been through an exhaustive process of archival research in order to identify and select appropriate materials to show to particular people (see below) the sessions usually centered on a particular suite of materials that related to a particular place or *Anengkerr* (Dreaming). The tremendous interest in the collection meant that those with close personal associations to the material or, alternatively, those with expertise in ritual matters would soon be gathered together in anticipation. Once the sessions had concluded, people's excitement generally spilled over into suggestions of trips to the relevant places referred to in the particular songs and ceremonies, or to suggestions of visits to see others with rights in the material. "When you come next time," Jimmy Haines commented after viewing one film, "we can go to Alekerang then, chasing after the *merek-artwey map* (all of the traditional owners). I'll go with you." This collaborative practice, I hoped, could further narrow the gap between the archive and the academy, and the communities that had a considerable interest in the content.

Selecting the relevant men to examine certain parts of the collection required careful consideration. Where possible, interviews were conducted with people who were either recognized as the most senior *merek-artwey* (traditional owners) or were *kwertengerl* (managers or assistants) of particular ceremonies. Being aware of the political issues that can arise regarding disputed ownership and control over sites, ceremonies, songs, and their associated ritual objects (see Anderson, 1995b; Batty, 2014), I was ever mindful of choosing the "right" content to discuss with the "right" people. I could not, for example, show the films Strehlow had made at Alcoota with men from the far distant community of Ti Tree. Local protocols and politics of information exchange, grounded in highly particularistic and personal ties to geography and Ancestral stories, had to be respected.

Given the restricted nature of these recordings, auditioning and reviewing this content would often transpire at a location far away from women and children. For example, in the community of Laramba (Napperby), it was customary to meet at a bough shelter on the western edge of the community where men would sit during their annual *apwelh* (young men's initiation) ceremonies. At Alcoota, we met in a dry riverbed not far from where Strehlow had filmed the Akwerrperl ceremonies in 1965. At Ti Tree, we usually assembled at the residence of one of the community's most knowledgeable ritual experts, Paddy Kemarr, located on the southern fringe of the Ti Tree Township in an area known as "Creek Camp." Since each of these sites was located away from general daily comings and goings in the community, the men were able to freely watch the films and listen to the recordings and also sing and act out parts of the ceremonies themselves.

The group sessions would typically begin with me handing out items such as photocopies from Strehlow's diaries or genealogies or presenting selected films or song recordings via a laptop computer. The interconnected nature of the material meant that discussion of one of the elements of the collection would inevitably lead into the discussion of another. For example, the screening of a ceremonial film could prompt the reading of a genealogy extract that detailed one of the featured performers and be followed by an auditioning of an associated song recording.

Largely unstructured and free flowing, these sessions allowed for a more equitable power dynamic in the researcher/researched interaction than if direct, one-on-one interviews had been conducted. Being mindful that structured or even semi-structured interviews might introduce relationships that are disadvantageous to collaborative modes of exploration (O'Reilly, 2009, pp. 78–82), I tried to ensure that sessions were led by the interests of the participants. The sensitivity of the ceremonial material being discussed meant that it was absolutely crucial that all participating men felt free to share or remain silent if they wished. I was not looking to pry into the concealed world of men's ritual without invitation and—in any case, as I was outnumbered—any moves on my part to do so would have been dealt with quickly. Rather than responding to a list of predetermined topics or questions, the men engaged with the material on their own terms, leaving me to respond to the themes generated from wide-ranging group dialogues and personal interests.

The older men would often serve as mnemonic aides to each other, while younger men, deferring to the authority of their elders on matters of "*tywerreng* law" (sacred rituals, but also land and Dreaming associations), tended to say silent and listen intently. Usually while the tea was being made, the cigarettes rolled, or the bush turkey or kangaroo meat was cooking in the coals, each person would have an opportunity to speak. Interjections were common, as people helped remember particular details or provide corrections. Each utterance would build on the other in a slow and cumulative manner to form a fuller picture of the meaning of a song, ceremony, or historical event. Speaking in groups also meant that people were conscious that their relatives could review their statements and make embellishments or amendments if required, especially if the person speaking could not utter a particular relative's name due to an avoidance relationship. (An avoidance relationship is a formalized and constrained familial relationship common in Australian Aboriginal societies.) Overall, the group approach was a natural fit with the usual mode of discussing ceremonial matters and encouraged an open discovery of the materials on people's own terms.

Another important aspect of this method was that it enabled men from a range of generations to come together and share in the dialogue. It was in fact a specific intention of mine to invite intergenerational discussion as a way of correcting the tendency in Aboriginalist anthropology to focus on the "knowledge" of senior men and women only. Under the perceived pressure to document societies in decline, research in these societies has tended to direct its energies toward the salvaging of languages, ritual details, and cosmologies from older generations and, as Ute Eickelkamp (2010, p. 157) has noted, this is often at the expense of understanding the viewpoints and experience of younger people. As will be shown in chapters 6, 7, 8, and 9, these cross-generational discussions revealed significant differences in the way song and ceremonial knowledge is understood across different ages, as well as how local history and genealogy is recalled and remembered. Many of the younger Anmatyerr men had been unaware of how much their fathers and grandfathers had shown to Strehlow, and they used these sessions as an opportunity to marvel at the remarkable ritual skill and achievements of the *angkwey map* (older generations).

Wrangling the Archive

Strehlow's archive is a wondrous collection of diaries, papers, maps, genealogies, audio recordings, films, and artefacts. Each item can be linked to other parts of the collection via Strehlow's meticulously kept and detailed documentation. Identifying and locating the relevant Anmatyerr material in the Strehlow collection, however, required an extensive exploration of the content and a careful appreciation of how each element might contextualize or inform another. Strehlow organized his collection in such a way that anyone with knowledge of the languages, sites, mythologies, and systems of kinship in Central Australia could reconnect its various elements. Without this familiarity, the cross references and linkages are difficult to recognize. Years of use, re-ordering of the collection, and cases of absolute sabotage (such as when Strehlow's second wife, Kathleen, cut the descriptive labels off a number of artefacts) had made these connections less apparent. In order to compile suites of material that belonged in a group (for example, all of the films, song recordings, artifacts, genealogies, maps, and diary extracts that pertained to a single area or ceremony), it was essential to first have an understanding of how they related to one another.

When I began this work in earnest in 2013, the work of comprehensively cataloguing the twenty-six hours of 16mm film (including over eight hundred ceremonial performances) had yet to occur. Cohen and Willis (2001) had produced a useful listing of the films produced up until 1962, but this source lacked time codes and cross-referencing with the digitized films held by the National Film and Sound Archive in Canberra. Other than the small number of anthropologists that had been employed at the Strehlow Research Centre over the years, no one had actively worked with the restricted ceremonial films or song recordings for quite some time. Identifying each of the films that specifically depicted Anmatyerr ceremonies was therefore a difficult undertaking, and one that required in-depth research into Strehlow diaries and notes.

Thankfully, Strehlow's duteous methods of documentation meant that identification and re-partnering of the material was possible. The ceremonies he filmed, though silent and without on-screen titles, were always fully described in his diaries and additionally photographed with a still camera. As each ceremony was being performed in front of him, Strehlow would label it with a title, usually comprised of the name or entity of the Dreaming ancestor being represented (e.g., a "fish," "possum," or "rain" ancestor), followed by the key site where the ancestor's actions were depicted in the ceremony. The Antenh Ceremony of Irrwelty, for example, referred to the *antenh* (common brushtail possum, *Trichosurus vulpecula*) ancestor from a place named Irrwelty.[1] Because there was often no indication in these titles as to whether a ceremony related specifically to Arrernte, Anmatyerr, or Luritja people, it was only by pouring over the related documentation that these relationships could be ascertained.

A similar method was required when looking for Anmatyerr song material among Strehlow's 150 hours of audio recordings. In this case, however, the process was doubly difficult because the collection had never been comprehensively catalogued and the hours of audio contained only Arrernte and Anmatyerr speech. Being completely fluent in Arrernte, Strehlow felt no need to elaborate his recordings with English introductions and clearly did not envision this material being revisited by people with limited or nonexistent Arrernte language capabilities. One can nonetheless listen to Strehlow and his informants as they talk between episodes of

---

1. Strehlow writes "Antana Ceremony of Erultja."

singing, but these interactions are usually quite brief and focused solely on the correct identification of words or phrases in a song text.

Originally produced on magnetic wire recorder technology and then reel-to-reel tape in the 1950s and 1960s, the recordings were later transferred to shellac disc and cassette tape. Today it is the cassette copies that are used for research purposes, and while it is clear from the accompanying inventories what the tapes contain, the lack of spoken introductions makes precise identification of discrete songs extremely difficult. Arandic songs, particularly those used in ceremonial contexts, are often esoteric and multidialectical (Ellis and Barwick, 1987; Koch and Turpin, 2008) and thus require extratextual explanations from knowledgeable people in order for them to be understood. Given these challenges, it was through the process of working with language speakers, singers, and holders of "Anmatyerr Law" that identifications were ascertained.

The process of reviewing various aspects of the collection—audio, visual, and textual—was intended as a deliberate form of "elicitation": a way of generating thick and rich descriptions and discussions. As an ethnographic technique developed since the 1950s (Prosser, 2011), elicitation continues to be popular when images, films, artefacts and sound material are used to stimulate discussion. Sociologist and photographer Douglas Harper (2002) described how visual elicitation methods tend to produce deeper analyses than those based on words alone. Nicola Allet (2010), working with people's reactions to music, has similarly noted the way that elicitation may additionally evoke important feelings and memories. Jane Lydon, a historian of Australian colonial photography, has used comparable methods to elicit responses to photographic collections among Australian Aboriginal communities. Lydon's work (2010; 2014) reveals how engaging with this material can facilitate the recovery of stories lost through the dislocations of colonialism or left undocumented in the official histories.

These methods, often incorporating the "return" or "repatriation" of not just photographic but other archival materials to Indigenous communities, are now recognized as important dimensions to a decolonizing anthropology. Many museum practitioners now commonly refer to the importance of discussing potential repatriation of physical objects with their "source communities" in order to enable better documentation and explanation of their collections (Brown and Peers, 2013; Allen, 2016), while anthropologists now regard the return of their own recently generated research results to Indigenous communities as a site of research in itself (Christen, 2005; Bell, Christen, and Turin, 2013; Treloyn and Emberly,

2013). What is clear from this growing body of literature is that the act of returning film, sound, or textual material, while it might be thought of as being relatively straightforward, is in fact an important and complex engagement involving not just technical solutions but careful sociocultural navigations.

The amount and depth of knowledge gained through these processes varies widely. In most cases, questions are provoked concerning the ongoing ownership of archival objects, and new perspectives on historical events are gained (Thomas, 2007; Palmer, 2013). Haidy Geismar and Anita Herle's (2010) comprehensive account of the return of the anthropologist John Layard's photographs to Malakula communities in Vanuatu stands as a particularly important exemplar. Their work not only brings the evolving nature of collaborative relationships between ethnographers and communities to the foreground, but also shows how important the performative aspects of people's engagement with ethnohistorical material can be. In Australia, the return of ethnographic films (Garde, 2013; Sweeney, 2006) and sound recordings (Campbell, 2014; Gibson, 2015a; Turpin, Green, and Gibson 2016) have similarly augmented the historical and ethnographic record.

If employed in a thoughtless manner, however, the return of archival material can easily produce inaccurate or distorted memories or, worse, result in serious hurt or distress to participants. The risk of offending is most pronounced when viewing ethnographic films from the past when restricted aspects of men's ritual were sometimes permitted to be filmed. In a number of instances accidental screenings of footage of restricted ceremonies have resulted in distress or anxiety in Aboriginal communities and led to threats of intercommunity violence (Thomas, 2007; Latz, 2014, pp. 161–163). I personally recall witnessing the distress and anxiety felt by women and children after having been exposed to this type of material. As families sat in the local library in Ti Tree viewing a documentary on the life of the Arrernte artist Albert Namatjira that had been produced in the late 1940s, the film suddenly cut to a vision of an elaborate and very secret ritual being performed by Luritja men. Shocked senior Anmatyerr women commanded the children to run from the library, and they too rushed for the doors.

Bringing Strehlow's recordings into Anmatyerr communities thus had to be carried out with extreme care and caution. Although I was careful in only showing this material to men of significant ritual standing, I knew that the arrival of this material was a risky intervention, and one for which I would be held personally responsible. Past experiences had taught me that presenting material to men who did not feel knowledgeable enough to see it or were not personally affiliated in some way to its Dreamings could lead to discomfort and accusations that they were meddling in other people's "Law."

When used in a cautious and responsive manner, however, collaborative screenings and listening sessions can be elucidating and may address sensitivities. Visual sociologist Jon Prosser has argued that participants in research will often feel less pressure when discussing sensitive topics if the focus of the interaction is nondirect, focused on the audio or visual content being examined, and diffused among a cohort of respondents (2011, p. 484). Strehlow's archive was thus used in this way, as a type of "intermediary" or "transitional object" through which dialogue could occur. People gathered around my laptop computer, or around photocopies of archival material, and used these items as a means to talk through or around important matters of ritual knowledge. They remembered historical events and made their personal connections to these things known.

It would be naïve to think that these discussions were in any way "natural" or routine. Although urged on by Anmatyerr interest in the collection contents, it was my intervention that had purposefully introduced this material back into these communities. Being involved as an active participant in the discussions, I was often asked to provide further information or clarify the background to Strehlow's work. This shared learning environment meant that I was able to benefit from the clarifications and descriptions provided by senior men, but they too could use me as a resource. As one of a small number of non-Aboriginal men to have been permitted to see these films and hear these songs, let alone share in the excited rush of commentary from senior Anmatyerr ritual experts, I felt enormously privileged to be able to record these responses, learn about their interactions with Strehlow, and deepen my understanding of Anmatyerr lifeworlds.

Reflecting on these experiences and the story of Strehlow's deep engagement with Aboriginal people in this part of Australia, it is critical to reconsider the history of how Anmatyerr people encountered ethnographers and *alhernter* in general. Strehlow was not alone in being asked to record song and ceremony, as others had done it before him, and still others have done so in more recent times. With this in mind, there needed to be a reconsideration of the agency and motivations of the people he was acquainted with. Were there longer historical relationships that informed these dynamics? Although Anmatyerr people had largely escaped intensive documentation over the years, they had nonetheless developed significant ties with settler society and appeared relatively comfortable with working out mutually agreeable zones of interaction. Far from being cut off from or exterior to Euro-Australian society, Anmatyerr people had been negotiating asymmetrical power relationships with Europeans for decades when Strehlow arrived on the scene in the 1930s. Central to these exchanges was the performance of "culture" under the gaze of the settler colonist.

Chapter 2

Early *Alhernter* Encounters

> Rather than cementing estrangement, culture contact always entails, in some measure, for each party, stratagems of reconfiguring the horizons of their own humanity.... Though every anthropological encounter begins in strangeness and separation, that gap is gradually, though seldom utterly, closed.
>
> —Jackson (1998)

Anmatyerr people will often refer to Europeans as *alhernter*, a term comprised of the words "*alha*" meaning "nose" and "*nter*" referring to the colors "red" or "pink." Interactions with the "pink nosed" date back to the arrival of the first explorers in the 1860s and have since been characterized by a long and unfolding history of coercion, inequality, and conflict as well as interaction and exchange. The earliest encounters between Aboriginal people and Europeans are now subject to detailed historical analysis, and the debates over what actually happened during these encounters now serve as important events where the moral foundations of Australian nationhood are questioned and defined (Manne, 2003; Macintyre and Clark, 2004). As historian Inga Clendinnen argued (2005), to understand more recent relationships between Indigenous and non-Indigenous Australians, one needs to grasp their foundation in the earliest interactions.

This chapter presents a number of historical episodes where Anmatyerr and *alhernter* met and interacted prior to T.G.H. Strehlow's arrival on the scene in the early 1930s. This historical purview is essential for seeing not only how transactions between ethnographers and informants developed up until this time, but also how expectations and tensions have persisted between *alhernter* and Anmatyerr since. The rough contours of intercultural relations had been established in the seventy years prior to the beginning of Strehlow's work, and these historical relationships built important preconceptions amongst both parties about how an exchange in cultural information might be mediated, structured, and negotiated. In her study of colonial travel writing, *Imperial Eyes*, Mary Louise Pratt describes these situations as "contact zones": spaces "where peoples once geographically and historically separated" came into contact with each other and established "ongoing relations" (1992, pp. 6–7). What is important about Pratt's concept here is her emphasis on how subjects and groups are constituted in their associations with each other within "asymmetrical relations of power" that include episodes of collision and misunderstanding as well as co-presence, interaction, and "interlocking understandings and practices." As Jackson notes in the epigraph, rather than "cementing estrangement," these encounters may equally be productive sites of struggle, mixing, improvisation, and dialogue.

Early colonial interactions between the Anmatyerr and *alhernter* were slow to build and at times ignited into bloody frontier violence. On the whole, though, it was people's long-term associations with pastoralism, combined with their irregular interactions with colonial authorities, that laid out important expectations of the newcomers. Tightly interwoven into the fabric of colonialism and the wider social settings of the nation, the history of ethnographic practice in Australia has been dealt with in somewhat generalized terms (Wolfe, 1999; Bennett, Dibley, and Harrison, 2014). These analyses have tended to highlight issues of oppositional frontiers and outright violence as well as structural, material, and discursive power (Lattas and Morris, 2010; Wolfe, 2006), leaving the finer details of micro-ethnographic, local or regional accounts and experiences unexamined. Taking inspiration from the more ethnographically oriented historical studies (Abercrombie, 1998; Austin-Broos, 2009), this chapter aims to explore the often deep intermingling of practices and worldviews in early encounters in particular. I begin with a discussion of exploration and conflict and the emergence of pastoralism as a significant "contact zone," before moving on to an examination of the early ethnographers and their interactions with Anmatyerr people.

"Discovering" the Known

The first *alhernter* known to enter into Anmatyerr territory was the Scottish explorer John McDouall Stuart in 1860. On his fourth inland expedition, Stuart and his small party traveled north from Adelaide and made their way to the center of the continent (Stuart, 1865). Following the Hanson Creek to the north, they headed toward a large mountain on the horizon, which they named "Central Mount Sturt" after the explorer Charles Sturt, although it was later renamed after Stuart himself as Central Mount Stuart. At the summit of this bulbous peak, Stuart and his second in command, William Kekwick, flew the British flag and claimed the surrounding country for the British Crown:

> We then gave three hearty cheers for the flag, the emblem of civil and religious liberty, and may it be a sign to the natives that the dawn of liberty, civilization, and Christianity is about to break upon them. (Stuart, 1865, pp. 165–166)

Unbeknownst to the explorers, the mountain was already known as Mer Amakweng and associated with Ancestral emus that moved across the country in the *Anengkerr* (Dreaming) and were honored in song and ceremony. As Stuart made almost no use of local Aboriginal guides and had little interest in ethnography, his interactions with Aboriginal people were mostly brief and insignificant (Finnane, 2010; Jones, 2012). His presence, however, did not go unnoticed by Aboriginal people, and stories of his party's arrival were later recorded in oral histories and artworks (Gillen, 1968; Strehlow, 1967; Gibson, 2015b). As Stuart passed through Anmatyerr territory in 1862 during his successful crossing of the continent from south to north, he marked the commencement of the colonial era for all of the people of inland Australia and heralded the beginning of an influx of settlers, mainly pastoralists, who gradually began moving their stock into the area.

By 1872, the newly constructed Overland Telegraph Line, built to establish communications with the British Empire and the rest of the world, effectively dissected the traditional territory of the Anmatyerr. Successions of telegraph repeater stations were constructed between Adelaide on the southern coast and Darwin in the north. In Central Australia, telegraph stations were built at Charlotte Waters and Stuart (later renamed Alice

Springs) in Arrernte territory and then at Barrow Creek on Kaytetye lands. Although a Telegraph Station building was never established within Anmatyerr territory, the poles and wires of the line ran directly through their country, and Anmatyerr people would occasionally encounter laborers and stockmen traveling between Alice Springs and Barrow Creek. These very early interactions were, according to historian Mervyn Hartwig, mostly insignificant and fleeting and thus left little mark on the historical record (1965, pp. 389, 247, 257), but as land was "settled," the transect of "the Line" and its telegraph repeater stations were used as bases from which to launch new expeditions and explorations (Gosse and Goyder, 1874). By the mid-1870s, Anmatyerr lands were being mapped from east to west by *alhernter* keen on expanding their own material and colonial interests, with very little interest in its Aboriginal inhabitants.

Frontier Violence

By the mid-1880s both Anmatyerr and Arrernte people to their south (who had borne the brunt of dispossession along the Overland Telegraph Line) became "the first to offer widespread resistance to the expansion of the pastoral leases" (Hartwig, 1965, p. 395). According to the various histories written of the time, conflict tended to flare up over the killing of cattle, which had become so prevalent that it was discussed as an "emergency" among authorities (Kimber, 1991; Hartwig, 1965; Nettelbeck and Foster 2007). The first serious instance of violent conflict, on February 22, 1874, occurred only two years after the Overland Telegraph Stations had been established. The northern neighbors to the Anmatyerr, the Kaytetye, had attacked the Barrow Creek Telegraph Station, killing two settlers and wounding a third in retaliation for the abuse and exploitation of Aboriginal women (Koch and Koch, 1993, pp. xiv–xv; Mulvaney, 2004).

The punitive response that followed saw people being shot far to the south in Anmatyerr territory, along the Hanson Creek and Skull Creek, a site apparently named after the skulls of the victims left there (Koch and Koch, 1993, pp. xv, 17; Strehlow, 1971a, pp. 590–593; 1967, p. 12). According to oral histories collected from two Anmatyerr men by T.G.H. Strehlow over forty years later, a "native police" unit consisting of Arrernte troopers led by Mounted Constable Samuel Gason had pursued the attackers (Strehlow, 1932, p. 119). At Arlwekarr (Lukara), a waterhole to the east of the present-day Stirling Community, the native police apparently scattered and destroyed the sacred objects (*tywerrenge*) kept at Arlwekarr. In Strehlow's estimation, the Anmatyerr had received "all the punishment" for an attack they had little or nothing to do with.[1]

Ten years later, the Anmatyerr launched an attack of their own upon a settlement homestead that had been established on their traditional lands. Anmatyerr men, with the help of some Western Arrernte, attacked the Anna's Reservoir homestead, first by setting fire to the thatched roof of the building and then waiting for the inhabitants to emerge (Kimber, 1991, pp. 10–11). As many as 150 Aboriginal men had waited outside the building with their spears at the ready. The head stockman rushed out, firing his revolver. The camp cook had already been badly wounded, and both men eventually died in the affray (Willshire, 1884). The exact reasons for the attack on Anna's Reservoir are not known, but there is reasonable evidence to suggest that access to resources (particularly water) or perhaps the rape of a young Anmatyerr girl had sparked the violence (Eylmann, 1908, pp. 462–463; Kimber, 1991). Whatever the reason, the attack was again followed by a brutal response from the authorities, led by the notoriously violent Constable Willshire (Nettelbeck and Foster, 2007; Roberts, 2009; Vallee, 2007) and his team of Aboriginal "native-police."

Over one hundred years later, the history of the Anna's Reservoir conflict is now part of the narrative of the Anmatyerr landscape. Driving between the Laramba (Napperby) community and the Stuart Highway, men have often pointed out the ranges of Angkwerl (Anna's Reservoir) and commented on the story. On one occasion, Huckitta Lynch and Ronnie McNamara called out over the din of the Toyota engine to recount the story of the attack. Ronnie bent over into the cabin where I was driving and, speaking loudly into my ear, remarked that this was the time of "the war." Ronnie was often blunt about the region's bloody history and had personal connections to it. His father, the white pastoralist William "Billy" McNamara, had shot Aboriginal people for spearing cattle in the 1920s (Bowman, 1989, pp. 36–37; Davis and Prescott, 1992, p. 92), and as a young man Ronnie was often confronted by descendants of the victims. Huckitta Lynch had also heard about the Anna's Reservoir incident and described how the Anmatyerr men had used fire as their primary weapon. "They made *ure* (fires) everywhere around the station at Mer

---

1. T.G.H. Strehlow in conversation with Curtis Levy, c. 1974. Levy audio-recorded this conversation whilst researching a film about the Overland Telegraph Line for the ABC that was never completed. Copy of the recording provided by Curtis Levy.

Angkwerl (Anna's Reservoir). Killed *warlparl* (whitefellas) too. We made trouble everywhere. That's *nwernekenh ayey, angkwey map* [That's our story, from a long time ago]."

The "war," or the "trouble," sent shock waves throughout the region during the late nineteenth century. Of the forty-five Aboriginal people officially recorded as having been killed during this early colonial period, at least eighteen were from the Anmatyerr and Kaytetye areas (Kimber, 1991). Local Central Australian historian and anthropologist Dick Kimber has noted that there were "undoubtedly" other reprisals "carried out by groups of stockmen working beyond the law, and others involving the police but not being officially recorded" (1991, p. 13). Ken Tilmouth Penangk, for example, has told of one such incident where his relatives were killed at the site of Itarlenty, a place now marked on maps as "Blackfellows' Bones Bore" after the human remains apparently left at the site following a shooting (see Bowman, 2015, pp. 91–92; see also Strehlow, 1967, p. 6; Kimber, 1991; Young, 1987, p. 160; Strehlow, 1971a, p. 588; Purvis, 1940, p. 176), and others speak of the fear that their ancestors had of violent whites.

Open and violent resistance to colonization following these brutal responses eventually faded in the late nineteenth century, leaving the local population with what Hartwig has described as a "refugee outlook" (1965, pp. 400, 413). The effects of frontier violence had been so great that by the turn of the century, one of the first anthropologists to visit the region, Walter Baldwin Spencer (see more below), declared that the Anmatyerr had been practically "wiped out" (1928, p. 412) by acts of "dispersal," a euphemism commonly employed in the colonial period to describe the enactment of violence against Aboriginal people (see Foster, 2009; Read, 1983). With their lands largely usurped and having spent decades in the company of the ever-increasing presence of settlers, the Anmatyerr had apparently given up on violent resistance. According to Mervyn Meggitt (1962, p. 335), Anmatyerr people made it known to their western neighbors, the Warlpiri, that the "whitefellows were there to stay, no matter what attempts the Aborigines made to dislodge them."

The violence of the early colonial period reappeared in August of 1928 in what was the last recorded mass killing of Aboriginal people by a police punitive party in Australia, the Coniston killings. As the details of this terrible event have been adequately described elsewhere (Cataldi, 1996; Cribbin, 1984; Kimber, 2003; Central Land Council, 2003; Wilson and O'Brien, 2003; Koch and Koch, 1993; Read and Read, 1993), only a very brief synopsis will be provided here. Following years of drought it was not uncommon for supplies and rations to be pilfered by opportunistic and hungry Aboriginal people (Kimber, 2003; Scherer, 1993, p. 24; Wilson and O'Brien, 2003, pp. 67–70; Strehlow, 1932, p. 15). Given the stresses of drought, Aboriginal people in the region were understandably angered by cattle spoiling scarce food and water resources, as well as encroaching upon important places for hunting game (Scherer 1993, p. 24). As tensions increased, a number of pastoralists were being threatened or openly attacked. When a "dogger" (dingo trapper) named Fred Brooks was killed by a Warlpiri man at *Arrwek* (Brooks Soak) on Coniston Station, the police response was brutal.

Between August and October of 1928, Mounted Constable William George Murray and a small band of local pastoralists terrorized the region. Although the number of people killed is unknown, oral history accounts suggest it was at least double the thirty-one deaths officially reported by the Board of Enquiry later set up to investigate the shootings (Cribbin, 1984; Kimber, 1991; Doyle, 1999). The biggest slaughter, according to Silas Ngal, a Anmatyerr/Warlpiri elder that spoke with T.G.H. Strehlow decades after the event (1968a, p. 60), was at a site called "Aloweija," where an *Urrempel festival* (the type of ceremonial gathering that Strehlow regularly documented throughout the 1950s and 1960s; see chapters 5 and 6) was underway.

Murders of Anmatyerr people by authorities ceased following the Coniston shootings, but Anmatyerr people continued to be used as indentured labor, suffered further maltreatment, and saw more sacred sites desecrated. The harsh times continued. Paddy Kemarr, born three years after the Coniston shootings, remembers being told about attacks made against a particularly brutal pastoralist, William John "Nugget" Morton, for his apparent mistreatment of Anmatyerr women:

> Well, Nugget Morton came from Western Australia. He brought bullocks from there. He came to Boomerang Hole [on the Lander River] through the desert. After that, well Nugget Morton gathered up some women and took them to his camp, taking them from the "old" people. He used to take women to work for him as stockmen. The white fellow (Morton) told them, "I'm going to shift camp to Mud Hut with these bullocks. Your mob can stay here at this fertile place with a waterhole!" Well, the old people were worried about their women. Well,

they gathered together into a fighting group, before attacking Nugget Morton. While he was sleeping . . . the fight started before daylight, at about 6 o'clock. There was a big fight. They smashed him about with boomerangs. Old Nugget Morton.

The tensions of these times remain vivid in the minds of many Anmatyerr people today. While growing up "in the bush" on Napperby Station, Janie Briscoe Mpetyan has explained that she and her family were anxious that "whitefellas" would kill them. "That was the olden days. We never went to the station homestead—only our father used to go to the homestead to get rations. We stayed in the bush" (qtd. in Bowman, 2015, p. 83). Unlike other Aboriginal groups in Australia that grew up on gazetted "Aboriginal Reserves" (see Howard-Wagner and Kelly, 2011), towns, or missions, the Anmatyerr came to know *alhernter* via the distinctive experience of living on a remote and largely unruly pastoral frontier.

Pastoralism

Amidst the tensions of this frontier, however, a contrasting dynamic of co-existence and adaptation began to emerge. By the 1890s, as substantial camps of Anmatyerr people congregated around station homesteads and close to the Overland Telegraph Line, the utilization of Aboriginal labor became commonplace. A kind of "middle ground," which historian Richard White (2010) describes as a space where Indigenous and European people attempt to reconfigure mutually understandable practices, began to materialize. These types of relationships emerged in settler-colonial environments that saw minimal state intervention, where the need to interact was present and where access to each other's labor, technologies, and resources was desired. While according to Hartwig, the demands that settlers and Aboriginal people placed on each other during this early period were so minimal that each was relatively free to pursue their own interests, increasingly the two came together. Bill Heffernan, a pastoralist that took up Ti Tree Station in the heart of Anmatyerr territory in 1914, explained that being largely "isolated and scattered," the early settlers needed to make concessions in order to accommodate Anmatyerr people (qtd. in Scherer, 1993, p. 19).

Having first tentatively and then violently confronted each other, the groups needed to find a way of cooperating and developing consent. So long as Anmatyerr people refrained from interfering with station infrastructure, chattel, or interests, and added their labor to the pastoral economy, settlers would not obstruct their religious or cultural lives (Hartwig, 1965, p. 450). Those gathered near station homesteads began to receive rations (food, clothing, and goods such as blankets and tobacco) in return for domestic work or laboring, which the Aboriginal community would then typically distribute among their local kin. These conditions, where men worked as laborer's/stockmen and women as "domestics," lasted well into the 1960s. The historian Mervyn Hartwig worked at Ti Tree Station over the summer months of 1959–60 and explained to me that Anmatyerr people were paid in little more than "bully beef," flour, and tea slops poured from an old four-gallon kerosene tin. Conditions like these had been common across Central Australian cattle stations for decades and characterized the imbalance in Indigenous and non-Indigenous power relations.

This type of "rationing," as Tim Rowse has argued (1998), became a defining feature of the colonial experience in Central Australia. While undoubtedly a flexible instrument of social, economic, and cultural manipulation that surely cultivated dependencies, rationing also operated as a point of exchange and established degrees of familiarity. As more and more people came to live close to station homesteads, some pastoralists attained rudimentary knowledge of the Anmatyerr language and developed closer personal ties with the local population. Some even came to have families with Anmatyerr women, although taboos associated with co-habiting with Aboriginal women, known as "combo-ism," were so great that these relationships were often concealed (Strehlow, 1968a, p. 54). Randall Stafford, a pastoralist involved in the Coniston shootings, for example, later had children with an Anmatyerr woman (Alice Stafford Pwerrerl) and developed obvious sympathies with the Anmatyerr.

> I've been good to them on every station I've been on—I've fed them—I've treated them well. I've never interfered with them on their walkabouts; and yet I feel sure that they like those other whites who treat them as though they were dogs. But it doesn't matter to me. I know that these *myalls* (bush people) sometimes spear one of my bullocks; but as long as it doesn't happen too often, I say nothing about it. It was their country before I came into it, and I know they often have a pretty tough time in making a living for themselves. (Strehlow, 1959, p. 312)

Stafford's thinking may have been ahead of his time, but by the 1950s other station owners in some places began to acknowledge that, while they owned the stock and the infrastructure, Aboriginal people owned the land itself (Sandall, 1972; McGrath, 1997; Bowman, 1989, p. 31). Eric Penangk, who was born in the same year as the Coniston shootings (1928) and whose family members fled for their safety during the chaos of the "killing times," was told as a young man that some pastoralists had actually defended people. Looking at one of the photographs taken by the missionary Ernest Kramer in the late 1920s (figure 2.1), Eric recalled the efforts of Mr. Thomas Moar at Pine Hill Station who protected his workers from the punitive party led by Constable Murray:

> They worked for Moar as sheep shepherds . . . because he looked after them from that one all the time. That Moar growled (became angry) at that whitefella without shooting. Mr Moar, he looked after them. (Constable William) George Murray came there, but Moar looked after them all. They all lived at Ilyelepwenty (Woodforde Well) because they looked after the

Figure 2.1. Ernest Kramer's photograph of some of the men who worked for Thomas Moar at the Woodforde Crossing, c. 1927 (SAM, Aborigines Friends Association Collection, item AA 1/59/3).

sheep. Old man Moar looked after them with a shotgun, from that other white fella. That's what happened.

Aboriginal workers—men, women, and children, throughout remote areas of Australia—became indispensable to the pastoral economy (Laufer, 2001; McGrath, 1997). Though undoubtedly exploited and receiving only meager rations in return for their hard labor, pride in their work nonetheless constituted a form of defiance against the oppressive paternalism entrenched in mainstream social attitudes (McGrath, 1987; 1997; Rose, 2005; Sandall, 1972; Hokari, 2002). The seasonal nature of stock work also meant that ceremonial obligations, often involving weeks away in isolated ceremonial camps, could be accommodated within the demands of the pastoral economy, and droving or mustering enabled people to visit important ancestral sites whilst "on the job." At stock camps, too, people would meet and share stories, exchange ritual knowledge, and perform public songs and dances (Mulvaney, 1976; Harney, 1946, p. 38; Gibson, 2015a). As Peter Sutton argues, it was these qualities that made pastoralism "the form of colonization most compatible with the maintenance of traditional Aboriginal connections to land" (1998, p. 35).

First Ethnographic Encounters

It was precisely against this socioeconomic and cultural backdrop that the first ethnographers encountered the Anmatyerr. Neither "traditional in the pre-contact sense nor assimilated," the Anmatyerr, like so many Indigenous groups across Australia, had negotiated their own place within a complex contact zone (Rolls, 2010, p. 194). The first interactions with ethnographers began in the mid-1890s, thirty years after Stuart's explorations and twenty-five years after the arrival of settlers. It was German *Forschungsreisender* (traveling researcher) Erhard Eylmann who apparently made the initial fieldwork incursion into Anmatyerr lands in search of anthropological insights (Schröder, 2004; Monteath, 2013; Courto, 2004). In his *Die Eingeborenmen der Kolonie Sud-Australien* (1908), Eylmann writes of journeying and hunting with people on Anmatyerr country, but makes no reference to the Anmatyerr ethnonym (Eylmann, 2011, pp. 261, 284–285). His map of tribal territories instead identifies only the "Arunta" (Arrernte) and the "Katitje" (Kaytetye) and omits any reference to the Anmatyerr (normally positioned between these two groups).

The next ethnographers to work in this area, Francis James Gillen and Walter Baldwin Spencer, were also initially silent on the presence of the Anmatyerr. Although they focused primarily on the ceremonial lives of the Arrernte (see Spencer and Gillen, 1899), Spencer and Gillen's work did nevertheless make reference to places and mythologies that we would now regard as being clearly identified with the Anmatyerr. What is confusing about Spencer and Gillen's first publication is that much of the information is attributed to a group they label as the "Ilpira," or "Ilpirra" (pp. 90, 645–657), an Arandic term (spelled *Arlpere* in modern orthography) for the Warlpiri cultural group that resides much further to the northwest. A careful reading of Spencer and Gillen's ethnography also reveals that the subsection terms listed for the "Ilpirra" are undoubtedly Arandic, as they lack the suffixes and prefixes used in the Warlpiri and Western Desert languages. Moreover, the geographic region they associate with the "Ilpira" is located where we might expect the Anmatyerr to be today, adjoining the Arrernte "on the north," or "*immediately* to the north" of the Arrernte (pp. 72, 276).

It wasn't until Spencer and Gillen's historic anthropological expedition across the continent in 1901 that the "Unmatjira" (Anmatyerr) were finally recognized in the literature (Gillen, 1968, p. 126). Primarily interested in gathering information on "primitive" people in order to advance an appreciation of social evolution, Spencer and Gillen followed the Overland Telegraph Line north from Oodnadatta in South Australia all the way to the Gulf of Carpentaria, producing detailed ethnographic records of Aboriginal groups in Central and Northern Australia (Spencer and Gillen, 1904). Although they traveled through Anmatyerr territory past Ti Tree and Central Mount Stuart, they did not meet any Anmatyerr people until their arrival at the Barrow Creek Telegraph Station. Here a man named "Jack" Arlpalywerrng Pwerrerl (Illpaliurkna Purula), a senior Anmatyerr man from the Arlwekarr area, provided them with their first insights into the Anmatyerr people.

Word of approaching anthropologists interested in trading rations for artefacts and information had been sent along the telegraph line, and Arlpalywerrng was just one of the many Kaytetye and Anmatyerr people who came looking to participate (Mulvaney, Petch, and Morphy, 2000; Gillen, 2001). Writing to his family back in Melbourne, Spencer described Arlpalywerrng as "a very remarkable looking individual," dressed in ragged clothes and donning a hat made out of an "old hoop rim and calico" (Spencer, 2013, p. 56). Giving an indication of Anmatyerr people's

Figure 2.2. Jack Arlpalywerrng Pwerrerl wearing the hat made for him by F.R. Scott (Spencer Collection, Museum Victoria, XP 14577).

early integration into the rural economy, the hat had apparently been made by the local pastoralist, Francis Robert William Scott, and given to Arlpalywerrng as protection from the sun while he tended Scott's stock. In annotating an accompanying photograph of Arlpalywerrng kept in the Baldwin Spencer Collection at the Melbourne Museum (figure 2.2), Spencer noted that Arlpalywerrng was "in charge" of a cattle "station" on the nearby "stirling Creek."[2]

Eliciting information from Arlpalywerrng and the others at Barrow Creek was made possible via a number of means. After twenty-five years in the region, Gillen had attained a working knowledge of Arrernte (Jones, 2005; Gibson, 2013) (a language closely related to Anmatyerr), and Arlpalywerrng had presumably learnt enough English to communicate with *alhernter* such as Scott. But as John Mulvaney (2001) has noted, Spencer and Gillen's talented interpreter Jim Alyelkelhayeka (Erlikilyika) Kite also played a key role at Barrow Creek, enabling discussions with informants that

---

2. Item XP14578 and also XP14577 in Spencer's photographic collection at Museum Victoria.

spoke any of the Arandic languages (Arrernte, Anmatyerr, and Kaytetye). With Kite's help, the duo obtained the earliest information on Anmatyerr burial and mourning practices, mythologies, kinship, and "tribal boundaries" from Arlpalywerrng. The other Anmatyerr people present at Barrow Creek, who according to Gillen had "never been near a white settlement" and knew nothing of the English language, proved far less forthcoming (Gillen, 1968, p. 165). In exchange for food, tomahawks, knives, pipes, and tobacco, these people were simply photographed and later submitted to having their heads measured with Spencer's anthropometric instruments.[3]

Perhaps most striking about this early interaction is the way in which sacred ceremonial knowledge was shared so liberally. Not only was the sacred ceremony concerning the *anyemayte* (witchetty grub) of "Intiara" that personally belonged to Arlpalywerrng discussed with the anthropologists, it was also performed and permitted to be photographed (Gillen, 1968, pp. 134, 140–142).[4] Although Arrernte people had given Spencer and Gillen permission to witness and photograph their sacred ceremonies five years earlier, after years of collaboration with Gillen, this appears to have been the first time Anmatyerr people had done so (Morphy, 1997; Kimber, 1998). Without preexisting relationships of trust or familiarity, it was a remarkably open exchange.

Future interactions with ethnographers would later build on this model of congregating groups of people together, utilizing local connections with pastoralists or colonial authorities, and providing rations and other resources in exchange for cultural information. The performance of ceremony and song was emerging as a critical zone of cultural interaction and translation.

The "Government Mob"

It wasn't until an unusual group of prominent men from Melbourne arrived at Ti Tree in the winter of 1927 that Anmatyerr people were again subject to intensive examination. Known as the "Victorian Railways 'Reso' Tour to

---

3. See annotations for the following images in the Spencer Collection at Museum Victoria: XP14390, XP14388, XP14389, XP14391, XP14392, XP 14393.

4. See also Spencer's Journal XM5856 (p. 116) and photograph XP9022 (Museum Victoria).

Central Australia," the group consisted of over sixty individuals, including "influential" businessmen, journalists, graziers, politicians, naturalists, doctors, dentists, and chemists. The primary interest of this entourage was to investigate the economic prospects of the arid interior's natural resources (hence "Reso"), but exploring the exotic "outback" of Central Australia that featured large in the imagination of urban Australia (Sutton, 2009b) was also on the agenda.

Among the party was author, journalist, and connoisseur of Aboriginal culture Charles Barrett, as well as Leonard Keith Ward, a geologist who had traveled with Walter Baldwin Spencer to Alice Springs four years earlier (Barrett, 1940; Barrett, Croll, and Elkin, 1943; Barrett, 1939, pp. 206–207). The group traveled by train to Oodnadatta and then by car convoy to Alice Springs and on to Tea Tree Well (on Ti Tree Station), where they had been promised a "big corroboree" as a finale to their journey. Exactly who planned these events is difficult to determine, but it appears that a range of colonial authorities played their part. Instructions were first sent to the Chief Protector of Aborigines stationed at the Barrow Creek Telegraph Station, Mounted Constable William George Murray. Murray, of course, was soon to be notorious for his leading role in the Coniston shootings the following year.

As Murray traveled south to Ti Tree Station to join them, he ordered Anmatyerr people from the nearby cattle stations to congregate at Bullocky Soak, at the base of Central Mount Stuart, and await further instructions.[5] Clearly accustomed to having Aboriginal labor available to them at all times, some pastoralists complained that their workers had been "taken away" by Murray simply to "attend a corroboree" (Spierings, 1984, p. 20). To the south of Ti Tree, another group of Anmatyerr people living with the solitary Methodist missionary Miss Annie Lock at Arden Soak (Mer Ilpereny) were also on their way to play their part in the performance for the "Resos (Turner, 1930; Cartwright, 1995; Gibson, 2007; Bishop, 2008.

Annie Lock claimed that the Anmatyerr were fearful of the order from the authorities to see "all the natives of the district . . . take part in a dance." It had only been the promise of plentiful food that had eventually swayed them to participate (Turner, 1930, p. 11). Horrified by the encouragement of this "pagan" behavior and distressed to see Constable

---

5. See "Northern Territory Police Journal Barrow Creek," Feb. 27, 1926–Aug. 31, 1932. NTAS Series F258/Box1/ItemA305.

Murray "roar" at the Arden Soak group for singing any Christian hymns, Lock labeled the event as a sham and went as far as claiming that the ceremonies later shown to the visitors had been inauthentic (Turner, 1930, pp. 12–13). On the other hand, Bill Heffernan, owner of Ti Tree Station, was quick to fulfill his role in the event, and ensured that a number of bullocks were slaughtered to feed the "Reso" party and the Aboriginal performers. According to newspaper coverage, two hundred Anmatyerr people had been rallied together for the "most interesting spectacle" of the tour (Anonymous, 1927).

The "Resos" were not interested in serious anthropological or ethnographic enquiry. Their documentation was more in the mold of earlier nineteenth-century descriptions of curious or exotic people. In this vein, Aboriginal people and their ceremonial performances were often poorly understood, regarded as temporally and spatially distant, and thus seen as "savage," "strange," and "exotic" (Casey, 2012, p. 3). The photographs and film produced at the time reveal images of curious onlookers, dressed in suit coats and hats, standing at a careful distance from the performers with cameras at the ready (Edwards, 1927). The meaning or purpose behind the ceremonies was probably lost on the audience.

Sharing some of the photographs taken during the event with Anmatyerr men in 2014, it was clear that the ceremonies on display were, contrary to Annie Lock's assertions, entirely genuine.[6] Sitting only meters from the site of the "big corroboree," Paddy Kemarr and Jimmy Haines flicked through the black-and-white photographs, identifying what they could. It was clear from the body paint adorning both men and women that among the ceremonies performed were *althart* (male public dances) (figure 2.3), *awely* (women's public ceremonies), and at least one sacred men's ceremony, featuring a ground painting (*Irlpanter*).[7]

---

6. Motion picture film taken at the time is compiled in "A Reso Tour to Central Australia," National Film and Sound Archives, Title 9400. See also the Northern Territory Library's "Reso Tour" Photographic Collection. The H.R. Balfour Collection at the Melbourne Museum also contains a similar photographic print (see item XP 16633).

7. The term "Irlapnter" appears to consist of "Irlpa" (ear) and "anter" (fat) in what is likely a metaphor for "knowledge." Original photographs from the Reso Tour reproduced here were taken by one of the drivers employed on the tour, Mr. Roy Renfrey (kindly supplied by Roy's grandson, Glenn Boerth). Other photographs from the tour can be found in the State Library of Victoria and the Northern Territory Library's photographic collections.

Figure 2.3. Anmatyerr men decorated for althart (a public ceremony) at Tea Tree Well in August 1927. Photograph taken by Roy Renfrey. (Image courtesy of Glenn and Rosemary Boerth).

Arguably the Resos' most ethnographically oriented team member, Charles Barrett made the only serious attempt at engaging with the performers. His endeavors reveal just how shallow, and potentially offensive, these interactions could be when *alhernter* rushed in without first being attuned to cultural and linguistic differences:

> When I approached and bent down to examine the ground-picture, the greybeards with bald foreheads and hair done a la chignon, waved me away with angry cries. They had not a word of English, while I was ignorant of the Arunta or Aranda language. We resorted to gesture language and got on very well. I pointed to the red and white circle, then placed a hand over my eyes. They smiled approvingly, and laughed as I walked slowly away. (Barrett, 1939, p. 207)

Barrett eventually came to understand that the circular red and white ground painting was restricted to men, but on the whole, the "Resos" lacked sensitivity in the way they approached the Anmatyerr. *Tywerrenge* (sacred objects) were also collected from the performers by Barrett, but they were treated as curios, with little contextual information being taken down about their significance or meaning.[8] The "Resos" claimed that the event was one of "the greatest" corroboree(s) ever seen by white people in Central Australia" (*The News*, 1927), but for the Anmatyerr the encounter was remembered in less effusive terms and represented the interests of colonial authority.

Speaking with linguist and anthropologist Jennifer Green in the early 1980s, an elderly Jacob Petyarr recalled the "big corroboree time":

> A big mob of men went, and they camped at Bullocky (Soak). From there they went to Ti Tree, and they had a big meeting, a big corroboree. That's when I was a kid, a long time ago. The station was there, only the station, no pub, and that old whitefella (Heffernan) was there. The Government came up from the south, they had those cameras with legs (on tripods). They photo'd people, with some rubbish clothes, some naked. The station mob killed two bullocks to feed us, and we ate bullock. The Government mob brought food, oranges, lollies, everything. That's big corroboree time, long time ago. (qtd. in Spierings, 1984, pp. 20–21)

Though short-lived and shallow, the performance for the "Government mob" had reinforced a developing mode of interaction and exchange. As with the earlier Spencer and Gillen expedition, pastoralists and local colonial authorities had again encouraged Anmatyerr people (more forcibly this time) to come together to demonstrate their cultural wares in exchange for food and access to other resources. The symbolic labor of ceremonial performance, song and dance, as well as trade in ritual artefacts became an acknowledged currency, alongside labor in the pastoral economy, in exchange for material resources.

The Cockatoo Creek Expedition

The University of Adelaide's Board for Anthropological Research expedition to Cockatoo Creek in 1931 continued with these themes of building

---

8. See item X 087589 at Museum Victoria.

congregations and trading resources in exchange for information and ritual knowledge. The Board had already carried out a number of similar expeditions into other parts of Australia, and would often seek out "contact" with Aboriginal people in remote locations by bringing them together in a proposed camp so they could be subjected to intensive examinations (Jones, 1987; Batty, 2013a; 2006a).

Led by medical and physical anthropologists John Burton Cleland and Thomas Draper Campbell, the team adhered to a rather outmoded evolutionary approach already under fire from Functionalism's theoretical shift away from speculative, evolutionary chronologies of human development. In studying the so-called "pure-blood natives" living on the pastoral stations to the northwest of Alice Springs (Cleland, 1932, p. 369), the Board was unashamed in its intention to gather physiological, psychological, and cultural data that might shed light on the place of Aboriginal people within this evolutionary paradigm.

Prior to the arrival of the expedition, Swiss-born missionary Eugene Ernest Kramer and his Arrernte assistant Mickey Akwerre Dow Dow had been engaged to spread the word of the upcoming event. Not unlike the Spencer and Gillen expedition and the "Resos" event, the Cockatoo Creek expedition utilized local expertise and resources to promote the coming together of people for the purposes of ethnographic study and curiosity. An expert bushman who had already traveled extensively in the Anmatyerr and Arrernte areas, Kramer was an obvious choice as expedition "fixer," and Dow Dow could easily converse with the predominantly Anmatyerr-speaking population in the area; they were the perfect duo for the task (Jones, 2011, pp. 71–92; Batty, 2013b). Anmatyerr residents at Napperby Station were first entertained with lantern slide picture shows and bible readings, before seeking out further potential participants camped along the creeks to the north, encouraging them to "follow on" to Anartelh (Cockatoo Creek). To bolster the gathering, several parties of chosen Station "boys" (Aboriginal stockmen) from Napperby and Coniston Stations were also sent out on "riding camels" with Dow Dow to call in additional people.[9]

As news of the gathering spread, the camp soon swelled to close to 150 individuals. Kramer entertained the first arrivals with more Christian songs, lantern shows, and bible readings, and began to distribute rations as they waited for the academics from Adelaide to arrive. Seeing it as his "duty" to "befriend" the "natives" to the researchers, Kramer hoped the

---

9. Kramer's Northwest Journey Report, August 1931. SLSA, PRG1322/2, p. 4.

congregation would function as something of a reconciliation between the settlers and the local "tribe" who in his view had been "deeply disturbed" by the "murderous reprisals" of the Coniston shootings only a few years earlier.[10] Most of the team set to work with psychological and physical tests while Norman B. Tindale, the expedition member from the South Australian Museum most interested in sociocultural anthropology, began noting the particulars of each of the participants. Numbers were assigned to each individual, and with help from Kramer, Dow Dow, and the expedition's Arrernte-speaking interpreter, Tom Wheeler Tjungala, people's genealogies, age, sex, and "tribe" were recorded on "sociological data cards," along with other cultural information.

The majority of people who came in to Cockatoo Creek identified themselves as "Anmatjera" (Anmatyerr), with the remainder describing themselves as either Luritja or Warlpiri. Learning that the Anmatyerr spoke "an Aranda type language," Tindale appreciated having Arrernte speakers at hand.[11] Just as Jim Kite had assisted Spencer and Gillen in their discussions with "Jack" Arlpalywerrng at Barrow Creek, Wheeler and Dow Dow also played critical roles as interpreters. Wheeler even knew some of the songs and *Anengkerr* (Dreaming) mythologies being alluded to in conversations and, with help from these interpreters, Tindale drew up the first extensive record of Anmatyerr vocabulary. The linguistic differences across the region were not always easy for Tindale to comprehend, however, and when Wheeler referred to the language spoken at Cockatoo Creek as being "Nanna" (*nhenhe*), Tindale assumed this to be the name of a local dialect (Tindale, 1931, p. 202). In fact, *nhenhe* simply meant "here," meaning the language spoken by the people in the immediate locality.[12]

Just days into the expedition, Anmatyerr and Warlpiri men "offered" to perform a number of restricted ceremonies "for the benefit of the cameras."[13] Urabuta Ngwarray, an Anmatyerr man aged in his sixties (figure

---

10. Kramer's Northwest Journey Report, August 1931. SLSA, PRG1322/2, p. 5.

11. Tindale's journal and field notes, AA 338/1/7, Expedition G. Expedition to Cockatoo Creek, Central Australia, August 6–27, 1931. Journal and field notes by Norman B. Tindale, 1931, South Australian Museum, p. 175.

12. Tindale's journal and field notes, AA 338/1/7, Expedition G. Expedition to Cockatoo Creek, Central Australia, August 6–27, 1931. Journal and field notes by Norman B. Tindale, 1931, South Australian Museum, p. 202.

13. Tindale's journal and field notes, AA 338/1/7, Expedition G. Expedition to Cockatoo Creek, Central Australia, August 6–27, 1931. Journal and field notes by Norman B. Tindale, 1931, South Australian Museum, pp. 22–23.

2.4), organized the younger men to first perform an *atyelp* (Western Quoll) ceremony that personally belonged to him, before revealing a number of other ceremonies. This was now the third time that Anmatyerr sacred ceremonies had been photographed or filmed, but the first time that their associated songs had been audio-recorded.

In 2008, I had the opportunity to listen to these recordings and watch these films with James Glenn Mpetyan, then Chairman of the Anmatyerr Regional Council. James, in his early thirties, claimed to have no great insights into the recordings, but with his help we were able to work with the South Australian Museum to see digital copies returned to Anmatyerr communities. While the songs were difficult to decipher because of the scratch and pop of the wax cylinder recordings, the films had clearly captured aspects of men's initiation still practiced by all Anmatyerr. Since that time, numerous men have approached me to express their surprise that highly restricted ceremonies were recorded by the expedition.

The historical context of these recordings is partly explained by Tindale in his diaries. After many of these performances had taken place, a group of "mostly Anmatjera (Anmatyerr) men" approached Tindale offering a small collection of *tywerreng* (sacred objects). The objects being offered, Tindale was told, pertained to the main site in the Cockatoo Creek

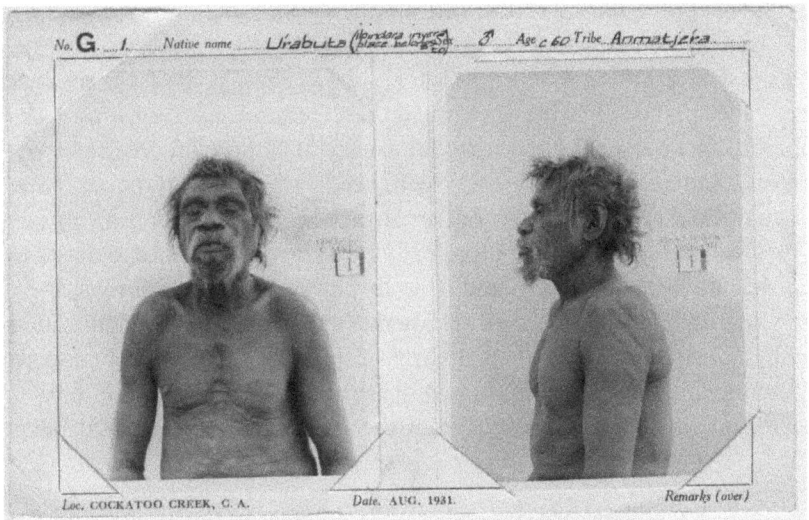

Figure 2.4. Urabuta, one of Tindale's Anmatyerr informants (South Australian Museum).

area, Anartelh (Anatila) (Tindale, 1931, pp. 25–36, 49, 50). As the South Australian Museum's principal representative, Tindale dutifully received the objects, but at the same time tried to justify his actions with reference to what he understood of Central Australia hierarchies. Presumably being familiar with the Western Arrernte concept of an *Ingkarte* (a ceremonial "chief," "leader," or "boss") from his experiences at Hermannsburg during an earlier Board for Anthropological Research expedition in 1929, Tindale attempted to employ this concept amongst the Anmatyerr.

Seeking to build an analogy between the responsibilities of the museum curator and the ritual owner of ceremonial objects, Tindale identified himself as being equivalent to an "Inkatai" (Ingkarte). Though we cannot be sure how this notion was received, a ritual exchange then took place whereby sacred objects were pressed against Tindale and others from the expedition:

> The old men pressed three of the *tjurunga* (*tywerreng*) upon us; we had already told them on a previous occasion that I was the man who was *inkatai* (Ingkarte) or "boss" of all the *tjurunga* at Adelaide (Museum).[14]

This method of handing over sacred objects after pressing them on a man's body (usually on his stomach) was first experienced and described by Spencer and Gillen at the turn of the twentieth century (1904, pp. 265–266). Known among the Arrernte as *atnerte ulpe-ileme*, literally the mashing or grinding of the stomach (Wilkins, 2001, p. 496), the practice was often practiced at the termination of ceremonies and seen as a way of creating a personal bond with the Ancestral beings embodied in these objects. Unlike Europeans, who regard the heart as the emotional center of an individual, Central Australians tend to regard the stomach this way (Turpin, 2002; Gibson, 2013, pp. 61, 70). By inviting anthropologists to participate in these rituals, and to even physically take *tywerreng*, these acts can be interpreted as sincere attempts at conveying the significance and import of people's "Law" (their deeply felt personal connections with ancestors and the country they created). Trading of these objects increased in Central Australia from the end of the nineteenth century

---

14. Tindale's journal and field notes, AA 338/1/7, Expedition G. Expedition to Cockatoo Creek, Central Australia, August 6–27, 1931. Journal and field notes by Norman B. Tindale, 1931, South Australian Museum, p. 48.

(Jones, 1995a), and also became an aspect of Strehlow's work in the decades to come.

The performance of these rituals, as well as Tindale's enlistment of the *Ingkarte* concept, invited, at least in a symbolic sense, the elevation of some Central Australian principles. Finding proper ways of classifying and positioning each other was critical to the exchange at hand. For example, the presence of "observers" to secret rituals was unlikely to have existed prior to the arrival of settlers, and the trading of religious objects with unrelated and utterly disconnected people was a relatively new phenomenon that obviously required cultural translation. Individuals who showed sincere interest in ritual and ceremony, in "Law," were being accommodated to some degree in order to legitimate their interactions. More than this, though, the notion of an *alhernter ingkarte* (a non-Aboriginal ritual leader) taking artefacts away to their "museums" was also being introduced. These were significant precedents to the far more advanced and personally invested form of participation from T.G.H. Strehlow (and others) in the years to come.

After two weeks of intensive data collecting, recording, and experimentation, the expedition party departed amid shouted "goodbyes" and the waving of hands. One old Warrmarla man from the far western desert, Tindale noted, approached the group and "made quite a speech asking us to come back again to his country and have a big series of ceremonies."[15] Silas Antenh Ngal, whose family had been present at the Cockatoo Creek camp at the time, explained to T.G.H. Strehlow many years later that the expedition had been remembered in largely positive terms (1968a, pp. 57–64). While the names of most of the academics present were forgotten in the oral history, Silas described the event as an *urumbula* (*urrempel*) festival that had been supported by men named "Kramer" and "Tini" [Tindale]. Their provision of food stuffs and other resources had enabled the coming together of people from disparate locations to perform and share ceremonial and cultural knowledge.

Rather than seeing the expedition in *alhernter* terms, either as an exercise in scientific exploration or even colonial coercion, for the Anmatyerr the event marked a demonstration and sharing of cultural knowledge. Even the bags of rations handed out by Kramer and the others

---

15. Tindale's journal and field notes, AA 338/1/7, Expedition G. Expedition to Cockatoo Creek, Central Australia, August 6–27, 1931. Journal and field notes by Norman B. Tindale, 1931, South Australian Museum, p. 56

were remembered as "tjaurelija" (*tyewarrely*), a traditional payment of food usually offered in exchange for ritual knowledge by novices (Strehlow, 1968a, p. 57). As Anmatyerr people transposed the *urrempel* concept on to the interrogations of the *alhernter*, and men like Tindale tried to build analogies between the authority of the *Ingkarte* and the authority of the anthropologist, the participants came to a negotiated understanding of these events. This does not mean, of course, that the experiences and recollections of the expedition were the same, or that inequality was overcome. What I have tried to show, however, is the ways in which the Anmatyerr (and Warlpiri) looked to gain value from the circumstances that confronted them and anthropology sought to justify its actions in Aboriginal terms.

Episodes of colonial violence and coercion, as well as the exchanges of labor and resources on the pastoral frontier, provide an important backdrop to Anmatyerr and *alhernter* encounters. Anmatyerr people's limited yet meaningful experience with ethnography and ethnographers had provided their own unique "theatre of contact," "enlivened by the agency of each troupe of actors—European and indigenous" (Jones, 2015, p. 90). In this particular "contact zone," both parties exhibited a preparedness to engage. Even where the enquiry was driven by the affectations of colonial and scientific exploration, or produced rather limited linguistic and ethnographic accounts, the relationships that ensued often awkwardly and unevenly progressed toward a meaningful exchange of objects, knowledge, names, and concepts. These local experiences established important anticipations and expectancies that were taken up and developed further in the following decades.

By the early decades of the twentieth century, the Anmatyerr and many other Aboriginal groups in remote Australia had experienced a period of enormous adjustment. The violence of the early period wrought terrible tragedy and social trauma, but also gave rise to complex interpersonal and intergroup relations. When ethnographers arrived looking for "un-spoilt" or "uncontaminated" "natives," they often encountered individuals who had already intermingled with settler society to varying degrees. The colonial infrastructure of the Overland Telegraph Line cutting through the remote center of Anmatyerr territory had meant that the form of ethnography that developed during this time was particularly reliant on networks of preexisting relationships among settlers, missionaries, and local Aboriginal people. Early cultural translation was achieved with the help of Arrernte speaking interpreters and guides.

Particularly significant was the way in which Anmatyerr people's symbolic and cultural capital, in these cases men's ritual knowledge, was at the center of these exchanges. Instigated by ethnographers with ties to government administration and universities, but crucially enabled by local pastoralists and missionaries, the "big corroborees," or what the Anmatyerr regarded as *urrempel* festivals, brought with them opportunities for meaningful intercultural dialogue as well as access to material resources. At the same time, the idea that *alhernter* taking some kind of responsibility for ritual information and objects was also an emergent idea among Central Australian men during the late nineteenth and early twentieth century.

These historical events and social engagements prefigured Strehlow's arrival on the scene in the 1930s. Generally, these early colonial interactions have been scrutinized for their inequalities, romanticism, or shallowness, but in the zones of translation described above, there appears to have been room for varied interpretations and purposes. While Anmatyerr people may have been seen as objects of curiosity by the inquiring *alhernter*, I suggest that their participation in ethnographic encounters was not entirely defined by this gaze. Although "performing their Aboriginality" within discursive and material conditions set by others (see Myers, 2002, pp. 255–276), Anmatyerr people also made sense of these interactions. Meeting with Anmatyerr people for the first time in 1932, T.G.H. Strehlow's fieldwork would partly build on these earlier experiences and expectations. His methods and conceptual interests, however, would be quite distinct from many of his predecessors.

Chapter 3

Strehlow's Scope

> Experiential authority is based on a "feel" for the foreign context, a kind of accumulated savvy and sense of the style of a people or place. Such an appeal is frequently explicit in the texts of the early professional participant-observers
>
> —J. Clifford (1983)

From the late nineteenth century up until the 1920s, anthropologists across the globe saw themselves as explorers, moving into virgin and exotic territories occupied by "primitive" peoples. By the 1930s, though, the discipline had begun to move away from the model of scientific expeditions and fleeting exchanges on frontiers, and social evolutionism was on the wane (Stocking, 1983). While some of the earliest anthropologists had certainly acknowledged the difficulties of seeing the world in the same way as "the natives themselves" (Gardner and McConvell, 2015), the emerging ethnographic methods took this objective far more seriously. Building on the innovative participant observation work of Frank Hamilton Cushing in North America and Spencer and Gillen in Australia, far more intensive fieldwork was now increasingly expected of ethnographers (Kuklick, 2012; Young, 2004). It was at this historical juncture that T.G.H. Strehlow began to make his first forays into a still rather nascent field of ethnography and Indigenous language documentation in Australia.

Understanding the underpinning theoretical influences and the intellectual style of T.G.H. Strehlow is essential for appreciating the personal and professional orientation he brought to interactions with informants. While analyses of Strehlow's moral character and intriguing life are plentiful

(Hill, 2003; McNally, 1981; Morton, 1995; 2004; 1993), far less has been written about his conceptual and methodological approaches to ethnography. The breadth of his career as a collector and translator of Arandic (and to a lesser degree Luritja) language material (McNally, 1981; Hill, 2003; Rowse, 1999; Rubuntja and Green, 2002, pp. 116–119; Morton, 1995; Moore, 2008), an administrator and activist in "native affairs"(Long, 1992; Rowse, 1992, 2012; Inglis, 2002), and his associations with Christianity (Austin-Broos, 2009; Moore, 2016) have all aroused significant attention.

Ward McNally's *Aborigines, Artefacts and Anguish* (1981), an authorized biography written only months before Strehlow's death in October 1978, was the first text to bring the drama of T.G.H. Strehlow's life to light. A relatively slight manuscript, McNally's account provides the general reader with a chronological account of the major events in Strehlow's life with insights from friends, colleagues, and relations. Over twenty years later, Barry Hill's *Broken Song: T.G.H. Strehlow and Aboriginal Possession* (2003) considerably extended and deepened this biographical narrative, and notwithstanding a number of philosophical ruminations and detours, was mostly concerned with the challenges of translation. Hill's work has undoubtedly become the most important biographical piece on T.G.H. Strehlow to date, but remarkably, neither he nor McNally made any serious attempts to examine his ethnographic methods or anthropological inspiration.

Barry Hill's biography of T.G.H. Strehlow's life does nonetheless tell us a lot about his development as an ethnographer. Despite being overshadowed by a primitivism borne of his training in the Classics and literature, Strehlow's work overwhelmingly relied on the stuff of ethnography, what Ingold describes as the desire to describe the lives of a living people with an "accuracy and sensitivity honed by detailed observation and prolonged first-hand experience" (2011, p. 229). In Strehlow's case, this involved decades of intensive study into the mythic, linguistic, and ritual underpinnings of Arrernte speaking peoples. Understanding the specific theoretical lenses and methodological influences he took into the field helps us recognize the scope and intent of his research and how this may have affected his interactions with Anmatyerr and Arrernte people.

Plotting a Complicated Life

Theodor George Henry (T.G.H.) Strehlow (1908–1978) was born at the Hermannsburg Mission, Central Australia, on June 6, 1908. He was the son of Carl and Frieda Strehlow, Lutheran missionaries who had emigrated from Germany in 1892. Before arriving in Australia, Carl Strehlow had trained at the Neuendettelsau seminary in southern Germany in preparation for his missionary work overseas (Strehlow, 2011; Kenny, 2013). Upon being posted to the Bethesda Mission at Killalpaninna in remote northern South Australia, Carl Strehlow worked with the Reverend J.G. Reuther on a translation of the New Testament into the local Diyari language (Stevens, 1994). In 1894, the Strehlow family headed northwest, further into the interior, to take over the dilapidated Hermannsburg Mission established in 1877.

Carl worked diligently to first learn the Diyari language spoken at Bethesda, and then the Arrernte and Luritja languages spoken at Hermannsburg. Through producing translations of Christian hymns and the Old Testament, Carl Strehlow's interest in the Arrernte and Luritja people at Hermannsburg extended well beyond his missionizing. Becoming one of the first ethnographers in this part of Australia, and producing outstanding written records of local traditions, songs, and mythologies, Carl Strehlow's contributions to Australian anthropology were substantial, though not well recognized at the time. Written in the German nineteenth-century humanistic style, predominantly out of step with the British evolutionist approach to anthropology prevalent in Australia at the time, his work remained under-recognized. Over ten years after first arriving at Hermannsburg, Carl published his first volume, *Die Aranda- und Loritja-Stamme in Zentral-Australien (The Aranda and Loritja Tribes of Central Australia)* with support from the Städtisches Völkermuseum in Frankfurt. The following year, young T.G.H. was born.

T.G.H. Strehlow was raised in an environment where his parents often spoke a combination of German, English, and Arrernte and where close relationships with Aboriginal people were the norm. He learned the local Arrernte dialect spoken by his childhood companions, and his father also taught him Greek and Latin, giving him a passion for the Old World of Europe.[1] Undoubtedly a significant figure in T.G.H. Strehlow's life, when Carl Strehlow died whilst traveling down the Finke River to receive medical attention, the event became the theme of his sole literary publication, *Journey to Horseshoe Bend* (Strehlow, 1969a). Written in the third person,

---

1. Upon listening to recordings of T.G.H. Strehlow's voice, some Anmatyerr men have commented that he spoke with a Pertame (Southern Arrernte) accent. Pertame is an endangered language spoken by people living along the southern reaches of the Finke River, immediately to the south of Hermannsburg.

the novel is a cathartic recounting of the journey of the fourteen-year-old son "Theo" as he ponders a landscape eternally animated by *Altyerre* (Dreaming) ancestors while witnessing his own father's own mortality.

Following his father's death in 1922, Strehlow moved away from Central Australia and relocated to Adelaide with his mother, Frieda. He was fourteen years old at the time, the approximate age that many of the Aboriginal boys he had grown up with at Hermannsburg would have begun to be initiated (Strehlow, 1978a, p. 150). As his male Arrernte peers started their instruction in song and ceremony, Strehlow commenced his studies at the Lutheran Immanuel College and later enrolled to study the Classics and English literature at the University of Adelaide. Having excelled in his studies, he was subsequently awarded an Australian National Research Council grant to study "Australian Native languages," and returned to Central Australia in 1932 to begin his fieldwork. Strehlow's return began what would become a lifelong enterprise in documenting Arrernte languages, songs, and ceremonies (see chapter 5).

In his reflections many decades later, Strehlow described how it had been the legacy of his father, and his conception and birth at Hermannsburg, that had opened doors for him across the region:

> Once my credentials—son of Mr. Strehlow of Hermannsburg, and Aranda (Arrernte) tribesman, Kamara class, conception site Ntarea—had been announced, there was no question of my being treated as an ignorant white man any longer . . . Even Anmatjera (Anmatyerr) men at Aileron, Leramba and Mt. Allan, also Walbiri men, had spoken to me with respect as soon as I had been introduced as "the" tjurunga (*tywerrenge*) leader, who knew all about men's tjurunga everywhere. (1968a, p. 114)

A "Famous Father"

Being the son of Carl Strehlow not only made his research among the Arrernte easier, it also prefigured his engagement with the scholarly community. The highly influential social anthropologist Raymond Firth, for example, referenced these patrilineal "credentials" when introducing T.G.H. as the son of a "famous father" at a conference in London, and other academic advisors often noted his father's work (Strehlow, 1950a, p. 165). Carl Strehlow's influence on his son was not just personal and psychological, as has been noted in the literature (Morton, 2004; Hill, 2003), it also had a significant impact on the approaches he developed in ethnography and linguistics. Like his father, T.G.H. Strehlow shared a deep interest in language and myth, and adopted a style of mostly descriptive ethnography that avoided grand theorizing. The original manuscripts of his father's work, along with Carl's unpublished dictionary and over 150 "family trees," stayed in the possession of T.G.H. throughout his career (Kenny, 2008, p. 43). Although he rarely admitted it, his father's work had set an important precedent for his own research. Father and son even shared "informants," with men such as Wapiti (or Talku), Arawe-irreke (Rauwiraka, Nathanael), (figure 3.1) and Moses Tjalkabota providing information to both men.

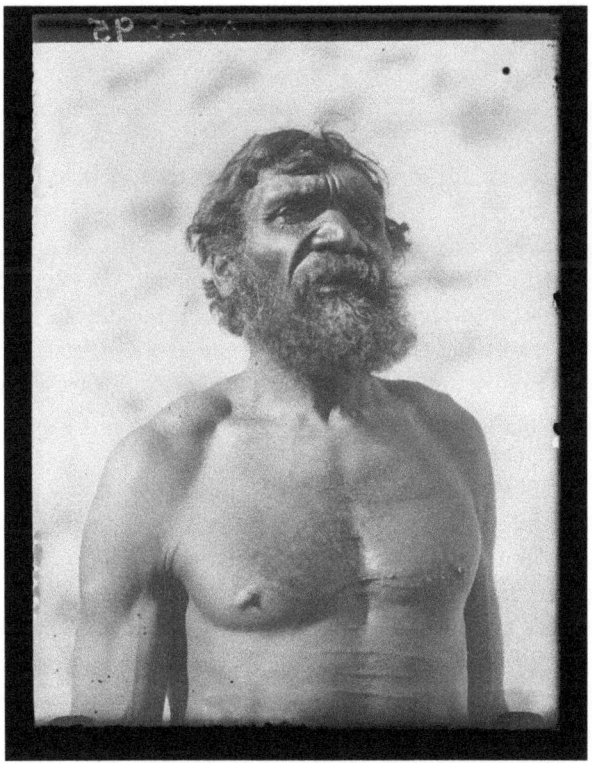

Figure 3.1. Arawe-irreke (Raueruka) or "Nathanael," photographed by Herbert Basedow at Hermannsburg in 1920 (National Museum of Australia).

In her recent assessment of Carl Strehlow's scholarship, anthropologist Anna Kenny (2013) has shown how different his approach was to that of his Australian contemporaries. Carl Strehlow was largely marginalized by the anthropological establishment in Australia and Britain, with Walter Baldwin Spencer suggesting that he was inescapably tainted by his missionary background (1927, pp. 584–596), and Bronislaw Malinowski referring to him as "incompetent" (Young, 2004, p. 435). The Anglophone nature of Australian anthropology and its general desire to be a contrast to the "amateurish" ethnography of missionaries was undoubtedly a factor in this assessment of Strehlow's work, but as Kenny points out, equally important was the different "German" intellectual position that he represented.

Carl took his inspiration and guidance from his editor in Frankfurt, Baron Moritz Von Leonhardi. A German intellectual with an interest in philosophy and a humanistic tradition in anthropology, Leonhardi encouraged Strehlow to make strictly empirical observations and records and resist the temptation to make theoretical suppositions about the song or myth traditions of the Arrernte and Luritja compared to those of classical antiquity (Kenny, 2013, p. 121). Following the works of influential German anthropologists such as Rudolph Virchow and Adolf Bastian, Leonhardi's antagonism toward anthropological theories that hierarchically stratified "races" complemented Strehlow's Christian conviction in the unity of humankind (Kenny, 2005). Grounded not in social evolutionism, then, but in the intellectual spirit of German Romanticism, Christian theology, and philology, Strehlow's work focused on building a record of the language and traditions of Aboriginal people as a way of understanding their worldview. As a Lutheran missionary, his task of course had been to develop these linguistic skills in order to translate and preach the gospel in the local vernacular.

Far from being "incompetent," as Malinowski had claimed, Strehlow was able to produce excellent language, myth, and song translations of considerable depth. Although principally focused on the Western Arrernte and Luritja people residing in or near Hermannsburg, Carl was also among the first to make reference to the "Imatjera" (Anmatyerr). *Die Aranda- und Loritja-Stamme in Zentral-Australien* includes some of the earliest references to Anmatyerr words, phrases, place names, songs, and mythologies (Strehlow, 1907b, pp. 56, 410, 412, 413, 701, 718), which he had presumably collected from men like Arawe-irreke (Rauwiraka), a Western Arrernte man who had been conceived in Anmatyerr territory.

Carl Strehlow's greatest weakness as an ethnographer, however, was his refusal to witness the sacred ceremonies that accompanied the song and myths that he had collected. As a Christian, Strehlow regarded these ceremonies as ultimately pagan in nature, and while he did collect some of their ritual paraphernalia, he was unable to produce eye-witness accounts of how they were used. While his contemporaries Spencer and Gillen lacked the type of linguistic competence needed to develop an accurate comprehension of ceremony and song, Strehlow's work lacked detailed photographic, filmic, and audio records.

As a student of both his father's and Spencer and Gillen's work, the young Strehlow began to bring these two strengths together. Throughout his career he would attempt a comprehensive documentation that combined textual work, ethnographic description, and the use of various recording technologies (see chapter 5). In the main, though, his focus remained squarely on the primary interests of his father: literature and language.

Literature and Language

T.G.H. Strehlow embraced classical studies and English literature at university. He studied Latin and Greek in his undergraduate years and emerged from the University of Adelaide with First Class Honors in English. Under the tutelage of Professor Archibald Strong, the author of an acclaimed translation of the oldest surviving Old English poem *Beowulf*, a keen interest in the literature and mythologies of Europe matured. Turning his mind to postgraduate studies under the careful guidance of Professor of Classics, John Aloysius FitzHerbert (1892–1970), Strehlow later devised a masters research proposal that went on to shape the remainder of his academic career and the overall trajectory of his life.

FitzHerbert, a Cambridge-educated professor of Classics, Comparative Philology, and Literature at the University of Adelaide, had been aware of Carl Strehlow's publications and quickly recognized the unique opportunity before the young Strehlow. His distinctive background and ability with languages meant he had the opportunity of making serious advances into the study of Aboriginal languages. FitzHerbert encouraged Strehlow to combine his knowledge of Arrernte and his passion for traditional literature in a concentrated study of the Central Australian language and poetry.

In hindsight, Strehlow's MA thesis proposal looks like an early sketch of the themes that came to dominate his magnum opus, *Songs of Central Australia*, published over forty years later. Grounded in his passion for literature, the original idea was to examine the "Primitive Elements in Old Icelandic Mythology and in Old English Heroic Verse, in the light of Aranda Myths and Legends" (Hill, 2003, p. 121). While the research into Icelandic and Old English traditions could be carried out using library and archival sources, discovering the oral traditions of Arandic "myths and legends" required extensive fieldwork. His first task, therefore, was to make a record of the Arrernte language in terms of phonetics and grammar, and second, to map out the geographic territories and linguistic variations of the various Arrernte dialects. It was these objectives that took him beyond the familiar territory of his upbringing in Arrernte (specifically Western Arrernte) country and to circumnavigate the Anmatyerr region during his initial fieldwork (see chapter 5).

In these formative stages of his career, Strehlow found additional guidance from a number of individuals associated with the University of Adelaide's Board for Anthropological Research. Some of these men had conducted fieldwork with the Anmatyerr and Warlpiri at Cockatoo Creek in the previous year (as discussed in chapter 2), and many of them had also been to Hermannsburg, Alice Springs, and other places in Central Australia during the 1920s and early 1930s. The medical anthropologists John Burton Cleland, Thomas Draper Campbell, and Henry Kenneth Fry, as well as Norman Tindale from the South Australian Museum, supported Strehlow, each providing advice on method and theory (Jones, 1995b; Strehlow, 1932, p. 203). The Board would also later enlist Strehlow to work alongside the men who coordinated the Cockatoo Creek gathering so efficiently, Ernest Kramer and Mickey Dow Dow, in order to track down Aboriginal people living across the remote Western Desert for an upcoming expedition to Mt. Liebig in 1932.

After returning from extensive fieldwork throughout the wider Arandic region in 1932 and 1933, FitzHerbert arranged for Strehlow to obtain a junior lectureship position at the University (Jones, 2002). Now able to devote time to writing up his research findings, Strehlow first published a detailed account of a Northern Arrernte song and myth (Strehlow, 1933a). He then began compiling his thesis, the first grammar ever produced of Arrernte (Strehlow, 1938), which was later published as *Aranda Phonetics and Grammar* (1942). This manuscript concentrated on the form of Arrernte Strehlow knew and spoke best, Western Arrernte, making only scant references to other Arandic dialects such as Northern Arrernte, Southern Arrernte, Central and Eastern Arrernte, or Anmatyerr (Wilkins, 1989, p. 18; Moore, 2008). Aside from his contributions on Arrernte, Strehlow also become the first scholar to describe features of the type of English used by Aboriginal people (Eades, 2013, pp. 106–107), what he called "Northern Territory English."

Subsequent Arrernte language specialists, while praising Strehlow's pioneering work, have come to re-assess his linguistic contributions on a number of fronts (Wilkins, 1989; Breen, 2002; Moore, 2003; Green, 2012). There was common agreement that his work was seminal in its treatment of Arrernte as a language of great complexity and subtlety, which made it very hard for arguments to persist that Aboriginal languages were crude or unsophisticated. However, inconsistencies in the way he rendered Arrernte sounds, and his tendency to maintain spellings in their Western Arrernte form instead of changing them to reflect the different Arandic dialects, were just a few of the limitations that make his work somewhat difficult to interpret (Breen, 2002, p. 57). At the time of Strehlow's training there were no departments of linguistics in Australian universities, and the conceptual approach that he took with him into the field was grounded more in the historical study of literary languages, texts, and written records. His work thus sits awkwardly between nineteenth-century philology and twentieth-century structuralism (Moore, 2008). By continuing to cast his work in the "classical Indo-European model," Strehlow had failed, according to Wilkins (1989, p. 18), to draw on many of the analytical practices already well known in linguistics by the 1940s.

Strehlow's work was interrupted throughout the late 1930s and 1940s because he was engaged as a Patrol Officer with the Northern Territory Administration initially, and then later in World War II military service. As the first Native Affairs Patrol Officer, Strehlow was charged with ensuring the welfare of "natives" in the Central Australian region (Long, 1992, pp. 5, 16–22). As he traveled across Aboriginal Reserves and pastoral leases, he made important personal connections both with pastoralists and Aboriginal people across a large area. Soon after returning to his academic vocation, with an appointment as senior research fellow in Australian Linguistics at the University of Adelaide in 1946, his study of ritual and related social organization, *Aranda Traditions* (1947), was published. Two years later he was able to take up a postgraduate fellowship at the Australian National

University. On the advice of Professor A.P. Elkin he attended the London School of Economics (LSE) to undertake his first studies in the discipline of anthropology.

At the LSE, Strehlow sought support and guidance from the then head of the anthropology department, the eminent ethnographer of Oceania Raymond Firth. Strehlow hoped that Firth might confer on him a doctorate in recognition of his existing publications, which included his manuscript for *Songs of Central Australia*. He soon realized, however, that Firth, like Elkin, remained unconvinced of his appreciation of social anthropology (Hill, 2002: 472–473). Strehlow's opinion was that the training in linguistics and anthropology being offered at the LSE was largely irrelevant to his work. Instead of bending his work to fit the strictures of social anthropology, Strehlow was unwavering in his commitment to Classics as his primary source of intellectual stimulation, and spent considerable time at the British Museum's Assyrian, Egyptian, and Greek collections during his time in London (Strehlow, 1950a).

Returning to Australia in 1954, Strehlow remained uninterested in the British school of social anthropology most dominant at the time and became a reader in Australian linguistics at the University of Adelaide. Toward the end of his career he received an honorary Doctor of Letters from Adelaide University as well as an honorary doctorate from Uppsala University in Sweden; he was also made Professor of Australian Linguistics (1970–1973). His in-depth knowledge of the Arrernte language and its dialects, as well as his deep interest in ritual, religion, dance performance, material culture, song, and cultural geography, meant it was difficult to confine his work to a single discipline. As well as producing his own writings on Arandic literature, arts, and song practices (Strehlow, 1971a; 1964), he appears to have found some affinity among *alhernter* artists with an interest in Indigenous Australians. The sculptor William Ricketts (Strehlow, 1965b), the poet Roland Robinson (see his foreword to Robinson 1956), and the painter Rex Battarbee (Strehlow, 1961a) each received important public support from Strehlow due to their shared interest in seeing Indigenous culture elevated in the Australian national identity.

For these writers and artists, only the incorporation of an Indigenous sense of place, mythology, and poetry could make the Australian nation distinct from that of Britain or Europe (see Elliott, 1977; 1979). Described by Nicholas Thomas as "settler primitivism," these ideas emerged across numerous colonial states during the mid–twentieth century and looked to affirm settler relationships with their own particular, local "native" cultures

(1999, pp. 12–13). Exhibiting these tendencies, Strehlow hoped that the material he was gathering would play a part in giving the "new Australia" a "heart" of her own (1964b, p. 57). While these ambitions are now easily recognized for their appropriation or "looting" of Indigenous forms and styles of representation (see Sansom, 2006; Langton and David, 2003), "settler primitivism" was nonetheless part of a longer process of recognizing Indigeneity in colonial states (see McGregor, 2011; Thomas, 1999; Myers, 2006). Notwithstanding its framing within European bourgeois notions of religiousness, aesthetics, and environmental purity, this viewpoint improved the appreciation of Indigenous cultures and worldviews. Strehlow's work on literature and aesthetics gave considerable support to these endeavors.

Anthropology

Strehlow's intellectual engagement with the discipline of anthropology was always secondary to his interests in language and literature. While he certainly wished to be better recognized in this field, and exhibited expertise in this area, Strehlow never aspired to be an anthropologist (Jones, 2004, p. 37). Recent reappraisals of his contributions to anthropology, however, reveal a style of analysis somewhat ahead of its time. Largely disinterested in the abstracted models of social organization typical of British/Australian anthropology during the 1940s and 1950s, Strehlow's analyses were more akin to the "interpretive" anthropology of the 1960s and 1970s (Austin-Broos, 1997). Committed to detailed observation and prolonged firsthand experience, Strehlow attempted to portray Arandic song, language, and ritual experience from their point of view. Like Ronald Berndt, one of the few anthropologists in Australia who persistently supported Strehlow's work in the discipline (Berndt, 1979a; 1979b; Hill, 2003, pp. 743–744), Strehlow similarly strove to present material in ways that were true to their original context in Aboriginal society (Morphy, 2009, p. 78).

Defiantly describing himself as having been "trained by natives" and not by "armchair anthropologists," Strehlow balked at what he saw as a privileging of theory over local concepts (Strehlow, 1950a, p. 129). The disconnect between his approach and that of his contemporaries in British and Australian anthropology, who were largely preoccupied with social institutions, their structures, and functions, was made apparent during his aforementioned time with Raymond Firth in London. As he would later write in *Songs of Central Australia* (1971), "in a hundred years future research scholars will be much more interested in knowing what" Aboriginal people themselves had to say rather than "any explanatory theories advanced by Freud, Malinowski, Frazer, Róheim, and the rest" (Strehlow, 1971a, p. xxxix). His version of social research resonated with what American sociologist C. Wright Mills (2000, p. 215) described as "the individual social scientist" working in the "classic tradition," who in seeing their efforts as the "practice of a craft" are "made impatient and weary by elaborate discussions of method-and-theory-in-general."

Anthropology's preoccupation with corporate structures, kinship terminologies and marriage practices during the mid–twentieth century were far too removed from reality for Strehlow's liking. He derisively referred to the practices of "algebraically abbreviated kinship terms" and the systematization of field data used by most anthropologists as confusing for general readers, whom he believed should be the primary audience for work of this kind. He also thought these practices disregarded the "emotional overtones" inherent in "social relations" (Strehlow, 1966). Likewise, when reviewing the work of others in the field, he generally approved of those who approached their subject/s in a way that was "humanitarian" and/or "emotional" (Strehlow, 1970a; 1966, p. 75). Despite these aversions to social anthropological theory, his research did nevertheless engage with some of the conceptual apparatuses of Functionalism and made significant contributions to the Australianist literature on social control, agency, geography, and social structure (e.g., see Strehlow, 1950b; Theodor George Henry Strehlow, 1956; Strehlow, 1965c; 1970b).

When writing on these topics, Strehlow's own tendency toward systemization becomes apparent. In the face of his contemporaries in Australian anthropology who described a range of social institutions such as patrilineal clans, moieties, phratries, tribes, bands, and economic groups (Warner, 1964; Meggitt, 1962; Elkin, 1970), Strehlow instead insisted on only three such units: language/territorial groupings (such as Arrernte, Anmatyerr, etc.), the family group, and in particular, *anyenhenge* (*njinaŋa*) groups (1947; 1965c). The *anyenhenge* concept, an Arandic term that translates roughly as "father and child together," underpinned Strehlow's appreciation of land tenure and emphasized the centrality of patrilineal descent groups (Strehlow, 1947, p. 139). These groupings, now generally referred to in anthropological parlance as "estates" (Peterson and Long, 1986, p. 55), were according to Strehlow the "only political structural unit of Central Australian native society" (Strehlow, 1999, p. 7). Even though he understood the multiplicity of ways that people, land, and *Anengkerr/*

altyerre (Dreaming) would intersect and produce different relationships and rights in land, resources, and ritual knowledge, Strehlow defined the Arandic region as distinctly estate focused. As anthropologists John Morton (1997) and Peter Sutton (2003, p. 124) later observed, Strehlow had streamlined his own dense, ethnographic evidence to broadly fit a Functionalist program.

This rather rigid *anyenhenge* model sits somewhat uncomfortably with the genealogies that Strehlow recorded. Unlike his contemporaries in anthropology, Strehlow's genealogies were never collected in order to discover a social "system" of "kinship," but were used as a way of mapping the *specificity* of Arandic custom and culture. Labeled as "family trees," these documents typically followed the male members of an *anyenhenge* (estate) group and emphasized the place and Dreaming of each person's *aknganentye* or "spiritual conception," described as the process whereby a "Dreaming" being would animate a child in the womb (see Pink, 1933; Merlan, 1986; Hiatt, 1996, pp. 120–141). These events were not necessarily tied to the inheritance of Dreamings from either matrilineal or patrilineal ties and therefore did not necessarily have a direct relationship with one's *anyenheng* estate. Strehlow emphasized that a person's conception site and its story amounted to a form of "individuation among patrifilial relatives" (Austin-Broos, 2009, p. 109). It served as a significant marker of personal identity.

By taking his understanding of the person, place, myth relationship further, Strehlow was able to make his most notable contribution to the discipline. He was among the first Australian ethnographers to give central importance to Aboriginal beliefs about, and experiences of, the living, "mythically inscribed landscape" (Rumsey, 1999, p. 177). Strehlow's accounts gave rise to an appreciation of Aboriginal lifeworlds that show deep connections among individuals, their personal relationships to mythological Ancestors, and narratives of Ancestors that animated and gave shape to the land. Going beyond both his father's discussions of "totem-gods" (Strehlow, 1907a) and Spencer and Gillen's references to the "wanderings of the various totems" (Gillen, 2001, pp. 37–41), Strehlow wrote in more detail about the inseparable, personal, and collective bond to an overarching "totemic landscape" (Strehlow, 1970b). As with the contemporaneous writings of Róheim (1945) and later Munn (1973) and Stanner (1979), Strehlow produced significant insights into the person-land-myth interconnection as well as its expression in ceremony and song.

It was the emphasis on "land-based" (Strehlow, 1970b, p. 98) myth and ritual and in particular the commemorative songs honoring ancestors

(Strehlow, 1971a) that provided direct inspiration for the now popular notion of the "songline." First used by anthropologist Bob Tonkinson (see Moyle, 1966, pp. 165, 227) and ethnomusicologists (Ellis, 1985; Ellis and Barwick, 1987) and later taken up by British novelist Bruce Chatwin (1988), the term fit with Strehlow's characterization of the ontology of Central Australian Aboriginal people and the way in which ritual songs would reference a sequence of places in an animated physical environment (Shakespeare, 2000, pp. 409–411). Strehlow described these paths as the "trails of wandering ancestors" but never used the descriptor "songline" itself (Strehlow, 1978b, map 2). The term has since become a neat shorthand for what Bradley describes as a complex "way of knowing," where the act of singing arouses "both country and kin" and imparts multiple layers of cultural knowledge (2010, p. xiii). Understanding the importance of geographic, mythological, and ritual links, Strehlow produced one of the most detailed records of Aboriginal place names, Dreamings routes, individual sites, song texts, and myths ever made in Australia.

Continental Connections

Despite these significant contributions, Strehlow was on the periphery of mainstream Australian anthropology. His preoccupation with myth and ritual as opposed to kinship and marriage relations left most of his contemporaries in British and Australian anthropology genuinely perplexed by his work. The British Australian anthropologist John Barnes, for example, recalled the "odd frame of reference" used by Strehlow, which he "did not understand" (qtd. in Gray, 2007, p. 224). As both Austin-Broos (1997) and Kenny (2013, pp. 238–240) have argued, Strehlow's Lutheran missionary heritage, his focus on European literature, and his almost myopic interest in the Arandic world meant that he was far more at home among the romanticism and historical particularism of the German-speaking tradition in anthropology. Seeing the importance of a holistic documentation of both language and culture, his research continued the practice of earlier German missionaries and extended it.

Despite speculation that Strehlow may have been significantly influenced by the writings of German philosophy and anthropology (Austin-Broos, 1997, p. 54), careful attention to his diaries and personal book collection suggests that this is unlikely. Contrary to Hill's suggestion (2003, p. 23), no evidence shows that Strehlow read philosopher and founder of German anthropology Johann Gottfried von Herder, and nowhere does he cite the work of the German-American anthropologist Franz Boas. If Strehlow had traveled to Yale University in 1932, however, to study with Edward Sapir (Boas's student), as had been originally suggested by Raymond Firth, he could have discovered likeminded peers (Jones, 2004, p. 37). Strehlow would have agreed with their rejection of social evolutionism and their emphasis on the holistic study of culture and language, as well as their "activist science" (Beals, 2000, p. 316) that converted Indigenes into a people with histories and an inherent value of their own.

Inheriting this disposition from his father, perhaps "unconsciously" as Anna Kenny (2013, p. 240) has suggested, Strehlow remained attentive to "German" ideas throughout his career. He felt a connection to scholars associated with this brand of German diffusionist ethnology, who shared an interest in human creativity, myth, and ritual. Very early on he was contacted by members of the Frobenius Institute in Frankfurt (Beinssen-Hesse, 2004) and later met with Helmut Petri while in Europe (Strehlow, 1950a, p. 130). His associations continued later with a contribution to the *festschrift* for another Frobenius Institute associate, Adolf Ellegard Jensen (T.G.H. Strehlow, 1964c) and correspondence with the American comparative mythologist Joseph Campbell.[2] Many of these writers were more speculative than Strehlow in their ideas about the circulation of language and culture across the globe, but their "late-Romantic," and "fieldwork-oriented" approaches (Gingrich, 2005, p. 108) resonated with Strehlow's interests.

The allure of psychoanalysis, an intellectual tradition with deep connections to German-speaking countries (Ermann, 1999), is recognizable in both Strehlow's personal and public writings. During the first years of his fieldwork he read a German edition of Freud's *Totem and Taboo* (1922) and avidly annotated the Hungarian anthropological-psychoanalyst Géza Róheim's *Australian Totemism* (1925) and contributions to the *International Journal of Psychoanalysis* (1932).[3] Strehlow referenced Carl Jung in the introduction to *Aranda Traditions* (1947, p. xv), and stated his

---

2. Strehlow also wrote a favorable review of Frobenius Institute member Andreas Lommel's "humanitarian" and "emotional" *Fortschritt Ins Nichts* (see Strehlow, 1970a).

3. See Strehlow's personal library collection at the Strehlow Research Centre. The inside cover of the *International Journal of Psychoanalysis* volume XIII (1932) reads "T.G. Strehlow June 25th 1933, Alice Springs." Strehlow has heavily annotated this text. In the same year he also read what he called "a very convincing study of native mentality" (Strehlow 1932, p. 9) by Stanley David Porteus (1931). Porteus's work has since been heavily criticized (Anderson, 2005, pp. 216–18).

interest in the possible "parallels" and common '*subconscious* drives" across cultures in *Songs of Central Australia* (Strehlow, 1971a, p. xvi).[4] Although careful not to make definitive statements in support of psychoanalytic theory, Strehlow concluded that "the Freudian school" had produced some "excellent suggestions" (1971a, pp. xvi–xvii) that could help explain the themes and content of Arrernte traditions.

Parallels and Comparisons

T.G.H. Strehlow felt far freer than his father to go beyond pure descriptive ethnography and entertain comparative investigations.[5] In what is arguably his most influential body of work, *Songs of Central Australia* (1971), Strehlow compares the traditions of Australia's desert peoples with those of Europe's past. Regarded as a kind of "Bible" of Australian Aboriginal verse and religiosity (Jorgensen, 2010), this hefty 775-page tome has come to assume canonical status in Australianist scholarship (see Elkin, 1975). Its examples of Central Australian (male only) song verse are often used to demonstrate the poetic or literary qualities of Aboriginal "literature." The translations highlight the plaintive and inspiring elements of Australian Aboriginal song, and go well beyond the paltry descriptions of Aboriginal song existing in earlier literature (see Spencer and Gillen, 1899; Davies, 1932; 1927; Moyle, 1959).[6]

Songs of Central Australia is not the grand compendium of Strehlow's fieldwork career that its size and scope might suggest. He wrote the bulk of the text between 1946 and February of 1953, and of the subsequent eighteen years of fieldwork only a very small selection was later incor-

---

4. Freud understood that "inadequate observation" and "misinterpretation" of Indigenous "manners and customs" by anthropologists in the late eighteenth and early nineteenth centuries was a concern for the development of psychoanalytic theory (Freud, 2014, p. 36).

5. Others influenced by comparative mythology, psychoanalysis, and cultural diffusion, such as the American mythologist Joseph Campbell, received support from Strehlow (Campbell, 1974, pp. xii, 185).

6. Ronald Berndt's (1952) work on the Djanggawul ritual in Northern Australia had also provided important translations of song.

porated into the manuscript.[7] But it was during this period that most of his work on the Anmatyerr was carried out (see discussion in the next chapter). *Songs of Central Australia* contains only one-fifth of the song material he recorded (1971a, p. xxxix), and is tightly focused on the form and content of songs alone. While the social context of these song traditions are generally explained, their linked ceremonies are left virtually untouched in this analysis. Detailed descriptions of the ceremonies were never published, and rarely were analyses offered of the material qualities or visual aesthetics that informed their ritual paraphernalia, iconography, or dances (see T.G.H. Strehlow, 1964).

Like his work in linguistics, heavily influenced by the intellectual traditions of the late nineteenth and early twentieth centuries and resistant to new developments in theory, Strehlow's anthropology was similarly cast with reference to studies in Classics. Anthropology had partly emerged out of comparative studies in Classics and folklore such as James George Frazers's *The Golden Bough* (1890), but by the early to mid–twentieth century this connection was distinctly on the wane (Ackerman, 2008). Anachronistically, Strehlow continued with comparisons of ritual and religious material during this period, but utterly rejected the earlier evolutionary epistemological perspectives of British anthropology by suggesting that Central Australian Aboriginal song and myth could be equivalent to that of classical antiquity.

Making this comparative point was not purely a scholarly exercise for Strehlow, but also a political one. The "parallels" given in *Songs*, he claimed, were "designed to achieve a more sympathetic attitude in the world of ideas," toward Aboriginal Australians (Strehlow, 1971a, p. xl). Strehlow was anxious to convince his readers that these songs were of equal quality to "our own" early poetic works from Europe, and he gave considerable space in *Songs of Central Australia* to comparing Aboriginal songs with poetic verses from the Greco-Roman world, the Anglo-Saxons, Norse/Scandinavian mythology and Judeo-Christian traditions. Using these texts as the benchmark, Strehlow uncritically accepted the classic tradition's fixation on the cultural development of the West. By the 1960s there was an advanced body of anthropological and folkloric literature

---

7. The map included with *Songs of Central Australia* contains sites recorded after 1953, and there are some song texts collected from Mick Werlaty at Alcoota, for example, in the 1960s, that were later inserted.

from North America, Africa, India, Asia, Central America, South America, and elsewhere in Australia, but Strehlow bypassed most of it. However, unlike most classicists, he had already accepted (based on his own ethnographic experience) that the human mind operated in a similar fashion everywhere, regardless of history or geography. The Athenians and the Arrernte were comparable.

Relying on comparisons with Europe alone, however, meant that Strehlow had accepted a Eurocentric form of criticism and analysis. He defined Arrernte song by modernist assumptions about the centrality of aesthetics and language, and when combined with his Lutheranism, this meant he assigned value to the "Word," with all the resonances of the Christian term. This perspective was not, however, as literary theorist Devlin-Glass has unfairly suggested, a "racist" position, exhibiting a "pervasive disgust" for the culture he documented (2005, p. 135). It is more a consequence, as previously mentioned, of his settler primitivism. From this viewpoint, Indigenous cultures offered an insight into a lost domain of European cultural heritage, and could create the cultural capital needed to establish a unique nationalist, cultural identity in colonial states.

This preoccupation with the cultural history of Europe also led to a particular view of social change. As a student of classics, Strehlow understood that the so-called "primitive" or "primary" literature of earlier European societies had been eventually overcome by French forms, with their roots in the Latin models and Greek originals. These introduced forms of language had proven "too strong" for what he described as the pre-Latin "native verse" of Europe (Strehlow, 1971a, pp. 5, 15), and their documentation was carried out too late and too carelessly. His work in Central Australia was thus an historic opportunity to document Arandic "native verse" before it too was overcome by external influences.

The Authentic Value of Culture

If there was any one task that defined Strehlow's investigations across disciplines, it was his aim of uncovering the cultural "soul" of Central Australian Aboriginal people through their language, song, and mythologies. Having inherited this focus from his father, Strehlow was unequivocal; the "soul" of people was "enshrined in its legends" (1947, p. 46). Although not a missionary himself, T.G.H. Strehlow's work bears the mark of what Clifford (1980) describes as the mission-oriented ethnographer engrossed in locating the "soul" of "their" people and strives to understand their "culture." Given his background, Strehlow imagined *culture* as something inherent in the ontological domains of "mind" and 'spirit,' and primarily expressed through language and most significantly connected to religious ritual. Being focused on text and translations, Jorgensen (2010) has astutely observed that Strehlow "simulated" the sacred of Central Australian people by rendering it in the cerebral language of poetry and literature.

The completely physical, embodied, and visceral nature of Aboriginal lifeworlds that caught the attention of others at the time (Róheim, 1988; 1974; Berndt and Berndt, 1951) were subordinate to Strehlow's interest in the conceptual and linguistic characteristics of human social existence. Captive to a notion of "culture" as something found in language, poetry, and song, Strehlow was limited by what critical theorist Herbert Marcuse has described as an "idealist cult of inwardness," where "authentic culture" is regarded as an expression of spiritual or psychological states (Marcuse, 1968, p. 70). Typically associated with the German romantic tradition, this viewpoint sees culture as an "interiorised property" (Denby, 2005, p. 58) and leaves the *immediacy* of the human condition, its somatic, mundane, and everyday experiences largely unexamined.

Further evidence of this tendency to aestheticize and etherealize "culture" is found in Strehlow's meager record of material culture and, perhaps even more surprisingly, his lack of published works about the hundreds of dance and other ritual performances he filmed. Strehlow certainly collected material culture objects, in particular *tywerrenge*, both the sacred objects associated with ancestors and the ritual paraphernalia made during sacred ceremonies. These were collected less for their material culture qualities than for their associations with the songs, rituals, and myths recorded. Rarely were the more mundane aspects of domestic or family life ever filmed or photographed. Even films made of "everyday" scenes at the Hermannsburg mission were staged for the camera and captured little of the immediacy of people's lives, perhaps because film, wire, and tape was expensive at the time of his fieldwork, and one needed to be economical and selective when making recordings. Strehlow's gaze was firmly fixed on the conceptual domain of religious cultural practice.

"Informants" and "Friends"

As noted above, Strehlow's authority as an ethnographer was most often evoked in reference to his personal biography. This has been a common theme in the history of anthropological writing, with authors commonly defending their accounts by citing either the amount of time they spent in the field or their successes in establishing close rapport with their informants. Through these personal experiences, claims are made about a cumulative deepening of knowledge, in situ and over time. In his critique of how "ethnographic authority" is produced, James Clifford pointed out that experiential claims often work to sanction an ethnographer's "real" but nonetheless "indefinable, feel or flair" for his or her people (1983, p. 130). Long-term personal experience and deep linguistic skills gave rise to the notion that he had some kind of privileged access to the souls of Central Australian people (Morton, 2004, p. 44). As Clifford has argued, though, if based on such foundations and expressed in an unreflexive way, such representations of a "people's" "world" will inevitably be

> *subjective*, not *dialogical* or *intersubjective*. The ethnographer *accumulates* personal knowledge of the field. (The possessive form, "my people," has until recently been familiarly used in anthropological circles; but the phrase in effect signifies "my experience.") (Clifford, 1983, p. 130, my emphasis)

This kind of subjective/personal accumulation of a people's worldview is most directly attested in Strehlow's self-identification as an "Arrernte tribesman" (as noted above), as well as his persistent claims to have personally, almost exclusively, taken possession of sizable repertoires of ritual knowledge. Working in this way, Strehlow's ethnography became a serious personal obligation, involving prolonged and deep attachment with the region and its people, but leaving its relational foundations unexplored. While the benefits of this personal investment were evident in the fine-grained analyses and detailed language studies that he produced, it also contributed to an unfortunate, proprietorial attitude that intimidated other researchers interested in conducting their own research in the region (Hill, 2003, p. 336; Marcus, 2001, p. 111; Green, 2001, pp. 33–34). Typifying what Stocking (1989, p. 211) has referred to as the "one ethnographer/one tribe" phenomenon in anthropology, or the "my people" 'syndrome,' Strehlow aggressively guarded his "patch" and his accrual of ethnographic detail led to a hubris that marred his appreciation of wider social experiences and processes.

Before delving into deeper analyses of his fieldwork interactions with Anmatyerr people in the chapters to come, it is important to consider how Strehlow's informants were represented within his published works.

It is true that Strehlow emphasized his own authoritative status, but both *Aranda Traditions* (1947) and *Songs of Central Australia* (1971) open with genuine acknowledgments of the men who so trustingly provided him with information. Unlike past researchers in Central Australia, such as Spencer and Gillen, who failed to recognize the identities of their informants in their published works (see Bradley, Adgemis, and Haralampou, 2014), Strehlow both named and thanked them, insisting they "should get the full credit for their own information" (Strehlow, 1971a, pp. xxxv–xxxviii). But how this was done reveals a great deal about the limitations of Strehlow's approach. In *Aranda Traditions*, for example, both the age (antiquity) of the informants and their subsequent passing into "memory" is highlighted:

> Many of the legends and much of the information contained in these three studies were obtained from old native informants under a promise of secrecy during their lifetime, and that is why these papers were not published earlier . . . This book is dedicated to their memory. (Strehlow, 1947)

A similar sentiment also concludes his introduction to *Songs of Central Australia*:

> I must not close without acknowledging by far my greatest debt—that which I owe to my *old* native friends who supplied me so liberally with their secret lore and admitted me to so many of their totemic rites . . . Many of them were, in fact, *pathetically eager* to pass on their totemic secrets to someone whom they trusted, and in whom they placed their confidence that he would do his best to *preserve* these secrets from *oblivion*; for they all knew that their own young men would not carry on the traditions of their fathers. (Strehlow, 1971a, p. xlv, my emphasis)

Leaving aside for the moment the expectation that these traditions would not be "carried on" (as I discuss this in detail in the coming chapters), Strehlow's language evokes both an indebtedness to his informants as well as the personal accrual, perhaps even final usurpation, of their deep knowledge. Despite convincing evidence in his own field diaries and from my discussions with Arrernte and Anmatyerr people (see coming chapters), to suggest that numerous men were indeed "eager" to share their ritual expertise, the impression given here of a group of "pathetically eager" people, seemingly incapable of handling the changes around them, is undeserved. The range of responses to colonization from Anmatyerr people in the early twentieth century, outlined in the previous chapter, are testament enough to the dynamism and creativity of a people under pressure. Numerous illustrations of how this ceremonial and song knowledge persists into the current period are detailed in the following chapters.

These critiques aside, the presentation of the informant voice in Strehlow's work nevertheless often gave rise to particularly poignant passages. Quotations from the Northern Arrernte man Akwerre (Gurra, also known as Mickey Dow Dow) (figure 3.2) in *Aranda Traditions*, for example, have given this text a value beyond its original intent. Translations of Dow Dow's words have since been used to describe the affective relationships of Central Australian Aboriginal people and their relationships to land (Das et al., 2014, pp. 12–13; Campbell, 1974, p. 185; Gammage, 2011, pp. 123–138).

Some aspects of Strehlow's portrayal of his informants, however, do deserve scrutiny. In the face of others working in the field at this time,

Figure 3.2. Mickey Dow Dow gathering *alangkwe* (bush bananas) at Apwerte Irretyepe, northwest of Alice Springs, April 28, 1932 (SRC).

such as W.E.H. Stanner and Olive Muriel Pink, who openly explored issues of "culture contact" and the "contemporaneity" of Indigenous peoples (Hinkson, 2005, p. 202), Strehlow instead portrayed his informants as exemplars of the past. Akwerre, or Mickey Dow Dow as he was more commonly known, had already worked as an enabler and interpreter to the missionary Ernest Kramer and anthropologist Norman Tindale (see Marcus, 2001; Jones, 2011, pp. 74–76), and was pivotal to the important ethnography produced by Olive Muriel Pink among the Northern Arrernte (Pink 1933; 1936). Pink would also describe Akwerre as being expert at explaining "sections" and "subsections," as having enough English literacy to scan Spencer and Gillen's publications, and that he had too much anthropological knowledge to be a good "informant" (Marcus, 2001, p. 109). Obviously a significantly intercultural figure, he was nonetheless portrayed by Strehlow in his publications as "Gurra," the authoritative "native" expert in ritual knowledge. These representational strategies rendered informants as exemplars of an authentic "Other" from another time.

With minimal attention given to the shared histories with settlers, pastoralists, colonial authorities, and missionaries, these published texts effectively removed men like Dow Dow from the workings of broader social and political life. The age of informants was also stressed as being critical to obtaining the most authoritative material. Indeed, the ages of Strehlow's informants are listed in the index to *Songs of Central Australia*. Those, like Dow Dow, who had been born before 1875 he argued (1971a, p. xxxv), were a better source of information because they had been less influenced by settler society and thus embodied a tribal past. As those born after this period represented a far more uprooted or acculturated *present*, the contemporaneous and ongoing application of song or ritual material was never seriously entertained by Strehlow.

Rendered in mostly sympathetic ways, these informants would always be representative of a disappearing authenticity that in his estimation was doomed to "utter and final oblivion" (Strehlow, 1953a, p. 147). This *denial of coevalness*, as Johannes Fabian (1983) has famously described the temporal distance imagined between ethnographer and informant, ultimately disavowed the shared experiences of Strehlow and the people he wrote about. The decision to locate Central Australian culture wholeheartedly in the past contributed to the primitivism that marred Strehlow's work.

Somewhat out of step with his Anglo contemporaries in Australia, Strehlow's interests in literature and the Classics produced a focused and empirical form of ethnography. His intellectual roots played an enormous part in shaping his interactions with people, determining his ethnographic focus and framing his scholarly contributions. Although his interest in "parallels" and "comparisons" was a constant motivating theme in his research, they did not dominate his findings. However, empiricism, modernism, settler primitivism, and an intense focus on language and song "texts" did put limits on his appreciation of the material he collected, and the people he collected it from.

Strehlow committed himself to the collection and translation of this material, not in order to create a bank of cultural knowledge for the people of Central Australia, but for the greater edification of an ignorant nation. As each song text was recorded, each myth written down, and each ceremony filmed, Strehlow imagined his records would one day be used by future scholars, much in the same way that Greek or Norse mythologies are scrutinized for cultural and historical insights today. Writing about what he regarded as the eventual decline of these traditions, Strehlow used a religious phrase in Latin to express his despair, "*sic transit gloria mundi*" (thus passes the glory of the world). His theoretical biases were clear.

Understanding Strehlow's work, and more importantly its standing among Anmatyerr and Arrernte communities today, requires a far deeper analysis of his time as a fieldworker. How Strehlow met with his informants in the field, how he worked with them and negotiated with them, is discussed in the following chapter. Specifically focused on his exchanges with Anmatyerr men, the next chapter draws upon Strehlow's meticulously kept field diaries to present a picture of his evolving ethnographic methods and the active role of Anmatyerr informants in the production of the Strehlow collection.

Chapter 4

A Balancing Act

Iparrpe lyang pepeke arrirtnye arrernetyenhe (Sing it quickly, so that the correct song can be put down in the book)

—Tom Lywenge

I first had an inkling of the critical role played by Strehlow's informants in September of 2005, after interviewing senior Arrernte man, the late Rupert Max Stuart Kngwarraye. Max, as he was known to most, had grown up on the Jay Creek Aboriginal Settlement, an Aboriginal Reserve to the west of Alice Springs that T.G.H. Strehlow and his wife, Bertha, ran in the 1940s. He had also performed in sacred ceremonies in front of Strehlow's cameras in 1955. Later, Max was helped by Strehlow when famously convicted of murder in a case that caught the nation's attention and sparked a Royal Commission (Inglis, 2002). I would occasionally run into Max over the years, either when he visited the Strehlow Research Centre to advise on the collection, or on the streets of Alice Springs. On this particular day, I was interviewing Max in the Strehlow Research Centre's boardroom, recording his commentaries on some of the nonceremonial photos in the Strehlow collection from the 1930s.

Among the pile of photos stacked on the boardroom table was an image of Tom Lywenge (Ljonga) Perrurle, Max's *atyemey* (mother's father). Lywenge had been an important fieldwork assistant to Strehlow in his early years, and as we looked at the black-and white-prints, Max began reminiscing about their relationship:

> Tom Lywenge my grandfather . . . He was right under late Professor Strehlow. Camel man and a bit of a goat shepherd . . . They went everywhere! They went out to the Hale River and everything these two. He (Tom) didn't know the country, didn't know the people, but they were talkin' and he could understand . . . he could talk Luritja and Arrernte. He talked Western Arrernte . . . (He was) very, quite cunning (clever) . . . I think he showed Strehlow more than he showed me, ya know? Taught him how to understand the people. He was a pretty hard man.

Max's description of Lywenge suggested a person with the confidence to venture into relatively unknown areas, but also to act as an interpreter and cultural intermediary. He clearly possessed deep ceremonial knowledge and had apparently shared a great deal with Strehlow:

> He taught him (Strehlow) a lot. His own ceremony he showed [to Strehlow] but other ones he keep quiet . . . Nobody knew Strehlow *properly* like this old fella did. And nobody knows my grandfather like what I did.

According to Max, Lywenge was in no way passive in his exchanges with Strehlow and would often tell him to "sit down over there" and to give the performers "room" to prepare. "You can sit down in the shade," he would instruct Strehlow, and "I'll call ya when we're ready." As they worked together, Max imagined, these two men would have created a "*balance* . . . like this one on a scales" (Max moved his hands as if balancing scales). But if he witnessed Strehlow "getting a little bit cheeky," meaning aggressive or coercive, "he'd pull him down . . . pull him back." He would also communicate in a discreet and concealed way with the other Aboriginal informants, using "finger-talk" (hand signs and gestures) so as to avoid detection by Strehlow. Max's story made me think that men like Lywenge had not only been critical as intermediaries but essential to promoting and carrying out the recording of this material.

In this chapter, I take Max's insights into the agency, ability, and confidence of men like his grandfather, using these as a lens through which to view Strehlow's fieldwork interactions. It was these initial comments that inverted the story of Strehlow as the principal figure in this history for me. I wanted to know more about how Strehlow's informants influenced and shaped the documentation of their own rituals and songs.

How much agency did they really have? But I also wanted to know how these relationships may have changed over time, particularly as Strehlow's methodologies developed, relationships evolved, and larger sociohistorical forces affected interactions.

In examining these questions, I returned to Strehlow's field diaries, looking for evidence of Indigenous "agency," and for signs of a significant intellectual exchange. While recent studies of colonial encounter often focus on how Indigenous intermediaries—when acting as guides, translators, hosts, performers, or facilitators—exercised degrees of autonomy in these encounters (Konishi, Nugent, and Shellam, 2015; Torrence and Clarke, 2011; Harrison, Byrne, and Clarke 2013)—I wanted to also consider how these interactions shaped everyone involved. Archaeologist Mike Smith (2013) comes close to this idea with his consideration of Baldwin Spencer and Francis Gillen's significant ethnographic work among the Arrernte in 1896. According to Smith, Spencer and Gillen's intensive documentation of the Angkwere (Engwura) ceremonies in the summer months of 1896–97 marked a moment of "profound intellectual exchange between elite members of two very different societies" (2013, p. 341). While not as pioneering as Spencer and Gillen's early work, the engagements between Strehlow and his interlocutors were equally if not more "profound" and had effects in both directions.

Strehlow's interactions spanned four decades, involved the participation of hundreds of individual informants, covered an expansive region, and benefitted from a depth of linguistic and conceptual comprehension that evaded the earlier ethnographers. In depicting the history of these exchanges and the dialectical interplay between researched and researcher, this chapter draws principally on Strehlow's own written record of events. As the quote from Tom Lywenge in the epigraph demonstrates, these diaries do not simply emphasize Strehlow's role in the process, but if read judiciously, can also illuminate more complicated collaborations. Strehlow's diaries, for example, reveal a great deal about the vigorous and interested roles that Anmatyerr and Arrernte people played in the fieldwork, and show the various challenges faced by all when negotiating the inequities and vicissitudes inherent in colonial relationships.

First Lessons

Strehlow's first year of fieldwork in 1932 consisted of four trips across Central Australia. His principal aim was to ascertain the boundaries of the

Arandic languages. After arriving in Alice Springs on April 2 and spending close to two weeks at the Hermannsburg mission going over his father's work, he began to make preparations for his own sojourns to the north. Planning to travel by camel across the northern boundaries of the Arandic language region, his first task was to secure the necessary beasts, as well as a "camel boy" (an Aboriginal man expert in camel wrangling) to act as a guide. Missionary Ernest Kramer recommended that Strehlow take Max's grandfather, Tom Lywenge Perrurle (c.1880–c.1940) (Strehlow, 1971a, p. 753). Of course, Lywenge was not a "boy" at all, but a man in his fifties who, as noted above, possessed excellent social skills and, like most Central Australian men, was knowledgeable in a range of languages and dialects.

Two very senior men, Moses Tjalkabota at Hermannsburg and Mickey Dow Dow in Alice Springs, explained to the young Strehlow that Arrernte language was spoken as far north as Tea Tree Well and Central Mount Stuart. So it was in this direction that he first headed to make a study of a northern dialect barely described in the anthropological and linguistic literature (Strehlow, 1932, pp. 7, 14). Fortunately for Strehlow, the Reverend T.G. Lithgow was driving north in his vehicle and agreed to take the young scholar and his assistant to Barrow Creek, where they could purchase camels for their planned fieldwork expeditions. Before they could leave, they needed a "license" for Lywenge because, under the protectionist policies of the "Aboriginals Ordinance" Legislation of the time, the mobility of Aboriginal people was closely regulated (Summers, 2000; Howard-Wagner and Kelly, 2011). With the paperwork complete, the group motored north along the Stuart highway, before diverting northwest toward a far-remote cattle station at Mt. Peake (Strehlow, 1932, p. 13). Here Strehlow chatted with the white pastoralists while Lywenge quickly befriended those in the station's "blacks camp," including an elderly man named "Jacky," or, as he was properly known, Urarty.

Lywenge explained to Strehlow that Urarty was universally respected in the region, a "proper" *Ingkarte* (ceremonial leader or boss) and thus someone worth knowing (Strehlow, 1932, p. 22). His "country" was Amakweng, Central Mount Stuart, "where his father, an Aranda (Arrernte) too, had lived all his days" (Strehlow, 1932, p. 14). Strehlow penned a further explanation from Urarty himself, "*Itne nhele kwetethe neke nyentamanyente ware*," but not did not provide a translation (Strehlow, 1932, p. 15).[1] Trans-

---

1. Written by Strehlow as *etna nala kutata naka njintamanjinta wara*, without an English translation.

lated as "They were always living here, just one by one, separately," Uraty's words gave the impression of distinct and slightly autonomous groups of people, existing side by side across the landscape in what would later be described as "estates." This was a concept only just beginning to be understood by anthropologists at the time (Radcliffe-Brown, 1918; 1930) and one that would feature prominently in Strehlow's work in the years to come through his emphasis on estate or "local groups" (Strehlow, 1965c; 1970b).

Although Urarty clearly spoke an Arandic language and could be mostly understood by both Strehlow and Lywenge, his "strange" "accent" (presumably his use of Anmatyerr rather than an entirely different language) caused some communication difficulties (Strehlow, 1932, p. 15). Seeing the opportunity of benefitting from Urarty's elite knowledge, the duo made plans to return to Mt. Peake once they had secured their camels and the necessary supplies for their longer expedition.

Just under a month later, Strehlow and Lywenge returned to Mt. Peake, this time on camels. Strehlow was again largely reliant on Lywenge to interpret and translate Urarty's information. In relaying his "totem-story," Urarty spoke quickly in a mixture of Arrernte and what appeared to be "Ilpara," possibly the Ngalia Warlpiri dialect, and although Lywenge could understand the gist of it, he found it too difficult to translate (Strehlow, 1932, p. 26). Urarty also sang his sacred songs concerning an ancestral *arrwekety* (woman) from a place called "Katna" in the Black Hills, but Lywenge found it extremely difficult to slow him down in order to dictate the individual words and songlines for Strehlow to record. Even with Lywenge's help, being unfamiliar with Anmatyerr, and recording his first-ever song text, Strehlow was struggling. He later recalled the event in this way:

> These Unmatjera (Anmatyerr) men spoke a dialect akin to Northern Aranda (Arrernte) but at that time I did not know any Northern Aranda, and I was still having difficulty even in understanding Ljonga's (Lywenge's) translations of Unmatjera sentences. . . ." (Strehlow, 1959, p. 132)

For the elderly Urarty, the task of slowly reciting and then providing free translations of the songs tired him out. "*Rtwekert ikwer kel arrewem!* (I can't stop my heart from trembling)," he finally exclaimed (Strehlow, 1932, p. 27).[2] Similar language difficulties cropped up with other informants

---

2. Written by Strehlow as *tukuta ekura kalla erouma*. The presented translation is mine.

at Napperby and Woodgreen Stations, where one man complained that his *aleny* (tongue) was *kwern* (not functioning properly) (Strehlow, 1932, pp. 41a, 88). Although the informants tried valiantly to modify their expressions so they could be understood, Strehlow complained that they would often "break down under the mental effort involved" (Strehlow, 1932, p. 90). It seems that Tom Lywenge also grew impatient at times, but instead of asking people to slow down so that Strehlow could better hear each of the words more clearly, he demanded that the singers speed up. Obviously frustrated by some of these exchanges, he encouraged singers to "*Iparrpe lyang pepeke arrirtnye arrernetyenhe* [Sing it quickly, so that the song can be put down in the book]" (1932, p. 102).[3] Intensive language documentation of this kind was new to all involved, and placed each of the participants under considerable strain.

The following morning, Urarty persisted with his explanation of his "totem-story" (Strehlow, 1932, p. 26) before leading everyone to the site where the associated sacred objects were kept. Urarty went ahead in search of the objects amongst the rust-colored boulders at the Black Hills. After a short time, he returned in despair:

> "Nating, nating" [Nothing, nothing] exclaimed the old man. He searched again. In vain; all had disappeared. Perhaps some atua kurka (*artwa akwerrk/akwek*, young men) or some atua wailbela (*artwa warlpal*, white man), or some arugutja (*arrweketye*, woman) had stolen them . . . (Strehlow, 1932, p. 29)

Speechless and saddened by the obvious distress caused by the theft, Strehlow diarized the event as a tragic but predictable result of colonialism. It was "disgusting" that a "white man" would steal "from an old native the last and most precious things which still remained to him" (Strehlow, 1932, p. 29).

Over seventy years later, I climbed these same boulders at the Black Hills with Jimmy Ngwarray, searching in vain for the very same objects. This was before I had read Strehlow's diaries and knew of Urarty's loss. At the conclusion of our search, I filmed Jimmy telling the same stories and Paddy Kemarr singing of the same ancestral woman and moon man as Urarty had done many decades earlier. Because the objects remained

---

3. Strehlow writes *Parpa ljang, pepaka retnja renitjanatanga*.

elusive, the country was one of those "wounded spaces" (Rose, 2004; Kearney, 2016), torn and fractured by colonial expansionism and haunted by (what I later found out) the theft of the objects by the pastoralists from Mt. Peake Station (Strehlow, 1963, pp. 129–130). Having joined in this search so many years later, I can imagine how this episode, so early in Strehlow's career, could have influenced his negative opinion of colonialism and produced gloomy predictions for Central Australian Aboriginal traditions.

Strehlow's sense of urgency to salvage as much as possible in the face of colonialism's march and a fracturing ritual order was only further confirmed throughout the remainder of his time on Anmatyerr lands in 1932. At Stirling Station, Strehlow and Lywenge again met men whose objects had been desecrated and broken into pieces, this time by a police punitive party after the Kaytetye attack on the Barrow Creek Telegraph Station in 1874 (see Strehlow, 1971a, pp. 590–593; 1959; Mulvaney, 2004; also see chapter 3). "Deeply moved" by the event, Strehlow had been invited by one of the owners of the objects, a man named Arlpalywerrng Kemarr, to join him in singing the associated songs for the damaged objects. At other places, objects were being constantly moved, relocated to safer destinations away from possible theft by pastoralists or opportunistic Aboriginal people.

These events were clearly having an effect on people's attitudes toward their *tywerrenge*. As evidenced in chapter 3, sacred objects, songs, and stories were being sold or traded with interested white men in the face of the changing sociocultural milieu. The fact that "men everywhere wanted to sell their "*tywerrenge* to the whites," Tom Lywenge commented, had come about because "the bad whites . . . lorded it over their natives, took their wives away from them, and threatened the men with their rifles." Even though this disempowerment was real, Lywenge also felt that it was mostly "bluff" and complained that his peers "*Itneke iterlarenye kapertele itya* [had not thought about this properly]" (Strehlow, 1932, p. 23).[4] The changing attitude toward sacred objects, he concluded, was not only the direct result of these power dynamics, but also due to the temptations of alcohol and other settler goods. Sacred ritual and objects had become a tender of sorts in a rapidly changing world, in which missionaries, policemen, museums, anthropologists, and private collectors all desired to possess them (see Jones, 1995a). In fact, the arrival of Strehlow and Lywenge in their quest of the same materials similarly represented this change.

---

4. Strehlow wrote *etnaka etalerinja kaputala itja* without English translation.

Atyewe-nhenge (The Age-mate)

At this time in Strehlow's career, the collection of material culture was in no way central to his methods. Chiefly interested in determining the dialectical differences between the Arandic languages and the documentation of people's song and mythic traditions, he often balked at the offer of objects from informants unless he could also collect their songs and stories. Most of the objects that came into his possession during these early years were not kept in his private collection but on-sold to the South Australian Museum.

At Tea Tree Well, for example, when he was approached by Paddy Kaltyirrpek and his nephew Tommy Ngal, Strehlow asked the men to first "recite" their *tywerrenge-arritnye* (sacred songs, or literally, "sacred name") before any object transaction could occur. Once this was done, though, the men nevertheless continued with their invitation to take Strehlow to the site so that he could acquire their objects. It is important to point out here that objects were not necessarily being traded with Strehlow due to any exceptional relationships. Hermannsburg was hundreds of kilometers away from Anmatyerr territory, and it's unlikely the legacy of his father had much sway here. Rather, it appears to have been his language abilities, his upbringing in Central Australia, his obvious cultural sympathies, and his willingness to enter into a reciprocal exchange that made these interactions more efficient.

On their way out of Ti Tree, Strehlow noticed the younger man, Tommy Kaltyirrpek, following close behind. Looking to align himself with the more senior men in the group, Strehlow dismissively referred to the younger man as an "*artwe akwerrke* [a little/young man]" and a "hanger on." Lywenge, however, who was twenty-five years Strehlow's senior and stood as a classificatory father to Strehlow, recognized the age similarities between the two men. The trailing man was in Lywenge's words, Strehlow's "*atyewe-nhenge*," an Arandic term meaning an "age mate," often used to refer to men who have passed through the rites of initiation at the same time (Strehlow 1932, p. 35).[5] The point was made with great subtlety. Strehlow was young, he had never been (and would never be) initiated, and while he had read and heard about senior men's knowledge of ritual and Dreaming, this trip was his first *experience* of it.

---

5. Strehlow writes *tjo:ananga*.

At the rock holes of Arwengkereny (Aranggurunja), Paddy and Tommy explained the significance of the *ahakey* (native currant, *Psydrax latifolia*) objects in an eloquent fashion:

> *Nhenh tywerreng altyerreng ngampekarl akwet ahakeyarl aknganekarl: itya artwel intelh-ilek, rarrp mpwarelhekarl* [These sacred objects manifested themselves in the dreaming/eternal times and are enduringly of the native currant dreaming; not designed by men, they are self-made]. (Strehlow, 1932, p. 35)[6]

The quote, again with no translation in his diary, captured a radically different ontology. When understood in its original language, Strehlow's firsthand experiences, hearing these words and being at the site with these people, gave central importance to Aboriginal people's own beliefs and experiences. It highlighted the living, mythically inscribed landscape they inhabited as well as what Arrernte elder M.K. Turner (2010, pp. 12-15) has more recently described as its "*angampeke-arle*" (i.e., the way in which existence continually arises out of itself). The details of this distinctively Aboriginal ontology and epistemology are now reasonably well articulated in the literature (Morphy, 1992; Myers, 1991; Rose, 1992), but at the time Strehlow was discovering this for himself via empirical experience. It was, first, through the combination of his informant's willingness to have their worldviews understood, but also Strehlow's keen interest in the conceptual and linguistic, that such insights could be apprehended.

Following this first foray, Strehlow's formative learning experiences were soon diverted. He had been asked to assist with the University of Adelaide's Board for Anthropological Research Expedition to Mt. Liebig. It was here among the predominantly medical and physical anthropologists that he was able to witness a very different mode of anthropological research, one that significantly contrasted with his own. Just as they had done the previous year during the Cockatoo Creek expedition, the University team organized a short-term large gathering of people for the purposes of intensive examination. They numbered their subjects and subjected them to a range of scientific experiments and empirical tests (Batty, 2013a; see also Jones, 1987). Their methodology could not have been more different from Strehlow's intimate style of fieldwork, which

---

6. Strehlow writes *Nana tjuruna altjiranga nambakala kuta agiala knanakala; itja atula intalelaka, era arpa mbaralakala*, without translation.

was supported by a single Aboriginal assistant and devoted to the comprehension of myth, ritual and language.

At the conclusion of the Mt. Liebig expedition, Strehlow and Lywenge immediately returned to Anmatyerr territory in order to resume their studies. As they headed north through pastoral leases, elders again approached Strehlow with objects, songs and mythologies, and comparative wordlists of Anmatyerr, Warlpiri, and Arrernte were made (Strehlow, 1932, pp. 95–97). At Stirling Station, an Anmatyerr man named Arimerlareny Pwerrerl began energetically expounding another story concerning *ahakey* (native currant) ancestors. As he spoke, he began to use a distinctively "multimodal" style of communication, using a combination of hand signs, song, and sand drawings to convey his narrative (Munn, 1973; Wilkins, 1997; Green, 2014). As he "tossed his hands about him, and lifted up his voice . . . nothing could restrain him" (Strehlow, 1932, p. 116). Tom Lywenge and two other Anmatyerr men who had been watching and listening intently refused to relay the details of the story for Strehlow, who was left somewhat perplexed. The story was specifically Arimerlareny's to tell.

Upon realizing that his own personal "totem place" (concpetion site) was connected to Arimerlareny's story, however, Lywenge sat down in the soft red sand with the old man, and together they used their fingers to map out various ancestral paths and make iconographic depictions of the story. The drawing depicted key places to which various Ancestors traveled, marked by circular motifs, and showed the paths of the Ancestors represented by dotted and wavy lines. Sketching this sand drawing into his diary (figure 4.1), Strehlow not only captured important mythological detail, but revealed the extent to which he was learning from the dialogues and interactions between his informants.

The Era of Festivals

Strehlow would only intermittently set foot on Anmatyerr country again over the next twenty-five years. Having been permitted to record secret-sacred songs and ceremonies with Northern and Western Arrernte for the first time in 1933, his research then concentrated almost exclusively on the Arrernte. Between 1933 and 1936, his fieldwork focused on photographing and producing written accounts of these ceremonies at a number of ceremonial camps, and between 1936 and 1948, his energies were diverted first toward a new role in government administration and later

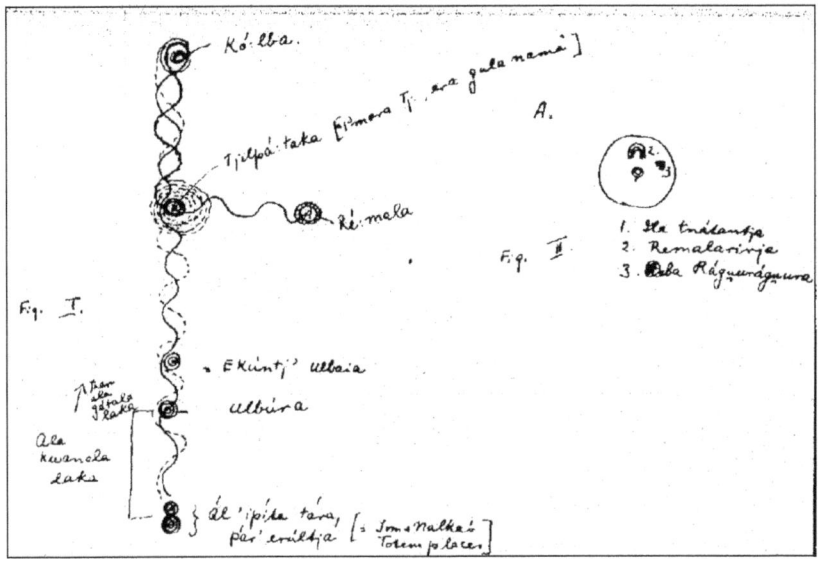

Figure 4.1. Strehlow's recreation of Aremelareny and Lywenge's drawings of the *ahakey* story (Strehlow Field Diary, 1932). "Fig. I" depicts the route of the *ahakey* men between places on Anmatyerr and Arrernte land and was drawn by Tom Lywenge. "Fig II" shows the positions of two ancestors and a ceremonial pole.

military service. Appointed as the first Patrol Officer in Central Australia in 1936, Strehlow often worked with the police and the judicial system to investigate Aboriginal welfare (as we will see in chapter 8) and between 1937 and 1942 established and ran the Jay Creek Aboriginal settlement, forty kilometers to the west of Alice Springs.

As Rowse has noted, Strehlow switched from his primary experience of recording expressions of Indigenous authority to personally enacting it within the "reforming colonial practice" of government administration (1992, pp. 102–103). In this respect, he struggled with a synthesis and though he wrote on matters of Aboriginal policy throughout his career (1956; 1958a; 1961b; 1975) he later regretted his time in "native affairs":

> I should have stuck to my collection of myth, songs and ceremonies in 1936 and never sacrificed any years of my life—or the enthusiasms of my wonderful and educated old men—for my foolish dreams of seeing a regenerated dark population . . . They

would have to learn self control first and determine to work hard for their own future. (Strehlow, 1968a, p. 72)

It was only with the aid of a postgraduate fellowship toward the end of 1948, that he was able to resume his documentation of "legends and chants" (Strehlow, 1948) before embarking on his studies in anthropology at the London School of Economics. Following this largely unsatisfactory venture (see chapter 3) and a quick tour of Europe, Strehlow returned to Australia ready to reignite and renew his fieldwork methods.

This new period of fieldwork, he later reflected, was defined by the "new ways of preserving" song and ceremony that were now available to him—color film, color slide photography, and wire audio recording (T.G.H. Strehlow, 1964b, p. 110). Beginning in 1953, he started to produce color films of ceremonies in the style of "objective" "data gathering." They were made with a single camera fixed to a tripod and positioned so that only the ceremonial ground and the principal performers were in shot. While at times films were made of men making ritual objects, or traveling to sacred sites, the vast majority of these films were taken at ceremonial camps and focused intensely on capturing the enactment of ritual alone. Other ethnographic filmmakers during this time—such as Ian Dunlop, who met and discussed filmmaking with Strehlow in 1965—began to gradually move beyond the focus on "traditional life" and became more interested in documenting 'societies in change" (Deveson, 2012, p. 21; Strehlow, 1965a, p. 2). Striving for the most authentic record of the precontact ceremony, though, Strehlow encouraged his performers to represent their ceremonies as they would have been precontact and to remove from the shot any accoutrements of modernity (shoes, hats, billy cans, etc.).

Turning this raw film "data" into something that could be understood and explained to a wider audience was a costly and time-consuming exercise. Illustrated "film scripts" were made for a small a number of ceremonies in order to describe and explain their contents, but these were only ever drafted and never published. Moreover, of the "kilometres of film" produced of hundreds of ceremonies, only three edited versions, complete with associated song and voice over soundtracks, were ever made.

With ceremonies being revealed in succession, Strehlow perched on the edge of the ceremonial ground with his cameras at the ready. Film and color photographs were taken of each performance and a full description of each ceremony was later noted in his diary, along with sketches of ritual paraphernalia, body paint designs, and the positions of different performers. Embracing the nomenclature of the theater, each ceremonial performance was described as having been "staged," and each part of a ceremony was classified as an "act." For Strehlow, an "act" was a single performance from a larger series of performances that constituted a complete ceremonial cycle. Though Strehlow never defined these terms, it appears that he regarded each major sacred site (*apmere kwetethe*) as possessing a ceremonial cycle made up of numerous performances and songs. The Anmatyerr ceremony of the *tyelk-aperrertety* (rufous songlark, *Megalurus mathewsi*) from Awengatherr (a place near Bushy Park Station), for example, consisted of three separate "acts." Continuing with his theatrical taxonomy, which had evidently originated in his background in Classics, Strehlow described the suite of related songs or ceremonies pertaining to a single estate or site as constituting a ceremonial "cycle." His methods of documentation, although somewhat idiosyncratic, were being carefully perfected in order to be as descriptive and systematic as possible.

Importantly, this period of fieldwork was characterized by the organization of ambitious ceremonial "festivals," often involving large numbers of participants. Ceremonial gatherings like this, where Strehlow had been permitted to attend, had been organized by Strehlow in the past, first at Nywente (Njonta) close to Alice Springs in 1933, and again at Arltunga in 1935. But between 1950 and 1962 these so-called "festivals," sometimes also referred to as "*urrempel*" or "ceremonial camps" were held regularly at two sites close to the Alice Springs township at Werlatyatherre (Wolatjatara) and then at Ajura (map 4.1 on page 110). Gatherings were also hosted beyond the Alice Springs district, often with assistance from local pastoralists on nearby cattle stations such as Maryvale, Hamilton Downs, Todd River Station, and Alcoota. Having cultivated a friendly relationship with many pastoralists, and being recognized as a "native-born" Central Australian, pastoralists often assisted Strehlow with these gatherings by granting leave to some Aboriginal stockmen to attend ceremonies, and in some cases providing logistical support.

In some respects these festivals resembled the previous gatherings of "the Resos," the Board for Anthropological Research and Spencer and Gillen. Provisions were provided to participants in return for access to ceremonial knowledge, and the proceedings were documented. But Strehlow's festivals were far more embedded in, and shaped by, the dictates of Aboriginal interests. These festivals brought men together from

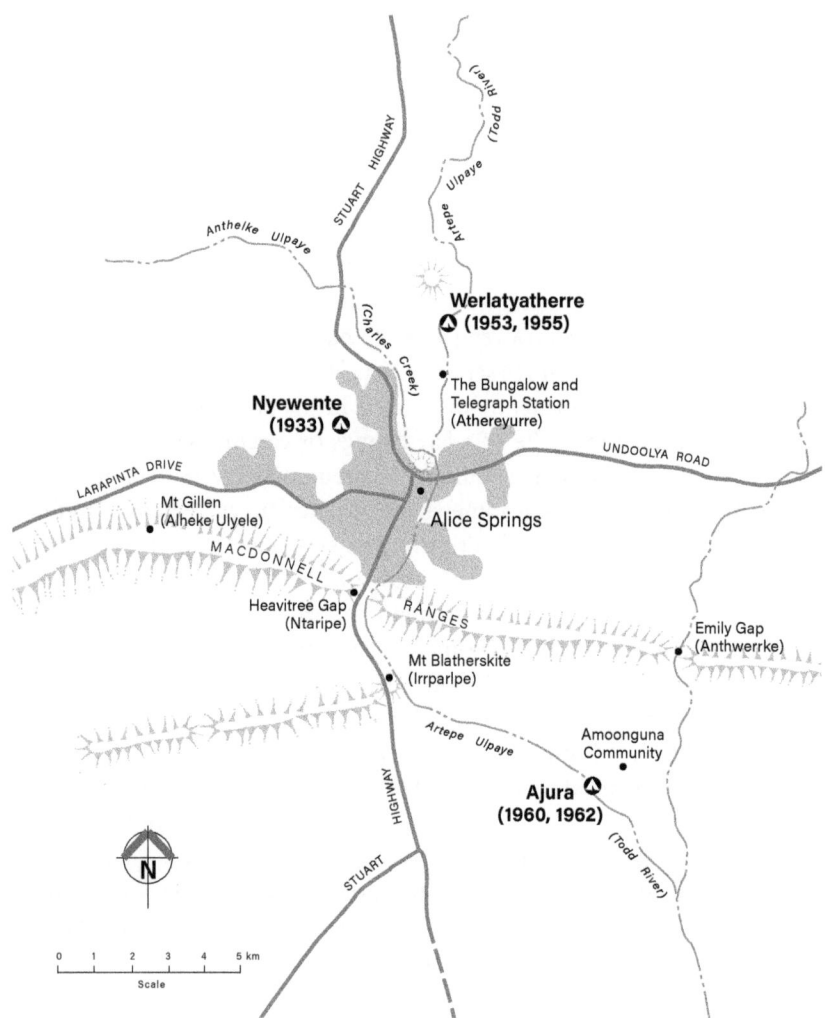

Map 4.1. Ceremonial festival sites near Alice Springs. Grayed-out area represents Alice Springs township area.

far afield in order to share selected parts of their ceremonial patrimony, and as the ritual education unfolded, Strehlow was there, ready to capture what he could on his new recording devices.

Interestingly, much of the material recorded between 1950 and 1962 was effectively omitted from his most influential tome, *Songs of Central*

Australia. Mostly based on the songs he had collected during the 1930s and 1940s, Strehlow had taken the manuscript for this book with him to London and put the finishing touches on it in the early months of 1953. Although *Songs* was not published until 1971, and only the occasional snippet of information from fieldwork after 1953 made it into the publication, it is the years between 1950 and 1962 that are best remembered by Arrernte and Anmatyerr people today. The earliest memories I could find of Strehlow's presence in the region began with the Werlatyatherre "festival" of 1953.

The site of Werlatyatherre is extremely well known to Arrernte and Anmatyerr people. It is one of the key places associated with a significant and partly restricted Dreaming that travels from south to north through the Alice Springs Township, on to the Anmatyerr estate of Ilkewartn and beyond. Translated as "two breasts," Werlatyatherre refers to two ancestral women being pursued by a group of *urrempel* men led by a man named Kwekatye (Wilkins, 2002, p. 36; Wootten, 1993). Werlatyatherre had been chosen as the venue for two of the "festivals" sponsored by Strehlow principally because of its proximity to the camps of Aboriginal people living nearby on the Alice Springs Telegraph Station Reserve, known as "the Bungalow." Accommodating local Arrernte and other Aboriginal people from across the region, the Bungalow had become a site of considerable social and cultural exchange. Arrernte people hosted and shared in ceremonies involving Aboriginal people from across central Australia (Meggitt, 1962, pp. 31, 40–41; Rubuntja and Green, 2002, pp. 47–48). Ironically, the colonial reserve designed to control and monitor Aboriginal populations had become a focal point for ceremonial exchange. It was an ideal place for Strehlow to source informants and performers.

"The King" and the "Akiwarenye"

The person most instrumental to the success of these events was the Northern Arrernte man, Bob Rubuntja Penangke. Just as Tom Lywenge had enabled Strehlow's work in 1932, Rubuntja now assumed a similar role as facilitator, go-between, and intermediary. The significance of Rubuntja's associations with Strehlow, although noted by both his son and grandson (Rubuntja and Green, 2002; Rubuntja, 2011) has generally been missed by those writing about Strehlow's legacy. Barry Hill's *Broken Song* (2003), for example, contains only a single reference to Rubuntja, and McNally

(1981) makes no mention of him at all. Nonetheless, Rubuntja was a man of considerable ceremonial authority, and was comfortable working with *alhernter*. As a youth he had been one of the initiates involved in the ceremonies recorded by Spencer and Gillen in 1896, and he was involved in Strehlow's earlier work. Even though the older men in the 1930s referred to him as "*awerre akweke ware* [just a little boy]" (Strehlow 1933b, p. 6), Rubuntja had become a well-regarded ritual expert.[7]

By the 1950s, Rubuntja was eager to show Strehlow some "very important" ceremonies in a "big festival" that could last "months" (Strehlow, 1953a, pp. 116–117). Predominantly orchestrated by Rubuntja, the 1953 and 1955 festivals introduced for the first time a significant number of Anmatyerr-related ceremonies. Rubuntja's genealogical and *Anengkerr* (Dreaming) connections partly explain the inclusion of this Anmatyerr content. Both his mother and father had been conceived in the shared Anmatyerr/Northern Arrernte country near Native Gap, and he himself had been conceived on the Urepentye (Rubuntja) estate neighboring Anmatyerr country to the south (Rubuntja and Green, 2002, p. 27).[8] Significant Dreaming ancestors such as the fish from Alherramp (Napperby) for example, had traveled out of Anmatyerr territory and moved into Rubuntja's country to the south, creating important links between them.

As is the case across most of Australia, different language groups were not as divided as the hard-and-fast lines drawn on tribal maps might suggest (see Peterson, 1976; Davis, 1989; Sutton, 1995). Anmatyerr and Arrernte ceremonies were often intimately interconnected. Four of the five "main series" to be shown at the 1953 festival, for example (Strehlow, 1953a, p. 129), and many of those shown in 1955, had direct connection with Anmatyerr people and country.

In addition to these Dreaming associations, Rubuntja had also traveled extensively throughout his life, driving wagons across large distances (Rubuntja and Green, 2002, pp. 21–22) and had established connections across the region. Like other "Aboriginal men of high degree," as Elkin (1977) described them, Rubuntja used these opportunities to meet with other Aboriginal men and develop deeper ritual expertise across an expansive region. Confident in his knowledge of these connections, Rubuntja would even go as far as describing himself as an "*apmere-ke ingkarte*" (a boss for the country), seemingly including sites in both Arrernte and

---

7. Strehlow writes *worra kurka worra*.

8. See also Rubuntja's genealogy on Family Tree IV, 1 at the Strehlow Research Centre.

Figure 4.2. One of the informants at Werlatyatherre (possibly Bob Rubuntja) and T.G.H. Strehlow, the "denizen of the ceremonial ground," in conversation. (Still taken from Film Reel No. 46, 1953.)

Anmatyerr territory (Strehlow, 1958b, p. 119).[9] Even senior Anmatyerr men living at Ti Tree, close to one hundred kilometers away from Rubuntja's traditional lands, were quick to remember his authority. Describing him as a "King," Paddy Kemarr remembered the Arrernte elder affectionately. "Old Japanangka (Penangk) from Rubuntja . . . That was a big boss! Old Urepentye (fire Dreaming place), he's the one. King! He was king for all that land . . . all over."

Strehlow's diaries similarly reveal how influential Rubuntja had been during the 1950s. It was often at Rubuntja's and not Strehlow's request, for example, that performers would begin to gather at the Bungalow in readiness for the ceremonies (figure 4.2). With his regular companion, the Northern Arrernte man Tom Arleyekwarte Pengarte, by his side, Rubuntja oversaw the coming together of grand gatherings, involving Arrernte,

---

9. Strehlow writes *pmaraka ingkata*.

Anmatyerr, and Alyawarr men "joining forces" with Pintupi and Luritja men from across the Western Desert (Strehlow, 1955a, p. 4). Rubuntja's idea was to see all ceremonies concerned with the traveling ancestral *yerramp* (honey ants) performed. Because these honeyants journeyed from Tatata in Pintupi country, through Luritja, Arrernte territory, Anmatyerr, and on to Ngkwarlerlanem in Alyawarr territory, performers and ritual experts from across cultural and linguistic regions were necessary. The plan required the coming together of men from the Aboriginal settlement of Haasts Bluff in the west, Anmatyerr and Alyawarr men from the cattle stations to the north, and Northern Arrernte men from Hermannsburg and Alice Springs.

Strehlow was convinced by Rubuntja to help host and record the ceremonies, and other *alhernter* too were recruited to help make Rubuntja's plan come to life. Native Affairs officers and mission staff at Haasts Bluff helped with the transportation of performers from the west, while the visiting Melbourne-based sculptor William Ricketts was "roped in" to pick up the Alyawarr and Anmatyerr men from the Sandover River area on the back of his truck. At the same time, Strehlow ferried people between Jay Creek, the Bungalow, and Alice Springs. Each of the *alhernter* would carry the message that Rubuntja had called together performers for these ceremonies. Organizing such a large-scale regional event stood as testament to Rubuntja's authority across cultural differences and his widely acknowledged standing as a ceremonial leader.

But if Rubuntja was the "leader" in these contexts, what was Strehlow? In a revealing exchange between these two men at the conclusion of the 1953 ceremonies, Rubuntja inadvertently "volunteered" a partial explanation. As Strehlow drove Rubuntja away from the ceremonial ground back into town after a successful event, Rubuntja turned to him and commented that the performers were all saddened to see Strehlow, the "*akiw-arenye*" returning to Adelaide (Strehlow 1953b, p. 50). This appellation "*akiw-arenye*" is worth considering in detail. Meaning someone "belonging to," "inhabiting," or being a "denizen of" (*-arenye*) a men's ceremonial ground (*akiwe*), this description contrasted with Strehlow's own idea of himself as an *Ingkarte*—a "leader" or "boss."[10] While it is certainly true that many Arrernte people referred to Strehlow using this term, we can"t be sure of their intended connotations. Rubuntja's more nuanced label, "*akiw-*

---

10. Strehlow spelled this term *kewarinja*.

arenye," recognized Strehlow's privileged participation in these events but importantly left room for the critical, leading roles played by men like himself. (Further perspectives on Strehlow and his role in these contexts are discussed in the next chapter.)

Colonial Interests

Legitimating such a regional gathering in the eyes of colonial authorities required careful inclusion and enlistment of the necessary administrations. In 1955, although Strehlow railed against Rubuntja's decision to yet again host the ceremonies at the site of Werlatyatherre, he eventually conceded. It was left to Strehlow to, first, negotiate use of the site (being within the bounds of an Aboriginal Reserve controlled by the NT administration) with the local Native Affairs officials, and second, to see that permits and transport for the Pintupi and Luritja performers could be arranged. Strehlow's ties to the colonial administration were needed to see Rubuntja's plan come to life. As writer Kim Mahood (2012) has cogently put it, white workers on the colonial frontier are now (as they were undoubtedly then) assessed according to how they might best assist local Aboriginal people carry on with their own concerns.

I suggest that men like Bob Rubuntja, in understanding that colonial authorities largely controlled the resources of their world, carefully assessed how best to utilize and exploit the situation. People like Strehlow, with their eager recognition of ceremonial expertise and desire to understand and record it, presented as opportunities. But, as Max Stuart observed at the beginning of this chapter, a need persisted for men at the coalface of these interactions to carefully "balance" the varying and competing interests involved.

In 1953 alone, the Native Affairs Welfare Branch of the Northern Territory contributed £676 in rations, clothing, and fuel to assist Strehlow's fieldwork.[11] When a similar amount was again contributed in 1955 and permits and permissions were granted for these "festivals," some staff asked for permission to see some of the ceremonies (Strehlow, 1955b, p. 41). Strehlow left the decision to Rubuntja, the actual convener of the gathering, and although he eventually agreed that a small number

---

11. See National Archives of Australia: A452, 1953/43, p. 169.

of male staff could attend, no photographs were to be taken (Strehlow, 1955b, pp. 41–47). Whether it was Strehlow or Rubuntja who introduced this proviso is uncertain, but clearly Rubuntja had allowed these men to attend in light of their notable influence over the local community. The interaction was a moment of "colonial stress" where unexpected pacts are made and where those in less powerful positions try to preserve their tactical relationships with holders of institutional power (Clifford, 2001, p. 478; see also Scott, 1990). The sole condition of no photography was nevertheless ignored by two of the officers, who assumed that if Strehlow was recording, they could too.

Seeing what offense this might cause and looking to preserve his privileged relationships, Strehlow negotiated with District Welfare Office Billy McCoy for the film to be publically burned. Rubuntja and the Lower Arrernte elder Fred Akngeyetneme (Kngeitnama) agreed this was an appropriate course of action, with Akngeyetneme adding that all of "the men had been saying that if any pictures of" the ceremonies "appeared in the Alice Springs picture show" (or were shown to women in Alice Springs) then three or four native women would surely "die" in Alice Springs—right before the whites' eyes" (Strehlow, 1955b, p. 45). With threats of violence in the air, Strehlow also hoped that by burning the film men who had "come from further afield," such as the Anmatyerr, would "return much more happily than they would have done otherwise" (Strehlow, 1955b, p. 47).

Unlike the Arrernte, whom had grown accustomed to Strehlow's presence at these festivals and in their communities for decades (figure 4.3), the Anmatyerr had been noticeably "reticent about their acts" early on and spoke "about them only in whispers" (Strehlow 1955a, pp. 149–150). Strehlow was a stranger to them and performing their most treasured ceremonies over 250 kilometers away from their homelands, close to the largest township in the region, and then seeing multiple people taking photographs, must have been disconcerting for the Anmatyerr to say the least.

The last of the ceremonial "festivals" that involved Strehlow were held at the Amoonguna Aboriginal Settlement, to the south of Alice Springs, in 1960 and 1962. Like the Bungalow it replaced, Amoonguna was both a settlement for the local Arrernte and a "transit camp" for other Aboriginal people passing through the township (Rowse, 1998, p. 199). Many of the settlement residents were registered in assimilationist-style employment programs designed to teach trades and get people "ready" for mainstream society (Coughlan, 1991). This is remembered by many of

Figure 4.3. "Last views of my Wolatjatara (Werlatyatherre) camp, 6th Oct 1955." Strehlow standing by his caravan located on the edge of the ceremonial ground (Strehlow Research Centre, PHO 00812).

the older Anmatyerr men I have spoken with as a period of being put to work for "them DAA (Department of Aboriginal Affairs) Welfare people." They worked as cooks and leared trades and were encouraged to live in the newly built homes as nuclear families (Rubuntja and Green, 2002, p. 97).

Strehlow's diaries from this time reveal the effects of the changing political and policy environment. Although openly critical of many of these assimilationist polices (Strehlow, 1958a, 1961b; T.G.H. Strehlow, 1964d), he simultaneously lamented the social dysfunction and decline in ritual activity among the Arrernte. Just as Tom Lywenge had in 1932, Tom Arleykwarte commented in the 1950s that colonialism, alcohol, and imprisonment were having disastrous effects on the local people (Strehlow, 1955a, p. 4). Even the now elderly Bob Rubuntja appeared dejected:

> He goes up to the town on most mornings and begs for some money (so the people say). Probably he drinks too. It is tragic to see an old man, who could be an honoured leader at an urumbula (*urrempele*) festival, being disregarded as though he

were already dead and of no account. His contacts with the white world have been his downfall. . . . (Strehlow, 1962, p. 141)

The era of the big ceremonial festivals in Alice Springs had come to an end for a disillusioned Strehlow. Seeing Rubuntja in this state merely confirmed for Strehlow the notion of a "disappearing object" of study. Like others working in "salvage" mode, Strehlow often assumed the "moral" and "scientific" position that social change inevitably led to the destruction of "something essential ('culture')" (Clifford and Marcus, 1986, p. 113). By conflating "culture" and "life," the supposed death of culture was assumed to also mean "social death" (Bessire, 2014, p. 7). For Strehlow, in the face of such lethal impacts from Euro-Australian society, only those making the recordings of these traditions could testify to their original authenticity and take on the responsibility for their future. His view hardened and intensified during the final phase of his fieldwork career despite conflicting evidence of an ongoing "social life."

Inner Cycles and Local Sites

In his third and final fieldwork period from 1964 to 1974, Strehlow spent more time looking to document what he regarded as "lost and forgotten" places, traditions, and songs (Strehlow, 1968a, pp. 45–49, 68). The landscape was, in his view, quickly becoming "empty and silent," and he was now "merely traveling through it in a final attempt to save the last scraps of the local traditions before complete oblivion settled down upon them" (Strehlow, 1968a, p. 92). It was this melancholy assessment that motivated the extensive "mapping trips" of sites that ultimately came to inform his large-format, fold-out map that accompanied *Songs of Central Australia*. But his pessimistic view was not entirely of his own making—it had been influenced significantly by his experiences with Arrernte people.

As early as 1958 he had been repeatedly told by men like Bob Rubuntja that knowledge of certain sites and their associated songs had been "lost forever" in the Northern Arrernte and Anmatyerr regions (Strehlow, 1958b, p. 116). The terrible violence of the region (see chapter 3) also suggested a decline in local knowledge.

It was with Rubuntja and Arleyekwarte, then, that he went "hunting" for what were presumed to be "lost and forgotten places" on the cusp of Northern Arrernte and Anmatyerr lands (Strehlow, 1958b, p. 121). To their surprise, the Anmatyerr men living nearby at Aileron Station were quick to identify each and every site. Ten years later, Strehlow returned to many of these same men, including Charlie Heffernan, Tom Uneynt, George Yerramp Rlwengapeltyey, and Bruce Campbell (figure 4.4), to discover that in their roles of *kwertengerl* (ceremonial managers and custodians) they had retained knowledge of many of the songs that he had presumed gone from the Ryan's Well and Aileron areas. In what was a purely working relationship, the men sang their verses in exchange for "raw meat and some bread" and at the end of the session walked back to their camp at the nearby Anwekeran (Laughton's Lagoon), declining Strehlow's offer for a lift in his Land Rover (Strehlow, 1968a, p. 82). That night, Strehlow camped on his own, as he usually did, and commented in his diary that a sense of "enthusiasm" had returned to his work. The Anmatyerr men had been "excellent and willing guides" and a "privilege" to work with (Strehlow, 1968a, p. 95).

Perhaps his most significant and detailed work with Anmatyerr people began at Alcoota Cattle Station in 1964. Strehlow had come to Alcoota at the request of Arrernte men who wished to recruit performers

Figure 4.4. Aileron informants, September 6, 1968. L-R George Yerramp Rlwengapeltyey, Tom Uneynt Pengart, Bruce Campbell Pengart, and Charlie Artetyerwenguny (SRC 03847).

for their ceremonies. Mick Kamperrkng Werlaty (Wolatja) approached Strehlow, asking for help (T.G.H. Strehlow, 1964a, pp. 49–50). The local pastoralist was constructing a road perilously close to an important sacred site named Akwerrperl (Korbula) and had threatened to shoot the men if they "trespassed" on his station run (Strehlow, 1965d, p. 11). Appealing to Strehlow as the *"ngkart ameke-arle-arey anthwerr* (the truly untouchable leader/boss),*"* presumably referring to his connections with the Northern Territory Administration and colonial influence more generally, Werlaty asked for help in protecting the site. Though Strehlow shared Werlaty's concern, he felt powerless to act:

> I sympathised with them, and promised to look them up again about this matter . . . Secretly, of course, I was rather worried by these pleas—I have no official standing in the N.T (Northern Territory) and Australian laws have never yet given the slightest protection either to aboriginal religion or the aboriginal sacred sites. (T.G.H. Strehlow, 1964a, p. 49)

Unprepared and unwilling to intervene, Strehlow left Alcoota, but true to his word, he returned in 1965 with an offer to help protect the site in the only way he knew: by filming its ceremonies and recording its songs. The Alcoota group immediately agreed and began to make preparations. Strehlow supplied the performers with some of the raw materials needed to manufacture their ritual paraphernalia (hair-string, spears, boomerangs, and red and yellow ochre) (Strehlow, 1965a, pp. 149, 151), but most of the materials were already at hand. Some of the men's methods of making these items were also highly inventive. For example, they had made a particular type of hair-string known as *"ndoitja"* not with the traditional possum fur but with sheep's wool purchased by pooling together station wages (Strehlow, 1965d, p. 36). Living in a small "native camp" on the fringe of a remote cattle station, over two hundred kilometers north of Alice Springs, these men were clearly ceremonially active, innovative, and fiercely independent.

Ten men were present at the ceremonial camp when the singing began. The older men in attendance—Sandy White Penangk, "Lame" Tom Ltarerlkek Ngal, Reilly Kwekaty Pengart, Tom Rayekwarr Pengart, Mick Werlaty Pengart, and George Yerramp Pengart—were all pensioners and largely reliant on station rations. Also participating were four younger men in their twenties and thirties, including Werlaty's son, Kenny Penangk, the man I would meet with to view these films over forty years later (figure 4.5). Over a five-week period, what Strehlow referred to as the "Inner Cycle" of Akwerrperl were enacted (1965d, p. 49), meaning the entire suite of ceremonies pertaining to this estate. Each of the twenty-seven "acts" divulged deeper layers of highly localized ritual and mythological knowledge, and often involved the production of highly "elaborate and constantly changing" ground paintings (Strehlow 1970b, p. 138). Quite possibly the most complete set of ceremonies for a single estate ever produced in Australia, these films are some of Strehlow's most intimate and thorough. Unlike the previous *urrempel* "festivals," which often featured only selected aspects of ceremonies from different locales (Peterson, 2000, p. 207; Curran, 2010, p. 100), these "inner cycles" specifically documented the rarely revealed ceremonies of a local *anyenheng* group.

Figure 4.5. Kenny Penangk Tilmouth at Alcoota Station in 1965 (SRC PHO-03971).

Strehlow's role during these ceremonies was by now well established and understood across the region. He would arrive in a community, make contact with the most senior men, and record as much as he was permitted to. At times, his presence would demand a degree of participation, and as his knowledge grew he felt justified in interjecting during ceremonial performances or joining in with the singing (though never on a recording). During the Akwerrperl ceremonies, for example, he sang along with the group, suggested changes to a performance, and often participated in the ritual handing-over and receiving of *tywerreng* (Strehlow, 1965d, pp. 31–32; 1955a, p. 103). At the conclusion of the first "act" concerning the *Alpwertek-alpwert* (Grey Butcherbird), three men in the same generational moiety to Strehlow (*anwakerrakeye*) joined him in the act of "pleading" for the associated objects (1965a, p. 150).

Despite only recently becoming acquainted with these men, Strehlow's subsection affiliation and his spiritual conception at Nthareye had enabled this ritual exchange (Strehlow, 1965d, pp. 8–10). Blinkered by his own self-aggrandizement, however, Strehlow saw himself as the sole heir to not only the material artefacts gifted or sold to him, but their associated knowledge as well:

> No one else will ever again be allowed to make another final Korbula (Akwerrperl) groundpainting or use again the designs done on its two shields and *alkata* unless I authorise such a thing. . . . *these are all my personal property from now on.* (Strehlow 1965d, p. 48, my emphasis)

Such was the hubris and self-deception that came to dominate Strehlow's later career.

The "duplicity" that anthropologist Johannes Fabian (2008, p. 6) has described as one of the defining characteristics of all ethnography ended up haunting Strehlow. He failed to think reflexively about his dual roles; he partook in ritual in the present, but simultaneously closed off the possibility of any contemporaneous or future trajectories. As is demonstrated in chapters to come, participating in ritualized handing over of material *had not* extinguished the rights of other men. As each of the inner-cycle rituals was performed at Alcoota, Strehlow's own diary entries note that both Kenny and Sandy White were being purposefully instructed in Mick Werlaty's expertise (Strehlow, 1965d, p. 9). Strehlow's presence, although it may have been a catalyst and opportunity to record the "inner cycle,"

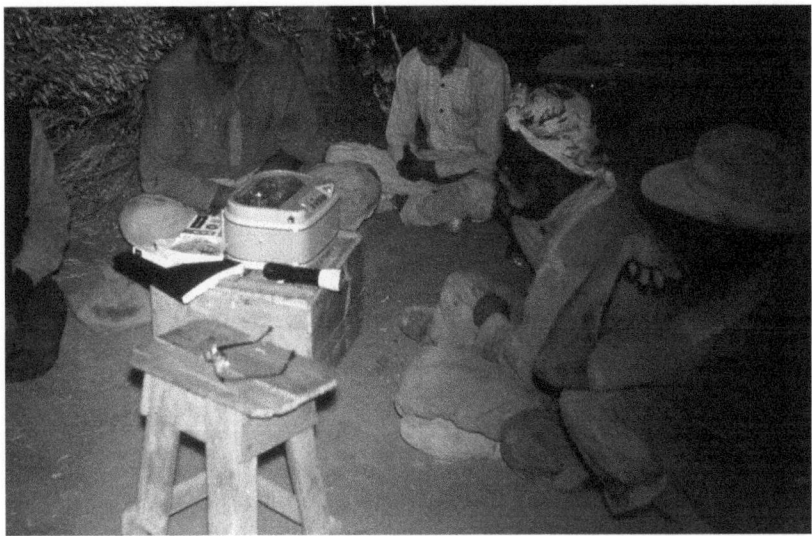

Figure 4.6. Alcoota men recording songs to tape in 1965. Mick Werlaty is seated immediately behind the tape recorder (SRC, image 03700).

was not a prerequisite for its maintenance, let alone preservation (see chapters 7 and 9).

There was nevertheless little doubt about the eagerness of this group in having their material recorded. The silent color films of the Akwerrperl ceremonies show performers gesturing to and conversing with the person behind the lens, and when the desert winds blew up making recording of songs difficult (figure 4.6) they joined together to sing *"arlke ultakemele,"* songs to break up the wind (Strehlow, 1965d, p. 34).[12] In spite of Strehlow's quest to accrue and amass knowledge, their cooperation and enthusiasm shone through.

"Disowned as Ingkata"

The "balanced" interactions between Strehlow and his informants came to an end during the tumultuous times of the late 1960s and early 1970s. Three decades after starting his research amongst the men of Central

---

12. See Film Reels TGH no. 17–41. Strehlow writes *ilka ultakamala*.

Australia, significant social and political changes were about to radically change relations between Indigenous and non-Indigenous peoples. Described as "a period of estrangement" between anthropologists and their subjects (Starn, 2011, p. 180), the rise of the Aboriginal rights movement and the emergence of new social policies effectively ended the way in which self-appointed non-Indigenous peoples could simply assume proprietorship over all things Aboriginal. Former "protectionist" regimes had given way to new strategies of "integration" or "acculturative assimilation," and by the end of the early 1970s they would morph again into policies of 'self-determination" (McGregor, 2005). By the early 1960s, Aboriginal people were granted voting rights, they were no longer regarded as "wards" of the state, and those working on cattle stations had finally been granted equal wages.

With a growing sense of independence in the air, Strehlow returned to Alcoota in 1968. This was a watershed year of important change across the desert communities. The Department of Social Security had begun paying cash allowances directly to the beneficiaries in settlement rather than seeing the money go to the superintendent of a community first, and Aboriginal stockmen were better paid (Bunbury, 2002; Martinez, 2007). Car ownership had become far more prevalent among Aboriginal people in this part of Australia (Peterson, 2000), and increased mobility led to greater movement between communities for the purposes of ceremony.

Finding it increasingly difficult to pin down his informants, Strehlow struggled to obtain exactly what he wanted. He had heard men from Alcoota sing the *ingwa* (night/darkness) songs at Arltunga over thirty years earlier, and was desperate to finally record them. But since Ned Kemarr, the head stockman at Alcoota and the owner of the *ingwa* traditions avoided him, it was left to Mick Werlaty to assist.[13] They headed out along the creek, mapping the *ingwa* sites, but much to Strehlow's frustration, this was soon cut short. News had hit the community of an impending *apwelh* (circumcision ceremony), involving a "red truck" carrying the initiate from Napperby. As soon as the *apwelh* "singing began," Strehlow understood the Alcoota men would be obliged to devote all of their attention to it, and his efforts to record the *ingwa* songs would be thwarted (Strehlow, 1968a, p. 101).

---

13. Strehlow to Tindale April 20, 1935. AA316 Strehlow Papers, South Australian Museum.

As Werlaty and Strehlow drove back toward the station homestead, they were passed by a Land Rover carrying Ned Kemarr and Tom Rayekwarr, who informed them that the young man to be initiated would be arriving at any moment. The youth, they explained, was Harold Ankatanga Mpetyan, the son of one of the key Akwerrperl performers in 1965, Lame Tom Ltarerlkek. Although Strehlow knew that the Alcoota men could no longer work with him, he became hostile and unsympathetic. These men, he complained, had reneged on their promise to provide him with the *ingwa* songs, and had thus "cheated" him (Strehlow, 1968a, pp. 111–112, 114). Instead of asking him to stay, as they would have done only a few years earlier, now they were "begging" him to leave. The Alcoota men, with a greater sense of autonomy and mobility, would apparently share their knowledge when it suited them, and not simply when Strehlow asked for it. Failing to appreciate the broader economic and social changes under way in Central Australia, Strehlow took it personally and declared that he had been dealt "a savage blow":

> On my travels this year even Anmatjera (Anmatyerr) men at Aileron, Leramba and Mt. Allan, also Walbiri (Warlpiri) men, had spoken to me with respect as soon as I had been introduced as "the" tjurunga (*tywerrenge*) leader, who knows all about men's tjurunga everywhere . . . But whatever the explanation was, yesterday morning, for the first time since 1932, *I had been disowned as ingkata (Ingkarte) by a section of the Aranda-speaking population.* (Strehlow, 1968a, pp. 114–115, my emphasis)

The dynamism and autonomy of Anmatyerr and Arrernte ceremonial life, completely independent of Strehlow's influence or concerns, was lost on the aging and humiliated anthropologist. Angry and hurt, he branded the Anmatyerr as cowardly "shrimps" (Strehlow, 1968a, p. 115), though he returned to Anmatyerr country one last time, in 1971 (Strehlow, 1971b, p. 73a). Mick Werlaty had passed away by then, but his son, Kenny Tilmouth, along with Harold Mpetyan, Ned Kemarr, and another man named Dick Alpwertekalpwert Purvis agreed to allow Strehlow to record not only their *ingwa* songs but also the *ikwelengk* (king brown snake, *Pseudechis australis*) songs of Ken's conception site (Strehlow, 1971b, p. 71a). Harold, whose initiation had disrupted Strehlow's visit only three years earlier, exhibited great familiarity with the song material, which surprised Strehlow. The way Harold joined in with the singing, Strehlow wrote, showed he had "learned quite a lot of the sacred traditions of this area in recent years," though Strehlow made no attempt to find out why or how (Strehlow, 1971b, p. 51).

As Strehlow left Anmatyerr country for the last time, Harold suggested that he return on another occasion in order to see some of his own cultural inheritance, in this case the *ahakey* (native currant) ceremonies from Arangwereny, an area to the east of Ti Tree that Strehlow had first visited in 1932. Contrary to Strehlow's overly negative perspective, some younger men were obviously still knowledgeable of their traditions, and after his thirty-nine years of research, ceremonies and songs that were new to Strehlow kept emerging. Always looking back and being content to simply mourn the passing of a "culture" and its "people," Strehlow had failed to comprehend how people were living in the present.

When Max Stuart first described the way that his grandfather used to "balance" T.G.H. Strehlow, it was difficult to imagine precisely what he meant. But as has been demonstrated via an examination of Strehlow's archival record, it was often important that intermediaries such as Lywenge and Rubuntja brought degrees of equity to the exchanges. These men actively assisted in the gathering of information and objects, organized and choreographed many of the ceremonial festivals, and in turn utilized Strehlow in ways that were not always evident to him. The zeal with which numerous men cooperated in this work is absolutely undeniable, as was the careful balancing of interests (personal, communal, and institutional) that they exhibited. As the *akiw-arenye* (denizen of the ceremonial ground), Strehlow's presence afforded those men living within a zone of changing cultural, political, and social relations not just the opportunity to "record" or "document," but more importantly, to demonstrate and reiterate their own cultural authority.

One could critique Strehlow's recording events as cases where informants had accepted a position assigned to them as "primitives," or that they had been corralled into the exchange. I contend, however, that substantial evidence supports they were not only attentive to the dynamics of these interactions but in part set the terms of the engagement. Although the precise motivations and interests of these informants can be only partially revealed via Strehlow's field diaries, it is clear that their interests in these exchanges often ran parallel to Strehlow's fixation on the documentation of an authentic Aboriginal ritual aesthetics. An obsession that positioned cultural/ritual vitality above the ongoing sociality of his subjects produced blinkeredness in regard to the sites where life is lived, meanings made, and cultural practice generated.

The following chapter delves into Anmatyerr people's own remembrances and stories of working with and witnessing Strehlow. These insights reconstruct the exchanges in ways that further tease out how they negotiated and engaged with colonial ethnography rather than simply being at the mercy of its gaze, which is, of course, the more standard story. In order to explore these engagements, we examine the various motivations of informants and the different ways that Strehlow's presence, and his endeavors, were perceived.

Chapter 5

Urrempel Man

> Strehlow had been coming around everywhere looking for all the man [*sic*] now. Strehlow had been coming around alright, that old Strehlow.
>
> —Paddy Kemarr

The campfire I most often sat by during my time with Anmatyerr people was the one belonging to Paddy Kemarr at Ti Tree. Paddy was born in the Arnmanapwenty area (to the north of Ti Tree) in 1932 and, like his father, Charlie Pwerrerl Kanajukurrpa (born c. 1895), had worked among the "wild cattle" most of his life. While growing up among all the "old people," young Paddy was apparently singled out and selected as someone to "learn more and more" and become what he described as a "knowledge man." Later in his life, Paddy traveled all over the Northern Territory working as a stockman and would often reside at the Bungalow and Amoonguna settlements in Alice Springs. It was here that he first became aware of T.G.H. Strehlow and met many of the senior men who had worked closely with him. In what must have been 1955, Paddy (then in his early twenties) remembered seeing Strehlow at the Werlatyatherre camp:

> I bin see him. He bin sit down with Arrernte people, on the Bungalow side, somewhere they bin sitting . . . There were three lots (three groups) sitting down . . . mixed up . . . *nhakw-areny map* (people from different places).

The "three groups" of people that had come together from all over the region were most likely those Arrernte, Pintubi/Luritja, and Anmatyerr/

Alyawarr men that Bob Rubuntja had "summoned" to Werlatyatherre in 1955.

I talked with Paddy about Strehlow's description of the ceremonies that were contained in his field diaries from the time, and he nodded patiently before launching into his own explanation. He knew perfectly well where the ceremonies of the *yerramp* (honey ant) ancestors pertained to, and pointed out their connections to numerous places in the Anmatyerr region, including his own birthplace, Arnmanapwenty ("the place of the worker ants") but also Arempey, Akwerrperl, and Alyape. Emphasizing the points of connection between people, sites, and ceremonies, he reminded me that it was fundamentally one's ability to "follow" these connections that made a person "*kalty*" (knowledgeable). This was not just a matter of tracing an objective story track, "line," or "path"—it meant understanding the links among a myriad of connected local *Anengkerr* episodes that could bifurcate or vanish, go underground or into the air, and most importantly, that belonged to individuals and local groups. Strehlow, Paddy posited, was someone who understood this. He was a "high school man"—someone who had actively accrued this inherently complex ritual knowledge by working along the points of connection.

At almost every Anmatyerr community I visited, I was told the same things. The older men had a nuanced or balanced memory of T.G.H. Strehlow that was fundamentally informed either by direct personal experience or oral histories. Strehlow, they explained, was a rare character, with unusual skills for an *alhernter*, and as such he stood out at the time. But it is the very specific way in which Strehlow is remembered that I want to feature in this chapter. As I traveled to these communities discussing his legacy and work with Anmatyerr men from across three generations, it was clear that Strehlow was remembered not according to the conventional narratives established in the literature, but through the lens of Anmatyerr people's own cultural categories and local histories.

As stated in the introduction, it was remarkable that neither of the two biographies written about T.G.H. Strehlow (Hill, 2003; McNally, 1981) contained any significant commentary from his informants. Considering that over fifty Anmatyerr men alone, and over one hundred Aboriginal men from across Central Australia, contributed to this long-lasting and thorough regional ethnography, it is astonishing to see how little of their memory has been incorporated into our understanding of this iconic historical figure. Where Aboriginal commentary on Strehlow has been inserted into the literature (Malbunka, 2004; Cohen, 2001b), it has primarily come from those connected with the Lutheran Mission at Hermannsburg (see Hill, 2003, pp. 728–730; McNally, 1981, pp. 38–40) and rarely concerns his ethnographic methods or relationships. As a result, very little detail has been unearthed about the nature of his relationships with the men he filmed, recorded, and photographed. The conventional wisdom that Strehlow was "no doubt" positioned "in the role of saviour" (Morton, 1995, p. 56), or that people "turned to him" as an *Ingkarte* (ceremonial leader, chief, or boss) so as to act as "a guardian of secrets" (Jorgensen, 2010, p. 22.6), has thus been left to linger without proper examination.

Even as Australianist anthropology increasingly turns in on itself, to trawl over its place in history (Gray, 2007; Cowlishaw, 2015, 1992) and in particular to consider the lives and contributions of its key thinkers (Hinkson and Beckett, 2008; Wise, 1985; Kenny, 2013; Monteath and Munt, 2015), the reflections or critiques of informants and participants remain marginal. And while there is growing recognition of Indigenous informants as "cultural experts" (Gardner and McConvell, 2015), as well as a sustained Indigenous critique of the production of anthropological knowledge (Nakata, 2007; Smith, 1999), few in Australia have followed the lead taken by those internationally (Geismar and Herle, 2009; Kan, 2001) to ask how ethnographers—and their practice of ethnography—is and was perceived, accommodated, and remembered by their interlocutors, a process that Geismar describes as looking "back up the lens" at the documenter (2009, p. 279).

Being a predominantly oral society and having little access to textual sources about Strehlow's biography, the Anmatyerr perspectives brought to the fore in this chapter emanate either from people's direct experiences or from locally circulating oral histories. Telling these stories allows people to shift attention away from previous narratives of a singular historical figure/agent and return emphasis to the points of interaction and relation, either in dialogue, conversation, singing, or traveling. Shifting focus, the chapter uncovers an account of these interactions as seen through Anmatyerr concepts of ritual responsibility, kinship, and relatedness.

Urrempel Man

Ronnie McNamara, a senior Anmatyerr/Arrernte man born at Tempe Downs Station in the mid- to late 1930s, was the first person to improve my understanding of how Strehlow was remembered among older men today. Ronnie was familiar with the Strehlow story, as he had spent his youth at the Hermannsburg mission, had passed through his initiation at the Jay Creek Settlement, which T.G.H. Strehlow had run, and later trained as a Lutheran pastor himself. When he came to the Anmatyerr region as a young man to work on Napperby station, Ronnie quickly established close connections with local families. Effectively adopted into the Ilewerr (Lake Lewis) group, he came to possess profound song, geo-mythological, and ceremonial expertise but remained committed to Lutheranism, as his nickname *Ngkart* (pastor) suggests. Despite this background, Ronnie remembers T.G.H. Strehlow not as a Christian figure primarily but as someone essentially defined by his involvement in men's ceremonies. Like Paddy Kemarr, Ronnie had seen Strehlow meeting with and recording the "old people" over the years and had come to understand him as being a part of the ritual scene at the time:

> Well he was on that *urrempel-thayt* [the domain of men's ceremony]. You know *Urrempel*? Like ah . . . *Amarleyarr* [the men's initiation ceremonies]. What they call 'em? He used to go around with all the *angerr-pat map* [all the senior men], and taking pictures of the old people, like on the *tywerreng-thayt* [the domain of secret men's Law]. *Kel ayeng iterlarem* [I know about it]. I know old Ted Strehlow.

Ronnie had seen Strehlow "everywhere" when he was a young man, but specifically at Hermannsburg, Haasts Bluff, and the Bungalow in the 1950s and 1960s. When I naïvely asked if he ever spoke with Strehlow, Ronnie shook his head and snickered. "No. He only talked to the old men. He was a *business man*!" Ronnie's use of the Aboriginal English term "business man" was unambiguous and clearly evoked a person deeply implicated in Aboriginal men's ceremony and ritual. "They didn't, you know, come near the women's side. They used to go a long way away and show him things like that one [sacred ceremonies]." At the time, though, everyone knew that the gatherings were at least in part intended for Strehlow's documentation purposes. As Paddy Kemarr explained, he could see that Strehlow was "right there, in that 'high-school business' [men's ritual education]," and while Paddy, Ronnie, and others of their age had attended similar ritual events throughout their lives, on those particular occasions in Alice Springs, he knew that they "*properly showed him* [Strehlow] *first.*"

I came to realize that it was Ronnie's earlier description of Strehlow as being someone "on the *urrempel-thayt*" (on the ceremony side) that best encapsulated the way people thought of him. It was similar to how Strehlow remembered being referred to by his informants, as an "Urumbulak" (*Urrempeleke*), meaning someone at or for *urrempel* ceremonies (1978c, p. 6). The term *urrempel* (or *urumbula*), though, despite its prevalence in the ethnographic literature for Central Australia, is difficult to define. In some parts of Arrernte territory and further south, it is often used as the name of a particular songline concerning western Quoll Ancestors who traverse the Australian continent from south to north (Ellis, 1964; Strehlow, 1947, pp. 153–157; Hercus, 2009). In more generic terms, though, it denotes a series of men's ceremonies, akin to the Engwura described by Spencer and Gillen (1899) and the Tingari of the Pintupi (Myers, 1991, pp. 59–64), where rituals from different places are shared among large, mobile groups of men. While this "travelling ceremony" also involved women's participation (Lovell, 2014, p. 187), it was primarily focused on male religious instruction. As Arrernte man Tom Williams described it to linguist Gavan Breen, the *urrempel* was equivalent to a "university" education . . . A main ceremony. Men only."[1]

The way Ronnie used the term clearly referred to the coming together of large numbers of men from across the region to perform ceremonies from a range of distinct places. The ceremonies and songs performed did not always intersect or directly relate to each other, but on the whole they pertained to stories that *traveled* through the country. Associating Strehlow with the *urrempel*, then, was noting his active pursuit of knowledge about the *traveling* songlines. As James Tewtew Mpetyan, a man in his late thirties, described Strehlow to me as a person who embarked upon "expeditions" into "other people's country . . . *following the country-lines*" as they passed through different estates. Rupert Max Stuart Kngwarraye, who performed for Strehlow's cameras in the 1950s, similarly characterized him as a person "always looking for that *big country*, ya know? *Big ceremony*. That's what he was doing."

This was overwhelmingly the way Anmatyerr men explained Strehlow's presence at the highly restricted ceremonies. He wasn't simply an "observer" or inhabitant of the ceremonial ground, as Bob Rubuntja's description

---

1. Personal communication with Jenny Green and Gavan Breen, January 2017.

"*akiw-arenye*" suggested (see previous chapter), but a person who "followed," "chased," and eventually "caught" (apprehended/understood) ritual knowledge. Importantly, this was and remains a category of person, and an activity, that persists in Central Australia. As Fred Myers's early biographies of Pintupi men from the neighboring Western Desert reveal, the notion of traveling with the intention of (among other things) attaining ceremonial knowledge was a common pre-colonial practice in the region (Róheim 1945, pp. 104, 124; Strehlow, 1978a, p. 151) and remains important (see Austin-Broos, 2009, p. 117; and Peterson, 2004, 2000). Although most Anmatyerr men reiterate that they are mostly concerned with their own localized cultural knowledge and, unlike their Western neighbors, do not "jump over boundaries," there are nonetheless small numbers of Anmatyerr men that do participate in this more expansive ritual accumulation. Sometimes referred to as *tyelkath-map* or *jilkaja* by Warlpiri speakers (see Peterson, 2000; 2004), these men travel to accumulate ritual knowledge throughout their lives, often by "following up" Dreaming tracks, visiting important sites, and attending numerous ceremonial gatherings.

Remembered as an "*urrempel* man," then, Strehlow's behaviors mimicked existing cultural categories and practices that remain relevant to contemporary lives. To the Anmatyerr watching him from afar, he moved metaphorically and physically through their cultural landscapes, as one of those people devoted to learning about the dynamic links between song, myth, and land. As Archie Mpetyan, whose father Friday Ankerr-raweny Ngal had sung for Strehlow in 1932, put it: "Strehlow was a 'high school man . . . Oh [he was a] good young fella!' . . . *Yeway* [Yes] he knew the Law. He's a 'high school' man that one." Others agreed that what Strehlow had been doing was recording and participating in the more advanced stages of male ritual, known among the Anmatyerr as *Akernenty* but often expressed as "high school" in English.

Others would be more specific, conjuring up memories of exactly which ceremonies had been filmed or recorded at different times. Tommy Thompson, a Kaytetye elder from the Barrow Creek area to the north of Ti Tree, for example, knew exactly which series of ceremonies Strehlow had recorded in 1955. Having heard about Strehlow's work from his Anmatyerr and Alyawarr relatives, Tommy made it clear that Strehlow's presence had been remembered across the wider Arandic region:

> Strehlow . . . He was coming there to Alyawarr country to catch 'em (to learn) whole lot, business! That *yerramp* (honey ant) and

all he bin catch. The whole lot. It started from Papunya, went right up to Ngkwarlerlanem. Different-different talking again, showing him (People of different language groups showed him).

Tommy's story clearly referred to the recording of the honey ant ceremonies with Bob Rubuntja that had drawn together men from "different-different" language groups, including Tommy's Anmatyerr and Alyawarr kin. Strehlow's "coming" to Alyawarr country, as Tommy put it, was not necessarily the act of *physically* traveling to the region (although he certainly did, in 1968) but the metaphorical visitation to the country via the revelation of ceremonies. This is what *urrempel*/ceremony men did.

Ingkarte?

But why hadn't any of the Anmatyerr men—or Northern Arrernte men, for that matter—ever referred to Strehlow as an "*Ingkarte*," a ceremonial leader or "chief"? Certainly, Strehlow's own writings had encouraged this view of himself, and others have since applied the term. While the men I knew seemed perfectly happy to accept Strehlow's presence and participation in ritual, none had ever elevated him to a status above them. Part of the reason for this omission can be found in the linguistic particularities of the term itself. Often used to refer to "missionaries," "priests," or "ministers," and by association "God" (Green, 2010), *Ingkarte/Ngkart* is never used by contemporary Anmatyerr speakers to refer to traditional ceremonial matters. The word also appears to have originated from the Western Arrernte language spoken at the Hermannsburg Mission and was only later introduced into both Anmatyerr and other forms of Arrernte via early missionaries (Dobson and Henderson, 1994, p. 493). As Central Arrernte speaker Mort Conway cheekily explained, *Ingkarte* had been "made up by the German monks!"[2]

These linguistic issues are not the only reason why the notion of Strehlow as an *Ingkarte* has not persisted. Nor is it associated with any ideological or political intentions, but rather the way in which Anmatyerr people fundamentally conceptualize ownership of ritual knowledge. To

---

2. Gavan Breen interview with Mort Conway, November 11, 1984. See also the entry for Ngkart in the Arrernte "megablend" document produced by the Institute for Aboriginal Development in Alice Springs.

raise a single individual to the status above all others seems untenable to most people today, especially when it concerns ceremonial knowledge that is never entirely confined to "personal property" but regarded as continually emerging from the non-labile Dreaming content objectified in land (Sutton, 1996, p. 23). For a single person to be a ritual "leader" *for all* is antithetical to the way in which these responsibilities are shared and distributed, particularly through the dual, complementary responsibilities of *merek-artwey* (owners) and *kwertengerl* (managers). One could certainly be knowledgeable, as suggested by Rubuntja's "King" status, but these people always founded their authority in the enactment of reciprocal duties and responsibilities.

At the Strehlow Research Centre conference in 2002, anthropologist John Morton quipped that if Strehlow saw himself as *Ingkarte*, then it needed to be asked who his *kwertengerl* (offsider, manager) was. While the intention of Morton's rhetorical question was justified, in that it pointed out the lack of checks and balances in Strehlow's dealings, it is not an entirely fair question to begin with. The proper, binary complement to a *kwertengerl* is not an *Ingkarte* at all, but a *merek-artwey*, someone who owns and inherits their own personal traditions. As Strehlow himself noted, while an *Ingkarte* or ceremonial leader might "strive" to possess expertise beyond his own traditions, he ultimately "had to become" a *kwertengerl* (custodian, protector) for others (Strehlow, 1971a, p. 248fn). While Anmatyerr men agree that Strehlow undoubtedly strove to possess expertise, they pay little heed to the *Ingkarte* title and reiterate that there were always senior men present to keep an eye on his powers from "*tyer-rty-kenh thayt*" (from the Aboriginal point of view). Stressing the critical importance of complementary rights and responsibilities for country, ceremonies, and songs, they insist that Strehlow was, and that his collection ought to continue to be, bound by these expectations (see chapter 8).

In addition to these clear ritual demarcations, the way that Anmatyerr people render social history also presents serious barriers to any elevation of Strehlow's status. As Jackson (1995) noted in his work with the Warlpiri, the western neighbors to the Anmatyerr, Central Australian Aboriginal people tend to prioritize a *relational* telling of local history that *de-emphasizes* the significance of individuals (Jackson, 1995; see also Jackson, 1998, p. 129). Jackson writes that contrary to conventional Western conceptions of social history that present individual lives as "heroically standing out from history and its social determinations" (1995, p. 162), individuals in the Aboriginal context usually placed within broader "skeins of relationship" that involve

Dreaming, landscape, and kinship. Historical figures are thus melded into a constellation of *social* relationships, as well as relationships to place and Dreaming, that downplay a self-contained individual actor. It is perhaps for this reason that T.G.H. Strehlow and his father—both *Ntharey-areny* (belonging to, or coming from Nthareye/Hermannsburg)—were conflated or their names interchanged during discussions.

It is therefore fitting that the various appellations ascribed to T.G.H. Strehlow by Anmatyerr men, "*urrempel* man," "high-school man," and "business man" suggest a non-hierarchical social status. Indeed, the suffix "*-man*" used with each of these descriptions appears to suggest instead a *commonality* and *sociality* among "men." In this way, Strehlow is remembered as being one among many rather than above or beyond. As has been observed in other parts of northern Australia, cultural categories and labels such as these can be "reworked" in ways that establish "workable degrees of relatedness" with non-Indigenous people (Redmond 2005, p. 242). With an atypical *alhernter* in their midst, people's pragmatism and desire to communicate led to an affiliation based on a shared encounter underwritten by Arandic concepts of relatedness.

Anpernerrenty (Relations)

Strehlow came to these interactions with the privileges and constraints of a *related* individual. At the very least, people who met with him often knew of his classificatory subsection affiliation as a *Kemarre*. They knew that he had been blessed with considerable knowledge of Arandic lifeworlds, and many also knew that being *Nthareye-arenye* (belonging to Hermannsburg), he had a personal conception site. Indeed, it was Strehlow's zeal to be positioned as kin that reinforced his Arandic social identity and ultimately enabled that most "mysterious," yet necessary quality in fieldwork, his personal *rapport* and point of connection with informants. Located within *anpernerrenty*, a term often translated into English as a "kinship system" or "relationship network" (Walsh, Dobson, and Douglas, 2013; Dobson, 2013; Green, 2010), Strehlow was made socially "real" or present to his informants. As with many ethnographers, this type of kin incorporation or adoption (Kan, 2001; Sutton, 2002), cultivated relationships and legitimated access to knowledge.

The significance of Strehlow's place within *anpernerrenty* can be seen in his participation in the Akwerrperl ceremonies at Alcoota, described in the previous chapter. As Strehlow ritually pleaded for ceremonial objects at the conclusion of the Grey Butcherbird ceremony, his *anwakerrakeye* (men belonging to his same generational moiety) joined him in what was an unmistakable recognition of his place with the kinship system (1965a, p. 150). Unlike most other ethnographers, Strehlow could also claim deeper relationships to people via his personal "conception" at Nthareye (Hermannsburg). In agreement with Arandic custom that regards a person's actual conception as the moment when a local ancestral spirit *angane-irreke* (spiritually conceives) an unborn child (cf. Merlan 1986; Montagu 1974), Strehlow asserted that he was related to the *Anengkerr* (Dreaming). As the ontological basis to Arandic lifeworlds, the claim could not be more momentous.

The *Anengkerr*, or *Altyerre* as it is referred to in Arrernte, that Strehlow was connected to was that of the *arathap* (newborn baby) Dreaming. Seeing this as part of his personal inheritance (Strehlow, 1950b, p. 47), Strehlow sought out knowledge of this Dreaming and its ceremonies and songs from senior Western Arrernte men throughout his life. When in Zurich, he searched the Australian ethnological collections, in vain, for the *arathap tywerreng* (the sacred objects embodying the newborn baby ancestors) (Strehlow, 1952, pp. 54–55). The cover of *Songs of Central Australia* featured a reproduction of one of the ground paintings used in the *arathap* ceremonies, and because he believed these traditions had been "handed over to him" as his "private property" (Strehlow, 1971a, frontispiece), he had no qualms about reproducing this usually secret iconography.

Anmatyerr men today make little comment about Strehlow's claims to spiritual inheritance, though those closer to his personal story often do support these claims. Intrigued by the notion that a non-Aboriginal person might be able to assert affiliation, perhaps even "rights" in Dreaming sites and mythologies, I raised the issue with a number of Arrernte people. I knew that Wenten Rubuntja, the son of Bob Rubuntja, had publicly stated that both Aboriginal and non-Aboriginal people born in Alice Springs could be spiritually connected to local Dreamings (Rubuntja and Green, 2002, p. 175). But did this really confer rights to ritual knowledge?

When discussing this with Western Arrernte men, they were often careful with their answers. Ownership of the Nthareye estate had been disputed for decades, resulting in a rancorous and seemingly intractable "factionalism" (Austin-Broos, 2009, pp. 179–182), and no one wanted to rekindle debates about ownership and rights. Mark Inkamala, whose patrilineal estate of Parirrweltye was to the north, agreed that Strehlow

Figure 5.1. With Mark Inkamala at Mpaltyartakerte, where some of Ted Strehlow's ashes were laid to rest. There were once two trees here, but fire has removed one (photo: P. Batty, September 2014).

was correct in regarding himself, first, as a man of the *Kemarre* subsection, and second, as someone connected to Nthareye via his conception. Journeying with Mark to Mpaltyartakerte, a related *arathape* site on the outskirts of Hermannsburg and the place where Strehlow's ashes had been spread, I asked if he thought Strehlow had exaggerated his connections to the area (figure 5.1). Mark insisted the connection seemed plausible, but it was impossible for him to know much more.

As one of the few Arrernte men to have spent considerable hours researching the contents of the Strehlow collection, Mark simply commented the recognition that Strehlow was granted by past generations was proof enough. He explained that a child born in the area might be related to the local *altyerre* (Dreamings), but he or she couldn't make claims over sacred/ritual material. They had to be bestowed responsibilities by senior men. Mark suggested this had been the case with Strehlow. "Just look at the way those old men treated him! He was a traditional owner for this country."

Further evidence of Strehlow's deep connection with the *arathape* Dreaming and his willingness to engage with his informants as kin is found in local oral history. Arrernte man Sandy White, one of the men present at the recording of the Akwerrperl ceremonies at Alcoota in 1965, for example, told both Pastor Paul Albrecht and the lay missionary Gary Stoll that Strehlow personally performed a ceremony from his conception site. White claimed that the ceremony was an act of ritual *akepenh* (reciprocity or "squaring up") on Strehlow's behalf, in return for being granted permission to record the Akwerrperl ceremonies. "He did a ground painting and everything," Stoll had been told. Strehlow's field diaries from the time do not reveal the occurrence of such a performance (see Strehlow, 1965d, p. 10). Other stories of Strehlow "dancing" in ceremonies for which he was "custodian" have also circulated with little supporting evidence.[3]

Writing of how English anthropologist John Layard was remembered by Indigenous people in the Pacific, Haidy Geismar documents a comparable story. Resembling Strehlow's case, the people of Malakula remember Layard performing and participating in ritual, even though evidence is absent from his own archive. In an insightful consideration, Geismar has suggested that the information documented by anthropologists can become "incontrovertible proof" not just of the important "relationships" that underlie the necessary dialogue to record these things, but of participation itself (2009, pp. 279–280). Where knowledge is embedded in sociality and most often actively performative rather than representational, it is expected that one could not "know" this information without having enacted it. Although Strehlow was never initiated, it seems anomalous to most Arrernte and Anmatyerr men that he could be permitted to observe and record rituals without being in some way a reciprocal participant.

Singing and Talking

When I discussed Strehlow and his work with Arrernte or Anmatyerr men, it was universally commented that he was like no other *alhernter* they had encountered. His fluency and commitment to language and the speed with which he became adept in communicating across Arandic dialects was striking. More than this, though, his ability to comprehend the esoteric

---

3. See Northern Territory Archive Service 1087/Item 1112, transcript of interview with Kevin Heintze recorded June 4, 2003, by Francis Good.

language of men's song and his ability to sing was extraordinary. In the words of Mick Mclean Irinyili, a highly knowledgeable Lower Arrernte/ Wangkangurru man who worked with Strehlow in the late 1960s, "Mr Strehlow is Arrernte himself . . . he *knows* Arrernte. He might translate it (song verse) better than me . . ."[4] These abilities, which must be noted are possessed by many senior Aboriginal men, were nonetheless particularly unusual and impressive for an *alhernter*.

After spending over five weeks with Strehlow during the filming of the Akwerrperl ceremonies, Ken Tilmouth was clearly impressed. "Oh yeah. He was *proper* hey! He was a good Arrernte bloke. He talked Arrernte all the time." It was these linguistic and cultural skills, then, that set him apart and afforded him deep relationships. Ronnie McNamara, similarly noting the significance of language to cultural identity, commented that these abilities made him "Arrernte-*anthwerr*" (really Arrernte). Others who had not met Strehlow but had heard stories about him claimed that he spoke "really hard Arrernte," or that he could speak Arrernte "right through" (fluently). And when listening back to recordings that included Strehlow in conversation with Anmatyerr men, Don Presley Pengart, the Lutheran pastor in Ti Tree, went so far as to claim that Strehlow appeared to speak *Pertame*, the dialect of Arrernte spoken to the south of Hermannsburg, although with a German accent. To Don it was "German Arrernte."

It is telling that these Aboriginal language abilities are perceived as exceptional in Central Australia to this day. Of the ten or so non-Indigenous individuals who presently speak an Arandic language, it is doubtful any would regard themselves as truly fluent. The rarity of this expertise, as well as the commitment and time it takes to attain these skills, makes individuals such as Strehlow particularly important local historical figures. But there are even fewer non-Indigenous people, not only in Central Australia but across the continent, who know how to sing ceremonial songs.

Harold Payne Mpetyan, or "Papelaw" as he is known among his peers, made a big deal about this. Harold had been away mustering cattle on a station in Eastern Arrernte country when Strehlow first arrived at Alcoota in 1965 to document the Akwerrperl ceremonies, but his father, "Lame" Tom Ltarelkek, spoke fondly of the white man. When Strehlow returned three years later, it was Harold's *apwelh* (circumcision ceremony) that had effectively forced Strehlow to leave the community (see chapter 5).

---

4. Mick Mclean, interviewed by Alan West, XAV1, Museum Victoria.

In 1971, when Strehlow drove back into Alcoota for the last time, Harold followed the lead of his father, as well as his *kwertengerl*, Ken Tilmouth, and trusted the Arrernte-speaking *alhernter* (figure 5.2). With his relatives by his side, Harold agreed to sing on both the audio recordings that were made. They sang the *ingwa* (night) songs belonging to Ned Kemarr and also Ken's *ikwelengk* (king brown snake, *Pseudechis australis*) songs relating to the site of Ulem, on Edwards Creek. Strehlow later commented in his diary how surprised he was to meet young men like Harold and Ken who exhibited such excellent knowledge of song and myth.

I met with Harold for the first time in 2015 at the remote community of Ahalper (New Store) on the edge of Anmatyerr and Alyawarr country (figure 5.3). I had specifically sought out Harold to learn from him about his time with Strehlow, but given his high mobility between the sparsely distributed communities of Mulga Bore, Alcoota, and Ahalper, he was often

Figure 5.2. Harold Payne in 1971 (SRC PHO-03972).

Figure 5.3. With Harold Payne Mpetyan at Ahalper, April 2015 (photo: Malcolm Heffernan).

extremely difficult to locate. Finally meeting him at Ahalper, I began clumsily with a broad question aimed at eliciting his opinion of Strehlow's character.

In Harold's estimation, Strehlow was essentially a "friendly bloke," someone who was "alright," but it was his ability to speak Arrernte and sing men's songs that most impressed him. He recalled sitting under the shade of a gidgea tree (*Acacia cambagei*) with Ken and his father while Strehlow photographed and filmed them decorating *alkwert* shields with Ken's *ikwelengk* (king brown snake) designs. As they painted (with "white lime" provided by Strehlow) they sang the necessary songs. As Harold remembered the occasion, he began to move his hand in a wave motion as if to indicate the design representing the movement of the snakes across the shields. Returning to my questioning, he explained that his principal concern was to fulfill his duties as a *kwertengerl* (ritual assistant) to Ken:

> Yeah, I met that one Strehlow. We were sitting down on the countryside, old Ken and me. I painted up some shields, *alkwert*. *Alkwert* [shields] we painted them with the *ikwelengk*, *ampwa Ikwelengk* [the king brown snake] designs. Me and old Ken. I was working with Ken as his *kwertengerl*.

Harold recalled that after "dinner" (actually lunch in stockman parlance), the trio were asked to sing the songs again, this time so they could be recorded on tape. Sitting up straight now and seemingly reliving the occasion in his mind, Harold began to sing a short burst of the *ikwelengk* song before stopping suddenly. "Ya. We bin singing . . . *alakenh*" (we did it just like that).

As a *kwertengerl*, Harold had to know these songs, but he could sing them only with the expressed approval of the rightful *merek-artwey* (owner). He continued by providing only a very basic outline of the places to which the song related and reasserted Ken's ownership:

> We sang like that you see. That's the *ikwelengk* [the king brown snake] that one. We went [the song's verses recounted the travels of the ancestor] from there to *Ayampe-thayt* [an estate in Northern Arrernte territory]. He [the snake ancestor] then meet that other *ikwelengk* that went there. Yeah, those two fellas met up on the Bushy Park plain on the east side from the station. And we pulled 'em right back [sang the verses that described his travel right back] to *Ulem* [on the Edwards Creek]. We were singing. Old Ken can sing that song for you. He knows that song. I know the song alright, but you might think bad about me [singing without permission from the owner].

The retelling of this event had also reminded Harold of not only Strehlow's excellent talents as a speaker of Arrernte but his abilities as a singer as well:

> He could talk Arrernte language and *he could sing too*. Ken and me bin hear him that one. He was singing. We all bin there. Three blokes. He would sing too [with us], *ya proper really one* that bloke! [He sang] that *apmwa* [snake] song now.

Laughing and shaking his head in genuine amazement, Harold continued to marvel at how an *alhernter* could become so adept in these esoteric songs. "He might know everything, that bloke!," Harold remarked. He had never seen such proficiency in song from a white person before, and in the forty years since, had never seen anything like it again. Although Harold didn't know it, Strehlow had in fact been trying to master what he called the "horribly irregular" singing style of Anmatyerr men for decades (Strehlow, 1955b, p. 37). He described one occasion during the Werlatyatherre festival of 1955, for example, when Anmatyerr men "came in close" to watch him transcribe their songs and then attempt to sing them. After singing "loudly" from his written notes, "everybody laughed," apparently enjoying "the fact that he had mastered it so quickly" (Strehlow, 1955b, p. 33). Serendipitously, the song that Strehlow was trying to learn on that occasion was part of the same *ahakey* (native currant, *Psydrax latifolia*) songline that traveled from Ahalper (where Harold and I sat) through to Harold's patrilineal estate of Ilkewartn.

There are a number of oral accounts of the speed and accuracy with which Strehlow would rapidly transcribe songs before singing them back to his informants. Gary Stoll, an excellent speaker of Western Arrernte and former employee of the Finke River Mission in Hermannsburg, for example, tells a similar story from Strehlow's final visit to Hermannsburg in 1977. Ever in search of new songs, Strehlow asked Stoll to escort him down to the camp of some of the old singers:

> So I took him down to the *kwaty lhere* [the river] and Old Luther, Jack Coulthard and Yankee, the ones that usually did the singing were there. Strehlow told them, he said, "I know the songs from up to Tempe Downs but I never learnt the ones that went on from there." And they said, "Oh no, well that's where we'll pick it up from then." Straight away they sang it around the back of the range, almost back to Areyonga. Strehlow said "That's amazing!" He was making a few notes . . . just a few notes. Then he'd say "Have I got that right?" and he read out the verses that he'd written down to them. But they said "Sing it." [After he had finished singing] They said, "Yep, never missed!"

Harold Payne and Ken Tilmouth recalled a similar exchange back at Alcoota in 1971. As Ken and Harold sang for these recordings, Strehlow again became involved. While Strehlow's diary remains silent on this exchange, Harold distinctly remembers Strehlow writing down each of the song verses while he, Ken, and Harold's father, Lame Tom Ltarerlkek, sang and decorated the *alkwert*. When it came to singing for the recording, though, Strehlow listened carefully to their performance, matching it with what he had written down earlier in his notebook. Looking out for any omissions or errors, he suddenly stopped them. Harold recalled:

He said "You two fellas just missed a line." We started to sing another song. And when we started another one, then he called out "Hey!" and he was looking down at his paper. [Strehlow said] "You missed that one (line) hey?" "You missed that one," he said. "Hey you bin . . . why you bin miss that one?" he bin tell me. "Oh we missed that one" we bin tell him.

Harold laughed about the irony of the exchange. "Was Strehlow right?" "Had you really missed a song line?" I asked. Shaking his head in disbelief, Harold replied, "*Yewe yewe* [yes, yes]. He was right. He's a singing bloke that one!"

"Strehlow-time" and "Three Law"

Beyond these personal aptitudes, though, Strehlow's name had also come to represent a distinctive phase in people's local history. "Strehlow time," as it was often referred to, signified not just Strehlow's role in recording and documentation but also his association with colonial authority. As with many other Aboriginal groups across Australia that describe important phases in their history with the suffix "time" or "times"—such as "Land Rights Time," "Killing Times," or "Wild Time" (Strehlow, 1969b; Kimber 1998)—the Anmatyerr identified "Strehlow Time" as a clearly identifiable historical period. Although the term was sometimes used by younger men, when older generations mentioned "Strehlow Time" it clearly evoked memories of a period in colonial history when the influence of the state began to assume a greater interest in and control over people's lives. The complicity of the Northern Territory administration in authorizing and assisting Strehlow in his efforts during this "time" was not undetected by Arrernte and Anmatyerr people.

Sitting by Paddy Kemarr's campfire at Ti Tree Creek Camp, Albie Mpetyan, a man in his sixties, explained that "Strehlow-time" was when "a whole lot" of men would be brought in to Alice Springs to perform for "the cameras" with the consent of local authorities. "*Yewe*, Amoonguna-*le* [Yes, it was at Amoonguna Settlement]. And he [Strehlow] let that policeman, manager know that they bin do "em [ceremony]." The consent of local authorities ("policemen") to stage ceremonies on Aboriginal Settlements meant that cultural practices that might otherwise have been deemed to be contrary to the objectives of assimilationist policies were effectively given free reign during Strehlow's stay.

In this sense, "Strehlow Time" is remarkably similar to what Arrernte people had earlier described as "Gillen Time" (Strehlow, 1969b; Kimber, 1998). Named after the anthropologist and Aboriginal sub-protector Francis James Gillen, who was the first *alhernter* permitted to record secret-sacred ceremonies, "Gillen Time" referred to a period in history whereby colonial authority and anthropological inquiry were encapsulated and combined within a single, charismatic individual. Much like Strehlow, Gillen had decades of experience among Arrernte, and although he did not possess anywhere near the same level of linguistic expertise, his personal affinity with the Arrernte was outstanding for the time. Not conceived on Arrernte soil like Strehlow, Gillen had nonetheless been incorporated into kinship as a man of the Peltharre subsection and bestowed with a "Dreaming" connection (Gibson, 2013). He also had "close emotional involvement in" rituals he documented and, at times, participated in (Morphy, 1997, p. 47). As historical labels, then, "Strehlow Time" and "Gillen Time" denote not only anthropology's historical (Asad, 1973; Stocking, 1993) and enduring embeddedness in colonialism (Lattas and Morris, 2010; Altman and Hinkson, 2010) but also the lasting significance of these exceptional relationships.

Oddly enough, the colonial milieu in which this ethnographic knowledge was being produced can also be evinced in the way some Anmatyerr people have come to pronounce "Strehlow." I first heard this pronunciation after spending time with Ray Nelson Penangke, a senior man who often resided at the community of Mulga Bore (Akay). I knew Ray through my work in the region over the years, and after stumbling into him on the streets of Alice Springs, I invited him to come to the Strehlow Research Centre to discuss the collection with me. The following morning we walked through the Centre's storeroom and archives discussing some of the *tywerreng* that had been collected by Strehlow in the vicinity of Ray's traditional country. Ray initially showed no signs of comprehending who the person responsible for this collection was. My conventional pronunciation of the Strehlow surname drew a blank. I could see that he obviously knew of an *alhernter* who matched the description of the person I was talking about, but he struggled to recognize the name. Frustrated, he began to probe his memory for clues:

> Oh, what's his name!? They bin sell 'em and give 'em away *tywerreng* [sacred material] hey? *Iwenhe* [what is] his name? He went all over the place . . . *Angwenh-athew*? [Who was it?] He went to Mer Athatheng [Woodgreen Station] and Mer Aleyaw [Ti Tree], everywhere . . . Oh, I forget his name . . .

Suddenly, Ray asked, "Oh! Do you mean *Threylaw*? We know *Threylaw*!" In fact, it was Ray's *angey* (father's brother) Paddy Kaltyirrpek Pengart, who had twice escorted Strehlow through Eastern Anmatyerr sites in 1932. Other men from the Eastern Anmatyerr area similarly explained to me, again using this distinctive pronunciation, that it had been "Threylaw" who "the old people had sold some of their *amek-amek* (dangerous possessions) to."

This articulation was previously noted by one of the few anthropologists to work extensively in this region, Jeannie Devitt, in the 1990s. According to Devitt, the name sounded something like "Threylaw," "Thrrelow," or "Thrreelo," and had come to resemble the words "Three Law" in English (see Strehlow 1968a, pp. 98–99).[5] Investigating further, Devitt asked the senior man Tommy Bird Mpetyan for a clarification. Bird, who had met Strehlow only once, during a mapping trip on the Sandover River (see Strehlow, 1968a, pp. 98–99), explained to Devitt that this was precisely how Anmatyerr people had understood Strehlow's name to be. It seemed to perfectly resemble his personification of three distinct "laws": his standing in "whitefella law," referring to his association with welfare and government administration; his well-known involvement in "blackfella law," meaning his deep involvement in men's sacred ritual; and his links to "God law" via his missionary background and bible translation work. The serendipitous twist of a German surname by Eastern Anmatyerr speakers had become a perfectly fitting encapsulation of the man in English.

A Specter in the Region

Embodying these qualities, Strehlow quickly became a well-known figure across the Central Australian Aboriginal community. Even people who had not personally met him, but rather had witnessed him working with their fathers and grandfathers, understood what was being exchanged. But in many cases, elders did not communicate with their sons and grandsons what was told or given to Strehlow. On a number of occasions, while reading over Strehlow's notes with groups of men, people expressed genuine surprise to learn of their fathers' or grandfathers' dealings with Strehlow. Lesley Stafford Pwerrerl from the Mamp/Arrwek estate, for example,

---

5. Personal communication, Jeanie Devitt, March 2, 2015.

was startled to learn that in 1932 his father, Sambo Rltwamparwenguny Kemarr, had permitted Strehlow to take many of his objects. In such cases, interactions were so short-lived that even though the discussions concerned deeply treasured ritual content, the exchange was ultimately insignificant in the broader scheme of things.

In other cases, it seems that stories of Strehlow may have been withheld or repressed due to the sensitivities associated with men's ritual. One could speculate that revealing the sale of sacred objects, in particular, or the revelation of vital song may have been too sensitive to admit among peers.

Eric Penangk's memories speak of this *specter* of Strehlow in the region rather than a direct memory of him. Born at Atnyemekwaty (Ryan's Well), where his father Tom Uneynt Pengart worked as a stockman, Eric became a station-hand himself and spent years mustering, droving, and breaking in wild horses in the area. When Strehlow drove into the "native camp" at Anwekeran (Laughton's Lagoon on Aileron Station) in 1958 looking for guides, Eric remembers watching him from afar. Strehlow and his Northern Arrernte guides, Bob Rubuntja and Tom Arleyekwarte, had approached Eric's elderly father Tom Uneynt as well as his brother George Yerramp Rlwengapeltyey. Eric's brief recollection of this occasion generally matches the account given in Strehlow's field diaries:

> I saw him one time, when he got all the older people together. They talked about "business" to old Strehlow. And they bin go in the bush to sing and see sacred sites. Well, I was a little boy then so I couldn't go. Cause it was a "man's" one [a trip that involved revealing senior men's business].

Numerous Arrernte and Anmatyerr men have explained similar situations to me when as young men they would quietly witness Strehlow's arrival in communities. They knew that older men were engaged in some kind of "men's business" with Strehlow, but never dared to ask about it. Eric would have been in his late teens at the time. Ten years later, Strehlow once again returned to Aileron and sought out Eric's father. As soon as I explained to Eric that I had found recordings of his father singing during Strehlow's visit, he immediately suggested that we move closer to the site of the old camp at Anwekeran. As we climbed into my car, Eric explained that we should listen to the recordings near to where they were originally made. After a short drive from the Aileron roadhouse, we arrived at the site of the old camp. I readied the laptop to play the songs, and Eric started to recall the occasion in more detail. "I saw Strehlow one time in the place that we're sitting now. [They were near] that *arrkernk* [bloodwood tree, *Corymbia opaca*], that way *ingerr-thayt* [to the east]. It was a long time ago that one. But I still remember."

Eric insisted that in both 1958 and 1968 his father, and indeed all of the other men at Aileron, had remained tight-lipped about the contents of their dealings with Strehlow. The type of information shared with Strehlow—"country-laws," as Eric put it—was imparted only to those fully qualified to share in it, and at the time Eric was too young or inexperienced. But Strehlow, he reiterated, had the credentials at the time. The old men didn't mind discussing this material with Strehlow because he had been "working all over the country, Anmatyerr-side, Eastern Arrernte/Anmatyerr, all mix up [people from lots of different areas]."

Eric's adopted grandson, Tony Ngwarray, marveled at how an *alhernter* could so easily be granted access to this type of information. I had shown him some of the related diary entries, including song transcriptions and maps of sacred sites, and his response was puzzlement and curiosity. "Why was everything passed on to him?" he asked. Before I could answer, though, Tony thought of a reply of his own based on the evidence before him. "Because he *knew* what old Tom Uneynt was talking about . . . Tom passed it to him. He must have been a pretty fucking brainy bloke hey?" It was clear to Tony that Strehlow must have possessed the skills to comprehend this information. While the archival evidence suggested that "everything" was "passed on" to Strehlow, he also knew that Eric possessed much of the same song and site knowledge, and in fact Tony had learned some of it himself.

"He took it dishonestly!"

What is most striking about the memories and accounts related above is that, on the whole, Strehlow was largely spared serious criticism from his informants and their descendants. Despite allegations of misappropriation and dishonesty being leveled against Strehlow as early as 1965, when the Northern Territory Administration's Director of Welfare, Mr. Harry Giese, made inferences that Strehlow had stolen *tywerreng* (sacred objects) (Strehlow, 1965d, p. 40), Anmatyerr men never made any such claims. During my conversations with people, however, there were observable differences of opinion regarding his avid collecting and personal accrual of ritual knowledge.

Some of these sentiments would arise while walking through collections stores with Arrernte men at the Strehlow Research Centre. Most men were unaware of Strehlow's outrageous claims to sole ownership of their material. As they perused the collection shelves, they were reminded of stories they had been told about Strehlow. One senior Peltharre man from the Anapipe estate, for instance, claimed he had been told by his father to desist from sharing with Strehlow. This man later claimed that while he had been away working as a stockman, Strehlow had been through his country, and with the help of other Arrernte men, had "emptied everything." Far more deeply embroiled in Strehlow's project than their Anmatyerr relations, the Arrernte had become more affected by his doctrinaire and possessive attitudes. His eager accumulation of *tywerrenge* (sacred objects) was particularly worrying for them. They argued that the decades of Strehlow's collecting had not only resulted in the "emptying out" of many of the sacred storehouses (where sacred objects were kept), but now meant they had a depleted ability to maintain the vitality and significance of "country" for younger generations.

As one of the few men alive who worked with Strehlow on a number of occasions, I regarded Ken Tilmouth's version of this history as particularly significant. I first broached the topic with him during his visit to the Melbourne Museum in May of 2013. Ken had traveled to Melbourne as part of a delegation of men from Central Australia interested in identifying secret-sacred objects that might be repatriated (incidentally, none of which had been collected by Strehlow). At the end of a long day of inspecting hundreds of objects, I asked Ken if he thought Strehlow had *arwengkel inek*, taken something without permission? Somewhat puzzled by my question, Ken reminded me that he and his father (Mick Werlaty) had participated freely in both the recording of their ceremonies and the handing over of objects. It was clear that Ken disagreed with the suggestion that he and his kin had somehow been deprived by Strehlow. "*Itya* [No]. I don't know *how* he *stole* those things?" Ken responded. "That old man, *angey-atyengenh* [my father] he still had them there in his *head!* And I *still* know it now." The very idea that they had been dispossessed of tangible or intangible cultural knowledge was, in Ken's view, entirely mistaken.

As with most suggestions of cultural appropriation, as Richard Martin (2013) has correctly pointed out, my question rested on the simplistic assumption of negligent or unequal unbalanced collaboration. Strehlow had certainly taken Aboriginal knowledge and objects and appropriated them into his own discourses, but this lay well outside Ken's specific interests. It was the distinctiveness of the local Anmatyerr lifeworlds, the arena where people learn and are bound together via social relations that mattered. Ken's experience and feelings on these issues derived fundamentally from a combination of his direct interaction with Strehlow, the roles played by his father, and the future position of his sons. The "Inner Cycle" of Akwerrperl, Ken reiterated, had certainly been presented for Strehlow's documentation purposes, but more important, it had been shown for the edification of all of the men present, particularly himself.

There were, however, some differences of opinion about the ethics of Strehlow's work *between* generations. Younger Anmatyerr men without Ken's experience or authority found it easier to be critical. After a number of hours of viewing Strehlow's films and discussing his collection with a group of five men at Napperby Station, I asked for people's opinions on the notion of appropriation. Peter Stafford Kemarr, the youngest man among them (mid- to late forties) was the first to respond. "*Ya, arwengkel inem!* [Yes, he took/stole it dishonestly!]," he asserted. Ronnie McNamara quickly interjected. Remembering more about Strehlow than anyone else in the group, and having witnessed him with the "old people" on numerous occasions, Ronnie wanted his particular reading of these events understood:

> . . . two ways [of thinking about it]. Whether he was stealing it, or whether he was just recording it? I reckon that he didn't really "steal" it because he was a big business man and he was asking about all the old people, the owners of the *tywerrenge*, and the owners of the songs. Because [to be] level with *tywerrenge* he's got to have song too, you know? He can't just take the *tywerrenge* without song. I think that was what he was doing. But some people really say that he was "stealing."

Following the older Ronnie's lead, Stafford altered his assessment. "*Arraty urlanem* song [This is the right way to study or make sense of the songs]. Song and all hey? *Lepel-akert. Arraty-ilem* [They make it level, equal, balanced or correct]." Both men agreed that it was right and proper to treat ceremonial designs, performances, and songs as inextricably interwoven, and thus any documentation or learning of them should treat them as such. Recording material in this way also meant that all of the interconnected elements could then be "given back afterward" to the next generation of legitimate person/s with rights to learn them. But it was precisely in this realm that Strehlow had failed, and his possessive treatment of these things stood in direct contradiction, indeed a violation, of what Anmatyerr men agreed was their established laws and customs.

After reading from a diary entry in which Strehlow claimed sole ownership of a ceremony, for example, Jimmy Haines, a key organizer of the annual young men's initiation ceremonies at Ti Tree, reacted strongly. "That's wrong way all right! When he was getting old he should have handed it back." Developing a detailed sense of the information for a period of time made sense—indeed, it was an important responsibility, argued Jimmy—but with the coming of age, men were equally responsible to hand on the material to others who were personally related to it's original source in *Anengkerr*. Knowledge and their associated artefacts were to flow between generations.

I began this analysis by demonstrating how contemporary Anmatyerr people thought of Strehlow as an individual with personal links to the Arrernte, and as someone who had become concomitant with the ceremonial events of the wider region. Commonly referred to as an *"Urrempel*-man," "high-school-man," or "business-man," Strehlow appears to have assumed, at least in the minds of many of the older men I spoke with, the familiar role of an individual who traveled widely to accumulate knowledge of ceremonies. Strehlow is also remembered as a person of highly unusual and exceptional linguistic skills and was renowned for possessing considerable knowledge of men's ceremonial songs and ceremonies. His language abilities enabled him to quickly develop rapport, grasp the details of the material he was recording, and eventually attain the necessary skills to personally perform esoteric songs and participate in ritual performance.

With these proficiencies at his disposal, Strehlow came to occupy an advantaged and widely acknowledged position as a documenter of ceremonial material across the region. It was his later failure to honor what Myers has described as the "vital responsibility" to "hand-on" or "pass-on" knowledge in Central Australian communities (Myers, 1991, p. 152) that spoiled his legacy. Among the Anmatyerr communities, attitudes differ toward these matters along generational lines. These attitudes, and this historical context, provide the backdrop to how Anmatyerr and Arrernte people respond to the various aspects of this collection today. The import of the material collected during "Strehlow Time" is discussed in the following chapters. I begin with contemporary reinterpretations and responses to the ceremonial films and the recordings of song.

Chapter 6

Declarations of Relatedness

"My family that one. I know that one."

—Huckitta Lynch Penangk

When I walked out of the Strehlow Research Centre with a portable hard drive full of Strehlow's recordings of Anmatyerr ceremony and song under my arm, I felt a tremendous sense of responsibility. After a formal application to the Strehlow Research Centre Board, I had been granted access to the material for the purposes of this research. Stated in the application was my intention to take digital copies of Strehlow's Anmatyerr-related films, song recordings, and manuscripts to Anmatyerr communities in order to garner contemporary responses, but also to document the interpretations and elucidations of senior men. Having seen some of the films with Anmatyerr men previously, I understood the sheer power and gravitas that these recordings conveyed. It was the first time that material like this had ever left the building and it was upon me to ensure that it was kept safe and revealed only to the appropriate senior Anmatyerr men. I knew these men would be eager to see and hear the material, but I felt slightly anxious about the range of responses that might ensue: delight, melancholy, surprise, disappointment, perhaps even anger.

Once I had driven through the gap in the Hann Range, Arwerlt Atwaty (Native Gap), and on to Anmatyerr country, though, my anxieties subsided. After several decades, these recordings were about to be shared with the people who knew most about them. Undoubtedly it was where these recordings belonged.

The secret-sacred nature of the recordings meant that researchers visiting the Strehlow Research Centre were generally denied access to this material unless they had specific permission from the pertinent Aboriginal men. Strehlow had also struggled with the dissemination of his photographic and filmic material, mostly opting to screen his films in international contexts or in closed sessions among academic peers. His publication of a small selection of ceremonial photographs in the German news magazine *Stern* in 1978, and their surprise republication in *People* magazine back in Australia, had provoked severe criticism (Kaiser, 2004; Hill, 2003, pp. 741–752). Although numerous anthropological publications had published such material in the past, by the 1970s the mood had changed considerably. The increased recognition of Indigenous interests and their rights to maintain confidentiality in regards to such ritual content (see Antons, 2009; Peterson, 2003) had resulted in a gradual reduction of access.

Prior to this period, though, Strehlow had allowed his research assistant, Catherine Ellis, to draw upon his extensive audio collection of song for use in her dissertation in ethno-musicology (later published as Ellis, 1964). His films, though never subject to any analysis per se, were last publicly screened (albeit restricted to "approved scientific and specialist audiences") around the same time in the late 1960s (McCarthy, 1966, p. 19). Largely off-limits to researchers since that time, Strehlow's audio and film collections have been cursorily noted, omitted from accounts of Australian visual (and aural) anthropology (Bryson, 2002; Morphy, 2012), or subject to generalized discussions of scope and form (Hersey and Cohen, 2004; Willis and Cohen, 2001; Cohen, 2001a). The only way of moving this material from the peripheries of Australian anthropology and delving into the significance of its contents was through collaborative review with senior Aboriginal men.

It was therefore in a spirit of collaborative and dialogic inquiry I began delving into this audio and visual material. To be clear, my intention was never to examine the technical form or linguistic contents of the songs as an ethnomusicologist might do, but to explore their meaning for Anmatyerr people. In this sense, I wanted to tease out the existential and social value and significance of this archival material in contemporary contexts. As touched on in chapter 1, the journey began when Tony Ngwarray rang me from a payphone in Alice Springs. "I've got Ken Tilmouth here," he said. "He worked with Strehlow, and he's probably on that film you mentioned." Within minutes, Tony had arrived at the Strehlow Research Centre with Ken and his son Kevin in tow. We sat in a darkened boardroom watching the silent color films for over an hour. This was a critical moment not only in the history of the collection—for it was seemingly the first time one of Strehlow's informant/performers had visited the Centre to watch any of the films they had helped create—but also for my own understanding of the relevance of this collection to contemporary individuals and families.

Like the vast majority of Strehlow's films, the raw footage of the Akwerrperl ceremonies had never been publicly screened, and had certainly never been seen by Anmatyerr men in the four decades since their making. In addition, the songs had been confined to tape copies and never played to any contemporary Anmatyerr singers. Strehlow's rhetoric, that there were "no successors" to the "band of singers" at Alcoota, for example, and that "when they die, their living song too will pass into eternity" (Strehlow, 1965d, p. 58) had relegated these recordings to the realm of ethnographic history. Apprehended in this way, the recordings were destined to sit lifelessly in museum stores or on library shelves awaiting recuperation from Western historians, who "could not dance or sing or live" this content, but only "dissect it" (Dening, 1980, p. 2). Ken's arrival at the Centre thus heralded an opportunity for a complete re-evaluation of not only the Akwerrperl films, but the entire collection.

As someone who *did* and *does* "dance," "sing," and "live" this material, Ken was able to bring the archive to life. Over the number of years since his reintroduction to these recordings, he has confidently explained the full significance of the ceremonies to the Strehlow Research Centre staff, building on what he and his father had told Strehlow in 1965. He has also assisted them in matching each of the film sequences with their associated song recordings using digital editing programs. This process is significant because it had long been assumed that the linguistic and cultural knowledge needed to properly understand the ceremonies filmed by Strehlow, as well as their associated songs, had effectively passed with Strehlow's death (Cohen, 2001a, p. 133). "It is tragic," ethnographic filmmaker Ian Dunlop (1979, p. 15) wrote, "that the remainder of Strehlow's footage could not have been fully documented, annotated and edited before his sudden death . . ." It seems that the assumption had always been that either these sorts of tasks were beyond the practical skills of senior Aboriginal men, or that they simply no longer possessed the ritual knowledge to carry it out.

When the Strehlow Research Centre was established in the mid-1990s these assumptions constituted the principal reason why collaborative research into the collection had never been seriously entertained. Largely accepting the narrative of cultural decline originally fashioned by Strehlow himself (see chapter 3), subsequent discussions of his work also tended to focus on "traditions" that have been fundamentally "broken" (Hill, 2003). Without denying the effects that colonization has wrought on the depth of knowledge surrounding much of this ritual, what this perspective glosses over is the regional variation in retention or relevancy of this material. Individuals from Anmatyerr, Arrernte, Alyawarr, or Luritja backgrounds will each come to this collection with varying degrees of ritual competency and familiarity. Moreover, without any ethnographic evidence to back it up, this perspective automatically accepts that notion that cultural knowledge will be depleted between generations. It also sidesteps the way that "traditions" in general, are not communicated in a rote-like fashion between people and generations, but creatively in a way that involves change and adaption (Weiner, 1999, pp. 205–206). There are a variety of ways that ongoing personal and collective identities are intertwined with song and ceremony in Central Australia as sources of social and symbolic capital.

As is evidenced in my discussions with men from a range of communities and age groups, even where tacit knowledge of actual performance has been attenuated, many people continue to possess both the ontological and epistemological premise upon which the song and ceremonial performance rests.

Dancing and Singing Warlapanpa

Ken had shown me an instance where song and ceremonial knowledge had been retained in an individual, but I wondered whether his expertise was anomalous. What about those songs and ceremonies recorded far earlier, say in the 1930s or 1950s, where the performers no longer lived? What would people know about them after decades of social change and disruption? I made the conscious decision to begin with a suite of recordings for a particular estate close to the country of the men I knew best at Ti Tree. Having located three films and a song recording for what Strehlow described as the Anmatyerr rain (kwaty) ceremony of Warlapanpa (Strehlow, 1953a, p. 152), an *Anengkerr* story and a place that I was vaguely familiar with, I decided to begin there.[1]

---

1. See "Unmatjera Kwatja of Walabanba." Video reel 3, 1953, TGHS No. 43, Strehlow Research Centre.

Warlapanpa is an important Rain Dreaming place located in the far northwest corner of the Anmatyerr territory (see map 6.1) and is well known to Warlpiri, Anmatyerr, and Kaytetye people. Located approximately three hundred kilometers north of Alice Springs, Warlapanpa was removed from Strehlow's primary focus on the Arrernte to the extent that he had even failed to mark it on the large-format map appended to *Songs of Central Australia*. The fact that Strehlow was able record these ceremonies demonstrates the diversity of ritual often on display at the "festivals" and the regional scope of his informants. It was only by chance that the owner of these ceremonies, Kwetyaney Ngal, had been present at Bungalow in 1953 and was willing to reveal his "acts."

Jimmy Haines Ngwarray was the first person to see the films of the Warlapanpa ceremonies. As Jimmy hailed from Akarn, one of the estates

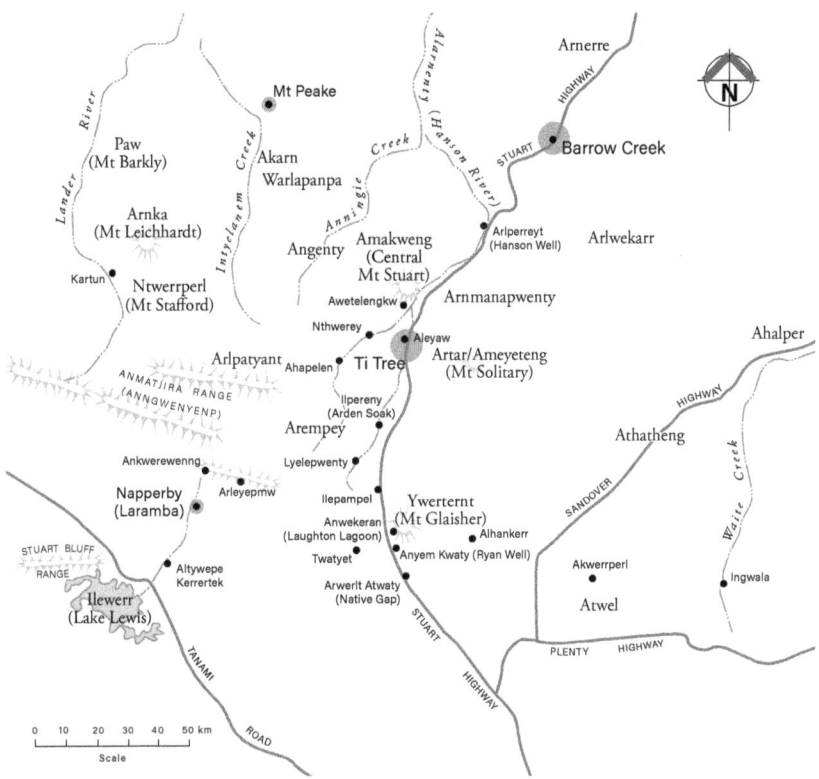

Map 6.1. Approximate location of a number of Anmatyerr sites and estates.

neighboring Warlapanpa, and because I knew that he had been central to the organization of the annual initiation ceremonies at Ti Tree over the years, I thought he would be an appropriate person to begin with.

Jimmy had also been to the Strehlow Research Centre with me in the past and had a good idea of what the Strehlow collection contained. At his makeshift camp comprised of corrugated iron sheets, tarpaulins, and boughs, we found some shade by his F-100 Ford and started to play back the first film on my laptop. As the film ran, I read out the names of the two performers, Kwetyaney Ngal and Bob Malpangk Mpetyan.[2] Jimmy stopped me immediately. "What was that old man's name?" he asked. "Ah, Kwetyaney . . ." I replied. A smile appeared on Jimmy's face. He had known Kwetyaney when he was a much older man in his seventies; in fact, Kwetyaney had married one of Jimmy's sisters at the Warrabri Settlement (now Alekerang Community). He also had fond memories of seeing the old man *"Ingkang kwart"* (walking barefoot) between Ti Tree and Anningie Station (over sixty kilometers) when Jimmy was "out bush, mustering with horses" on Ti Tree Station.

We proceeded to watch all of the Warlapanpa performances filmed by Strehlow. The first two showed Kwetyany as the sole actor decorated with *kwaty* (water) designs, advancing toward a group of six standing men, one of whom beats a shield with a large stick. The other "act" showed Kwetyaney and Malpangk performing together decorated with head dresses and body paint designs that represented the principal protagonists in this water Dreaming. Delighted to see "Old Kwetyaney" as a young man showing his ritual prowess, Jimmy spoke in whispers, explaining the various moves used by men in their ceremonies, such as *warrkuntwem* and *rrkwem* (actions that cannot be described due to the restricted nature of these ceremonies). The general outline of the Warlapanpa story, featuring two "kwaty *amarleyarr*" (new initiates of the rain Dreaming), Jimmy explained, was known to most Anmatyerr, Kaytetye, and Warlpiri men, but he did not personally claim any privileged or intimate knowledge of it.

Seeing that Jimmy had some familiarity with the material, I continued to read an extract from Strehlow's field diary. *"Warlapanpa artwa atherr alata akem-irrem"* (the two men from Warlapanpa rose up from the ground), I prompted. "Yeah, *"akantyer-akwek akem-irrem"* (the little storm clouds got up), he replied, but declined to say anything more.

---

2. Video reels 3 and 4, ceremony 12 from VR 3 TGHS No. 43, ceremony 46 from VR 4 TGHS No 8B (Final Act), Strehlow Research Centre.

While Jimmy felt relaxed about seeing the films, he suggested that senior men such as Paddy Kemarr (figure 6.1) would have a far more confident understanding of the ceremony and the linked *Anengkerr* story.

Paddy Kemarr and Don Presley were sitting together, warming themselves in the morning sun when I arrived at Paddy's camp. I had known both of these men for many years and appreciated just how close Don had become to the older man. Don often referred to Paddy as his "teacher" and admired him for his encyclopedic knowledge of local Dreamings, songs, and ceremonies. After exchanging pleasantries, I briefly told the two men about how I had met with Jimmy and shown him "films" of a man named Kwetyaney, and that Jimmy had suggested that I come to see Paddy to garner his response. Before I could describe the contents of the films, Don launched into further biographical details about Kwetyaney, a man he remembered as being much like others of the previous generation—an itinerant laborer who carted goods from Alice Springs to the railhead at Oodnadatta in South Australia with strings of camels. He was also remembered as an elderly man who owned and cared for a flock of "nanny goats" (*nanekwets*).

Figure 6.1. Paddy Kemarr at Ti Tree creek camp (photo: M. Turpin).

Similar experiences were repeated on almost every occasion where these audio and film recordings were introduced to Anmatyerr men. Explaining who individual performers were and recounting their genealogical and biographical stories was usually the first step in discussions. Men would often point to the screen and mutter Anmatyerr expressions of affection, such as "oh, poor buggers . . . *Terawath itya!*" (they had no trousers), and remarks about their obvious self-confidence in ritual such as "*aketh-anthwerr!*" (really naked!), "*tyelkath marnt map*" (all closed men's ceremonies), and "*angkweye nhenhek*" (this is the old days).

The way in which these biographical narratives intersected with Strehlow's archive is discussed in more detail in the chapter 7, but seeing and hearing these recordings brought up fond memories of the much-revered "old people" and their ceremonial proficiency. The men who danced naked, as well as those adorned with body-paint designs of pigment, feather, and portulaca, or who were carrying large ceremonial objects such as *atnartenty* (long ceremonial poles) were admired by their current-day relatives.

Continuity and Change

I had made a decision at this point to show these films to Paddy and Don without giving a description of their contents. As mentioned earlier, during the course of this research I came to realize that in 2007 Paddy and Jimmy had discussed and sung of the same *artwa anyenty* (moon man) and *arrwekety* (woman) ancestors at the Black Hills (Mer Akarn) that Strehlow had recorded with Jacky Urarty in 1932. If Paddy or Don could immediately recognize the ceremony depicted in this film, then the assumption that Aboriginal men no longer possessed the detailed knowledge to help edit and annotate this material could, yet again, be contested. As I readied the film on my laptop, I simply explained to both men that the film depicted Kwetyaney "dancing." Strehlow's title for the film and all other descriptive material was not revealed prior to the viewing.

Their first comment was not about the ceremonial performance itself but the landscape that provided the setting. Expecting to see country in which Kwetyaney would be associated, most likely within the Anmatyerr or Kaytetye areas where he was from, Don was immediately puzzled and surprised to see the iconic MacDonnell Ranges of Alice Springs in the background. "This is Alice Springs is it!?" he asked quizzically. His question was perfectly understandable given that ceremonies of this nature would usually be performed close to their country of origin. Many other men responded in the same way when first seeing the *mise-en-scène* of Alice Springs for ceremonies from the Anmatyerr region. It was clear that place, as Merlan has written, was never considered as a simple passive entity and certainly not an abstract "backdrop" upon which events occur (Merlan, 1998, p. 211). Rather it was something that afforded clues as to whose country the performance was enacted on and thus what possible connections and relationships between individuals and families may have been at work during the performance and during the production of the film.

The "setting" also told a story of how people traveled in the past to places like Alice Springs and became "mixed up" on Aboriginal reserves, settlements, and missions. Kwetyaney, everyone agreed, would have been in Alice Springs as part of his laboring duties, possibly when he was working with the "*Kamwerl-*team *map*" (the camel caravans that carried freight across arid Australia). For those without the personal experience of "Strehlow Time" or "Bungalow Time" (see previous chapters), however, it was slightly disorienting to see ceremonies enacted so far from the sites that they referenced.

Plainly curious about this film and the ceremony depicted, Don looked to Paddy for clarification. "What is that? Do you know it?" he asked Paddy. With his eyes fixed firmly on the screen, Paddy at first stayed silent. As the performers began to move closer to the camera and he began to recognize the performer's body paint designs and actions, he became animated. Speaking in an excited mixture of Anmatyerr, Warlpiri, and English, and pointing to Warlapanpa, he declared:

> "*Yewe, yewe, yewe*" [Yes, yes, yes!] . . . "*Warlapanpa! Warlapanpa! Ngapa! Ngapa* [Water! Water] dreaming! That's water dreaming that one! And *Awely-awely* [storm lightning]. *Yeway* [Yes], there! . . . That's *kwaty* (rain) . . . Oh, proper number one! Proper number one!"

Don excitedly called out to Archie Mpetyan, another very elderly man lying under a brush shelter nearby, to come quickly. The son of Friday Ankerr-raweny Ngal, a significant elder and one-time informant to T.G.H. Strehlow, and now aged in his eighties, Archie lifted his head to see what the fuss was about. "*Artwang-ay!*" (Old man look here!) "Old Kwetyaney, your old uncle. That's him now," called out Don. "*Yeway*. I'd been a young-feller for him," retorted Archie, referring to Kwetyaney's classificatory standing to him as a father. Paddy, however, remained transfixed by the film and waited for the first ceremony to conclude before he started to explain exactly what he knew.

He had not only seen this ceremony before but had seen it performed in situ at the "main center," or principal totemic site, of the Warlapanpa itself. He remembered seeing the performance during a time when Anmatyerr, Warlpiri, and Kaytetye people from across the region had been "gathered up" to work on the Anningie Tin Mines:

> I bin see it along Warlapanpa again. We had a big camp there . . . They bin working, old people, picking up all that tin. Working around. Well old people bin gather up there, for that painting [to produce sacred designs on bodies and objects for ceremonies]. They bin start painting now. Show 'em at night. All the young people, they bin learn 'em. Tell old story. With this old man [Kwetyaney] we bin sitting down [and] with Davey Pengart's father. We bin sing 'em there.

Given that Paddy was born around 1932 and that he would not have been privy to witnessing sacred ceremonies until he had been initiated (at approximately eleven years of age), this was probably in the 1940s or later. Paddy's firsthand memory of the performance, however, was slightly different from the version Strehlow had captured on film. Instead of there being two performers, as depicted in the filmed version, Paddy remembered three performers acting out the activities of the *akantyer* (storm clouds) and *awely awely* (lighting and thunder) ancestors. In Paddy's version, it was two men who accompanied or "shadowed" the main performer, presumably trailing behind him:

> I bin see it alonga Warlapanpa, a long time ago. This one. Well they been try it a different way. That three men had been dancing with *kwaty aken* [water designs and ceremonial objects]. And another, he's got two shadow [people following him]. When him go long way, he's got to keep going that way.

Given the speed with which Paddy immediately recognized this performance and the way in which he later proudly sang along with the recording of the Warlapanpa song, his deep knowledge of this tradition was unquestioned. Kwetyaney, Paddy continued, was the "right seed" for Warlapanpa, meaning he had inherited the traditions through his father, a man named Kwelanty Mpetyan. In fact, it had been Kwelanty (whose name alluded to a flat bootoms often seen on rain clouds) who had taught Paddy these rituals, songs, and stories at Anningie. "He's *kwaty-kartwey* [belonging to the rain Dreaming] that one . . . He's the one that bin show that painting [body paint designs] and all. Got all the story. That's Kwelanty. He's the rainmaker. He been boss for that place." Impressed with Paddy's account and wanting to convey the importance of the story to me, Don exclaimed, "That takes us back three generations!" But the version of the ceremony captured by Strehlow in 1953 in Alice Springs, hundreds of kilometers from its source, was seemingly different.

Having witnessed the ceremony being performed *in situ* and under the guidance of numerous senior men, including the owners of the tradition, Paddy's commentaries were of immense value. His memory of the Warlapanpa ceremony suggested that the filmed version may have been a slight variation from the norm due to the unusual circumstances in which it was produced—at a place far from its source its source and perhaps with a limited number of Anmatyerr performers available at the Bungalow Settlement. Most interesting about Paddy's comments, though, was his acceptance of the possibility of variation to a sacred performance often cast (particularly by Strehlow in regards to song) as being archaic, inert, and unchangeable. This observation had been made by other Anmatyerr men, but also Arrernte men who also noted "different versions" of ceremonies after watching Strehlow's films (Hersey and Cohen, 2004, p. 183). As Strehlow described it in *Aranda Traditions*, these sacred ceremonies and songs were governed by "the oppressive night-shadow of tradition" that in his view "stifled creative impulse" (Strehlow, 1947, pp. 35 and 6). It is exactly these degrees of ambiguity and indeterminacy, in what might appear as fixed traditions, however, that have come to the attention of both specialists in Aboriginal art (Morphy, 1989) and song (Sutton, 1987; Hale, 1984) in more recent times. Sutton had, for example, noted that while a "cultural ideology" among senior Aboriginal men might promulgate the ideal of cultural fixity, ritual has an inbuilt "mystery" that makes it somewhat more lithely.

The contexts within which people came to learn this material had changed considerably over the course of the second half of the twentieth century. While men used to acquire knowledge in the formalized settings of "*akernenty*" or "high school" gatherings that involved long periods of seclusion in ceremonial camps, in recent times men came to learn these rituals only during the relatively brief annual *apwelh* (young men's initiation) ceremonies. *Akernenty* was, according to Paddy, "the same like whitefella call them big high school. And after that they go and have another high school. That's how I been learn." Based on "*akern*," meaning "high," or "on top," Akernenty refers to a period of secluded, intensive, and higher-level instruction in ritual. Men learned ceremonies that were "dear," meaning that in order to learn these rituals one would have to make significant payments to those possessing the knowledge of them, and any contravention of the restrictions around this knowledge could be costly (not only in terms of local reputation and standing among men but possibly in terms of physical harm, even death).

Paddy had attended many of these ceremonies as a younger man and later in life had himself led aspects of these proceedings in order to teach younger men. But as *akernenty* stopped in many Anmatyerr communities around the 1970s, no other forum for learning about ritual life, in particular the ceremonial patrimony associated with specific sites or estates, has specifically replaced it. While some of these ceremonies continue to be revealed during the annual initiation events, many are now only remembered via the descriptions of older people. Strehlow's color films therefore added magnificent visual evidence to these descriptions and gave younger men a chance to learn more.

Despite never having seen this ceremony, Don Presley did nonetheless have an excellent understanding of its context and relevance to present-day generations. One of the rain-making sites associated with Warlapanpa, Don asserted, was in fact located at "an old sheep well" in his own country, Mer Angenty (in the Anningie Station area). Here, the leading old rain-makers—Don's father's "full uncle" and the gardener at Anningie homestead Percy Mpetyan, Paddy's father Charlie Kanatjukurrpa Pwererl, and another man referred to as simply "Old Jack" Pwererl—would perform their "*angerr-ilem*" (increase ceremonies) to make rain, with the young men looking on. They made the rain not just for the health of the country and its Aboriginal inhabitants, but as part of their station duties of shepherding and caring for livestock (sheep and cattle). Paddy continued the story:

> Yeah, they were dancing and they're making the rain. And all the young fellas bin see 'em old people. Oh! Old what's his

name was there at that station, Old Tony Chisholm [manager of Anningie Station in the 1950s and 1960s]. He bin make 'em want them to make rain for the cattle too. [Make it] Green . . . Yeah, it made it green. They make it water no worries! . . . Tony Chisholm tell 'em for *kwaty* [rain]. Make 'em rain for *pwelek* [bullock]. It worked. They do 'em straight out. Big rain coming up, big rain coming up.

Now blended within an intercultural history, Warlapanpa and its ceremonies were discussed in ways that accentuated the place of song and ritual in lived experience. As Francesca Merlan argues, "social experience," including socioeconomic marginalization, cannot easily be separated out from peoples' "mytho-religious content" (see Merlan, 1991). The Rain Dreaming of Warlapanpa in some respects is now intertwined with settler history, such as the "old sheep well," the gatherings of people in exploitative conditions at the Anningie tin mines, and the adaptive merging of pastoral interests and Anmatyerr rain-making rituals.

Declarations of Relatedness

One of the most important reasons Anmatyerr people sing their traditional songs or perform their ceremonies is to assert relationships to the country and the Ancestral beings. Originating from the eternal presence of the Ancestors, these songs and rituals bring forth the very power and presence of these beings and have the ability to affect not only the natural environment, but human and nonhuman animals as well (Koch and Turpin, 2008, p. 169). In addition, these repertoires are also reproduced to assert religious, moral, and political authority. People will therefore sing, reproduce a body-paint design, dance, or reveal ritual objects in order to make a statement regarding their social status and their rights and relationships to the ancestors or the land. Song and ceremony have also come to play significant roles in the enforcement of Australian law under the *Aboriginal Land Rights (Northern Territory) Act 1976 (Cth)*. In this Western legal context, the ability to perform a ceremony or sing a song (among other evidence of "spiritual affiliation") can be a key determinant in granting ownership of traditional lands (Koch, 2013).

I always considered Strehlow's recordings as potentially controversial. So when I sat down with people to play back songs or films, or discuss the names of performers, I was often apprehensive about the possibility of reigniting or perhaps even starting disputes. What if one of Strehlow's informants was regarded by people today as someone who did not have the authority to sing or dance a particular ceremony? What if I mistakenly exposed people to ritual material they did not have legitimate cultural rights to see or hear? There was also the very real possibility that if rituals were no longer known, hearing or seeing these recordings could cause embarrassment or sadness. The reintroduction of forgotten or unknown material could even cause confusion or conflict.

What I soon discovered, however, was that in most cases people came together in groups, and the responsibilities associated with seeing and hearing ritual content were shared. While material utterly unrelated to Anmatyerr people was quickly dismissed as irrelevant or improper to view or hear, such as the time when I accidentally played a snippet of a song from the Hermannsburg area, people generally looked for ways of making connections. Reviewing the Anmatyerr ritual material gave people the opportunity to declare varying forms of relatedness not just to the ceremonial content but to the performers and places.

The fish Dreaming (*Irrpenng Anengkerr*) song from the site of Ankwerewenng was among the first I played back to a group of six senior men at Napperby (Laramba) in 2014.[3] Having arrived at the community in the afternoon, I immediately sought out the two senior men I knew best, Ronnie McNamara and Huckitta Lynch. Excited to see and hear the recordings, they insisted we start immediately and began assembling the other older men from the *arnkenty* (single men's camp). As we drove past the camp, Ronnie called out from the passenger seat of the car, "*apety-alhay ampwang-ay! . . . akiw, apwer akwek*" (Come on elders! Come to the "bush camp"/ceremony ground). A small gathering of men aged fifty and up soon congregated under a bough shelter on the edge of the ceremonial ground used during the annual *anmanty* (initiation ceremonies). Each time I returned to Napperby, this was the preferred venue for our discussions because it was out of earshot of the women and children in the community and was respected as the domain of senior men.

As the afternoon light faded, we began listening to the songs directly associated with the country we were sitting on. As soon as I pressed play on the recording, everybody instantly pointed north along Napperby Creek

---

3. Strehlow writes "Irbannga of Ankurowunga."

in the direction of Ankwereweng, the specific fish Dreaming site to which the singing referred. Two of the men in their seventies, Harry Ngal and Bobby Tilmouth Pwerrerl, assured me that although none of the *merek-artwey* (owners) who descended from the singers "Old Irrpenng" and Jack Peltharr (see Strehlow, 1953a, p. 133) were present at our gathering because they were *kwertengerl* (ritual managers) from the neighboring estates, they had dutifully learned these songs and their related ceremonies.

The ceremony's body-paint designs and songs were also "used," Huckitta assured me, "every year" on the ceremony ground not far from where we sat. Knowing of my interest in this ceremony, a number of men later informed me that during recent initiation ceremonies at Napperby this fish ceremony was again performed. During this group session, some of the men refrained from singing along with the recordings. Like Harold Payne in the previous chapter, as *kwertengerl* they would not sing while the *merek-artwey* were absent. There was no doubt, though, that the actions of the principal ancestors referred to in the song, the *arlweng-rlpwerr* (desert mogurnda fish), *ntepirtny* (bony bream fish), and *ankeper* (waterbird—either a cormorant or a darter), were well known by all the senior men here, and they recounted the story of the songline as it moved south into Arrernte territory.

Hearing the fish (*Irrpenng*) song and also watching the film made of its associated ceremony was not simply an act of looking back at times past but also a way of demonstrating present-day connections. Men gestured to related sites along the nearby Napperby creek and acknowledged the past and present *merek-artwey* that embodied these *Anengkerr* ancestors. People's experience of this material was dually embodied as a spatial and social encounter. Whether hearing or seeing, perception of this material was much more than sensory stimulation; it was an action involving the construction of meaning. If, as Merleau-Ponty's phenomenology suggests, perception "occurs not in the head but in front of the subject and it brings the perceiving subject as well as the perceived object into being" (quoted in Crossley, 1994, p. 14), then Anmatyerr people (as perceptual subjects) and these recordings (as the perceptual objects) brought each other into being. More than this, it was the intersubjective knowledge garnered from dialogue, response, and exchange that almost always made apparent the interconnectivity of Anmatyerr place, person, song, ancestor, and ritual.

Even in cases where ceremonies or songs are no longer performed or well known, seeking out these points of connection remained paramount. When the film for the Awengatherr (Awungatara) ceremony was shown to

Ken, George, and Kevin Tilmouth at Alcoota, they all confessed they had never seen this performed before.[4] As they stared at the screen carefully to see what their relatives had shown Strehlow, I noted in my diary how they all watched in utter silence, only intermittently interrupting their viewing to point out a movement or to discuss a particular aspect of the body-paint decoration on a performer. While the ceremony was new to them and they marveled at the skill of the performers, all three knew the *Anengkerr* story and its connected site. Kevin, the youngest among them, spoke up first. Deferring to his father, but obviously knowing the answer himself, he asked "*Tyelk-aperrertety* [rufous songlark], isn't it?" "Ya. It's our country. Yeah it's my country, Atwel," Ken answered. No one asked to see Strehlow's diary entries or any other documentary evidence. The group's knowledge of the ritual designs, the body movements of performers, and the local totemic geography were enough to make sense of it all.

Mapping the connections between personal identity, kin, place, and songline were of course central to Strehlow's original ambitions, however, given the complexities of these interwoven relationships, which were often understood in changing ways throughout out a person's life time, his record could only ever be a static snapshot of active relationships. Some of the deeper relationships between song and country were serendipitously revealed to me when reviewing the aforementioned fish traditions from Napperby.

Having just finished watching the Warlapanpa films, Paddy and Don wanted to hear the wire recording made of the associated Warlapanpa song. The two men sat patiently as I grappled with the imprecise cataloguing of Strehlow's tapes, which often made the selection of specific songs from the (digitized) cassette compilations produced in the 1990s a very difficult task. As the original audio recordings rarely featured any spoken introductions, and in most cases each song is preceded only by a brief prompt from Strehlow in Arrernte, one must listen very closely to the brief glimpses of conversation or, alternatively, recognize familiar song melodies. Having found the beginning of the recording, or so I thought, I readied Paddy and Don to listen carefully, pressed play, and waited for their response to the Warlapanpa song.[5]

---

4. See Awungatara Ceremony of Tjilkalabirititja, video reel 5, VR 5 TGHS No. 15, Act 1, Tjilkalabirititja II from VR 5 TGHS No. 26, and Act 2 and Tjilkalabirititja III from VR 5 TGHS No. 27 and 28, Act 3 (final act).

5. Here I begin to play the recording from the beginning of side B of tape SOU 00141.

Upon hearing the first verse, Paddy immediately responded. "*Irrpenng* [fish] . . . at Napperby!" he confidently stated. Don quickly concurred with Paddy. "Ya, fish dreaming song!" Slightly embarrassed, I quickly returned to my notes and realized they were correct: the Irrpenng of Ankwerewenng song was indeed listed as preceding the Warlapanpa song on the original tape inventory.[6] Feeling uneasy that I had unintentionally revealed this song to the "wrong" men, I quickly tried to find the Warlapanpa song. Before this could happen, Don spoke up in a way that demonstrated both his legitimate hearing of the song and his personal relationship to it. "According to . . . well in Aboriginal way, *this is my grandfather. He shares* with this song." Given that Strehlow had titled this recording as a song relating specifically to a site far to the south of Don's patrilineal country (Mer Angenty), I was unsure of the connection, but nonetheless willingly accepted his claim. We listened to more of the recording, and at the twelve-minute mark the connections became clearer.[7] At this point, Don sprang to life as he recognized a particular part of this song that specifically referred to his country, Mer Angenty, and the *anterrng artety* (mulga seed) Dreaming that traveled from there to the Napperby area:

> That's my old man! . . . That song, it's belonging to my *arreng*, grandfather [father's father] . . . that's Mer Angenty. Mer Angenty that one. They're dancing.

Whispering the verses to himself, and leaving the more confident singing to the older Paddy, Don seemed pleased—not that a recording of the song existed, but far more importantly, that he could recognize with confidence his personal associations with it. Though Don had been living away from his country for many years due to poor water quality at his outstation, hearing and singing the song produced a type of intense closeness in which his individual identity was integrated with the external objects of song and place (see Munn, 1970). This closeness was not just with his *arreng* (father's father's) country but extended across the wider Anmatyerr landscape, following the songline that undoubtedly drew in other relationships along the way.

---

6. See tape SOU 0014, "Irbannga of Ankurowunga Song."
7. Time code at 12:24, side B of cassette SOU 00141.

Confirming Don's identification with this small song, the men at Napperby agreed that the song words referred to the mulga seed that traveled from Mer Angenty to Artetyelherel, a site close by to the fish site of Ankwerewenng, before moving further south to Lake Lewis (Ilewerr). What Strehlow had simply labeled as a song pertaining to the fish tradition of the Alherramp estate (belonging to people of the Peltharr and Ngwarray subsections) had in fact included within it a "small song" (see Ellis and Barwick, 1987) that referenced a tradition linking estates belonging to people of the Penangk and Pengart subsections of Mer Angenty and Mer Ilewerr.

The tradition told of an old man from Angenty who traveled to Ilewerr (Lake Lewis) collecting mulga seeds before returning to Angenty via an underground route. Huckitta Lynch Penangk, the senior owner for the Ilewerr estate, also knew this song. Upon seeing the filmed ceremony, Huckitta rather nonchalantly commented, "Yeah, I bin use 'em that one."[8] His *kwertengerl*, Lesley Stafford, added, "*Yewe yewe, artetye alyent atwem*" (Yes, you beat the mulga seedpods with a stick) in that ceremony, while Bobby Tilmouth, who hummed the tune, added, "I've got the music for that one too."

Over sixty years after Strehlow had recorded this material, the men at Napperby were able to identify or confirm Strehlow's records, and reveal further connections between people, estates, and Dreamings that were absent from Strehlow's record (Strehlow, 1953b, p. 40). Whether he had neglected to note these associations or they were not revealed to him is unknown, but these connections could have only been made known by contemporary Anmatyerr handling of the recordings. Their elaborations put to rest any suggestion that Strehlow had been comprehensive in his documentation, but also that contemporary Central Australian people found the collection "mysterious" (Smith, 2009, pp. 85–86). It is possible that Strehlow's emphasis on bounded estates, what he called *anyenheng* sections (based on father-son subsections), blinkered his apperception of these links, an observation suggested in Morton's (1994) critique of the *anyenheng* model (as noted in chapter 4).

Identification of more detailed and complex interactions between *Anengkerr* (Dreaming narratives) estates, and Dreamings associated with

---

8. See film titled "Mulga seed ancestor of Ititjalirala" (1953) on video 4, 1953 1:05:17–1:06:30N. My notes, Napperby June 25, 2014, part 1.

other patrilineal subsection pairs were not always clearly expressed in Strehlow's notes. In this case, Strehlow is seemingly aware, but makes no comment on the fact, that the mulga seed Dreaming that belonged to the Penangk/Pengart subsections had traveled to a site in Ngwarray/Peltharr country. However, Anmatyerr men were quick to note and explain these associations.

Back at Ti Tree, Paddy made his relationship to this song and ceremony clear by pointing out that his grandfather's wife had been a *kwertengerl* (manager for this country) and his father, Charlie Kanat-jukurrpa Pwerrerl, had also frequently participated in the singing of the Ankwerewenng songs during ceremonial gatherings. Just as he had done earlier with the Warlapanpa verses, Paddy effortlessly, and with great pride, sang along with the entire recording of the *Irrpenng* (fish) song, as did many of the men at Napperby.

Witnessing men sing over the top of Strehlow's recordings, and their frequent comments about how "clear" (recognizable) the recordings were, struck me as moments of creative mimesis. Song was taken up and re-enacted as an act of reverent remembrance of ancestors that are eternal in *Anengkerr* but fleeting when realized through their relatives. But more than this, people's responses to the material were more often than not declarations of present-time relatedness. People experienced these recordings as actors and not just receivers of information. These songs and ceremonies did not simply designate a preexisting relationship, but played a role in recreating relationships between people and places. As Anmatyerr men switched between singing along with a recording to describing the diverse array of partial entitlements to know and share in this material, their own lived experience also shone through. The recordings were being apprehended not as historical "objects" or even anthropological or literary "texts," as Strehlow would have them, but as embodiments of current connections between places, people, and their ancestors.

Valuable and Vulnerable

Across five different Anmatyerr communities, the vast majority of the seventeen ceremonial "acts" and over twenty different sound recordings were identified and well understood. The clear retention of knowledge of sites, estates, associated *Anengkerr* (Dreamings), the identification of performers, as well as their contemporary kin who have rights to many of these traditions in fact, made working with the Strehlow collection relatively straightforward. This does not mean that every filmed ceremony could be explained by people who had experience of enacting or witnessing them, or that every song could be sung. Songs were not always passed on between generations, and in many cases ceremonies have ceased to be performed.

The reasons for this attenuation in ritual expertise in Aboriginal Australia are numerous and have been well documented in the literature. Time spent away from specific sites and traditional lands (Peterson, 2000; Young, 1987), high mortality among senior knowledge holders, and language loss (Donaldson, 1984) are perhaps some of the most significant reasons. Although undoubtedly playing an important part in the social, cultural, and political lives of many Aboriginal people in both Central and Northern Australia, the gradual reduction of people who can sing and dance expansive repertoires is now a common tale. Appraising the "strength" or "weakness" of Anmatyerr song or ceremonial knowledge is, however, very difficult, and perhaps serves no useful purpose because it is what is remembered *now* that really matters. Anecdotally, people speak of a higher number of singers and performers across the Anmatyerr region than among the Arrernte, and yet despite this comparative strength, many Anmatyerr people remain anxious about the future. Younger men speak of an obvious decline in the number of senior men available to teach younger men and comment that with the passing of each elder, entire "libraries" or "archives" are being lost.

Don Presley's earlier reactions upon hearing the Mulga Seed verses from Angenty encapsulated this tension perfectly. Obviously excited to hear a song to which he belonged and see a film made of its associated ceremony, Don could not, however, disguise his melancholy. Segments of the song were clearly familiar enough for him to sing along with the recording in parts, but having witnessed the far more active ceremonial life "back in the 1970s" when it had "still been working," he lamented that now it was "all gone":

> I'm excited hey! It's true. Some of us doesn't know it [these ceremonies], but . . . Sometimes when I go out with this old fella [Paddy] you know I get really excited. He shows me other stuff. And that's the first time [that I had seen these ceremonies]. "Cause I never saw it before this, [these] sort of things, ever. Yeah. Anyway, he teaches me a lot. When's he's going (passes away), he's going to leave that stuff with us . . .

Ronnie McNamara, too, despite personally possessing an expansive knowledge of these songs and traditions, claimed that the frequency and significance of ceremonial activity for the Anmatyerr had certainly diminished. Some of the songs Strehlow had recorded with men who were Huckitta and Ronnie's "fathers" or "brothers" were apparently unknown to either of them. After listening to these recordings, Ronnie responded with great emotion and fragility in his voice. He looked to the ground and shook his head in disbelief. "That's the first time . . ." His voice trailed off. A number of the other men, also bemused and saddened that they had missed out on learning these songs, whispered *"Lyetant awem"* (The first time I've heard this). Like many Aboriginal men of this generation who grew up working pastoral leases all over the Northern Territory, Ronnie and Huckitta had been caught up in their roles as stockmen and laborers and had limited opportunities to learn from the senior men. Strehlow, on the other hand, had made following and accumulating knowledge of these songs and stories his life's work:

> Ronnie: In these years, like in 1958 [1968?] and the '70s, we were just moving down from the old [Napperby] station where used to live, near the station there. Moving to this place here [Laramba community]. Cleaning up all this one before the housing. Just half of it you know. Half and half. The other mob stayed at the old camp and another mob stayed here doing a bit of work you know? Cleaning it up . . . That was around 1968 now. Well Strehlow he was still travelling around about that time. '68 and the 70s. He still bin around.
> Huckitta: Everywhere he had been travelling around. Getting them [songs] everywhere . . . I don't know [these songs] cause I was working everywhere.

Just as Anmatyerr men—like many in Central and Northern Australia—had been inculcated into the work regimes of cattle stations in the twentieth century, so too they had been introduced to Christianity. On the whole, this environment seems to have produced, as anthropologist Diane Austin-Broos has noted amongst the Western Arrernte, a general "diversification of knowledge" (2006, p. 8) whereby men certainly sought out Christian knowledge but stayed in touch with their land-based traditions. Like the Western Arrernte, the Anmatyerr had been able to visit sites and thus promulgate this land-based worldview via their work on vast cattle stations (see chapter 2). But there is no doubting that across Central Australian Aboriginal communities Christianity has become a ubiquitous social, moral, and philosophical force (Austin-Broos, 2010; Myers, 2010). Traditional ceremonies are now largely confined to the initiation ceremonies held annually in the summer months, while Christian ritual, song, and prayer permeates everyday life. As a senior ceremonial expert, former Lutheran Pastor, and former fencing contractor and stockman, Ronnie acknowledged that the centrality of ceremonial activity had waned: "Ceremony side is just like the wind . . . Christian is alive all through the year."

Initiation ceremonies persist with regularity, however, and in the lead-up to the summer holidays and Christmas break period, Anmatyerr people begin to consider which communities will host these events. As has been observed among the nearby Warlpiri/Anmatyerr communities of Yuendumu and Mt. Allan, participation in these yearly initiation events is increasing (see Peterson, 2000; Curran, 2011). At Napperby and Ti Tree, some elders talk about the excessive numbers of initiates now "going through business." Jimmy Haines, for example, noted that whereas in the past approximately two to five young men would be initiated at once, today it was not unusual to see fifteen or more. As the number of initiates grows, so does the size of the gathering as associated kin travel from across the region to participate. These larger assemblies place stress on community resources (food, fuel, accommodation) as well as on the elderly ritual experts needed to sing and lead in the conduct of the ceremonies. Feeling the pressure, some men expressed a desire to return to the smaller gatherings they remembered from their youths.

"Country Business"

Outside of the initiation ceremonies, there has been a gradual reduction in performance of what people generally refer to as "country business" (ceremonial patrimony). These are generally the ceremonies and songs that honor the activities of ancestors from particular estates. The enactment of this "country business" requires highly specialized, localized, and expert knowledge of songs, ceremonies, and paraphernalia. While aspects of these performances are at times enacted in an abbreviated form during the initiation events, they were once fully revealed and explained during the course of the now very rare, if not defunct, *akernenty* rituals. This attenuation of "country business" and the growing pervasiveness of initiation rituals was something that Strehlow was acutely aware of (Strehlow, 1978a, p. 153; 1968b, pp. 15–16) and was part of the reason he focused his efforts on the documentation of the more vulnerable repertoires. More than this, though, Strehlow had also observed that initiation rituals in the Arandic region had been influenced by Western Desert practices (Strehlow, 1978a, p. 153; 1968b, pp. 15–16). Agreeing with Strehlow, senior Anmatyerr men note that annual initiation ceremonies have certainly been influenced in this way, but in communities like Napperby, distinctive Anmatyerr traditions that relate to local estates and Dreaming undoubtedly persist.

Gauging an accurate picture of exactly which of these restricted male ceremonial genres persist today is an extremely difficult task. The inherent secretiveness of these ceremonies means they are not easily brought up in conversation, and as noted earlier, experiences with the illicit distribution of recordings made of this material in the past has made people extremely wary of permitting further documentation (cf. Myers, 2014, who cites similar attitudes among the Pintupi). As a result, there has been a relative dearth of research into ritual in the Arandic region since Richard Moyle's *Alyawarra Music* (1986), and more recent research has understandably tended to focus on unrestricted genres of song and ceremony, primarily among women (Turpin, 2005; 2013; Turpin, Gibson, and Green, 2016; Turpin and Green, 2011). In light of these sensitivities, then, the process of reviewing audio and visual recordings enabled a relatively safe way of exploring these issues and making comparisons between "Strehlow time" and today. Without directly confronting the closed domain of contemporary male ritual, discussions could ensue about general changes in cultural practice over time.

With numerous experiences of listening back to Strehlow's recordings of restricted song and other similar recordings, it is clear to me that while some genres are being actively taught and learned, others are not. The more specific songs and rituals pertaining to particular estates, known as "country songs," as well as the less ritually charged *althart* (male genre of public song and dance) or *ilpenty* (songs associated with attracting lovers) are less well known by younger men. None of the Anmatyerr-related *althart* recorded by Strehlow (see 1949, pp. 85–91) were recognized by men today, although senior men did know many other public men's ceremonies (*althart*) that had not been recorded by Strehlow. As *althart* is a genre of song and dance performance traded between groups, and not "owned" by people from particular estates, it is not surprising that different repertoires would come in and out of style (Strehlow, 1968a, pp. 48–49).

Songs associated with the public and restricted aspects of young men's initiation ceremonies are, however, more widely recognized and learned by men from across the generations. When playing back recordings made of these initiation songs over the twentieth century, almost every man I worked with would immediately sing along, demonstrate related dance poses, or identify local sites or Dreamings associated with this tradition. These suites of initiation ceremonies and songs are shared across many Central Australian communities, ubiquitously known among initiated men and commonly heard throughout a male's lifetime.

These "Country" songs," Huckitta pointed out, although being less well known and often reserved for men's ceremonies, had aspects of them that could nonetheless be used in more everyday contexts. While listening to Strehlow's 1949 recording of Nathanael Arawe-irreke singing the songs of Huckitta's country Ilewerr (Lake Lewis), he noted that his Ilewerr songs were a "little bit different."[9] While Huckitta certainly "owned" the songs via patrilineal inheritance, some of the Ilewerr songs were sung ubiquitously throughout the western and central Anmatyerr communities during the *anmanty* (young men's initiation ceremonies). *Anmanty* is an opening stage of the initiation ceremonies, Huckitta explained, where both men and women participate, "When they hear this song, all the women go over there and make "em *apwelh*" (a cleared area of the initiation ground used for performance).

Later that year, Huckitta organized a camp at the site of Altywepe keretek, not far from the Tilmouth Roadhouse on the Tanami Highway, so that the *anmanty* songs of Ilewerr could again be recorded. Unbeknownst to him, Altywepe keretek had been the place where his older brother, Charlie Artetyerwenguny, had camped the night with Strehlow during a mapping trip in the region forty-eight years earlier (Strehlow 1968a, pp. 48–49). Over a number of nights, Huckitta, Ronnie McNamara, Lesley Stafford, Peter Cole, and the younger Martin Hagan sang the entire *anmanty* series (figure 6.2). During the days, we visited key sites referred to in the singing, Kwamparr, Nyepwat, and Alparr.[10] As the songs were sung either

---

9. The "Areanana verses of Iloara" area on SOU 00014 at the Strehlow Research Centre.

10. These recordings, made between October 31 and November 3, 2016, were instigated by Huckitta and facilitated by Shaun Angeles at the Strehlow Research Centre. They were funded by an Australian Research Council (ARC) Linkage project "Re-integrating Central Australian Community Cultural Collections" (LP140100806) and Myfany Turpin's ARC grant (FT40100783).

Figure 6.2. Singing Anmanty at Altywepe keretek, November 2016. L.R. Lesley Stafford, Peter Cole, Ronnie McNamara, Shaun Angeles, Huckitta Lynch, Martin Hagan (Photo: Ben Deacon).

late in the night or just before dawn, the senior men gave explanations of the different ancestors who featured in each of the "small songs." They spoke of burrowing bettong (*rtway*), the woma pythons (*ahenenh*) snakes, and an ancestral "old woman" named Arlerl-arlerl Penangk, who had last been "*angane-irrek*" (spiritually conceived) in Huckitta's sister. Some of the small songs, Huckitta also explained, could be used to heal those suffering from an illness. "These ones belong to the sick . . . I always use these songs when my grandson gets sick. I sing him with this one now. Every time I use 'em."

As Strehlow recorded "country songs" under the overarching rubric of specialized men's ritual, there was a tendency to miss the various ways in which these songs might be used in everyday social life. When listening to his sound recordings too, I was struck by the absence of background noise, conversation, barking dogs, the clanging of billy cans, and so on. With this "sociality in sound" (Feld and Brenneis, 2004, p. 462) absent, his collection evades any record of these everyday instances of performance. Strehlow certainly did acknowledge the different genres of song and their uses (1971a, pp. 254–261), but he remained largely aloof to the use of song, or even aspects of ritual, in less formal settings. As more recent work on Aboriginal song has shown (Wild and Jangala, 1990; Furlan, 2008; see also Rose, 1999), multiple genres are sung within ordinary life and not always shrouded in "high seriousness" (Bradley and Yanyuwa Families, 2010, p. 244). "Country songs" will be sung on the ceremonial ground, but aspects of them will also come out when inhibitions are low, while sitting quietly, feeling homesick, or when healing sick children.

Listening back to the audio recordings that I made of my discussions with Anmatyerr men during these group discussions, this sociality of song and ceremony is obvious. The voices of a critically engaged and inquisitive audience can be heard, against a backdrop of car engines, barking dogs, and children playing in the distance. People talk in whispers, for example, as a silent film was screened or when the lives of elders now deceased were discussed. During the playback of song recordings, the voices were often raised and excited, especially when senior men began singing along with the tapes. People didn't sing for my benefit to demonstrate or prove their abilities to me (why should they?), but to declare their relatedness to the people singing, the places, and the Dreamings.

Hearing the singing voices of the Anmatyerr men I worked with merge in unison with informants from the 1950s was an extremely powerful experience. It was an important reminder that these recordings, as they move from the archive back into the sphere present lifeworlds, can invite powerful local responses. Once understood outside of the archive, and placed within an Anmatyerr terrain of social activity, these recordings can take on extraordinary existential and practical value.

I had never intended to crudely "test" people's ability to sing or perform this material, but the discussions that ensued delivered remarkable insights into contemporary Anmatyerr song and ceremonial knowledge. Severely disrupting any assumptions that song and ceremonial knowledge might be so modified that contemporary Aboriginal elders had little to offer in the curation, interpretation, or use of this collection, these discussions revealed a changed, but ongoing, utilization of these traditions. Even where there has been an attenuation—or, gradual loss in intensity of ritual life—the recordings were seamlessly integrated and made sense of within a familiar web of social, personal, land-based, and mythological relationships.

Discussing and singing while film and audio were reviewed evoked a kind of metaphorical journeying through ancestral country; as *Anengkerr* stories were recounted, they were also located in the landscape.

As I listened intently to these discussions and followed what I could, it was clear that learning about song and ceremony could never be contained via simple rote acquisition. Each tradition exists as an element in a system of interrelations between landscapes and kin, and it was the experience of being with people that enabled different points of connection to be revealed. These recordings also sparked biographical storytelling, social memories, and detailed explanations of *Anengkerr* and ritual practice.

In the course of deliberating and examining the recordings, not only were direct personal identifications acknowledged, but broader sociohistorical contexts were recalled in order to recontextualize the material in a contemporary setting. It is precisely this intersection of local knowledge and the archival that occupies the following chapter, as we begin to reinterpret the genealogical and biographical material contained in this collection.

Chapter 7

The Intermingling of Intimate Narratives

This is a true story about them old peoples hey. Ya. You know that's where all the stories come from, them old people—or a bit further on (in history/Anengkerr)

—Don Presley Pengart

When my long-term friend and one-time Anmatyerr language tutor Malcolm Heffernan Pengart requested access to his family's genealogy from the Strehlow Research Centre in 2012, he already knew much about his own ancestry. But important questions nevertheless remained about the life histories of some of his grandparents. Beginning with his family's genealogy, Malcolm and I began a collaborative investigation into how Anmatyerr people, steeped in orality and social memory, come to grips with written accounts of their social, ancestral and family histories.

Indigenous people worldwide are increasingly turning to archival records of the past for answers to questions about their cultural heritage (Johansen, 2004; Jackson, 2007; 2010; Kasten and Graaf, 2013; Shryock, 1997). In Australia, the records of missionaries and early ethnographers are being used to revive languages (Thieberger, 1995; Thorpe and Galassi, 2014); reconstruct place names (Hercus, Hodges, and Simpson, 2002, pp. 157–201); reimagine cultural practices (Harris, 2014); and trace genealogies (Finlayson, 1998). In Malcolm's case, he wanted to see what information he could squeeze out of the Strehlow archive to further elucidate his family's history, while I wanted to discover how much authority the archival record had for him. I was interested in how Malcolm and other Anmatyerr men interpreted and contextualized this information according to their lived experiences and within their own cultural frameworks.

T.G.H. Strehlow's field diaries contain not only details of song and ceremony, but also carefully illustrated maps of people's traditional lands, stories of their recent ancestors, and accounts of their interactions and dealings with each other. Intimately linked to these narrative accounts are a series of carefully drawn-up and annotated "family trees" containing very specific information about people's relationships to place and *Anengkerr* (Dreaming). Being with Malcolm and other Arrernte and Anmatyerr people as they carefully examined these records, I came to appreciate the diverse ways in which these texts were discussed and understood.

Malcolm's Story

It was late one afternoon in Alice Springs when I decided to ring Malcolm with news of a discovery that I had made in the Strehlow Research Centre archives. I had dipped into one of the diaries that Strehlow kept while engaged as a Patrol Officer, hoping to find out more about his investigations into the exploitation of Anmatyerr people at the Anningie tin mines, to the north of Ti Tree, in the late 1930s. During the course of this reading, I stumbled across the story of how Malcolm's *arreng* (father's father) had been killed. I knew that having lost his father to pneumonia at a young age, Malcolm certainly had questions about his grandfather. In particular, he was unsure about when, where, and how he had died. Stories circulated in Malcolm's family that the old man, known either as *Ingkaparleparl*, Artetyerwenguny, or "Big Foot," had possibly been shot and killed during the frontier violence of the "killing times," but nothing specific was ever discussed.

Strehlow's 1937 diary entry revealed that Ingkaparleparl had not been killed by *alhernter* at all, but by a Warlpiri man from the near northwest. Unsure how to broach the topic of such a temporally distant death, especially the passing of a significant patrilineal ancestor from whom so much of one's identity and relationship to land are often based, I felt quite apprehensive about making the call. When I got through to Malcolm, he was at work at the Alice Springs hospital, where he served as an Anmatyerr and Arrernte interpreter. Feeling awkward about explaining my finding over the phone, I suggested that we meet up later to read through the diary extracts and genealogies together.

Though aged in his fifties, and thus quite a bit older than me, Malcolm had become a close friend over the years. I had particularly come to love his sense of humor, his very gentle spirit, and his openness. As someone who had grown up on the northern cattle stations, mostly on his Arrernte mother's country at Yambah Station, Malcolm's youth was spent in the bush. The family would, however, often make the trip into Alice Springs, where they would either stay at the rear of the pastoralist's town residence or at Lhenpe Artnwe (an Aboriginal camp known as Middle Park located to the south of the Alice Springs Telegraph Station). Following troubled times between his alcoholic parents, Malcolm was taken to the Santa Teresa Catholic Mission in Eastern Arrernte territory by his older sister.

As a young man, Malcolm would often return to Anmatyerr country to visit his relatives. He later underwent his initiation at Anwekeran (the old "native camp" on Aileron Station) under the close guidance of his uncle and Strehlow informant, Charlie Artetyerwenguny Heffernan Penangk. Charlie taught him about his patrilineal ties to Ilewerr (Lake Lewis), the large salt lake near Napperby Station, and as an adult Malcolm resided on the country of his *aperl* (father's mother) at Ti Tree for many years.

Orality, Literacy, and Historical Practice

Unlike most of the Anmatyerr people I knew who had grown up and lived "in the bush," Malcolm had been subject to Western education on the mission. As a result, he possessed a reasonable degree of English literacy, and after trying his hand at many different jobs, had become a well-respected, professional interpreter with various health services in town. Malcolm was therefore one of the relatively small number of Aboriginal individuals now in their late middle age whose level of Western education marked them out from the majority of Anmatyerr people. Described by some as "biculturalists" or "intercultural adepts" (Burke, 2013), these people were often adroit at working in different linguistic and cultural registers and comfortable with literacy. As one of these people, Malcolm found discussing the contents of Strehlow's archive, and in particular its textual material, a relatively straightforward exercise.

For most Anmatyerr people, though, living in remote, non-urban spaces and where literate culture is mostly a marginal presence, English literacy was poor. Continuing to speak their own language, and often being proficient in a number of other Central Australian languages, Anmatyerr people were often less confident conversing in English. Despite some exceptions (cf. Green, 2003; Campbell et al., 2015), most people also struggled with alphabetic writing, as institutional education tended to fizzle out at the secondary school level in the remote communities.

The promulgation of literacy among Indigenous peoples in the colonial era was often focused on religious conversion or social assimilation, but early on Aboriginal people in Australia began to use both reading and writing as a communication tool, a political weapon, and a means of creative expression (see Carlson, Fagan, and Khnanko-Friesen, 2011; Ong, 1988; Olson and Torrance, 1991; Goody, 1987; 2010a). Although the tensions between oral and literate societies are far more complex and varied than can be explored in this chapter (see Carlson, Fagan, and Khnanko-Friesen, 2011; Ong, 1988; Olson and Torrance, 1991; Goody, 1987; 2010a), some of these debates provide an important conceptual backdrop to the discussions that follow. In Aotearoa (New Zealand), for example, Māori were particularly quick to adopt print in order to contest colonialism (Ballantyne, 2014), build national cultural consciousness (Paterson, 2010), and contribute to intellectual debates (Carey, 2014).

In North America, too, there have been equally powerful attempts by First Nations people to use text in order to articulate and preserve their languages and cultures (Edwards, 2005; Cannizzo, 1983). Despite these pragmatic and creative ways in which some have taken up the culture of print, there are nonetheless key differences in the way that predominantly oral societies have experienced the arrival of print culture.

Unlike some Aboriginal groups in Central Australia who were introduced to text and literacy principally via Christian missions (Ferguson, 1987; Austin-Broos, 2003; Kral, 2000), the Anmatyerr had no such experience. Living beyond the influences of mission or government settlements, literacy remained rare up until the second half of the twentieth century when government schooling was eventually introduced. Prior to this, some of Malcolm's stockman relatives had certainly been exposed to topographical maps (Johnson, 1994, pp. 79–120) and biblical texts (Bowman, 2015, p. 55), but none of his parental generation (or beyond) had ever been literate. What linguistic anthropologist Inge Kral (2009, pp. 40–41) has described as the socially or culturally "meaningful textual practices" that accompanied the rise of literacy elsewhere in Australia were generally absent in this part of the Northern Territory.

The ability of Anmatyerr people to engage with print culture is undeniably critical to how they understand the textual elements of Strehlow's archive. Like other people living in predominantly oral cultures, Anmatyerr people tend to preserve their knowledge by embedding it in verbal formulae, by singing it, by finding it rooted in place, or by recalling it via other mnemonic devices. Concealed by what author and translator Robert Bringhurst has called "the lumpy colonial carpet," the achievements of oral poetics and of social memory have been severely challenged by the predominance of Western literacy (Bringhurst, 1994, p. 165). One of the more significant writers in this field, Walter Ong (1988) has similarly described these challenges as leading to a "shift" whereby both the psychology and social lives of oral societies are irreparably transformed. As much as anthropologists, linguists, and translators have tried to improve on the ways that print can convey the oral aesthetic (see Tedlock, 1983; Hymes, 1981; Blaeser, 1999) and its close relationship to bodily gestures and facial expressions (Kendon, 1988; Green, 2014), most scholars would agree that the oral can never be fully expressed in the written.

Writing specifically about the impact of Arrernte access to extensive genealogical and cultural heritage records of T.G.H. and Carl Strehlow, Anna Kenny, in line with Ong's hypothesis, has similarly suggested that although the Strehlow archive presents enormous opportunities for people to reconstruct cultural and individual identities, it has paradoxically led to a transformation of their "consciousness":

> No other Indigenous Australian group can draw upon such a rich cultural heritage record and deep and detailed genealogical documentation. Maybe ironically, this record has so *impinged* on Western Arrernte *consciousness* that it has become an artefact in their *modern* culture. . . . (Kenny, 2013, p. 242, my emphasis)

Other anthropologists working in the Arrernte area have similarly critiqued the use of the Strehlow genealogies on the grounds that they have been "appropriated" as sources of "written proof" in Native Title and Land Claim proceedings (Wilmot and Morgan, 2010). Underlying these concerns is a somewhat static, binary conception of "traditional," "oral" (and thus more "authentic") forms of "consciousness" on the one hand, and a "literate," more "modern" and thus a more "impinged" upon "consciousness" on the other. As Francesca Merlan argues, though, while it has been a preoccupation of Australian anthropology to demonstrate the "traditionality" of Indigenous peoples, this glosses over an "analytic understanding of "tradition" as an inherently reflexive category" (2006, p. 98). As more and more Aboriginal people from across Australia increasingly derive at least part of their cultural knowledge from written sources (see Walsh, 1995; Rigsby, Finlayson, and H.J. Bek, 1998) the traditional/modern dichotomy is harder to maintain.

Taking a view that challenges these hard-and-fast boundaries, others draw attention to the way in which writing will often intermingle with orality in a dialectical fashion (see Bradley and Kearney, 2011; Jones and Russell, 2012). Focusing more on the way in which people produce and reproduce social memories and a sense of history via numerous experiential, textual, oral, social, and embodied ways, these writers bring a heterogeneity to these processes that need not privilege or essentialize oral-indigeneity (Platt and Quisbert, 2007). As historical archaeologists Sian Jones and Lynette Russell (2012, pp. 270–71) have argued, orally transmitted social memories ought not be "romanticized" or "naturalized" as isolated sites of "subaltern resistance" to hegemonic print culture. Orality and literacy might better be conceived now as elements in a *generative* process whereby the past is continually being interpreted and negotiated (see Buchholtz, 2011; Climo and Cattell, 2002). Hokari (Strehlow, 1968a, p. 46) too sees this as "a dialogue and negotiation between two historical practices" (oral/memory and literate/archival) that can share ways of constructing the past.

It is precisely the elaboration of this *intersection* and *interplay* between the social, oral, emplaced, and documentary materials that forms the focal point of this chapter. Freed from conceptual binaries and grounded in ethnographic description, one can begin to apprehend the ways in which archival text, orality, journeying in place, and social memory intermingle in Anmatyerr ways of historical practice.

Finding "Big Foot"

The archival discovery of Malcolm's grandfather's death in Strehlow's diary began a chain of events that brought these intersections to the fore. To begin with, Malcolm wanted to make sure I had in fact correctly identified his grandfather, who most today referred to by the name of "Big Foot." Returning to the genealogy constructed by Strehlow in collaboration with Malcolm's uncle, we could see that both Malcolm's uncle (father's brother) and his grandfather (father's father) were all listed under the same name, "Charlie Ititjarungunja (Artetyerwenguny)."[1] The identical English first names were not unusual, as these were often uncaringly applied to people by pastoralists, and the name that nominally stood as a surname (in this case Artetyerwenguny, meaning "belonging to the mulga Dreaming") clearly indicated their patrilineal connection to an important *Anengkerr* for the Ilewerr (Lake Lewis) estate.[2]

A footnote to the genealogy indicated that Charlie Artetyerwenuny (Malcolm's uncle) reminded Strehlow that he had investigated the murder of his father (Ingkaparleparl) in the late 1930s. "It turned out," Strehlow wrote, that "*this* Charlie" Artetyerwenguny was in fact:

> the son of the Charlie Ititjarungunja who had been accidentally killed on the Hanson River" (allegedly at a placed called Ljoljaka [Alywelyek] or Atutagata [Artwertakert]) by Jamatjitjana in the late thirties: I had been present at the exhumation of his body by Sgt. Koop. (Strehlow, 1968a, p. 46)

When I read the above diary entry to Malcolm, he was immediately suspicious. Rumors often surrounded unexplained deaths, particularly those that occurred during the violent colonial past, and there were stories circulating in the family that "police" had likely murdered his grandfather. Huckitta Lynch, the youngest son of Ingkaparleparl, and Malcolm's *angey* (father's brother), alternatively spoke of the old man dying at the hands of an "*ngkekern*," a ritual assassin endowed with supernatural powers of flight, invisibility, and more. Being ambiguous about a death like this was, according to Malcolm, an intentional way of avoiding further retributive violence or family feuds.

As it was also customary to place a complete embargo on speaking about a person after their death, rumors and misinformation would often circulate unchecked. Perhaps because Ingkaparleparl's death had involved an inter-family conflict, it had been unmentionable and become suppressed and shrouded in mystery?

---

1. See Family Tree IX, 5 at the Strehlow Research Centre.

2. This suffix "rwenguny" does not feature in the contemporary dictionaries for any of the Arandic languages but is recorded in both Carl and T.G.H. Strehlow's work. Numerous Anmatyerr and Arrernte speakers have informed me that this is an older form of "ke-artwey" now used to indicate "belonging to" a particular Dreaming.

Encouraged by Malcolm and Huckitta's interest in unearthing more about the incident, I began looking more closely at Strehlow's archive and located a range of journalistic accounts written at the time (Strehlow, 1968a, p. 85a). From these sources, the following story of Ingkaparleparl's death emerged. At Artwertakert (also known as Ardell's Soak) on the Hanson River in November of 1937, a large group of Anmatyerr people had gathered for the initiation ceremony of a young man named Norman Tyapeyart Carter (Strehlow 1968a, p. 85a). One afternoon a Warlpiri man, known either as "Big Foot Jack" or Yamatjitjana ("Jamatjitjana"), approached from the north and attacked Malcolm's grandfather with a boomerang (Strehlow, 1937, pp. 61–64). Following Ingkaparleparl's eventual death a day or two later, his body was buried in a "shallow grave" partially formed by an "old rabbit warren" (*The Advertiser*, 1937) close to a mature *atyarnp* (Ironwood) tree.

Accompanying Sergeant A.E. Koop from Alice Springs as an interpreter, Strehlow arrived a few days later to help gather evidence from local Anmatyerr residents and witnesses.[3] Mampey Penangk, Malcolm's aunty and the daughter of the murdered man, was among those who spoke with Strehlow as he passed through Ryan's Well on his way to the scene of the crime on Ti Tree Station. When Strehlow arrived, he sketched a map illustration of the location of the burial and the direction from which the attacker had apparently approached. Koop and Strehlow then undertook the gruesome task of unearthing the body so the Government Residential Medical Officer could carry out a post-mortem. Weeks later, Strehlow appeared on behalf of the accused at the inquest in Alice Springs, and although he was not named in the newspaper reports, it seems likely that he also served as an interpreter for the seven Anmatyerr witnesses who gave evidence.

The reason for the attack, however, remained elusive, and accounts of the injuries that Ingkaparleparl had received differed, as did how long it took for him to die. Many of the Anmatyerr witnesses independently referred to the attack as being "*apalkel (balkala)*," meaning with no apparent reason or motivation. But there were some indications that an inappropriate sexual relationship between a relative of Ingkaparleparl's and a woman named Mary Tjirbmintiri Kemarr may have been a cata-

---

3. See also "Police Journal, Alice Springs 2/2/1936–30/4/1939" entries for November 21–26 and December 3–10, 1937. Northern Territory Archive Service, NTRS F255.

lyst. It is also clear from Strehlow's diary entries that he suspected that some information was being purposefully withheld from him. "The local people," he wrote, "had hidden" under their "usual veil of absolute ignorance." Mary Kemarr (a potentially key informant) had apparently been at Connor's Well but did not speak to him when he passed through, and this made him wary (1937, p. 62). There was clearly more to the story, and Malcolm wanted to dig deeper.

Questioning the Archival Account

I photocopied the relevant pages of the diaries and genealogies and left this information with Malcolm to read over and discuss with his family. His initial reaction to the story was mixed. Although pleased to discover more about the incident, he was understandably saddened by the revelation that his grandfather had been killed in what appeared to be an unexplained act of violence. There were important anomalies, too, that in Malcolm's mind needed exploring. Malcolm thought the timing of the attack, which according to Strehlow's account had been at "sundown," was suspect for in his experience elders normally aired their grievances, or fought, in the early morning only. Other aspects of the Strehlow report also seemed curious given normal kinship conventions. Men of the Penangk subsection such as Ingkaparlepar were usually prohibited from doing harm to their nephews (men of the Ngal subsection) and, similarly, these men (such as Yamatjitjana) were not permitted to "hit" their "uncles."

These minor yet noteworthy anomalies made Malcolm somewhat distrustful of the account. Coupled with the fact that the fight had occurred during the opening stages of an initiation ceremony, Malcolm became worried that the altercation could have originated in a quarrel over "men's *tywerreng* business" (secret/sacred rituals). Venturing further into the details of a tale that involved an indiscretion or violation of secret men's ceremonial Law—regardless of the antiquity of the story—could, he warned, "make men *mwekenh*"—a term specifically reserved for occasions when men became incensed about the illicit handling of their restricted cultural information. Malcolm also worried that if these documents were carelessly distributed they could exacerbate contemporary hostilities between Anmatyerr and Warlpiri families who had been warring at Ti Tree and Willowra in recent years (see Sinclair, 2013). Given these potential sensitivities, the photocopies of Strehlow's diaries were not shown to

Malcolm's *yay* (big sister), and it was understood that any further investigations, at least for the time being, needed to proceed with discretion.

Traveling to Artwertakert

As I regularly traveled between Melbourne and Alice Springs in my capacity as repatriation curator with the Melbourne Museum, Malcolm and I often discussed the Ingkaparleparl story, either in person over a cup of tea or on the phone. In September of 2014 Malcolm accompanied me on one of my research visits to Ti Tree so we could try to locate the gravesite of his *arreng*. I could understand why he wanted to be at the place, to feel and know its location and to survey the country and imagine his grandfather's presence, but I couldn't see how this would reveal anything more about the historical event.

Regardless, we headed off armed with the original hand-drawn "mud map" that Strehlow had produced in 1937, as well as a second map featuring the names of sites along the Hanson Creek that he had drawn during one of his "mapping trips" in 1968. Being largely unfamiliar with this part of Anmatyerr country, Malcolm saw these maps as being potentially very useful, although he knew we would need to call upon Anmatyerr people in Ti Tree, who had detailed knowledge of the local cultural and environmental geography, to pilot the way.

Illustrated in his field diaries, Strehlow's mud maps (sometimes labeled as "plans") plotted places of totemic significance. Created for innumerable locations across Central Australia, these maps are exceptional records of sites, mythological associations, and *anyenheng* (clan) connections down to the smallest details. They were not drawn to scale and lacked geospatial data such as latitude and longitude identifiers, but they did provide enough information to make them useful. Unlike the maps that Strehlow (1970b; 1971a; 1978b) and others produced in order to show the general trajectories and sites of Dreaming ancestors (Spencer and Gillen, 1899; Meggitt 1966; Yanyuwa families, Bradley, and Cameron, 2003), these drawings were made to specifically plot sites in relation to river courses, mountain ranges, water bores, fence lines, station tracks, and so on. As such, local geographic and geo-mythological expertise is often required to orient and contextualize their reading. For example, finding a concealed site like a soakage that has to be dug out of a dry riverbed (and rarely features on orthodox maps) could be accomplished only with the assistance of those who have been shown and told of the site's significance, have a working knowledge of the local geography, and know the station infrastructure.

On our way north to Ti Tree, Malcolm and I stopped in at the Aileron Roadhouse to show these maps to his classificatory father, Eric Penangk. Before the maps could be produced, though, both Eric and a younger man in his thirties began describing exactly where Artwertakert, the site of Ingkaparleparl's burial, was. As many of the men and women living between Aileron, Pine Hill, and Ti Tree stations traveled in that area when hunting and knew the area well, Strehlow's maps appeared to be superfluous. They did, however, spark eager explanations from Eric about the various Dreamings that featured in the Artwertakert area. Trying to get the conversation back on to his grandfather's death, Malcolm gently encouraged his "father" to talk about the story. Eric seemed to know something but refused to discuss the matter further. It seemed as if the story of one man's death was dwarfed by the recounting of bigger things, in this case local *Anengkerr* and place relationships.

As we left Aileron and continued north along the Stuart Highway, Malcolm reflected that knowledge of sites and Dreamings was robust partly because of people's increased regional mobility.

For someone like Malcolm, who now lived in town, away from Anmatyerr country, it was clear that those living in "the communities" continued to learn a great deal about their country. "You know how it is . . . *Mer* [the country], it is all connected. People move about, visiting families and they use all the roads. They tell stories all the way." It was something I had noticed before and that Minoru Hokari (2005) during his fieldwork with the Gurindji had also understood as being central to the "mode of historical practice" exhibited by Aboriginal people in the Northern Territory. Movement across and within interlinking networks of Dreaming tracks, kin relations, countries, and stories supported a "relationalized" telling of the past. This also produced a relational understanding of the "self," as exemplified in Eric's earlier emphasis on the connections and relationships involving country, kin, and Dreaming, rather than narrowing in on the isolated story of one person (Malcolm's grandfather).

This emphasis had clear resonances with the way in which Strehlow had been discussed as an historical figure in chapter 5, where, contrary to Western historical conventions that plotted life histories against a linear chronology, people were instead remembered within broader constellations of relationship, underscored by Dreaming, landscape, and kinship.

Anmatyerr people were regularly moving between communities in every direction. The people at Ti Tree would often be heading east to the Utopia homelands, but also west to Napperby, Willowra, or Yuendumu for funerals, football carnivals, ceremonies, or hunting trips. Private ownership of motor vehicles, as well as freer access to both pastoral and Aboriginal freehold leases in the region following a number of successful land rights and native title claims (Young, 1987), meant that mobility had remained an important feature of Indigenous sociality (see Memmott, Thomson, and Long, 2006; Peterson, 2004). This type of wide-ranging travel and kin relatedness, whether by foot, on horseback, or in cars, worked to keep tightly interconnected, mythologic, social, and genealogical information circulating among communities across generations (Austin-Broos, 2006, p. 12). Although many people now lived sedentary lives in communities far from their ancestral countries, young and old still moved across the region with great regularity (usually in packed cars that would often break down or run out of fuel). It was this mobility, as Malcolm was suggesting, that had played a key role in the learning of familial and *Anengkerr* relationships between people and places.

When we arrived at Ti Tree, Malcolm and I showed both of Strehlow's maps to Paddy Kemarr, but also to Jimmy Haines, who had just arrived with a delivery of firewood for the old man. "Ah, Mer Artwertakert. It's not far . . . *antekerr* [south] from Ahapelen. *Alhernter* call 'em Waterloo (Bore)," Jimmy confirmed. Exhibiting his customary mastery of local historical and cultural knowledge, Paddy indicated that he knew exactly where the Artwertakert was, but remarkably, he also claimed to have personally witnessed the attack when he was a young boy. Showing little interest in Strehlow's maps and diary entries, Paddy indicated that what we needed to do was make the short journey to Artwertakert so he could properly explain what he remembered, as well as what he had been told about the incident.

Discussions about the confrontation involving Ingkaparlepar ceased as we drove out of Ti Tree town and south along the eastern bank of the Hanson River. Much like Eric Penangk's earlier emphasis on *Anengkerr* and country, what was on the face of it an historical story quickly became subsumed within an overarching discussion of site names as well as land ownership. This propensity to read and name the landscape, described as "topographical gossip" by some (Lewis, 1976; Nash, 1998), was a common experience among Anmatyerr men and clearly played an important role in the regeneration of historical, social, and cultural associations (see Palmer, 1982). Both being in and journeying through *Mer* (place/country) was indeed part and parcel of *becoming* an Anmatyerr person (cf. Taylor, 2013). This was true not just in the ritual sense of "following" Dreaming "tracks," as discussed in chapter 6, but more broadly true where places were experienced as entities inherently animated by Dreaming.

Mer (country/home/land) was not something experienced passively, though. At specific places, such as Malcolm's country of Ilewerr, for example, people interacted with the *merlalp* (spirit beings of the country) who would, among other things, brazenly steal people's car keys or make them confused and lost. It was the presence of people, perceiving subjects, who enabled the land to, as Casey would describe it, "release" memories among the "intensely gathered landscape such as that of Aboriginal Australia" (Casey, 1996; 1987, pp. 182–194). It was clear from the experience of journeying with Anmatyerr people that palce (*Mer*) was something inherently mediated and constituted via social relations and practices (Rose, 1992; Myers, 1997; Merlan 1998). It was the act of *going to* or *being at* a specific place that generated a dialectical relationship between places and people and facilitated discussions and elucidations that otherwise would not have emerged.

Getting closer to Artwertakert, Paddy extended his arm from the vehicle and gestured toward a seemingly nondescript section of the Hanson River. Calling out over the rumble of the engine, he announced our arrival. "*Mer Atwertakert. Mer ahenpeny. Yanhel live-irretyart* [That's Artwertakert. An old, disused camp. We used to live over there] . . . People used to camp here . . . Make *anmanty* [young men's initiation ceremonies]." After crossing the dry riverbed of the Hanson at the Ti Tree and Pine Hill Station boundary fence, we approached the area where, according to Strehlow's map, Ingkaparlepar had been buried (see map 7.1 for a new map produced after revisiting the site in 2014). Explaining that this country belonged to an *arlewatyerr* (sand goanna, *Varanus gouldii*) ancestor of the Kemarr subsection, Paddy pointed out a collection of large sandstone boulders immediately to our north. While these boulders were absent from Strehlow's maps, an annotation on his 1968 map (presumably dictated by his informant Peter Ntaranga Ngal) described the site in this way: "on the western bank of the Hanson, from Etutagata (Artwertakert), there is a *makamaka, loatjira kwatala indama* [sacred site where a sand goanna laid its eggs]."

Paddy's description of the site in 2014 was almost identical:

Here's the *amek-amek. Nhenh arlewatyerr kwartel intem* [Here is the sacred place. This is where the sand goanna laid its eggs]. *Yewe* that *amek-amek* that's *ker arlewatyerr akeweny* [Yes, that site belongs to the Sand Goanna, the precious thing]. *Arlewatyerr* [sand goanna]. Belonging to him right through to Nthwerey. Right through to Pweray [Two sites further north along the Hanson]. *Kwerreng* [associated with] again. That is his own place. He bin big boss! *Mer akweteth* [a local ancestor and not one that travels widely].

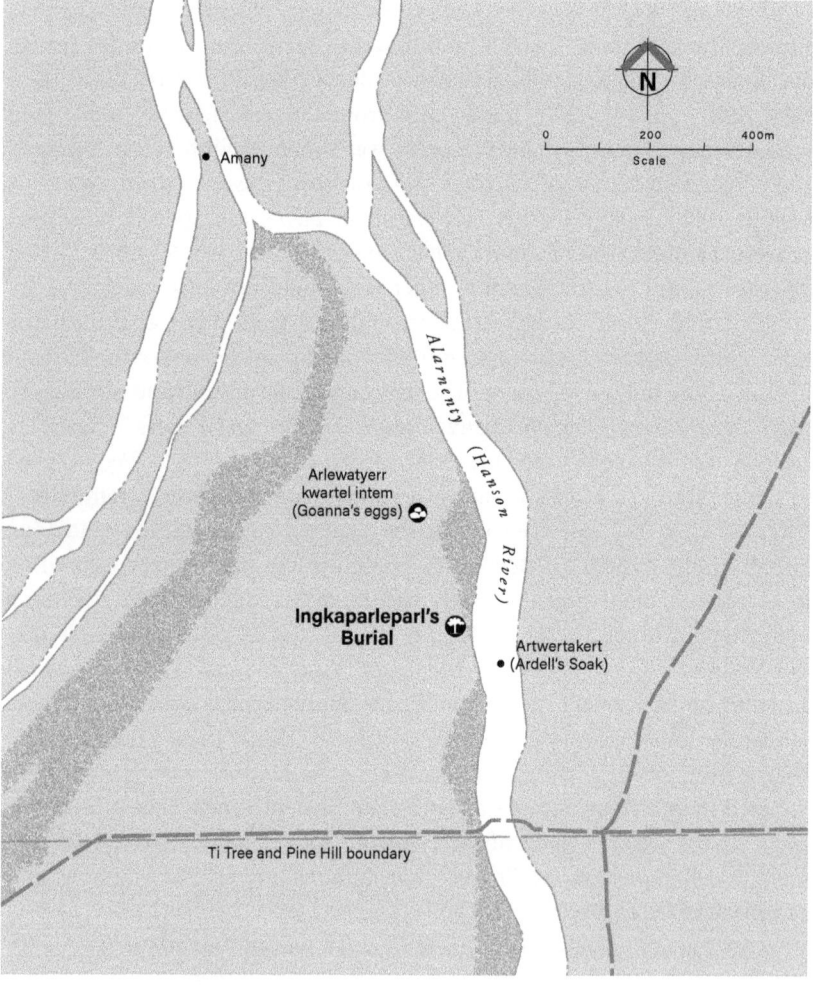

Map 7.1. Map of Ingkaparleparl's burial site on the Hanson Creek, south of Ti Tree.

Using place as their starting point, Paddy and the others began filling in the gaps left in Strehlow's descriptions. These acts of remembrance of past events were, as Miriam Kahn has nicely described in similar practices in Papua New Guinea, organized or anchored "spatially" rather than "temporally" (e.g., see Kahn 1990, 1996) and with little regard for dates, years, or chronology.

The "Written Down Story"

Paddy was about five or six years of age when Ingkaparleparl was killed, and his version of the event—including the direction from which the offenders approached and the context of Norman Carter's initiation—largely tallied with Strehlow's report. He agreed that the fight was certainly *apalkel* (without reason)—"He was killed right there! I don't know. *Apalkel*. No reason. No reason." He also recalled seeing Ingkaparleparl, whom he recalled as being "a big tall fella," and like many of the men from Ilewerr was known as "Bigfoot," being carried across the wide, deep sandy dry riverbed by many men to his burial under the *atyarnp* tree. Though Paddy had been very young at the time, he had clearly shared in, and been the beneficiary of, a tradition of orality that placed great worth in acts of memory and valued firsthand experience (as is evidenced in his knowledge of song and ceremony demonstrated in the previous chapter). As he constantly reminded us, he had been present—"I seen. We were witness. We bin witness. We bin looking at it . . . cause I bin look all the people. I bin look proper level."

There were some differences, though, between Paddy's and Strehlow's accounts and further details that had escaped Strehlow's diarizing. In Paddy's version of the incident, another man, Bill Ngal Twenperwenguny, had also been injured during the altercation and died later from an act of sorcery, though perhaps not until months or even years later. Instead of boomerangs, Paddy had heard that stone knives imbued with "*arrwengkelth*" (supernatural poison or sickness) had been used by the "*arlper* [Warlpiri] soldiers." Contrary to Malcolm's doubts earlier about the timing of the attack, however, Paddy confirmed that Ingkaparlepart did get his "hiding little bit *angwerrel* [mid-afternoon]," though he added that Bill Ngal was "murdered" (meaning attacked and fatally injured with the *arrwengkelth*) the following morning.

Paddy wanted the discrepancies between versions to be recognized, but also wanted his version recorded. Addressing me using my subsection name and thus reminding me of his fatherly status to me, Paddy stressed the need to record his version. "*Pwerrerl*, that [Strehlow story] is another one . . . But, you can put my story on that paper. I've been telling you straight . . . Oh yeah, you've got to get it right, right, proper right. *Arraty* [true]." Then, pointing to my digital audio recorder, he said, "We can put that one in there." While challenging the authority of the archive, he was simultaneously appealing to the perceived power of static recordings, both textual and audiovisual, to capture what was *arraty* (true). Just like all of the men who had worked with Strehlow in the past in having their genealogies, songs, and rituals recorded, Paddy also saw the value of these recordings. This was a way of seeing that his version of events—indeed, his knowledge—would be treated authoritatively when placed within the mnemonics of literate society.

The slight variance in the oral and written accounts nevertheless led to a lively discussion in the group about what *really* happened—about what was "*arraty*" (true) or "straight." Jimmy, approximately thirty years younger than Paddy, and personally unfamiliar with the story, appealed to the perceived truth-values associated with written accounts. Strehlow's version, he advanced, was surely correct. "But that's the *written down* story," he remarked. Still unwilling to accept this, Paddy responded, "No, that's nothing!" As was generally the case for people who had spent their youths in a more "classical" (though not precolonial) version of Aboriginal society (e.g., see Baker, 1999), Paddy saw oral sources as underscoring views of the past, whereas written accounts were inferior. "That's only . . . That's not really right . . . I reckon a little bit wrong there." It was his *memory* of the events that was "really true, *arraty* [straight, correct]."

After a break for lunch, we began searching for what could be the precise *atyarnp* (ironwood tree, *Acacia estrophiolata*) under which Ingkaparlepearl had been buried (figure 7.1). While the tree had probably died or been destroyed in bush fires since 1937, the plain along the western flank of the Hanson was dotted with hundreds of juvenile *atyarnp* trees.

We returned to Strehlow's maps for clues. Apparently, the burial had been slightly north of the Artwertakert soakage, close to where we were sitting and eating our lunch. Surveying the scene, Jimmy spotted a rusted bonnet of an old vehicle, possibly from the late 1930s or early 1940s, among the tall buffel grass. We gathered around as Paddy began to reflect on the likely scenario that Ingkaparlepearl's burial had been covered over with this bonnet after Strehlow and Koop had disinterred the body in their investigation. The bonnet would have protected the burial from

Figure 7.1. Malcolm Heffernan at Artwertakert, in the vicinity of where his grandfather was buried in 1937 (Photo: J. Gibson, September 2014).

the large number of cattle that once roamed Ti Tree Station. Though pure conjecture, it was well founded and, most important, enough for Malcolm to start planning the erection of a small headstone in honor of his father's father (*arreng*).

Reading the Family Trees

This interplay of text and social memory, and similar modes of historical practice, was again on display during our collaborative examinations of the genealogies collected by T.G.H. Strehlow. These documents, produced throughout Strehlow's fieldwork career, were based on a very similar methodology to his father's genealogies, and are now some of the most regularly viewed documents in the collection. Access to these documents began with the establishment of the Strehlow Research Centre in 1991, and since that time numerous people, mainly Arrernte men and women, have been able to obtain copies of genealogies that are immediately relevant to their particular families (see Malbunka, 2004). Very rarely containing any restricted ritual information, they are among the safest materials for people to copy, distribute, and openly discuss, though they have been wielded during disputes over family lineage and, thus, rights in land.

However, individual interest in these documents varies. Some are simply curious about their ancestry, while others (particularly those of Aboriginal and non-Aboriginal descent who have had little contact with their Aboriginal kin) see them as offering important information on colonial family histories negatively impacted upon by government policies (such as the removal of children) (see Kruger and Waterford, 2007). Others, however, have openly sought out "written proof" of their lineage for use in land tenure and related disputes over ownership and rights in cultural property (Wilmot and Morgan, 2010). During the course of this research, but also during the three years that I worked out of the Strehlow Research Centre, I was often asked by Arrernte and Anmatyerr people to help them interpret Strehlow's spellings of Arrernte terms and phrases, as well as generally decipher the contents of these idiosyncratic and potentially politically potent documents.

When Malcolm Heffernan first accessed his family's genealogy, which was essentially based on information provided by his uncle (Charlie Artetyerwenguny), he was initially perplexed. He had been listed by Strehlow as being "from" "Alice Springs."[4] "This is wrong," he protested, "I'm not from Alice Springs! I'm from Lake Lewis [Ilewerr], *arrengey atyenh* [my father's father] country. My country." Although the genealogy provided no information on his Dreaming or "totem" affiliation, Malcolm understood that because he was listed as being "from" Alice Springs, it would be assumed by anyone reading this that he "belonged" to one of the Dreamings that occupied this area. If taken at face value, mere inference of this association could lead to serious political repercussions. Turning to me with a cheeky grin, Malcolm wondered whether "people might think" that he was "claiming *merek-artwey* [traditional owner status] here!"

This was no laughing matter, though, as Malcolm knew well that many people had in fact misinterpreted these genealogies before and used them

---

4. Family Tree IX, 5 at the Strehlow Research Centre.

to make claims about belonging to land and Dreaming in ways they did not understand. The question remained in Malcolm's mind, though: how could T.G.H. Strehlow, and the relatives that informed this genealogy, have got this information so wrong? In analyzing his own genealogy further and after looking at numerous other Anmatyerr family trees, it became clear that this was in no way an error on Strehlow's part. It seemed to be an artefact of both Strehlow's particular empirical interests and the way in which past generations of Arrernte (and presumably Anmatyerr people) described personal ties to land, ritual, and Dreaming. Significantly, these genealogies were never produced by Strehlow as means of theorizing the origins of human social organization, as they had been by earlier anthropologists, nor were they designed to capture rules of kinship, social structure, or even land tenure, as they had been by Strehlow's contemporaries in social anthropology (see Warner, 1964; Hiatt, 1965; Meggitt, 1962).

Strehlow was certainly aware of social anthropology's theoretical interests in kinship, but this was not his concern in these genealogies. His "family trees" and the other genealogical records he kept (Strehlow, 1969c), are not abstracted, they have no "ego" reference point, and the people featured in them are named. The family trees often contain detailed footnotes on the location of their conception site, further biographical insights, and in some cases commentaries on the "mixed" or "full-blood" heritage of the person concerned. These were not records of kinship, but of what interested him most, the relationships among persons, myth, and land. By extension, they showed an individual's rights in ritual knowledge, which did not automatically confer "landholding" rights.

Most of the 150 genealogies drawn up by Strehlow concern Arrernte families. At the margins of this corpus, though, are a smaller suite of family trees for a number of other Aboriginal cultural/linguistic groups, including nine that pertain directly to the Anmatyerr. Within these nine documents, which usually begin with an apical ancestor and show membership of a particular *anyenheng* group, there are approximately 370 individuals listed from across the length and breadth of the Anmatyerr region. The name and subsection of each person is listed, as well as reference, first, to the place where they are "from" and, second, to their associated *aknganenty* ("knganintja," which Strehlow abbreviates as "kŋ/kng"), a term that generically refers to an individual's conception "totem" or "Dreaming." It is the information listed under these categories, "from" and "*aknganentye*," that resulted in the initial puzzlement mentioned above.

Without an explicit key or clarification about what these documents actually record, Arrernte people are often left unsure how to interpret them (see Kenny, 2013, pp. 189–193; Wilmot and Morgan, 2010). My experiences with Anmatyerr people, however, have been slightly different. I first began reading through and examining these genealogies with people in Ti Tree and was immediately taken by just how effortlessly they were interpreted. Once the ethnographic and theoretical background to these texts is explained, the data enter a new process of interrogation utilizing the knowledge of senior men and women. Contemporary understandings of descent, which as is shown below appear to have undergone some change during the twentieth century, are then applied in order to render these documents recognizable in their social context.

The Trouble with Terminology

The initial trouble begins where associations between a listed individual's *aknganentye*, their subsection, and the place where they are "from" appear incongruous. An example to illustrate: when discussing the genealogy of Bob Malpangk Mpetyan—one of Strehlow's informants from the 1950s—a number of people were quick to point out what appeared to be a mismatch. Jimmy Haines, for example, had no personal memory of Bob Malpangk, but he knew immediately from Malpangk's subsection (Mpetyan) that he could not be "from" the Pathantek (Batantaka), a site located with the Arempey estate area belonging to people of the Penangk and Pengart subsections. Where you were "from," almost every Anmatyerr person assumed, would be a person's patrilineal connection, their landholding association, which in this case would be country associated with the Mpetyan/Ngal subsections. As Jimmy Haines put it:

> Pathantek. Yeah, I know where that Pathantek is! It's that big hill there, near Arempey [Pine Hill], Penangk, Pengart country. But he's not the *owner* of that *mer* [place], that bloke. He might have been just *kwertengerl* [a ritual manager] . . . Strehlow mightn't . . . he never might be listen properly intit [do you think]?

Without denying the wide variety of modes of attachment to land and rights to ritual knowledge that feature in Anmatyerr and other Central Australian communities (Myers, 1991; Keen, 1997; Morton, 1997), it is clear that people generally *expected* that these family trees would provide information to help them to trace, or "go back" to, their father's father's country. Ordering these relationships in hierarchical terms, James Mpetyan, a man in his thirties, for example, explained that a person's father's father (*arreng*) has priority, followed by their *atyemey* (mother's father). The *atyemey* "come from the daughters. They become the *kwertengerl* [manager or assistants in custodianship of land and ritual]," but your father's father (*arreng*), James reiterated was the "main seat" or the "grass roots of your genealogy." If Strehlow had "listened properly" it was assumed that he would have documented *these* connections.

In order to better understand the distinctions between the inheritance of associations and the personal attainment of Dreaming affiliations, a fuller appreciation of the notion of spiritual conception is required. The literature on conception totems in Australia is extensive and embroiled in historical debates about Aboriginal procreative beliefs (see Malinowski's contribution in Montagu, 1974; Charlesworth et al., 1984, pp. 108–134; Hiatt, 1996, pp. 120–141; Merlan, 1986; T.G.H. Strehlow, 1964c). For the Anmatyerr and Arrernte, the notion of "conception" refers *not* to a baby's actual conception or birth but specifically to the moment of "quickening," as Olive Pink described it (1936, p. 288) when an ancestral spirit enters a woman and *angane-irrek* (spiritually conceives) the unborn child inside her. The process is often discussed by Strehlow as being akin to the "reincarnation" of an ancestor (e.g., see Strehlow, 1978b). As a person's moment of spiritual conception may occur at any locality while a mother is journeying, it follows that the Dreaming ancestor that animates the child may not be associated with one's father's country and in fact is more likely to occur in an area familiar to the mother (Hamilton, 1998, pp. 101–102) but in reality could occur anywhere.

As Anmatyerr families moved around the region, working, hunting, visiting relations and traveling to ceremonies, a given set of siblings could therefore potentially be spiritually conceived, colloquially known as being "found," in different places and thus acquire unrelated personal Dreamings (Rubuntja and Green, 2002, p. 15; see Austin-Broos, 2006, p. 111, for an excellent illustration of this). Although senior men played a role in determining which specific Ancestor entered the child at a particular intersection of *anengkerr* trajectories (Strehlow, 1947, p. 139; Gillen, 2001, p. 159), conception sites were/are ultimately an arbitrary attribution. Regardless, the tradition of spiritual conception according to Strehlow was enormously important to an individual's identity, rights, and duties in ritual (Strehlow, 1978b, p. 26), and as Austin-Broos has added, operated as a way of promoting "individuation" and diversification of relationships "among patrifilial relatives" (2009, p. 109). It was this diversification that bound people together within networks of mutual and overlapping ritual responsibilities.

Where you come "from" on these family trees is thus more correctly where one was "found," and the totem listed is the ancestor that *angane-irrek* (spiritually conceived) the person. Explaining this in a letter to Mervyn Hartwig in 1965, Strehlow wrote that the "genealogies can reveal at least certain features of the local organization in the pre-white days; the "conception site" is always included. It reveals where the mother was some seven months or so before the birth of each of her children."[5] Anmatyerr speakers, however, find Strehlow's use of the term *aknganenty* slightly problematic. *Aknganenty* can just as easily also refer to the "country" and Dreamings one inherits via their father's father, as much as it can to their personal conception "totem." Other terms like *anngirrem* or *alkngirrenty* are much more commonly used to denote spiritual conception (Green, 2010; 2013). As Malcolm explained, *aknganenty* could refer to the full range of personal "connections" to ancestral beings that could be associated either to one's grandparents or implicated in an individual's personal conception.

Biography and Becoming

When the particulars of these documents are understood, though, Anmatyerr people are relatively quick to make sense of them. I distinctly recall one occasion where a large number of people gathered at the bonnet of my car to read over extracts from Strehlow's *Handbook to Central Australian Genealogies* (1969c), a compilation of census data taken by Strehlow during his time as a Patrol Officer, as well as genealogies collected from his informants. Pointing to the documents as I sat in my car at the front of the Ti Tree store, Don Presley inquired "*Nthakenh. Pepe nhenh iwenheh?*" (What's happening? What is that document there?). We laid out the genealogies on the bonnet of the car, and on finding reference to his father, Don called over his wife and a younger woman. As people passed by us on their way to the store, more and more people began to

---

5. Strehlow to Hartwig July 29, 1965. Strehlow Research Centre.

congregate. Don read the documents aloud to a growing crowd. Although he struggled with what he called Strehlow's "German spelling" of Arandic terms, Don, another man keenly interested in these records, experimented with the text. Trying out various pronunciations for various words and phrases, they would at times add suffixes and prefixes to Strehlow's strictly Arandic text to see if the words might be more familiar in the neighboring Warlpiri language (e.g., the Anmatyerr word for emu, *ankerr* is *yankirri* in Warlpiri). This was done until an agreed-on interpretation of site names or Dreaming ancestors was found.

On almost every occasion, the group would at first express collective puzzlement over a person's listed *aknganentye*, before launching into intricate discussions about how particular people could be associated with the listed place or totem. The most senior people, who often personally knew many of the older generations listed on these family trees, were of course the quickest to realize that Strehlow had recorded non-patrilineal associations. As an example, the genealogy of Ingkaparleparl's killer, Jamatjitana, which described him as being "from" Puturlu (Mt. Theo) was immediately recognized by Paddy Kemarr as signifying what he knew was this man's *menh-menh*, mother's mother's "country." Indeed, on most occasions people attributed the *aknganenty* to a person's *kwertengerl* (ritual assistant) responsibilities or their "mother's country."

When Malcolm read his own family's genealogy, he similarly noted that the *aknganenty* and place listed for his older sister rang true with what she had been told by her parents about her conception:

> She told me that she was born . . . no, not born—*anganek*—at Mer Ywerternt [Laughton's Lagoon, near Aileron]. It happens before you turn up [before you are born, i.e., conceived]. She is *kwaty-ke-kartey* [belonging to the rain Dreaming] and she was given the nickname *ampelyerrk*. I thought *ampelyerrk* just meant a "newborn baby," but she told me that it also means "the small cloud that you see before rain."

As these genealogies were "worked through" with senior people, fuller biographies of the individuals listed would often emerge. Going well beyond the minimalist, data-focused records produced by Strehlow, people interspersed their analyses with memories of individual personalities, the stations they worked on, the places they traveled to, the type of work they did and, of course, their familial relationships to contemporary generations.

As others have pointed out (cf. Ong, 1988, p. 97; Rigsby, 1998, p. 108), the original statements made by informants about genealogies in oral societies are generally couched in "narrative terms" and are very rarely conceptualized in the itemized, tabulated, or fixed forms of the ethnographer. Having them re-read by contemporary descendants was thus a means of reinserting this orality and narrativity.

Discussing the aforementioned Bob Malpangk's genealogy, Paddy Kemarr again became insistent about patrilineal associations. He wanted to make it clear that Bob was first and foremost "*ahakey-ke-artwey*" (an owner of the native currant or bush plum, *Psydrax latifolia* Dreaming) "from" his father's father's country of Aleyaw (Ti Tree Township). Paddy explained that Bob Malpangk's father had been Ntapwet Ngal, a man briefly referenced in Strehlow's published work (1970b, p. 117) and now regarded as an important ancestor for the Ti Tree township area. Gesturing to our north, he pointed out a tall ghost gum tree (*pwernengk*) that embodied the "seed" of "Old Ntapwet" located between the Ti Tree Roadhouse Pub, and the local Shire office.

> That big tree standing there, that white tree, *pwernengk*, that's the "*seed*" for that Ntapwet. That's *ahakey* [the bush plum]. *Ahakey* travelling west. . . . There, look. Right along from the pub. Right along from that roadhouse. Big one. Olden time.

Wanting me to see "Old Ntapwet standing up," we drove over to the site, only a short distance away (figure 7.2). The ghost gum tree embodied the spirit of the person and the *ahakey* ancestor simultaneously. All those descendent from them participated in the same essence. But it was Paddy's use of the English word "seed" and not "*aknganenty*" to describe this concept that appeared significant to me. As the Anmatyerr words for spiritual conception—*anngirrenty* or *alkngirrenty*—have at their root the Anmatyerr term for "seed" (or eye)—"*annga*" or *alknga*—I assumed that he was specifically referring to Ntapwet's conception Dreaming. But since Paddy had previously described Kwetyaney as being the "right seed" for Warlapanpa, his patrilineal country, it seemed that this was an erroneous assumption on my part. Paddy used "seed" to refer to one's patrilineal inheritance.

It appears that the tradition of conception is in noticeable decline and will make the reading of these genealogies doubly difficult for future generations. At the moment, there are men and women who understand and

Figure 7.2. Paddy Kemarr at the "seed" tree of Ntapwet Ngal (photo: J. Gibson, 2014).

operate according to this tradition, but in some parts of central Australia the "ontology of conception," "reincarnation," or 'spiritual conception," as Austin-Broos variously refers to it, is almost totally gone. The "forces of inheritance," mostly along patrifilial lines, are taking on greater precedence (2009, p. 117). The principal reasons for this "ontological shift" have been the rise of monotheism/Christianity and the influence of pastoralism (with its highlighting of property/landowning rights), but also the way in which sedentary life has resulted in large numbers of children being conceived at a single location (community). The only way to maintain diversification, when large groups of children share the same site of conception and birth, is therefore to emphasize their inherited associations.

When gathering genealogies from his informants at Napperby (Leramba) in 1968, Strehlow was told that the "anmatjera children" from here usually "inherited their *father's totemic centres and their traditions*"

(1968a, p. 66). Although he believed that this information was "rather doubtful," as he was looking for the "older," "more traditional" emphasis on spiritual conception, to his credit he resisted the temptation to "tidy up" what he had been told. The genealogies were, "after all," he admitted:

> the property of the heirs that figure in them; and what they know—or believe to know—must take precedence over the doubts and theories of the person who collects" F.T.s [family trees]. (Strehlow, 1968a, p. 66)

Armed with their own in-depth knowledge of *Anengkerr*, family, and social history, these "heirs" are now ready and willing to make sense of this genealogical archive. Their interpretation is not straightforward, but like other ethnographic sources, when read socially among senior men and women and with careful explanation of their theoretical context, they can be important resources in the emergence of intimate histories.

The text-based records created by ethnographers are particularly significant sites in which the tensions between oral and print cultures play out for Indigenous groups. Dense ethnographic works, like Strehlow's, certainly have the propensity to "textualize" oral cultures by taking unwritten oral narratives, beliefs, or traditions and repositioning them as objectified assemblages of text (Célestin, 1996, p. 11). Whether it be genealogies or social histories, these texts create new learning contexts (Goody, 2010b, p. 153; see chapter 8) and challenge word-of-mouth communication between kin, and across generations. But Anmatyerr people generally come to this material ready to apply their own interpretative lens. They bring their local and orally communicated social memories, complete with the challenges of changing ontological frameworks and ideas about connection to land and Dreaming. People make sense of these documents on their own terms.

An important part of this process for Anmatyerr people was taking these texts back to the locales to which they referred. *Mer* (country) for Anmatyerr people is a highly local, social reality saturated in memories of deaths, births, conflict, peace, journeying, generations of families, and the disruptions of colonial history. As the processes of living and moving through *mer* revealed, these places did not simply "gather" meanings but, as Casey has put it, "beckoned" to its inhabitants to assemble and make meaning (Casey, 1996, p. 25; see also Myers, 1997). Situated in this way, Strehlow's textual archive was actively intermingled with the geo-mythologies, memories, and the noumenal forces of *Anengkerr*. I contend therefore that we move away from the notion that access to this material will necessarily negatively "impact" upon the "consciousness" of readers in oral societies, or act "as a new form of objectified authority" (Wilmot and Morgan, 2010, p. 1). Far from being authoritative, Strehlow's genealogies, maps, and diary extracts were often subsumed and reinterpreted within relational modes of historical practice and individual experience.

Chapter 8

"You're My *Kwertengerl*"

> The museum literally takes the world apart at its joints, collects the pieces, and holds them in suspension. Identified, classified, and arranged, objects withdrawn from the world and released into the museum are held in a space of infinite recombination . . . the museum puts people and things into a relationship quite unlike anything encountered in the world outside
>
> —Kirshenblatt-Gimblett 2004

When regarded as an ensemble of distinct archival types and housed in spaces withdrawn from the "world outside," the ethnographic museum collections might easily be described as above. The objects and information contained within these collections become disconnected, fragmented, and removed; in this case the ritual lifeworlds of Central Australian Aboriginal people are metaphorically taken apart at the "joints."

The Strehlow Research Centre, at least for some, has come to represent these reifying effects of museums in general:

> At the Strehlow Research Centre in Alice Springs, you descend a ramp into a subdued room. The lights are dim. There is a febrile intoning over an invisible speaker system, faking a spooky sense of the spiritual. But there is no evidence of human activity here. Only lifeless objects stripped of their contexts and reinstated in the reverential space of "art." (Jackson, 1995, p. 171)

Since these observations, though, there have been other engagements with this collection beyond its "objects" and outside the cold world of the museum "store." The museum context has undoubtedly put people and things into a relationship quite unlike anything encountered before, but there is certainly no absence of "human activity." Within this very same storeroom, numerous Aboriginal men have now sung, recounted stories, and interacted with their objects collected by T.G.H. Strehlow. In the upstairs offices, people visit the center to hear recordings and watch the ceremonial films of their fathers and grandfathers.

Over the last twenty years, the Strehlow Research Centre has come a long way amidst the general push toward greater Indigenous participation in the curation and management of ethnographic collections in Australia and other settler-colonial states (Hendry, 2005; Stanley, 2007a; Lonetree, 2012). In these settings, many museums have looked to develop "indigenous museological approaches drawing on local indigenous traditions, skills and forms of knowledge, which may complement mainstream, standardized, museum practices" (Varutti, 2013, p. 72).

At the time of writing, there are three representatives on the Strehlow Research Centre Board from the local Central Australian Aboriginal community, a number of initiated Arrernte men have been employed to work on the collection, and the *Strehlow Research Centre Act 1988* was amended in 2005 to allow for the repatriation of artefacts to occur. Yet, despite these advances, there is still, as anthropologist John Morton puts it, "unfinished business" when it comes to "putting the whole of the Strehlow Collection back where it belongs, in the hands of Aboriginal people" (Morton, n.d.). While it would be hard to disagree with these remarks on moral or political grounds, this chapter interrogates the complications of these issues in reality. How would this work in practice?

At the center of these discussions are a number of fundamental questions about how the collection might be utilized by present and future generations. What role might Central Australian Aboriginal men play in the process of managing and caring for this unique body of predominantly restricted material? Given the absolutely authoritative and in-depth responses to this material given by Anmatyerr men in the previous chapters, it seems fitting to now turn to their views on how the collection should be handled into the future.

The principal debates and issues surrounding the prospects of repatriation, Indigenous control, and management of museum collections are discussed with direct reference to how the Anmatyerr responded to these issues and opportunities. The description has been assembled by me in dialogue with Anmatyerr (and Arrernte) people, and in the course of a number of actual repatriation endeavors. Out of these experiences has emerged an appreciation that repatriation is more complex and nuanced than the conventional discourses surrounding the role of museums might suggest. The typical argument is that repatriation, meaning the return of objects pertaining to an Indigenous group, might go some way to correcting some of the past wrongs of colonialism. As one former Director of the Strehlow Research Centre noted, the sacred *tywerrenge* objects of Central Australian men simply "don't belong in museums" and ought to be returned to the traditional owners (Mitchell, 2012). Exactly what this "return" might look like, what effect it might have on those receiving the objects, and the variance in opinions among Indigenous groups are, however, far more difficult issues to address.

Suggesting that the primary interest of collecting institutions should be to ultimately empty their stores of Indigenous collections is short-sighted. This is not to say that the return of cultural heritage to Indigenous communities is not required or desired. Indeed, the process of dialogue and exchange that surrounds these negotiations has led to "mutually beneficial and restorative" outcomes for all involved (Jessiman, 2011). Going beyond the well-intentioned rhetoric, many Indigenous groups across the world now look for ways of engaging with collecting institutions (Chaat Smith, 2007; Stanley, 2007b) and call for greater recognition of the fact that these collections are inherently entangled. Others point to the "pragmatism" and "hope" demonstrated by many Indigenous elders, museum curators, and cultural-resource managers across the world (Brown, 2003, p. 252) who not only maintain a stand against cultural exploitation and insensitivity, but acknowledge the importance of intercultural, cooperation, dialogue, and negotiation.

Strehlow's Collection?

Exactly what T.G.H. Strehlow had in mind for the future of his collection is hard to determine. His writings on this topic reveal confused and contradictory ideas. On the one hand he promoted the interests of Central Australian Aboriginal people as "heirs" to their own heritage, and praised young men like Ken Tilmouth as being "future guardians" of their traditions (Strehlow, 1965d, p. 17). At the same time, though, he derided the general abilities of the younger generations to properly understand and care for this material, claiming they "would not carry on, or even value, the traditions of their fathers" and that "there were no worthy dark heirs" (Strehlow, 1968a, p. 40). He remained largely silent on the topic of *future* Aboriginal uses of the collection.

Amassing a large and intricate collection of material culture, audio, visual, and textual materials was never at the forefront of Strehlow's mind when he began his research in 1932. Many of the early objects he collected were sold to museums and private collectors (see Leo, 2008, p. 94; Rowse, 1999), suggesting that he originally had no intention of making a large collection of material culture. Strehlow was well aware that his father, and others at the Hermannsburg Mission, had been collecting and selling artefacts to museums and private collectors since the late nineteenth century, but this was not part of his plan. He initially focused on gathering texts, and any objects gathered were traded on.[1]

Over time, however, his private collection of ritual paraphernalia, including ceremonial poles, head dresses, and other ceremonial props, as well as wooden and stone sacred objects (*tywerreng*), became critical to his practice (Strehlow, 1978c, p. 6). In the final six years of his life, Strehlow and his second wife, Kathleen, worked toward the establishment of a kind of hagiographical monument to his work, the Strehlow Research Foundation. This was to be the place where all of his collection could be stored but also where the unfinished business of transcribing his field diaries and matching his song recordings and films could be carried out. Seeing himself as the "sole inheritor" of the ceremonies, songs, and objects he had recorded and amassed, he envisaged that Kathleen, and their son Carl, were to be the future "heirs" (Hill, 2003, p. 735; Smith, 2009, pp. 83–85; Morton, 1993, p. 38). Although the idea of establishing some kind of access to the collection for Aboriginal people in Alice Springs and Hermannsburg was initially discussed (Hill, 2003, p. 734), planning went no further than this.

Aboriginal relationships with ethnographic collections (and particularly the question of access to sacred objects) had already been a topic of conversation in Central Australia for a number of years prior to the establishment of the Foundation. Ken Tilmouth's father, Mick Werlaty, had previously discussed the idea of creating a "sacred storehouse" with

---

1. For example, see items X051378 and X051359 "obtained from T.G.H. Strehlow in September of 1937" in the Harry Rainy Balfour collection at Museum Victoria.

the Reverend Paul Albrecht in the late 1960s (Strehlow, 1968a, p. 41), and by the early 1970s a "Men's Museum" had been established at the Yuendumu community in order to house Warlpiri and Anmatyerr sacred items (Carmichael and Kohen, 2013; Campbell and Scott, 2006, pp. 26–28). The Strehlow Research Foundation, though, was intended to be something quite different. It would be located in Adelaide, 1,500 kilometers away from Central Australia, and its primary purpose would be to translate and then publish the entirety of the collected song texts (Hill, 2003, pp. 734, 751; see also Strehlow, 1978c, p. 7).

The future of the corpus would more likely resemble the great collections of antiquity that Strehlow so admired at the British Museum. It was envisaged that his materials would one day be used as aesthetic and intellectual inspiration in the development of national cultural identity. Favoring the well-established and founding discourses around museum collections that pitched ethnographic collections as part of an international cultural commons (Geismar, 2015; Bennett, 2013), Strehlow did not embrace the emergent notion of "cultural heritage" being promoted by organizations such as the United Nations Educational, Scientific and Cultural Organization (UNESCO) in the 1970s. According to this view, ethnographic collections were the legacy of a particular group or society and therefore carried direct relevance to their future generations (Roy, 2015). Convincing himself that the traditions he had recorded now "lived on only" in his "pictures and records" (Strehlow, 1978c, p. 8), Strehlow viewed his collection as being important to a common human history. The authenticity and value of his collection was also premised on his authority as a collector and expert on the subject of the ethnographic "Other" (Clifford, 1988, p. 233).

When Strehlow died suddenly of a heart attack, only hours before the launch of an exhibition celebrating his life's work, the fate of the collection became precarious. At the request of Strehlow's wife, Kathleen, proceedings continued and the exhibition was launched on the evening of his death. Ronald Berndt, one of Strehlow's few supporters within anthropology, delivered an address noting the extraordinary contribution that Strehlow had made (Kirby, 1978, p. 2), but was later more critical of his old friend for not having properly acknowledged the importance of the collection to present and future generations of Central Australian peoples (Berndt, 1978; 1979b; 1979a). The Strehlow Research Foundation soon became the property of Kathleen, and all of the materials remained with her in Adelaide.

Allegations soon emerged that the collection was in danger of being broken up and sold overseas (Hugo, 1997). With the passing of the *Aboriginal and Torres Strait Islander Heritage (Interim Protection) Act 1984*, which gave the Federal Government of Australia amplified powers to protect Aboriginal heritage, particularly in relation to sacred sites and sacred objects, the Foundation apparently panicked. The collection was allegedly secretly relocated to New Zealand, or some other possible overseas location, while others claimed that the collection never actually left Australian shores. Wenten Rubuntja, the son of Bob Rubuntja, Strehlow's key collaborator in the 1950s, was reported as saying in the local press that the collection "should not be scattered or allowed to be desecrated," and it was clear that Central Australian men wanted a say in setting the conditions of use and access to the materials (quoted in Hill, 2003, p. 733). There was also concern that the collection was being "wasted," perhaps even placed in danger, while in the hands of a person without any cultural authority or academic expertise (Morton, n.d.). Having a woman preside over men's *tywerreng* was also highly offensive.

Following years of protracted negotiations, which involved considerable but "mysterious" sums of money being paid to Kathleen Strehlow (Smith, 2009, p. 88), the Northern Territory Government eventually established the Strehlow Research Centre in 1988. The Centre opened its doors as a research repository, conjoined to the Museum of Central Australia, in 1991 (O'Byrne, 1993; Schulz, 1992), and although the collection now resided in Central Australia questions remained over Aboriginal access. Protesters gathered on opening day, doubting the value of a repository that did not encourage Aboriginal participation or allow for the repatriation of objects (Anonymous, 1991; Cohen, 2015, p. 93). The Centre was seen by many as a sterile, disempowering institution, removed from local Aboriginal concerns.

"Beautiful" Yet "Dangerous"

The last fifteen years have seen a shift in the way the Strehlow collection is perceived. Those Arrernte people who have had the opportunity to engage deeply with the collection tend to speak generously about its contents and the "extraordinary achievement" of its principal maker (Perkins, 2016). Shaun Angeles, an initiated Northern Arrernte man who has been working on cataloguing the secret-sacred film collection at the Centre for a number of years, sees the collection as a "beautiful body of knowledge" (2016). In Shaun's estimation, while Strehlow was undoubtedly "an amazing man," it is the "*akngerrepate*" (senior men) who worked alongside him as "co-creators" who provide contemporary inspiration. The time has come, Shaun argues, for the Strehlow Research Centre to work hand-in-glove with the *akngerrepate* again:

> It is important for us to work very closely with our Elders to realise the collection's true potential. We have to include our elders throughout every process as they are the ones—and the only ones I might add—who understand its content and are able to enrich it and enrich the lives of our young men who are coming through the ranks. Our elders were left out of the collection for so long, so now we have a perfect opportunity to rewrite this bit of history and involve them with everything we do. We need to find innovative cultural ways to unlock this potential. (Angeles, 2016)

Given the highly restricted nature of the majority of the content, unlocking this potential is fraught with difficulty. The collection is both "beautiful" and "dangerous." The Strehlow Research Centre itself is both a physical reminder of forward-thinking cultural exchange and of cultural dispossession. In the main, though, it is seen as a container of highly "dangerous," "*tikeley*" (of great sensitivity) material, and a place that needs to be approached with great care. The Centre and its contents are known by Arrernte people as being *amek-amek*, meaning a place associated with "sacredness" that must be "secured against violation or infringement." Such references draw obvious analogies with "restricted" places on traditional lands, which are "off limits" to the uninitiated, women, and children and are commonly known as "sacred sites" (Biernoff, 1978). As one Northern Arrernte elder expressed it, because the Strehlow Research Centre was known by everyone in the local Aboriginal community as "*amek-amek anthwerr*" (a highly restricted place), it was regarded by many men as the most suitable institution in Alice Springs to hold restricted cultural collections.

Many men therefore look upon any female staff or Aboriginal women visiting the Centre with a degree of wariness. While they generally do not suspect that anyone is trying to illicitly gain access to male ritual knowledge, they do nevertheless worry that women may be unintentionally exposed to it. They might stumble upon a photograph, walk into a room where films are being played, or accidentally read descriptions of restricted songs or ceremonies. Arrernte women are doubly aware of these protocols of gender segregation, and although their visitation is less common and cautious, they will come in to the Centre to access family genealogies (see Malbunka, 2004) and "open" (non-ceremonial) photographs of their male kin (cf. Wallace and Lovell, 2009). But on the whole, most Arrernte women refrain from visiting the building. Just as Strehlow's publications are understood as being "closed" to them (Perkins, 2016), so too the Strehlow Research Centre and its surrounds are to be approached with caution. In order to reduce the chance of being exposed to "men's business," or being accused of attempting to do so, some Arrernt women will send in *alhernter* (non-Aboriginal) friends or other family members on their behalf to request materials.

Because the Centre holds *tywerrenge* (sacred objects) from all over the region, its concentration of *amek-amek* material makes it a potentially volatile place. It is for these reasons that Anmatyerr and Arrernte people tend to see this location as an unusually powerful place: a confluence of *Anengkerr* (Dreaming) vitality from across the region, but also a site where "lost" objects congregate and linger. Like when visiting sacred sites in the landscape, younger men are encouraged to avoid the building unless they are chaperoned by knowledgeable elders. When intending to access ceremonial recordings or objects they will often bring with them the rightful *merek-artwey* ("owners") and *kwertengerl* ("managers"). Centre staff will also request that these cultural protocols are upheld.

The Logic of Repatriation

In 2005, the *Strehlow Research Centre Act* was amended to allow for the repatriation of "objects," defined in extremely broad terms as "artefacts, notes, diaries, records, films, publications and sound recordings" to their "traditional owners."[2] Since the 1980s and 1990s, museums in settler states such as Australia, the United States, and Canada have increasingly developed policies aimed at advancing the return of both human remains and secret-sacred objects to Indigenous groups (Bray, 1996; 2001; Fine-Dare, 2002). In the United States, the Native American Graves Protection and

---

2. See www.legislation.nt.gov.au/en/Legislation/Strehlow-RESEARCH-CENTRE-ACT

Repatriation Act (NAGPRA) of 1990, provided a framework for this to occur (Brown, 2003, pp. 17–18; Nash and Colwell-Chanthaphonh, 2010). In Australia, the Commonwealth Government's Policy on Indigenous Repatriation supports similar objectives (Australian Government, 2013, pp. 5, 7). Once the great accumulators of ethnographica for museums (Peterson, Allen, and Hamby, 2008b), museum curators and anthropologists are now increasingly tasked with the job of "de-collecting," taking objects back to the sites where they were originally collected (Anderson, 1995a; Turnbull and Pickering 2010). It is in this changed policy context that Anmatyerr and Arrernte today now deal with the Strehlow Research Centre, other museums, and their staff.

The complexities involved in the repatriation of objects first occurred to me when Donald Campbell Peltharr, an elderly Anmatyerr man with considerable cultural knowledge, visited me at the Strehlow Research Centre in 2006. Two younger men whom I knew well had asked Donald to accompany them to the Centre. They knew of the ritually charged material contained within the Centre and understandably did not feel comfortable being in the place without a senior man present. When Don arrived, I began to explain the nature of the Strehlow Research Centre and its collections. Soon after, Don asked if I could help him locate an object he knew had been "missing" from a site near Napperby Station for many years. Staff from the Centre were immediately called in and responded to Don's query by quickly searching their listings for the object that Don described. Unable to find it, the Strehlow Research Centre Director then wrote letters to the other museums on Don's behalf asking that they also search their collections. I was reminded of the alacrity of the staff of the Centre when I stumbled across one of these letters in the Melbourne Museum archives nearly a decade later.

Although this object was never "found," the process of working with Don and the museum staff started me thinking about the prospects of repatriating this type of material. Did all men want their objects back? What would they do with them once they had been returned? Were museums really comfortable with seeing these items relinquished? These were questions not peculiar to this case nor to the Central Australian context. Issues like this had hung over the relationships between museums and Indigenous communities worldwide since the notion of "cultural property" had been established in international discourse at the end of the twentieth century (Ames, 1992; Geismar, 2015). Whether it be the repatriation of the G'psgolox totem pole to the Haisla First Nations groups in Canada

(Jessiman, 2011), or the return of ancestral human remains to the Māori of New Zealand (Stumpe, 2005), negotiations between Indigenous groups and collecting institutions were notoriously complex, involving contrasting perspectives on the value of objects and their futures. For many in the museum and archaeological community, these objects represent a common, inclusive, human history that deserves transparent and objective study (Mulvaney, 1991; Allen and Murray, 1996), whereas for many Indigenous groups, these items are regarded as their personal or collective cultural property.

Since this time, I have been pulled aside by many men aware of my links to museums, asking for help in tracking down items now lost from their country. On one occasion I drove all day with a man of the Pengart subsection to the far Western edge of Anmatyerr territory so that we could visit the site where an object was once located. At this place we would feel the presence of the Ancestors. At this place we would feel the presence of the Ancestors and needed to "look after ourselves from the Ancestors of our land (*"Anwern arntarnt-arelhetyek, anwern-kenh merlalp map"*). Sadly, one of the objects that embodied these ancestors had been removed, and while most guessed that the culprit was a local pastoralist, with no evidence people felt powerless to act. This journey to Pengart's country underlined the sense of loss and subjection that people felt when this type of theft occurred. These objects were important in terms of their religious and political significance (Spencer and Gillen, 1899; Strehlow, 1947; Batty, 2014) and carried undeniable affective value to personal identity. Much like the grief that Strehlow had witnessed among Anmatyerr elders who searched in vain for stolen objects in the 1930s, Pengart felt as though he had failed in his responsibilities to care for these things for future generations.

Some, but certainly not all, of the sacred objects now residing in museum collections were undoubtedly taken via similarly illicit channels. In the case of the Strehlow collection, however, it was clear from the stories of exchange and participation described here that the vast majority had been originally sold, gifted, or traded. They had not been "removed" or "stolen" but had been acquired within the asymmetrical contact zone of the colonial frontier. Trade in these objects had been an important feature of early colonial relationships and lasted up until the 1960s and 1970s (see Anderson, 1995b; Jones, 1995a). Aboriginal men that participated in this exchange did so in order to gain access to power, better treatment, rations, foodstuffs, clothing, or cash payments. In some cases, men reportedly "made special trips by camel to fetch" objects to sell to the Lutherans at

Hermannsburg, who would in turn sell them to private collectors and museums.³ Encouraging this type of enterprise not only helped destabilize local religious beliefs and advance Christian conversion (Rowse, 1998, p. 82; Austin-Broos, 2009, pp. 69–70; Batty, 2014, pp. 306–310), but also assisted in raising much-needed funds for the mission.

Most senior Anmatyerr and Arrernte men today acknowledge this complicated history and speak of the difficult position their elders found themselves in. "A long time ago I think they sold them for tucker and tobacco, poor buggers," explained Paddy Kemarr. To Paddy, these men were simply struggling to adjust to a rapidly changing cultural, religious, and economic world. Evidence of this can be seen in Tom Lywenge's comments to Strehlow during their first fieldwork journey together in 1932 (see chapter 5). Perhaps conflicted by their decisions, many of these men appear to have failed to inform their sons of the fate of these objects.

When I revealed to the elderly Archie Mpetyan at Ti Tree that his father Friday Ankerr-raweny Ngal had sold some of his personal *tywerreng* to Strehlow, he was clearly disappointed and surprised. As I read from Strehlow's diary, Archie sat up straight to get a good look at the sketch illustrations that Strehlow had made of them. The shape and the specific iconography depicted on each object would reference particular associated *Anengkerr* (Dreaming) ancestors and sites. As he stared at the drawings, I could see he was struggling to make out the markings due to his very poor eyesight. But the information noted by Strehlow made him wonder if these were the same artifacts that his older brother had in fact been searching for in vain. "Bring him back!" Archie insisted. "My old brother was looking for him [the object]. That must be *that tywerreng* now. We've been looking for that one!" To the men who wanted their objects back, the original payments made to Strehlow were superfluous to the ongoing, continuous claims they had as senior descendants and owners. If they were returned to their owners, the objects could be brought out again at "business" and used in various aspects of the initiation ceremonies.

For others, though, asking for the return of objects that were knowingly sold or traded was inappropriate. Eric Penangk, for example, suggested that some sort of recompense ought to be made not to Anmatyerr people but to the museums that had in recent times repatriated objects. Knowing

---

3. Letter from F.W. Albrecht to A.S. Kenyon, February 7, 1934. Melbourne Museum Indigenous Cultures. Correspondence "Bunker" Archives, Box 29.

full well the unequal conditions in which his "old people" had mostly traded or sold these items to Strehlow, Kramer, and others, Eric maintained that the moral imperative was to uphold the original agreement. "They [past elders] sold them for tucker and rations. We can't ask for them back. You can't take back what you sold." In a similar tone, Chris Anderson (1995a, p. 12), a former repatriation anthropologist with the South Australian Museum, documented cases where senior men insisted on making some sort of compensation to museums for any objects returned to them.

When faced with lists of objects that museums might potentially repatriate, men like Eric understand that repatriation is not entirely about the amelioration of past injustices. In the past, men have been called together for meetings (a typically Western form of group information sharing and decision making), presented with photographs of objects, and then than asked to make identifications in a relatively short time. It is also not uncommon for the anthropologists involved, who often work in communities across linguistic regions, to be less than proficient in Anmatyerr and thus produce rather dubious pronunciations of key *anengkerr* association or place names. In scenarios like this, it is very difficult for people to dwell on the contents being presented, to share the material with others who were not present at "the meeting," and come to considered decisions. As a number of people experienced in the return of this material have acknowledged, in these circumstances it is usually the "non-Aboriginal people working in cultural institutions" who feel anxious about seeing objects returned (Galt-Smith, 2001). For these reasons, repatriation, perhaps the most undertheorized aspect of museum policy, is now being discussed as a "ritual" (Batty, 2006b; Peers, Reinius, and Shannon, 2017) that offers not just opportunities for Indigenous claimants but a partial "redemption" for settler-colonial states.

There is also an expectation that if barriers to access are removed, Indigenous people will naturally reconnect with materials kept in museum collections. Museum policies have certainly shifted in recent times to encourage this type of engagement with "source communities" (Brown and Peers, 2013) and to create exhibitions and research that is far *less* object-focused and *more* people-focused (Griffiths, 1996, pp. 95, 278–282; Edwards, Gosden, and Phillips, 2006; Hendry, 2005), but interaction with collections will come in different guises. Brett Galt-Smith, a particularly proactive former Director of the Strehlow Research Centre, had initially hoped for a type of deep engagement. When the Centre was established, however, senior men did not flood in—in fact, they stayed away (Galt-

Smith, 2001, p. 5). While Galt-Smith speculated about some of the reasons for this, he failed to consider the possibility that maintaining *distance* as well as *silence* over this material could be an entirely legitimate reaction. The expectation that Indigenous "communities" would want to have something to "say" about museum artifacts, and furthermore publicly reassert their custodianship over them, may well be a preoccupation peculiar to Western "rights" discourse, a point made by curator Liz Bonshek in her dealings with Papuan communities (2015, p. 33; see also 2008). The shift in museum policies toward greater community engagement and their attempts to focus on developing personal relationships (see Scott and Luby, 2007; Hafner, 2010; Allen, 2016) should be applauded, but room must be made for nuanced responses that might appear an anathema to these expectations.

In my experience, it is not uncommon for people to feel uneasy in museum stores, especially when invited to make statements in regard to these highly charged ritual objects. People often ask that their anonymity be protected. Afraid of being accused of prying into other people's "business," they often prefer to leave no trace of their interaction and publicly "say" little. Most men refuse to touch secret-sacred objects that do not belong to them, and on one occasion I was even asked to turn the pages of a photographic album containing images of sacred ceremonies so as to avoid the person's fingerprints being left on the object. The fingerprints, my companion advised, could be ensorcelled by the people who owned the rituals depicted in the photographs. Only where a personal or kin connection to an object can be established will people feel comfortable about physically interacting with the object or making a public utterance about it or asserting any claim.

Yet another complicating issue is that some objects in the ritual domain of Central and Northern Australian Aboriginal culture are simply too dangerous or anomalous to return to communities. This is particularly the case with head dresses and ceremonial poles in Central Australia that would normally be made for a single performance or rite and then disassembled soon after. People will often express surprise and shock at seeing ritual paraphernalia like this preserved on museum shelves, and in some cases find them so aberrant that, much to the dismay of museum curators, call for these items to be destroyed (cf. Bradley and Kearney, 2011, p. 35). Once preserved, objects meant to be inherently ephemeral and temporary take on a geographically removed and atemporal life completely at odds with their original cultural contexts (Classen and Howes, 2006, p. 215).

Being anomalous in this way, they fall outside of the usual rules of care and management for cultural objects and are difficult to work back into contemporary lives and contexts.

Ken Tilmouth's views on the objects contained in the Strehlow collection are particularly significant. Many of the thirty-two objects either gifted or sold to Strehlow during the recording of the Akwerrperl "inner cycle" in 1965 were made with Ken's assistance. Together with his father and a small number of other men, Ken produced numerous fine examples of ritual paraphernalia used in men's sacred ceremonies. Without going into the details of what these objects consist of or signify—for they are highly restricted—Ken explained that most had been replaced with "fresh ones" soon after their handing over to Strehlow in the 1960s and used in the enactment of the same ceremonies at a later date. While some objects had been offered to Strehlow because they were "old" and in need of replacing, others could simply be remade and dismantled again in accordance with local custom. The objects, stored in acid-free paper cardboard boxes and wooden crates at the Strehlow Research Centre, were a frozen-in-time exemplar of what these different types of paraphernalia looked like, as well as a testament to the interactions with Strehlow.

The idea of "giving back" this type of material does not adequately account for these many complexities. On a number of occasions, Strehlow Research Centre staff have asked Ken if he would like to see the return of objects collected via himself and his father. Ken's responses have always been both cautious and guarded. "What are you going to do?" he asked the Centre's anthropologist during a meeting at Alcoota in 2013. The very concept of "repatriation" itself needed clarification, especially as Ken had never himself requested that the materials be put in his physical possession (though he had asked for copies of the film). The option to "repatriate" was mostly presented to senior men as a positive opportunity by the Centre's staff who, of no fault of their own, had put unintentional pressure on the senior men (*angerr-pat*) to respond. Even if the "repatriation" was to occur only "on paper," meaning that they would be registered as belonging to Ken but continue to stay in the Centre's store, there was uncertainty about how recognition of his rights to the material by the Northern Territory Government would work in the long term and in a practical sense. Ken was also unsure how future generations might be affected by these decisions.

To date, Ken has reasoned that these objects should be kept at the Strehlow Research Centre. Here, these fragile items can be cared for and kept alongside all of the films, photographs, and audio recordings that documented the Akwerrperl ceremonies as they were enacted in 1965. Like the men at Napperby who had agreed that Strehlow's collecting had been conducted appropriately because he brought together suites of related songs, objects, and ceremonies, Ken reiterated the importance of keeping the collection united. His preference would be to visit the collection with his sons whenever necessary, and most importantly to ensure that their ongoing rights to the material were documented and recognized by the Centre:

> Well, we can go in there next time. We can have a look and we can tell you three [referring to myself, and two SRC staff]. We'll tell "you can look after this one," and we can put that *arreyn* [name, description], that name there [help you provenance and document the collection]. You've got a good place there you know . . . We can go around there and have a look and sort them out, see?

Given all of the complexities associated with the idea of simply repatriating Indigenous cultural materials, James Clifford is right to point out that the process of "decolonizing" collections will not be an "all or nothing, once and for all, transition" (2001, p. 473; 2013, pp. 302, 306). The entangled and intertwined histories of these collections make their reintegration and revivification in contemporary social lives inherently complex. There are signs, however, that alternative approaches to dealing with these matters are emerging among Anmatyerr and Arrernte considerations.

"You're my *kwertengerl*"

Acknowledging the aforementioned complexities and ambiguities, many senior men now tilt toward an alternative model of care and responsibility that does not necessarily demand the return of objects. This alternative is most desirable when either direct repatriation is not sought or possible, where definitive ownership cannot be ascertained, or when the knowledge needed to control powerful items exceeds the abilities of present-day ritual leaders. In these cases, most men indicate that they expect collecting institutions and their staff to care for the materials in the long term. Critically, though, the way in which this was envisioned by Anmatyerr and Arrernte men was not informed by the discourses of collecting institutions or state-sponsored repatriation initiatives, but in terms of Anmatyerr or Arrernte notions of rights, responsibilities, and care: specifically, the idea that museums should accept the responsibilities of a *kwertengerl* (ritual manager). Before I can assess what this process might entail and how it might work, a thorough definition of the term is required.

The term *kwertengerl*, and its equivalent in other Australian Aboriginal languages, has been the subject of considerable attention in the past few decades. Often translated into English as "managers," "guardians," or "offsiders" of land and ritual who work in tandem with their "owners," the idea of a *kwertengerl* denotes an important social role often found in many parts of Australia (Pink, 1936; Meggitt, 1962; Nash, 1982). For Sutton, the dual roles of the "manager" and "owner" are a "ritual based system of formalized complementary filiation" (Sutton, 2003, p. 194), whereby (using the Arandic terminology) the *kwertengerl*—who are related to the *merekartwey* (traditional owner) via their mother's and their mother's brother's country—manage, advise, and protect the ritual knowledge and sites possessed by the *merekartwey*. The *kwertengerl* thus play an important role in helping the *merek-artwey* to maintain the integrity and long-term transmission of their estate-based rituals, songs, dances, and so on. Likened to a "governance structure" by some Warlpiri people (Pawu-Kurlpurlurnu, Holmes, and Box, 2008), these complementary occupations ensure that everyone within *anpernerrenty* (the network of relatedness) has a role.

I first heard museum staff and their institutions being likened to *kwertengerl* during Ken Tilmouth's visit to the Melbourne Museum with six other Arrernte men in 2013. These men had been invited by the museum, using funding allocated by the Commonwealth government's "Indigenous Repatriation Program," to explore the large holdings of *tywerrenge* collected between the 1890s and the late 1960s. As is the case with many Australian museums now, these objects were stored in a way that mimicked the traditional sacred storehouse: kept in a separate storage area accessible to only a small number of male staff (including myself) (Anderson, 1996; Kaus, 2008; Stanley, 2007a). When the men were first introduced to the primary collection manager who cared for the objects, they immediately identified him as "our *kwertengerl*." As the curator and I were responsible for the research and community consultations relating to this material, we too were described as "*kwertengerl*," and in effect were being invited to see our professional roles through the complementary *merek-artwey/kwertengerl* dynamic.

But it was not until I visited Ken at the Alcoota (Engawala) community later that same year that I began to consider the use of this designation more seriously. As we discussed the potential of the Strehlow collection for coming generations, Ken reiterated the importance of *kwertengerl* in maintaining the complexity and reciprocal fundaments of these traditions. Pointing directly at me as I wrote down his thoughts on ownership and rights, he tried to explain the expanded cultural responsibilities of everyone now working with these collections. "You're my *kwertengerl* again. You write this one [with pen and paper]. You make 'em *arraty-ilem* [accurate/ truthful documentation]." Turning to Adam MacFie, the anthropologist working for the Strehlow Research Centre at the time, Ken reiterated his position. "You're my *kwertengerl* too. Same. Your hand does this one [making writing motion/gesture] on this one . . . paper . . . paper-one . . . That's *kwertengerl* now. They do it that way. *Alakenh* [that is how it is done]."

The inference was clear. Adam and I (or, indeed, anyone else in comparable positions) were to act in a similar way to Ken's *kwertengerl* in the ritual setting. By writing down what Ken as the *merekartwey* had to say about the collections, and upholding his rights in the objects (but also the associated audio and film recordings), we would be honoring his social and cultural status. The act of writing, too, it must be added, has parallels with one of the key responsibilities of *kwertengerl*—the art of decorating, often referred to as "painting up" the *merek-artwey* prior to the enactment of a performance and helping to construct ritual objects (Pink 1936, p. 302). In order to do this, *kwertengerl* must have knowledge of the designs and other aspects of these rituals so they can properly oversee the custodianship of the traditions. By sharing in this knowledge, they uphold an "owner's" rights over it.

Assimilated into these local frameworks of social relatedness, museums and their staff were often regarded as "working for" Anmatyerr people. Similar to what Myers observed in Pintupi sentiments toward Western forms of authority being responsible for "looking after" or "caring for" Aboriginal people and their interests (1980; 1991, pp. 283–284), the Anmatyerr expect the same from collecting institutions. I had this pointed out to me by a group of senior men at Napperby after playing them recordings of some restricted songs associated with highly secretive aspects of male initiation. It was a dark, still night, and the glow from the firelight only partially revealed people's facial expressions, but as the songs played I could hear the men talking quietly among themselves about how many of these songs should never have been recorded. I asked what should be done with these recordings. "Burn them," one of the old men replied. "Give them to a *warlparl* [whitefella] to look after. Aboriginal people in town can't be trusted with these things. They're too dangerous."

In addition to challenging the discourses of cultural preservation (as mentioned above), these statements run counter to the idea of Indigenous *self-determination*. In its place was a notion that all of the managers (the *kwertengerl-map*) who "work for" Anmatyerr people would fulfill their role in protecting the rights of senior ritual experts. Some Arrernte men have even gone as far as suggesting that museum staff be issued with official "*Kwertengerl*" identification badges so that their role in communities is properly defined!

If one applies the logic of complementary filiation to the management of the Strehlow collection, then the community of ritual "owners" for the collection are undoubtedly the particular *merek-artwey*, while the collecting institution(s) and their staff become the quasi-*kwertengerl*. I describe this as quasi-*kwertengerl* because it would be folly to take these suggestions too literally. An institution, composed of men and women mostly unrelated to these Aboriginal communities, can never operate as the genuine *kwertengerl* themselves. The metaphor is worth pursuing, though, for even where "misunderstandings" or "misinterpretations" may occur, these types of interactions can nonetheless cultivate a useful space of new cultural production in cross-social and cross-political contexts. As White's theorization of the "middle ground" posits, this is not necessarily "acculturation" or "compromise," but a process whereby people adjust their differences through a process of creative, and often expedient, misunderstandings and misinterpretations (see Deloria, 2006, p. 16). Writing of similar "disjunctive spaces" between different interpretative communities and their approaches to museum collections, Morphy (2010a, p. 281) similarly suggests that new ways of caring for these collections may be emergent.

As challenging as it may be for *alhernter* individuals and institutions to satisfy local Aboriginal governance and epistemological frameworks, the expectation that they will at least make the attempt persists. Writing about the "intellectual toughness" of Aboriginal people "steeped in the classical traditions," Sutton correctly points out that most will expect scholars working in their domain to uphold the integrity of these traditions (2010, p. 81). But what would it really mean then for the Strehlow Research Centre, or any other collecting institution, to take on a *kwertengerl* role? The relationship between the *kwertengerl* and the *merek-artwey* is fundamentally a reciprocal one centered on "ritual co-operation," so if taken seriously neither the *merek-artwey* (the ritual owner or community of owners) nor the *kwertengerl* (in this case, the collecting institution) would predominate. As the *kwertengerl/merek-artwey* system works to integrate and bind together the two groups in accordance with their distinct roles and responsibilities (Pink, 1936, p. 300), both would have to share in the responsibilities of caring for the tangible and intangible cultural material contained in these collections. In the context of managing ethnographic collections, "ownership" would need to unequivocally remain with the *merek-artwey*, while the collecting institutions, anthropologists, or museum specialists would have to act as *kwertengerl* by caring for ceremonial knowledge, artifacts, and recordings. Perhaps with the addition of some specific items being returned to "owners," this model comes close to what many Anmatyerr men expect to see from the Strehlow Research Centre and other museums today.

"We Still Working"

It is the ongoing ritual lives of individuals, outside of any dealings with collecting institutions, that takes precedence in the care of ceremonial matters. Senior ritual specialists who are *kalty anthwerr* (very knowledgeable) and confident in their ceremonial knowledge see the Strehlow and other relevant collections as ultimately peripheral to their everyday lives. These men are not in a position where they need to look to Strehlow's collection for "meaning," and make it very clear that their energies are focused squarely on *current* and *ongoing* ceremonial responsibilities. Unlike other Indigenous groups who now use archival sources to revivify song, language, or ceremonial traditions (Kahunde, 2012; Treloyn and Emberly, 2013; Thorpe and Galassi, 2014), for these older Anmatyerr men like Ken Tilmouth, the collection, while certainly edifying and important, is secondary to more immediate concerns:

> Just leave it [Strehlow's collection] there. This mob [the men of Alcoota] are alright. Everyone knows this country, our country. No worry because this mob *know* you see? All the youngfellas. We're teaching them all the time you see? We teaching them *akiw* [in the ceremonial camp for young men]. *Akiw!* They can work with us like that now.

Ken reiterated his point again during another conversation in the previous year:

> We got everything there. *Mer* [In the land]. We've got all the songs from there [the site of Akwerrperl]. I got all the songs from the bush [sites, away from the community] too, on my side anyway . . . We still *working*. Same again [as when Strehlow was here]. We still got it all. We got song and all. He's right here . . . *Artwampw map alyelhem arreyn* [The senior men sing these songs]. We got all the song here. We can *alyelhem* [sing] anyway.

Many other senior knowledge holders, while happy to receive copies of recordings if offered, reiterated that it was better if this material was kept safe in collecting institutions. "*Kele* [No], Leave it there . . . more better if you leave it there," Harold Payne commented on the films and song recordings made of his father. Like Ken, Harold continues to educate younger generations in contexts that have little or nothing to do with collecting institutions, and much of this ceremonial activity endures in social spaces now rarely observed by *alhernter*.

This is not to suggest that male ritual knowledge is not under considerable strain in Central Australia, just that sending archival recordings into these contexts will have limited effects. Tamara Bray (1996), an anthropologist working on similar issues with First Nations people in North America, makes a similar point with her assessment of repatriation and "the politics of the past." According to Bray, the idea that the return of museum artifacts will do much to help maintain cultural practices is ultimately "misguided" (1996, p. 442). Cultural identity, she argues, does not reside in either artifacts or recordings, and the preservation of these materials is often not a high priority for marginalized groups. What takes greater precedence is the upholding of the underlying relationships, social contexts, and practices that ultimately give meaning to this archival material. Moreover, the idea of simply returning cultural content (be it objects or recordings), of putting them "back in their place" in an act of cultural "restoration" (Forrest, 2012, pp. 132–223), supports an ideological view of Aboriginal culture as impervious to change.

The social forces of pastoralism, settlement, and Christianity alone in remote Aboriginal Australia have, however, produced considerable change. The return of ethnographic materials that were collected in pervious historical contexts therefore need to proceed in ways that are very much aware of contemporary assumptions. "Acting as if nothing had happened," Jean Baudrillard warns of repatriation endeavors, is a type of "subterfuge" or "retrospective hallucination" where the complicated past is "effaced" (1994, p. 11). Tasked with returning ceremonial objects to Aboriginal communities in Western Australia, for example, the anthropologist Kim Akerman found a remarkably changed attitude to ritual when he was told, "You Keep It—We are Christians Here" (2010). In the Anmatyerr region also, in the decades since Strehlow's recordings, people made choices about which traditions to carry on with. As discussed in chapter 6, certain genres of song and performance were sustained, some were known only to a handful of senior men, and in other cases only knowledge of the relevant sites or ancestral stories remained.

These sociocultural changes are most apparent when museums try to reintroduce materials that can no longer be definitely claimed by senior people. This scenario usually arises when items with provenance to sites or estates that no longer have contemporary senior knowledge holders are discussed. While the presentation of this material might spur significant interest, ultimately Anmatyerr people appear to be focused on what is currently in social circulation and being actively performed. A number of the ceremonies and songs recorded by Strehlow, for example, relate to places (estates) that no longer have active ceremonial leaders. When discussing the prospect of returning film and song recordings from sites nearby to Aileron with Eric Penangk, he was noticeably saddened by the situation. He and his father's generation had "held" the knowledge for these places for decades, but as they were strictly not *merek-artwey*, he felt very uncomfortable with the idea of receiving responsibility for objects or recordings from the area:

> They're all gone! *Merekartwey ityakwet* [There are no owners left]. You can't see [any] young generation. Their father's, their mother's all bin finished [have died] in Alice Springs somewhere. They never turned back to country . . . No one is alive for that country. Everybody's been going that way [to Alice Springs] and they finished-up [died] somewhere there.

Although some of the mythologies and sites relating to these recordings or objects were well known to people associated with these areas, an absence of senior experts who "belonged to these places" has effectively created what Deborah Bird Rose (2004, pp. 34–52) has described as a "wounded space" both in terms of landscape and social fabric. Though these "wounds" can sometimes be mended by expert *kwertengerl* and others who assume responsibility and care for certain traditions (see Young, 1987; Morton, 1997, p. 114; Sutton, 1995, p. 151), for most Anmatyerr men the preference is to remain focused on nourishing practices and performances that remain central to present-day ceremonial responsibilities.

Teaching with "Content"

This is not to say that the revivification of traditions from archival material is a completely repudiated idea. On the contrary, there is growing interest, particularly among younger generations of men, in utilizing every resource available to them in order to fill gaps in their learning. Men aged in their thirties, for example, who in addition to having been initiated and educated by elders, are equally eager to retrieve whatever additional material they can, including archival song recordings, films, and ethnographic texts, to help augment their learning. The changed nature of Indigenous social life, including its "darker side"—alcoholism, unemployment, incarceration, domestic violence, and declining health conditions (Starn, 2011)—has undoubtedly led to declined opportunities for the teaching and learning of song and ceremony among people of Central Australia. Exactly what the Strehlow collection might actually offer future generations, and how it might be used to educate younger men in ritual performance, is difficult to predict.

Despite the confidence and authority exhibited by some senior men in regard to song and ceremony, there nevertheless remains an anxiety for many others. The anxiety is felt by both young and old. The elders feel both the responsibility of teaching younger generations and the pressure of younger men wanting to learn. The younger people, too, feel apprehensive, not only about the frailty and small numbers of their senior people, but about their abilities to carry on these traditions. This type of anxiety appears to plague every generation, and even senior men with considerable knowledge, such as Eric Penangk (now in his eighties), comment on the absence of "strong leaders" like they knew in their youth. What both generations admit is that as fascinating and edifying as Strehlow's collection may be, its contents can never replace the performativity and tacit knowledge at the heart of song and ceremony. As Bradley, an anthropologist who has devoted decades to seeing his own in-depth documentation of language, song, and myth returned to its relevant communities (Yanyuwa families, Bradley, and Cameron, 2003; Bradley and Yanyuwa Families, 2010; Kearney et al., 2012) has noted, this type of content can only ever act as an "aspirational motivator" (2011, p. 9) and its effects will be determined by larger social factors.

It was precisely these issues, and the way that future generations could potentially misuse this material, that occupied Malcolm Heffernan Pengart's mind during one of our trips on Anmatyerr country together. Malcolm and I had just set up our camp in the dry creek bed at Queensland Gully (Mer Atwelengkw), an old stockmen's camp under the shadow of Central Mount Stuart (Amakweng), when we started discussing the songs that his uncle Charlie Artetyerwenguny had recorded with Strehlow in the 1960s. Reclining on his swag, Malcolm was in a reflective mood and began talking about his childhood. He remembered the way that old men such as the Rice brothers (Freddie and Willie) and Tim "Cowboy" Riley used to "sing lots of different country lines" during the early morning. They would do this with young men like Malcolm sleeping close by at the *arnkenty* (single men's camp). "I was only twelve or thirteen at the time. Before my *apwelh* [circumcision ceremony]. The singing would begin in the morning, before the sun had come up, *aherlkenty-aherlkenty* [pre-dawn]. They would end when the sun was just up." At the time, Malcolm resented being woken so early, but he realizes now that this had been the manner in which he had acquired song knowledge and it was thus their way of trying to teach him in spite of changed social rhythms found on settlements.

Learning songs from recordings made by Strehlow, however, was a very different proposition. It was clear to Malcolm that men like his uncle were aware of the changes that were taking place in Anmatyerr and Arrernte society in the mid to late twentieth century. Younger generations were increasingly being brought into Western educational contexts and missing out on a particular style of learning that had been modeled by past generations. One of the reasons Malcolm resented being woken by the old men was that the interruption caused him to go back to sleep and consequently be late for school at the Santa Teresa Mission. His uncle's recordings with Strehlow, then, in Malcolm's view, were a "good" or "safe" option of preserving material that, if in the hands of those not properly educated in men's Law, could potentially be very "dangerous."

As ceremonial material was potent and mercurial, it could only ever be properly understood when its context, significations, and linkages were explained and governed by senior ritual specialists.

In Malcolm's view, the older men had been mindful of the social changes occurring around them and had used their time with Strehlow as an opportunity to free themselves of a burden. "I think that's why they were trying to get rid of it." They wanted the recordings put in "a safer place . . . they told Strehlow that it was sacred, and they wanted to get it locked away somewhere." At the time of our conversations, rumors were circulating that some Arrernte men were accessing the collection as a way to attain ritual knowledge and using it for malevolent ends. These stories made many men extremely anxious.

To my knowledge, the Strehlow collection has to date never been used to revive a neglected song or ceremonial tradition. Some people can certainly see the tremendous opportunity that the collection offers in this respect, but to do this would be extremely brave given the considerable "power" embedded in these practices. More than this, though, questions persist about exactly how the performative, linguistic, and other deeply affective aspects of practice can be taught via mediated content. These questions are often asked by those working on projects aimed at assisting the "intergenerational transfer" of "knowledge" in remote Aboriginal communities (see Holcombe, 2009; Verran et al., 2007; Christie, 2005). Crucially, most agree that "knowledge" is fundamentally inseparable from its instantiation in practice, not something that can be parceled and delivered to subjects in a mediated form.

The concept of "tradition" is equally bound to its reproduction in these contexts. As folklorist Barry McDonald (1997) has argued, traditions are based in *personal relationships, shared practices,* and a commitment to the endurance of *both*. In order to learn the complex interrelations between totemic geography, song, body paint, and more, one must not only *listen* carefully and *observe* patiently but also allow the cumulative effect of *being-with others* to enable *knowing* (Jackson, 1998, pp. 180–181). As indicated by the significance of spatiality (journeying and being in place) and interpreting (via oral memory and other means) described in chapters 6 and 7, the continuance of a tradition rests on the ability to *socialize* the next generation of learners so they can identify these relationships (Myers, 1997, p. 109). Malcolm fears that where these underlying factors and commitments are absent, the "unlocking" of the Strehlow collection will be fraught.

Tin Boxes and Digital Files

Indigenous communities across Australia and the globe now find themselves in a position whereby collections are being returned to them at a steady rate. Not only are collections being made more and more accessible via the ubiquity of digital technologies (Devlin-Glass, 2002; Glowczewski, 2005; Gibson and Batty, 2014), but contemporary researchers are being encouraged to return their raw data to "source communities" as a part of decolonizing research methodologies (Harris, 2014, p. 8; Barwick, 2004). Database solutions have also been designed specifically to hold digitized Indigenous cultural materials for improved local access (Christen, 2005; Christie, 2005; Gibson, 2007; Dallwitz and Hughes, 2007). While the search for local technological solutions are important, there has been a dearth of ethnographic research on the existing strategies people have put in place to store, manage, and utilize repatriated or returned objects and recordings in their local communities.

In Central Australia, and particularly among Arandic speakers, the idea of ethnographers making photographic and other recordings of ceremonial material is not new. It was in the 1890s that Frank Gillen presented prints of some of the photographs of men's sacred ceremonies to his Arrernte interlocutors in Alice Springs. Being afforded a similar status to the stone and wooden *tywerreng*, these photographs were soon after secreted in a remote location and protected in a "shallow tin case" (Gillen, 2001, p. 157). Over one hundred years later, cassette tapes, DVDs, and USB flash drives are being managed in similar ways. Copies of Strehlow's films, for example, have been "buried" or stored in caves for safe keeping (Hersey and Cohen, 2004, p. 183), and I have seen "repatriated" CDs of song and archival maps of sacred sites stored alongside *tywerreng* recently repatriated from museums. Galvanized metal tool boxes, lockable and secure, are often the vault of choice for Anmatyerr men, and it is not uncommon for these mini-collections to be further hidden away in dilapidated caravans, broken-down cars, or the homes of senior men.

Over time, though, these boxes and their contents become dirty, dusty, and worn in the extreme desert climate. In the winter the boxes reach freezing point and, in the summer, they boil. Museum curators and archivists everywhere would be aghast. But without adequate storage infrastructure and conservation skills in these very remote and small communities, it is likely objects will be kept in this grassroots way for many years to come. More important, though, as much as men express interest in establishing a "cultural center" or some other facility to store their collections, the very notion of "preservation" as advanced by bodies such as the United Nations Educational, Scientific, and Cultural Organization, and museums in general (see Edwards and Stewart, 1980; Stanton, 2011), sits uncomfortably with their purposes. Over the past decade, I have sat with men in their camps discussing the various schemes and ideas hatched by local and territory governments to establish museum-like facilities, and yet at the same time have witnessed these men using these collections in ways that are antithetical to preservation.

Managed in these ways, ethnographic materials are elaborated on by Anmatyerr men and employed in their everyday lives. These items aren't just being stored away, they are being circulated and shared. Anmatyerr men who have been given access to very specific aspects of the Strehlow collection have, for example, taken DVD copies of filmed ceremonies and shared these between ritually affiliated men across geographically disparate communities. Films like this are also finding their way into the primary, large-scale initiation events held annually across Central Australia. Because these ceremonies bring people from multiple communities together, large groups of men are able to sit in secluded "bush camps" and discuss and respond to these recordings in ways that explain their significance to younger generations. At this grassroots level, people are indeed taking it upon themselves to personally look after this material and manage its dissemination.

The logic of repatriation nonetheless remains the primary rhetorical device through which the return of sacred materials is often discussed in academic and institutional circles. Anmatyerr, however, clearly think about these materials and interact with them in far more nuanced ways.

Collecting institutions and their staff are now being quietly encouraged to alter their ways to accommodate—in fact, emulate to some degree—the systems of complementary filiation (the *merek-artwey/kwertengerl* system) that governs the handling and dissemination of secret-sacred material. If collecting institutions wish to handle such restricted material with sensitivity, they must develop protocols that not only incorporate local Aboriginal epistemological frameworks (see Myers, 2014), but acknowledge the entangled relationships between collectors, collecting institutions, and contemporary "owners" and "managers" of ritual practice. By extension, this will require ongoing negotiation rather than occasional consultation and requires more than simply "handing back" specific objects. As Morphy has noted, the integration of Aboriginal concepts and interests like these could in fact lead to a "transformation of the concept of the museum" (2010b, p. 159; see also 2006) and result in greater mutual understanding of each other's motives and objectives.

The Strehlow collection sits at the periphery of far more significant factors in Anmatyerr people's everyday and ritual lives, but if the trajectory of other Indigenous groups in Australia and elsewhere is anything to go by, there may be a time when these collections assume a greater significance. If the Strehlow Research Centre is to shift from being a *research center* to a *resource center* for Central Australian Aboriginal people, it seems clear that not only will formal policy changes be required, but long-term relationships will need to be fostered across the Arandic region. It will undoubtedly be a significant challenge for a bureaucratic institution, and its staff, to handle the fluid and relational ways in which practices of custodianship over ritual knowledge are conferred. As interest begins to coalesce around the collection, particularly from younger men, there is a real need to find ways of responding. The responses from Anmatyerr men give an indication of some of the potential ways forward.

Conclusion

I opened this book with reference to a discussion I had with two men regarding the history of ethnographic inquiry and collecting in their region. As we looked through museum collection stores, ferreted through the archive, and discussed people's attitudes toward these collections, the stories uncovered were always found to be complex. Like so many of the Anmatyerr and Arrernte men I have spoken with over the years, these men knew that the Strehlow collection had emerged out of a deeply difficult relationship between *alhernter* and their ancestors. The most complicated of these relationships was that between T.G.H. Strehlow and the large numbers of Central Australian Aboriginal men he worked with over four decades.

I have presented an account of the relationships established, evoked, and negotiated in the course of making arguably the most complete collection of cultural material of any Indigenous people in Australia. But there are two stories conveyed here. The first is the story of how this collection was made via a prolonged and deep interplay with an idiosyncratic ethnographer and an array of Aboriginal participants. The other story addresses what these events meant, and continue to mean, for those either implicated in the original exchanges or culturally invested in the collection's contents and future. Inspired by Anmatyerr men who spoke with confidence and pride about their knowledge of *mer* (place), *tywerreng* (sacred objects, rituals, and songs), and *Anengkerr* (Dreaming), I wanted to know to what degree Anmatyerr (and to a lesser extent Arrernte) people aided Strehlow in his project. Just as important, I also wanted to know what relevance the collection held for them today. This introduced my proposition that the Strehlow collection could most fruitfully be understood as a *co-production*, originally emergent from dialogical encounter and best interpreted in *relational* terms. The resulting analysis focused on Anmatyerr people's relationships to each other as well as to T.G.H. Strehlow and his legacy, but also to myself, a researcher whose intervention brought this material to people's attention.

In the final phase of drafting, colleagues and friends often asked me what my research had covered. I usually gave a pared-down answer: the research was fundamentally about the relationships between an Aboriginal group in central Australia, an ethnographer, and the collection they produced. I explained that I wanted to understand how Aboriginal people had contributed to the making of this collection, but also how they understood and responded to its contents today. After being prompted further, and often asked to define what these relationships *were* like and what *did* Anmatyerr people make of the collection, I often struggled with producing a neat summary. Having been immersed so deeply in the intricacies of this story, I was naturally wary of the kind "specious mastery" that Adorno (2006, p. 82) warned of, when the contradictions and ambiguities of social reality are glossed over. My synthesis needed to accept contradictions, interminglings, and ambiguities.

Those who knew the rudiments of the T.G.H. Strehlow story, his controversies, and the drama of his biography would nod and signal their understanding of the topic, but they often had little idea that he had worked with the Anmatyerr. Coming at Strehlow's ethnographic work from this angle, I was aware of the need to build a better picture of Strehlow as a regionally focused researcher who followed traveling stories and focused on a socially saturated landscape entwined in networks of ritual knowledge. His Anmatyerr ethnography was not as extensive as his work among the Arrernte, nor was he as personally invested in it. But this is its charm; it sheds light on previously unexplored aspects of this significant collection and adds to a rather meagre body of literature on the Anmatyerr.

After all this time spent with Anmatyerr men—traveling with them, hearing them sing, and sharing in their explorations of the field diaries and recordings—I had to ask myself if I had come any closer to an answer to these central questions about agency, dialogue, and co-presence? When considering this, an array of poignant imagery came to mind. Each was suggestive of the numerous archival and fieldwork findings that gave partial answers: the congregations of Anmatyerr and Arrernte people interpreting anthropological inquiries as *urrempel* festivals; Tom Lywenge urging and prompting informants to sing for Strehlow in the 1930s; Bob Rubuntja, "the King," organizing truckloads of Anmatyerr men to attend the ceremonial festivals at Werlatyatherre in the 1950s; Ken Tilmouth providing explanations of the films that Strehlow had made of he and his father in the 1960s; Paddy Kemarr singing along with Strehlow's wire recordings; and standing with Malcolm Heffernan at the site of his grandfather's burial. Taken together, these historical and contemporary experiences exemplified the links between the making and interpretation of this collection.

"The relationships with Strehlow weren't as bad as people might imagine," I would try to explain to people. Yes, it seems that he was haughty and officious in his dealing with people, and there were undoubtedly unequal power relationships, but this had not negated the interests and motivations of his many informants. Their interests, as varied and complex as they were *then*, as they are *now*, were perceptible. But it was my experiences with Anmatyerr people that made me read Strehlow's collection in a new light, looking for traces or insights into their agency as well as evidence of the way that Anmatyerr people negotiate these histories and interactions on their own terms.

Coming to understand the way Anmatyerr people saw their exchanges with anthropologists enabled me to understand that this collection, and the history of its making, could never be reduced to simple political pronouncements. Nor would they contain its explanation and interpretation within historical chronologies. The Anmatyerr and Arrernte men that I knew tended to speak quietly about these exchanges, remained focused on their own local knowledge, and interpreted this material through their own personal life experience. Anmatyerr participation in Strehlow's project was not an exemplar of hegemonic compliance, domination, or even collective agency and "resistance." Although historically located and socially constituted, this collection was created out of particular encounters between Strehlow and his various informants.

The biographies and commentaries written about Strehlow over the years had nevertheless largely ignored the story of his informants. Assuming that present-day Arrernte people knew too little to contribute to illuminating this corpus, and confronted by the protocols and restrictions surrounding the majority of the contents of the collection, few had ever ventured to ask what these people might think of the collection today. Moreover, past emphasis on Strehlow's biography and his connections to the Arrernte at Hermannsburg meant that no one had envisioned broadening the scope to include people from neighboring and related groups like the Anmatyerr.

The serendipitous events that led me to see this collection in a new light were in many respects catalyzed by Anmatyerr elucidations. Their perspectives urged me to resist dwelling on the biography of this controversial linguist and anthropologist, and to instead explore the "human encounter between researcher and researched" (Toren and Pina-Cabral, 2011, p. 2). The contents of the collection and its production was as much a part of their story as it was a part of his. The erroneous belief that only Strehlow possessed the skills to understand and interpret this collection clearly grew out of a fixation on the biography of the collector and a failure to engage with the contents of this collection itself. Assessing what has been "lost" or "retained" in a culture ought not therefore be generalized from broad historical impressions but considered in light of exposing primary sources to interrogation in contemporary social contexts.

Strehlow was just one person in a long procession of ethnographers throughout the years who have sought to record and understand the ritual lives of Aboriginal people. His arrival on the scene was prefigured by social and historical conditions defined by early colonial violence and dramatic social change. As his work continued throughout a less violent, but still tumultuous, period for Central Australian Aboriginal people, it documents a changing social milieu. However, despite the vicissitudes of these decades, Anmatyerr people today continue to discuss their knowledge of kin, country, and ceremony in comparable ways to their forbears. Furthermore, the utterances of past generations retained in Strehlow's archive are made intelligible and confidently interpreted by their descendants today.

But had I actually grasped the character of the relationships at the heart of ethnographic encounter? By analyzing the historical archive, I could see the contexts in which people interacted. Occasionally Strehlow's diaries revealed the humanity of both the *observed* and *observer*. But the gravitational pull of the prevailing *alhernter* narrative is strong, and maintaining a focus on informant agency and motivations was a challenge. Their story can be easily overwhelmed by the specter and scope of such an enigmatic figure as T.G.H. Strehlow. It was only by welcoming the nuanced perspectives of Anmatyerr people, as they recalled, imagined, and affirmed their own entangled participation in these events, that a fuller picture of this ethnographic encounter could emerge.

In 1968, Malcolm Heffernan's uncle, Charlie Artetyerwenguny, traveled from Napperby to Coniston Station with T.G.H. Strehlow in his Land Rover. On the way out of Napperby, near Gidgee Bore, Charlie pointed to a number of possum and other sites. Reading the landscape and the people like historical sources, Strehlow described these sites in his diary as something of the past: "all this country *had been* possum country," he wrote

(Strehlow, 1968a, p. 47, my emphasis). The fact that they were significant for Charlie at the time, and that they might be of some ongoing importance for Anmatyerr people, was never seriously entertained by Strehlow. As shown repeatedly throughout this study, Anmatyerr men forty years later point to many of the same sites, sing many of the same songs, and relay many of the same stories. Thus, when I read Strehlow's diary entries I wonder why he, someone with considerable linguistic ability and an eye for detail, had failed to notice the sharing of information between generations.

We know that Strehlow had a deep knowledge of Arandic ritual and song, and in some cases significant personal ties, but it was his personal *accrual* of ethnographic information, his denial of *coevalness*, and a primitivism that spoiled his efforts. Framing his interactions as a kind of crossing of cultural divides in order to salvage cultural data, he overlooked the conditions of everyday existence. Ethnographic projects construed in this fashion spend little time grappling with the concepts of sociality that draw in and hold researchers and their interlocutors together over time. I am not suggesting that Strehlow did not understand the significance of being incorporated into the world of his informants—he clearly did. What I contend is that he stopped short of theorizing the basis of this incorporation, his reciprocal response to it, and how this shaped his knowledge of that world.

Strehlow's commitment to particularism, transcription, and translation has nonetheless provided a tremendous resource for professional scholars and oncoming generations of Central Australians. Just as he had argued during his time in London in 1950, his work concentrated on what his informants themselves considered to be of critical importance: the social "laws" and "customs" grounded in Dreaming and conveyed in song, dance, story, and ceremony. These particular aspects of Central Australian tradition remain central to group and individual identity today, if not always in practice, certainly at the ideological level. The historical period following Strehlow's time, the era of land rights anthropology where Aboriginal people all over the Northern Territory were required to demonstrate their traditional links with land, accentuated this emphasis. Song and ceremony were accepted as evidence in land claims and discussed as "title deeds" to land (Rose, 2000; Merlan, 2007; Koch, 2013). Given this currency of Indigenous value and belief now present in Western legal-political contexts, it is unsurprising that Strehlow's work continues to have tremendous salience, either as a form of evidence or simply as "grist for the mill" in local discussions.

As shown throughout this study, description is never a naïve or innocent procedure. The genealogies produced by Strehlow, for example, were read by Anmatyerr people today in ways that introduced additional and unexpected layers of social memory. They also revealed evidence of "shifting ontologies" (Austin-Broos, 2009) associated with inheritance of Dreaming affiliations. Cartographic, audio, and visual materials were also seen as requiring a filtering through the contemporary perspectives of senior experts. Rather than producing an infallible repository of cultural and linguistic knowledge, Strehlow's commitment to the "full details" of "mythological and sociological information" (Strehlow, 1971a, p. xviii), eventuated in an oeuvre ripe for critical interpretation and reuse when intermingled with the orality and social memory.

The name "Strehlow" carries with it a number of connotations across Central Australia that cannot easily be encapsulated. It references a family lineage associated not just with anthropology and linguistics, but also with missionizing, biblical translation, and literature. Members of the Strehlow family continue to write about the legacies of their forebears in Central Australia (Strehlow, 2011), and even use the collection's content with either little knowledge, or regard for, contemporary Aboriginal sensitivities (Strehlow, 1996). For the Anmatyerr, however, the name represents a period in their lives when salvage ethnographic filming and recording of men's ritual was often supported and encouraged by colonial authorities. "Strehlow-time," as they refer to it, signifies not just the presence of the linguistically adept T.G.H. Strehlow as the principal documenter, but a period in history when Anmatyerr, Arrernte, and other Central Australian men would readily share their ceremonies and songs. Their motivations appear to have included a willingness to document and preserve and, just as important, a desire to demonstrate, proclaim, dialogue, and share.

If we consider these collections as not derived solely from the toils of a solitary, "heroic" scholar, but as co-produced via active engagements of informants, then the future handling of all of this material needs to be reassessed. This includes thinking deeply about the moral imperative to "repatriate" or "return" ethnographic collections to their traditional owners. While in some cases repatriation may be desired, in others we need to leave space to reinterpret these collections as the outcomes of long-term intercultural processes. Being part of what Merlan describes as the liberal states "project of recognition," whereby Indigenous minorities are defined "in determinate ways, not unboundedly" and continuing to ensure that the worlds of Indigenous and non-Indigenous people are kept apart (2006, pp. 98–99), museum policies often fail to acknowledge this entanglement. Repatriation initiatives, then, although well intentioned, were often met with ambiguous responses from senior men. The adoption of Christianity, sedentary lifestyles, changed ceremonial practices, and intergenerational differences have influenced the way these returned collections are received (Batty, 2006b; Akerman, 2010). There is a need to address, more openly and intelligibly, questions of the qualitative diversity in historically shaped, Indigenous–non-Indigenous relations in different parts of Australia and new ways of caring for these complex collections.

As this research shows, it was often those men who actually made ritual paraphernalia or sang for Strehlow who showed the least interest in having this material returned to them. There are two principal reasons for this. First, men like Ken Tilmouth and Harold Payne made their exchanges with Strehlow with their eyes wide open. They had watched their fathers interact with Strehlow and understood the terms and conditions of these dealings. Reflecting on these interactions today, they accept that what now resides in the Strehlow collection stands as a kind of historical testimony to the exchange. Second, as these men are armed with the detailed knowledge of "the Law" and possess song and ritual knowledge to reproduce these objects, teach these songs, show younger people the significant sites and help enact ceremonies, they look forward rather than backward. In spite of Western society's continued obsession with the "primitive" and "preservation," "hope does not lie in the reproduction of the past," as Bessire has observed, but in people's "capacities to endure and transform the worlds they inhabit" (2014, p. 21). Senior Anmatyerr men see their primary role as one of supporting current younger generations in learning the songs and ceremonies that are currently pertinent and enduring. Rather than resurrecting aspects of traditions that may have fallen to the wayside or can no longer be reintegrated into networks of social relatedness, they look to maintain cultural traditions with little or no influence from the outside.

In many cases, reintroducing this material when there are no longer younger people with the full requisite knowledge to contain its power presents serious dangers. Songs and ceremonies, particularly the type recorded by Strehlow, as much as they may be learned in pragmatic fashion, conceal a myriad of meanings beyond the literal. Songs will contain an esoteric language that needs to be explained so that their hidden associations, their "super-vital" powers (Bradley, 2014), can be apprehended. There are fears among some that recordings of song can turn into dangerous forces if used in ignorance or with malice. Seemingly innocent songs, such as songs for the rain, can turn into dangerous forces if used with malice, as Eric Penangk explained at Mer Ywerternt. As we walked through a site where large chunks of quartzite representing hail stones were left scattered in the Dreaming, Eric explained that those who owned these songs had the power to unleash storms as weapons against their enemies. Having knowledge of songs and ceremony therefore came with a tremendous responsibility. It is for this reason that some Anmatyerr men would prefer to see the ritual content collected by Strehlow confined to the Strehlow Research Centre.

But it is not just the abilities of contemporary generations to contain the power of these rituals that concerns some senior men. They also want to safeguard the integrity of this collection and expect collecting institutions, and their staff, to help them do so. Public and professional debates about repatriation have however reinforced the broad perception that most ethnographic collections in colonial states were both unfairly acquired and unjustly kept. Despite all the examples of collecting and recording mentioned in this study, there are very few examples of blatant theft of objects or the coercive extraction of information, although as Thomas has noted (2000, pp. 273–274), the fairness of the original exchange often matters little to Indigenous people who want access their materials today. Strehlow's collection was certainly amassed within unequal conditions of power, but we cannot ignore the active participation of his informants. In fact, this is partly the reason why Anmatyerr people feel so sure of themselves in making the case for the Strehlow Research Centre to respond to their epistemological frameworks and protocols.

The task now is for institutions like the Strehlow Research Centre to respond. Meeting this challenge will require what Morphy (2010a) calls a "stepping back" from the usual "dispositions and pre-suppositions" of the institutions that administer these collections, and entering into the "disjunctive space" between Arandic and *alhernter* communities. The ethnographic account presented here, of how this collection is valued and interpreted, is just the first step. While some progress has been made in this area, the Strehlow Research Centre will need to reconfigure its practices to ensure that it responds to Indigenous understandings of ownership, responsibility, and care. Under this rubric, objects and information derive their value not via their *accumulation* but their dissemination across generations. In Central Australia, this includes a willingness to work within dimensions of complementary filiation, upholding the rights of both *merek-artwey* (owners) and *kwertengerl* (managers), and further, adding the museum itself or the museum professional to an adoptive responsibility of *kwertengerl* (manager, caretaker). Accepting such a proposal would not only defend the rights and interests of traditional owners but increase an acceptance of the relational and fluid ways in which Aboriginal ideas of custodianship are negotiated. The ongoing social and ritual activity of the Anmatyerr (and Arrernte) will make tracking and understanding these relationships an extremely challenging task for the institution.

When Strehlow began his documentation work, Aboriginal people all over Central Australia had already begun explaining their religious life to outsiders and allowing photography and filming. Of course, this sincerity and general enthusiasm to display one's own prowess as a singer, performer, or guide through country had to find ways of fitting within existing cultural protocols. Anmatyerr and Arrernte men allowed uninitiated men like Strehlow—and earlier, Spencer, Gillen, and Tindale—to record their most-treasured and secretive material. Within the "contact zone" of ethnographic practice, conventions around gender segregation and initiatory status were suspended or reworked to enable interaction and to enhance people's positions in relation to *alhernter* as opportunities arose.

All of this is suggestive of a people looking to recognize crucial others, and shape them as responsive, sympathetic interlocutors. Critical to these interactions succeeding, though, was at least a partial willingness on the part of *alhernter* to recognize and at times deploy Central Australian concepts such as an *ingkart* (a ceremonial leader) or *urrempel* "festivals" (ceremonial gatherings). As much as these terms may have been misunderstood or misappropriated, they did nonetheless operate in a way that aided dialogue around ritual matters. Strehlow took things much further than this via his willingness to promote his "spiritual conception" at Nthareye to legitimate his handling and reception of ceremonial knowledge. For the Anmatyerr, though, when *alhernter* wanted to record their ceremonies, this was seen as either a form of support for their *urrempel* gatherings, or in the case of Strehlow, was further justified in more intimate terms involving kin and Dreaming relationships.

A key point that emerges from this observation is that the cultural traffic between actors produced new contexts of exchange. The cultural and social changes that eventuated in relation to the sharing of ritual knowledge were thus partly borne out of the assertion of precolonial, Indigenous concepts. Cultural continuity and change are not, therefore, clear-cut opposites but intimately interrelated and co-exist. In fact, as Sahlins would argue, "the transformation of a culture is a mode of its reproduction" (1985,

p. 185). New forms emerge to deal with novel interactions while old ones also continue to exist; cultural categories and concepts are amended and changed. Anmatyerr men responded to probing ethnographers according to their own customary conceptions and interests. By encompassing these ethnographic documentation events in traditional cultural forms, they recreated and reinforced the relationships that originally defined the diffusion of this knowledge. But once the conditions of contact with *alhernter* progressed, new forms of ritual teaching developed, as well as an unexpected reification of tradition in the form of museum collections.

With the passage of time, Aboriginal people in many different parts of remote Australia have become deeply and rightly distrustful of ethnography's gaze. Strehlow's errors and hubris have played a significant part in this, but he was not alone in his insensitivity. A long history of appropriation has had its toll, where knowledge and objects have been taken away as possessions without recognition of ongoing relationships. Despite early participation in a program of salvage anthropology, from the mid-1970s onward Aboriginal people in Central Australia began to refuse access to their secret-sacred ceremonies and content (Morphy and Morphy, 2013; Merlan, 2013). As discussed in chapter 4, growing socioeconomic independence and mobility had given people the confidence to, at least from Strehlow's perspective, "disown" him as someone with ceremonial authority.

The Anmatyerr today adopt a far more stringent attitude toward the sharing of the ritual knowledge. Fiercely guarding that which is considered "proper dear" (meaning revealed only to those that make significant ritual payments), or *tikeley* (dangerous), the filming or recording of secret-sacred material is now rare. To my knowledge, restricted ceremonies have not been professionally filmed in the region since Strehlow's time, and the contents of this collection, I suspect, will be *amek-amek* (off limits) for many years to come.

It goes without saying that the exchange between Strehlow and his informants involved people from different cultural backgrounds, but conceiving of this interaction in binary terms, involving "Indigenous" and "non-Indigenous" worldviews, is far too simplistic. While I have not specifically addressed larger debates about whether these interactions are best categorized as involving "relative autonomous" groups or those enmeshed in pure interculturality (Merlan, 2013; Morphy and Morphy, 2013), I have clearly tried to stress the importance of intermingling and relationality. As this study has shown, neither Strehlow nor his informants existed in self-referential or autonomous domains during their original interactions but occupied a shared social field. Strehlow was undoubtedly influenced by his deep involvement in Arandic lifeworlds, while at the same time trying to create distance from it. His interlocutors also were keenly influenced by the dominant society around them, but these interactions did not negate their agency, their social relations, and general value orientations.

The manner in which Anmatyerr people engaged with this collection today did nonetheless reveal entangled, long-term intercultural processes. Anmatyerr people, like Strehlow, grew up on the colonial frontier, spoke an Arandic language (as well as English), and shared an experience of remote, arid Australia. Strehlow certainly came to these interactions with an idiosyncratic conceptual and personal purview, with links to colonial authority and a regional history of missionizing, but his induction into ritual and classificatory kinship makes his involvement far more ambiguous. The Anmatyerr too clearly embodied a radically different ontology, but they had eked out a marginal place in the local pastoral economy over a number of generations. It was this type of cultural "traffic" that produced the unique local and regional cultural identities that typified colonial interactions (Beilharz, 1997, pp. 46–47) and continues to express itself in the way that Aboriginal people in Central Australia have responded to the dominant Euro-Australian society.

Anmatyerr people today uphold the ideal of transmission of knowledge from the old people through orality and memory, but they also willingly respond to written and other sources. Added to this is an environment where Europeans have been inducted into ritual, classificatory kinship and imbricated into social relationships, and it seems difficult to dispute the idea that "natives" and "settlers" are indeed interdependent and mutually constituting (Sullivan, 2005; 2006; Merlan, 2005). While "cultural difference" certainly exists, the complex entanglement of Indigenous and non-Indigenous lifeworlds, generations of shared lives, and the mutual occupation of country in the Anmatyerr region cannot be unseen.

It may seem that by arguing for the recognition of the entanglement in ethnographic collections I have inadvertently minimized the claims that Indigenous groups might make over these materials in the long-term. On the contrary, what I am suggesting is that Strehlow's informants did not exist as "Indigenous subjects," "out of time" or beyond the influences of social and historical processes. The historical and contemporary explorations of this collection reveal that while anthropological and museological discourses might stage the appearance of neatly divided groups or people (between researcher/researched or collector/object), the reality is often far messier.

There was something distinctive about the way in which these historical and ethnographic objects were dealt with by Anmatyerr people. Each item was voraciously taken up and used in a kind of mimetic performance, either by visiting ancestors embodied in the country, re-enacting song performances, or gesturing to, or journeying toward, particular places where memories and stories could be revived. The collection's contents were interleaved into social spaces where people experienced life and where reflection took place. Trying to understand this collection from the viewpoint of Anmatyerr men, and not simply from the perspective of the observer, I strove to recount the processes whereby meaning was made.

The collection was *not* first and foremost apprehended as an exemplar of an authoritative past, as Strehlow may have liked, or others have since worried that it might become, but as a source from which a range of relationships could be *explored* and *declared*. As these recordings and artifacts traveled with me to different places, their substance flourished among the sites, people, and ancestors they referenced. "Old Kwetyaney's" dancing, captured on film at Alice Springs in the 1950s, for example, was reanimated as soon as the dancer's identity was known, and people could re-imagine the ceremony as it was performed in its proper locale. From here, connections were quickly made to the related estates and sites connected to the two traveling rain Ancestors that the song and ceremony honored. Social histories of the assimilationist period and the amalgam of anthropological and administrative power known as "Strehlow-time," as well as biographies of individuals and families, also surfaced.

The layers of meaning supplied by Anmatyerr responses certainly enhanced and added complexity to Strehlow's original documentation, but the actual collection items themselves offered something back. The return of Strehlow's sketch maps of Artwertakert, for example, were used to stimulate the unexpected retelling of an unspoken and concealed family story of violence and death. As we revisited and traversed the country with these documents in hand, the intertwined nature of social held memories, personal recollections, and *Anengkerr* narratives became clear. The process also revealed intra-community and inter-generational debates about the efficacy of oral and written testimony. Anmatyerr people's questioning of this collection involved a kind of triangulation, or reeling-in, of relationships between various aspects of Anmatyerr lifeworlds. A person's response or critique was thoroughly dependent on their own (kin) position within an interlocking set of affiliations, involving the axiomatic *Anengkerr* narratives, but also their personal associations through spiritual conception, inheritance, seniority, and residence.

Much more than simply inserting "missing histories" or "counternarratives," these perspectives offered a way of enlarging our understanding of how ethnographic collections might be alternatively understood. Hokari (2005) comes close to describing something similar to this in his "mode of historical practice" exhibited by the Gurindji in Northern Australia. Focused on a conceptualization of "history," Hokari described how these people tended to create and maintain a sense of the past through a complex web of relationships between entities, such as people and ancestral beings and significant places. These would be reaffirmed and brought into the present via performative acts such as storytelling, singing, and traveling. Similar characteristics are also evident in the ways that Anmatyerr people make sense of the past. But rather than confining this "mode" to the purely *historical*, I suggest that this is a more holistic, *relational mode of inquiry* that incorporates not just the temporal, but a wider nexus of relationality that is anchored in *mer* (place/country). As a methodology for making sense of both past and present phenomena, this mode of inquiry first locates entities within this web of associations, and then strives to realize their points of interconnection.

Throughout my research, I was continually reminded of the ongoing relevance and currency of song and ceremony to Anmatyerr men across the generations. I rarely went looking for this evidence, but it was often hard to miss. On one such occasion, a middle-aged man from the Coniston area whom I had not seen for many years and his *atyewe* (agemate) approached me at the Ti Tree Roadhouse. He had been out most of the day working on a nearby cattle station and was rounding the day off with a beer with a friend. As I knew both men, we started chatting, and although we began by reminiscing about our past travels together to Aboriginal communities in the "Top End" (Northern Australia) a decade earlier, we soon moved on to more local matters concerning country, song, and Dreaming. In this unlikely place, this young man in his early thirties spoke about an ancestral *pelyakw* (gray teal, *Anas gracilis*) from the Coniston area and began to sing a snippet of its song. He described the bird's peregrinations as it moved between a number of sites and named some of the senior men who had taught him these things. He spoke softly so that others in the pub nearby wouldn't be able to hear. Both men were earnest in what they communicated and smiled with pride.

It would be naïve and inaccurate to suggest from these vignettes, and the other examples presented in this book, that these traditions are not severely threatened. The entire Australian continent was once alive with song and ceremony, and the diversity and number of these traditions have been greatly diminished. The status of Anmatyerr traditions are far from secure. The situation for the Anmatyerr is not, however, as dire as some might expect. At Ti Tree, Napperby, Alcoota, and Aileron, there are men of all generations knowledgeable of significant sites (including many never mapped by Strehlow), and local *Anengkerr* mythologies are reasonably well known. Detailed ceremonial knowledge and the ability to sing numerous songs for "country" are, however, known only by the most senior men, and even in these cases their full repertoires are often recalled in an attenuated form.

As so many older Anmatyerr men reiterated, there is now far less depth of learning. Reviewing these recordings made with their fathers and grandfathers, these men made it clear that while they had retained a great deal compared to some of their neighbors, the opportunities for young men to learn are now greatly reduced. As young men they would learn while gathered together with older men in stock camps or when traveling the country on foot or on horseback—all in a time before the ubiquity of television, radio, and all of the other accoutrements of Western society. Young men are now primarily learning and being exposed to song and ritual at the annual initiation events, which, according to Ronnie McNamara, merely come and go "like the wind" and compete for ontological primacy with Christianity. Beyond this there are limited opportunities to practice, and there are fears that one day there will not be enough young men confident in these traditions for them to continue in any form.

As I sit at the computer writing the final paragraphs to this conclusion, I get a phone call from Malcolm Heffernan. He has bad news. Jimmy Haines Ngwarray, one of the men who so kindly befriended me, showed me his country, and shared in these explorations of the Strehlow collection, passed away at the age of sixty-three. Jimmy was one of those people who quietly possessed his expertise and never pretended to be an authority, but whose passion for local cultural knowledge was infectious. His familiar greeting, "Hey *pwerrerl, nthakenh-athek*?" (where you going?) and his constant reminders to "*ingkwernem-ilem*" (put it in writing) make me think of the energy of Strehlow's interlocutors such as Tom Lwenge, Ken Tilmouth, Mick Werlaty, and Bob Rubuntja. I hope that this book will help reframe the Strehlow collection as a testament not to a heroic individual but to the cohort of *urrempel* men who both made the collection and continue to make sense of it.

References

Abercrombie, T. 1998. *Pathways of Memory and Power: Ethnography and History among an Andean People*. Madison: University of Wisconsin Press.
Ackerman, R. 2008. "Anthropology and the Classics." In H. Kuklick (ed.), *A New History of Anthropology*. Malden, MA: Blackwell Publishing, pp. 143–157.
Adams, W.Y. 2016. *The Boasians: Founding Fathers and Mothers of American Anthropology*, Lanham, MD: Hamilton Books.
Adorno, T. 1951, *Minima Moralia: Reflections on a Damaged Life*. New York: Verso.
Adorno, T.W. 2006. *History and Freedom: Lectures 1964–1965*. Cambridge: Polity.
The Advertiser. 1937. "Body of Native, Believed Murdered, Disinterred Alice Springs, November 23," p. 15.
Akerman, K. 2010. "'You Keep It—We are Christians Here': Repatriation of the Secret Sacred Where Indigenous World-views Have Changed." In P. Turnbull. and M. Pickering (eds.), *The Long Way Home: The Meaning and Values of Repatriation*. New York and Oxford: Berghahn Books, pp. 175–182.
Allen, J., and Murray, T. 1996. April. "The forced repatriation of archaeological materials," *Australian Humanities Review*. australianhumanitiesreview.org/1996/04/01/the-forced-repatriation-of-archaeological-materials
Allen, L. 2016. "On the Edges of Their Memories: Reassembling the Lamalama Cultural Record from Museum Collections." In J.-C. Verstraete and D. Hafner (eds.), *Land and Language in Cape York Peninsula and the Gulf Country*. Amsterdam: John Benjamins Publishing Company, pp. 435–454.
Allett, N. 2010. "Sounding out: Using music elicitation in qualitative research," *ESRC National Centre for Research Methods*, 4(10): pp. 2–15.
Altman, J., and Hinkson, M. (eds.). 2010. *Culture Crisis: Anthropology and Politics in Aboriginal Australia*. Sydney: UNSW Press.
Ames, M.M. 1992. *Cannibal Tours and Glass Boxes: The Anthropology of Museums*. Vancouver: UBC Press.
Anderson, C. 1995a. "Politics of the Secret." In C. Anderson (ed.), *Politics of the Secret*. Sydney: Oceania Monographs, Oceania Publications, University of Sydney, pp. 1–14.

Anderson, C. 1995b. *Politics of the Secret*. Sydney: Oceania Monographs, Oceania Publications.
Anderson, C. 1996. "The Economics of Sacred Art: The Uses of a Secret Collection in the South Australian Museum." In C. Anderson (ed.), *Politics of the Secret*. Oceania monograph. Sydney: Oceania Publications, University of Sydney, pp. 97–107.
Anderson, W. 2005. *The Cultivation of Whiteness: Science, Health, and Racial Destiny in Australia*. 2nd ed. Carlton, Victoria: Melbourne University Publishing.
Angeles, S. 2016. "'This beautiful body of knowledge' at the Strehlow Centre." *Alice Springs News Online*. www.alicespringsnews.com.au/2016/09/30/working-with-this-beautiful-body-of-knowledge-at-the-Strehlow-centre
Anonymous. 1927. "Reso train returns: Party pleased with trip." *The News*: p. 7.
Anonymous. 1991. "Protesters disrupt opening of $3m centre for sacred objects." *Koori Mail*.
Antons, C. 2009. "*Foster v. Mountford*: Cultural Confidentiality in a Changing Australia." In A.T. Kenyon, M. Richardson, and S. Ricketson (eds.), *Landmarks in Australian Intellectual Property Law*. Port Melbourne, Victoria: Cambridge University Press.
The Argus. 1937. "Aborigine for Trial Allegation of Murder," p. 2.
Asad, T. (ed.). 1973. *Anthropology and the Colonial Encounter*. New York: Humanity Books.
Austin-Broos, D. 2003. "The meaning of 'pepe': God's law and the Western Arrernte," *Journal of Religious History*, 27(3): pp. 311–328.
Austin-Broos, D. 2006. "'Working for' and 'working' among Western Arrernte in Central Australia," *Oceania*, 76(1): pp. 1–15.
Austin-Broos, D. 2009. *Arrernte Present, Arrernte Past: Invasion, Violence, and Imagination in Indigenous Central Australia*. Chicago: University of Chicago Press.
Austin-Broos, D. 2010. "Translating Christianity: Some keywords, events and sites in Western Arrernte conversion," *Australian Journal of Anthropology*, 21(1): pp. 14–32.
Austin-Broos, D.J. 1997. "On Reading Theodor Strehlow's 'Agencies of Social in Central Australian Aboriginal Societies.'" Occasional Paper no. 1. Alice Springs, NT: Strehlow Research Centre, pp. 51–56.
Australian Government. 2013. *Australian Government Policy on Indigenous Repatriation*. Canberra: Department of Communications and the Arts.
Baker, R.M. 1999. *Land Is Life: From Bush to Town, the Story of the Yanyuwa People*. St. Leonards, NSW: Allen and Unwin.
Ballantyne, T. 2014. "Contesting the Empire of Paper: Cultures of Print and Anti-Colonialism in the Modern British Empire." In J. Carey and J. Lydon (eds.), *Indigenous Networks: Mobility, Connections and Exchange*. New York: Routledge, pp. 219–240.

Barrett, C. 1939. *Koonwarra: A Naturalist's Adventures in Australia*. London: Oxford University Press.
Barrett, C. 1940. *Our Aboriginal People*. Carlton, Victoria: United Breweries.
Barrett, C., Croll, R.H., and Elkin, A.P. 1943. *Art of the Australian Aboriginal*. Melbourne: Bread and Cheese Club.
Barwick, L. 2004. "Turning it all upside down . . . imagining a distributed digital audiovisual archive," *Literary and Linguistic Computing*, 19(3): pp. 253-263.
Batty, P. 2005. "Private politics, public strategies: White advisers and their aboriginal subjects," *Oceania*, 75(3): pp. 209-221.
Batty, P. (ed.). 2006a. *Colliding Worlds: First Contact in the Western Desert 1932-1984*. Tandanya, Carlton, Victoria: Museum Victoria and National Aboriginal Cultural Institute.
Batty, P. 2006b. "White Redemption Rituals: Repatriating Aboriginal Secret-Sacred Objects." In T. Lea, E. Kowal, and G. Cowlishaw (eds.), *Moving Anthropology: Critical Indigenous Studies*. NT, Australia: Charles Darwin University Press, pp. 55-62.
Batty, P. 2013a, " 'Primitive Blacks Face White Man's Laws': The 1932 Anthropological Expedition to Mt. Liebig, Central Australia." In J. Bell, A. Brown, and R. Gordon (eds.), *Recreating First Contact: Expeditions, Anthropology, and Popular Culture*. Washington, DC: Smithsonian Institution Scholarly Press, pp. 197-239.
Batty, P. 2013b. "Murder, infanticide and the moral certainty of Ernest Kramer," *Journal of the Anthropological Society of South Australia*, 37: pp. 107-125.
Batty, P. 2014. "The Tywerrenge as an artefact of rule: The (post)colonial life of a secret/sacred Aboriginal object," *History and Anthropology*, 25(2): pp. 296-311.
Baudrillard, J. 1994. *Simulacra and Simulation*. Ann Arbor: University of Michigan Press.
Beals, A. 2000. "Boas, Kroeber, Lowie: American anthropology comes of age," *Journal for the Anthropological Study of Human Movement*, 11(2): pp. 313-324.
Behar, R. 2008. "45 Anthropology: Ethnography and the Book That Was Lost." In *Handbook of the Arts in Qualitative Research: Perspectives, Methodologies, Examples, and Issues*. Thousand Oaks, CA: Sage, pp. 529-542.
Beilharz, P. 1997. *Imagining the Antipodes: Culture, Theory, and the Visual in the Work of Bernard Smith*. New York: Cambridge University Press.
Beinssen-Hesse, S. 2004. "Correspondence of Leo Frobenius and Colleagues with Ekkehard Beinssen Concerning Proposed Activities of the Frankfurt Institute for the Morphology of Culture in Australia." In W.F. Veit (ed.), *The Struggle for Souls and Science: Constructing the Fifth Continent: German Missionaries and Scientists in Australia*. Strehlow Occasional Paper. Northern Territory Government, Alice Springs, NT, pp. 152-182.

Bell, D. 1984. "Women and Aboriginal Religion." In M.J. Charlesworth, H. Morphy, D. Bell, and K. Maddock (eds.), *Religion in Aboriginal Australia: An Anthology*, St. Lucia: University of Queensland Press, pp. 295–303.
Bell, D. 1985. *Daughters of the Dreaming*. Melbourne: McPhee Gribble.
Bell, J.A., Christen, K., and Turin, M. 2013. "Introduction: After the return," *Museum Anthropology Review*, 7(1–2): pp. 1–21.
Bennett, T. 2013. *The Birth of the Museum: History, Theory, Politics*. London: Routledge.
Bennett, T., Cameron, F., Dias, N., Dibley, B., Harrison, R., Jacknis, I., and McCarthy, C. 2017. *Collecting, Ordering, Governing: Anthropology, Museums, and Liberal Government*. Durham, NC: Duke University Press.
Bennett, T., Dibley, B., and Harrison, R. 2014. "Introduction: Anthropology, collecting and colonial governmentalities," *History and Anthropology*, 25(2): pp. 137–149.
Berndt, R., and Berndt, C. 1951. *Sexual Behavior in Western Arnhem Land*. New York: Viking Fund.
Berndt, R.M. 1952. *Djanggawul: An Aboriginal Religious Cult of North-Eastern Arnhem Land*. Melbourne: F.W. Cheshire.
Berndt, R.M. 1974. *Australian Aboriginal Religion*, E.J. Brill, Leiden.
Berndt, R.M. 1978. "A time for remembering," *Australian Nurses Journal* (November): pp. 17–19.
Berndt, R.M. 1979a. T.G.H. Strehlow 1908–1978. *Aboriginal History*, 3, pp. 84–88.
Berndt, R.M. 1979b. "Obituary: T.G.H. Strehlow, 1908–1978," *Oceania*, 49(3): pp. 230–233.
Bessire, L. 2014. *Behold the Black Caiman: A Chronicle of Ayoreo Life*. Chicago: University of Chicago Press.
Biernoff, D. 1978. "Safe and Dangerous Places." In L.R. Hiatt (ed.), *Australian Aboriginal Concepts*. Canberra: Australian Institute of Aboriginal Studies, pp. 93–105.
Bishop, C. 2008. "'She Has the Native Interests Too Much at Heart': Annie Lock's Experiences as a Single, White, Female Missionary to Aborigines, 1903–1937." In A. Barry, J. Cruickshank, P. Grimshaw, and A. Brown-May (eds.), *Evangelists of Empire? Missionaries in Colonial History*. Melbourne: University of Melbourne eScholarship Research Centre. www.msp.esrc.unimelb.edu.au/shs/missions
Blaeser, K.M. 1999. "Writing Voices Speaking: Native Authors and an Oral Aesthetic." In K. Rice and L.J. Murray (eds.), *Talking on the Page: Editing Aboriginal Oral Texts*. Papers Given at the Thirty-Second Annual Conference on Editorial Problems, University of Toronto, November 14–16, 1996. Toronto: University of Toronto Press, pp. 53–68.
Bonshek, E. 2008. "When speaking is a risky business: Understanding silence and interpreting the power of the past in Wanigela, Oro Province, Papua New Guinea," *Journal of Material Culture*, 13(1): pp. 85–105.

Bonshek, E. 2015. "Making Museum Objects: A Silent Performance of Connection and Loss in Solomon Islands." In A. Dessingue and J. Winter (eds.), *Beyond Memory: Silence and the Aesthetics of Remembrance*. London: Routledge, pp. 31–52.

Bowman, B. 1989. *A History of Central Australia, 1930–1980*. Alice Springs, NT: Author.

Bowman, M. (ed.). 2015. *Every Hill Got a Story: We Grew Up in Country*. Richmond, Victoria: Hardie Grant Books.

Bradley, J., Adgemis, P., and Haralampou, L. 2014. "'Why can't they put their names?': Colonial photography, repatriation and social memory," *History and Anthropology*, 25(1): pp. 47–71.

Bradley, J., and Kearney, A. 2011. "'He painted the law': William Westall, 'stone monuments' and remembrance of things past in the Sir Edward Pellew Islands," *Journal of Material Culture*, 16(1): pp. 25–45.

Bradley, J., Kearney, A., Norman, L., and Friday, G. 2011. "That's the choices we make: Animating Saltwater Country," *Screening the Past* (August). www.screeningthepast.com/2011/08/these-are-the-choices-we-make-animating-saltwater-country

Bradley, J., and Yanyuwa Families. 2010. *Singing Saltwater Country: Journey to the Songlines of Carpentaria*. Crows Nest, NSW: Allen and Unwin.

Bradley, J.J. 2014. "'Singing through the Sea': Song, Sea and Emotion." In S. Shaw, and A. Francis (eds.), *Deep Blue: Critical Reflections on Nature, Religion and Water*. New York: Routledge, pp. 17–32.

Bray, T. (ed.). 2001. *The Future of the Past: Archaeologists, Native Americans and Repatriation*. New York: Routledge,

Bray, T.L. 1996. "Repatriation, power relations and the politics of the past," *Antiquity*, 70(268): pp. 440–444.

Breen, G. 2002. "The Ingkarte's Ear: A preliminary Evaluation of T.G.H. Strehlow's Hearing and Writing of Aboriginal Languages." In M. Cawthorn (ed.), *Traditions in the Midst of Change: Proceedings of the Strehlow Conference*. Alice Springs, NT: Strehlow Research Centre, pp. 52–60.

Breen, G., Rubuntja, E., Armstrong, G., and Pfitzner, J.C. 2000. *Introductory Dictionary of Western Arrernte*. Alice Springs, NT: IAD Press.

Bringhurst, R. 1994. "Point-counterpoint: The polyhistorical mind: A story as sharp as a knife, part 3 (19th century Haida poets)," *Journal of Canadian Studies*, 29(2): pp. 165–175.

Brown, A.K., and Peers, L. 2013. *Museums and Source Communities: A Routledge Reader*. London and New York: Routledge.

Brown, M.F. 2003. *Who Owns Native Culture?* Cambridge, MA: Harvard University Press.

Bryson, I. 2002. *Bringing to Light: A History of Ethnographic Filmmaking at the Australian Institute of Aboriginal and Torres Strait Islander Studies*. Canberra: Aboriginal Studies Press.

Buchholtz, D. 2011. "Telling stories: Making history, place, and identity on the Little Bighorn," *Journal of Anthropological Research*, 67(3): pp. 421–445.

Bunbury, B. 2002. *It's Not the Money, It's the Land: Aboriginal Stockmen and the Equal Wages Case: Talking History*. Fremantle: Fremantle Arts Centre Press.

Burke, P. 2013. "Warlpiri and the Pacific—Ideas for an intercultural history of the Warlpiri," *Anthropological Forum*, 23(4): pp. 414–427.

Campbell, A.P., Long, C.K., Green, J., and Carew, M. 2015. *Mer Angenty-warn Alhem: Traveling to Angenty Country*. Batchelor, NT: Batchelor Press.

Campbell, G. 2014. "Song as Artefact: The Reclaiming of Song Recordings Empowering Indigenous Stakeholders—and the Recordings Themselves." In A. Harris (ed.), *Circulating Cultures: Exchanges of Australian Indigenous Music, Dance and Media*. Canberra: The Australian National University, pp. 101–128.

Campbell, J. 1974. *The Mythic Image*. Princeton, NJ: Princeton University Press.

Campbell, L., and Scott, D. 2006. *Darby: One Hundred Years of Life in a Changing Culture*. Sydney: ABC Books for the Australian Broadcasting Corporation.

Cannizzo, J. 1983. "George Hunt and the invention of Kwakiutl culture," *Canadian Review of Sociology/Revue canadienne de sociologie*, 20(1): pp. 44–58.

Carey, J. 2014. "A 'Happy Blending'? Maori Networks, Anthropology and 'Native' Policy in New Zealand, the Pacific and Beyond." In J. Carey and J. Lydon (eds.), *Indigenous Networks: Mobility, Connections and Exchange*. New York: Routledge, pp. 184–215.

Carlson, K., Fagan, K., and Khnanko-Friesen, N. (eds.). 2011. *Orality and Literacy: Reflections across Disciplines*. Toronto: University of Toronto Press.

Carmichael, B., and Kohen, A. 2013. "The forgotten Yuendumu men's museum murals: Shedding new light on the progenitors of the Western Desert Art Movement," *Australian Aboriginal Studies*, 1: pp. 110–116.

Cartwright, M. 1995. *Missionaries, Aborigines, and Welfare Settlement Days in the Northern Territory*. Alice Springs, NT: Author.

Casey, E.S. 1987. *Remembering: A Phenomenological Study*. Bloomington: Indiana University Press.

Casey, E.S. 1996. "How to Get from Space to Place in a Fairly Short Stretch of Time: Phenomenological Prolegomena." In S. Feld and K. Basso (eds.), *Senses of Place*. School of American Research Advanced Seminar Series. Santa Fe: School of American Research Press, pp. 13–52.

Casey, M. 2012. "Colonisation, notions of authenticity and Aboriginal Australian performance," *Critical Race and Whiteness Studies*, 8: pp. 1–18.

Cataldi, L. 1996. "The end of the dreaming? Understandings of history in a Warlpiri narrative of the Coniston massacres," *Overland*, 144: pp. 44–47.

Célestin, R. 1996. *From Cannibals to Radicals: Figures and Limits of Exoticism*. Minneapolis: University of Minnesota Press.

Central Land Council. 2003. *Making Peace with the Past: Remembering the Coniston Massacre, 1928–2003*. Alice Springs, NT: Central Land Council.

Chaat Smith, P. 2007. "The Terrible Nearness of Distant Places: Making History at the National Museum of the American Indian." In O. Starn and M. de la Cadena (eds.), *Indigenous Experience Today*. Wenner-Gren International Symposium Series. Oxford: Berg Publishers, pp. 379–396.

Chandra, U. 2015. "Rethinking subaltern resistance," *Journal of Contemporary Asia*, 45(4): pp. 563–573.

Charlesworth, M.J., Morphy, H., Bell, D., and Maddock, K. 1984. *Religion in Aboriginal Australia: An Anthology*. St. Lucia: University of Queensland Press.

Chatwin, B. 1988. *The Songlines*. New York: Penguin Books.

Chisholm, J. 1999. *Destined for the Desert: Memoirs of 35 years in Central Australia*. NT, Australia: Charles Darwin University Press.

Christen, K. 2005. "Gone digital: Aboriginal remix and the cultural commons," *International Journal of Cultural Property*, 12(3): pp. 315–345.

Christie, M. 2005. "Words, ontologies and Aboriginal databases," *Media International Australia Incorporating Culture and Policy*, 116(1): pp. 52–63.

Chronicle. 1937. "Fatal fight between Aborigines: Murder finding by coroner" (December 16): p. 40.

Classen, C., and Howes, D. 2006. "The Museum as Sensescape: Western Sensibilities and Indigenous Artifacts." In *Sensible Objects: Colonialism, Museums and Material Culture*. Oxford: Bloomesbury, pp. 199–222.

Cleland, J.B. 1932. "The blood-grouping of Central Australian Aborigines, 1931 series," *The Journal of Tropical Medicine and Hygiene*, 35(24): pp. 369–371.

Clendinnen, I. 2005. *Dancing with Strangers: Europeans and Australians at First Contact*. Melbourne: Text Publishing.

Clifford, J. 1980. "Fieldwork, reciprocity, and the making of ethnographic texts: The example of Maurice Leenhardt," *Man*, 15(3): pp. 518–532.

Clifford, J. 1983. "On ethnographic authority," *Representations*, 2: pp. 118–146.

Clifford, J. 1988. *The Predicament of Culture: Twentieth-Century Ethnography, Literature, and Art*, Cambridge, MA: Harvard University Press.

Clifford, J. 1997. *Routes: Travel and Translation in the Late Twentieth Century*, Cambridge, MA: Harvard University Press,

Clifford, J. 2001. "Indigenous articulations," *The Contemporary Pacific*, 13(2): pp. 468–490.

Clifford, J. 2013. *Returns: Becoming Indigenous in the Twenty First Century*. Cambridge, MA: Harvard University Press.

Clifford, J., and Marcus, G. (eds.). 1986. *Writing Culture: The Poetics and Politics of Ethnography: A School of American Research Advanced Seminar*. Berkeley: University of California Press.

Climo, J., and Cattell, M.G. 2002. *Social Memory and History: Anthropological Perspectives*. Walnut Creek, CA: Altamira.

Cohen, H. 2001a. "The Filmworks of T.G.H. Strehlow: Commodities of the Sacred." In G. Turcotte and G. Ratcliffe (eds.), *Compr(om)ising Post/Colonialism(s): Challenging Narratives and Practices*. Sydney: Dangaroo Press, pp. 129–139.

Cohen, H. 2001b. *Mr. Strehlow's Films*. Film Australia.
Cohen, H. 2015. "Film as Cultural Memory: The Struggle for Repatriation and Restitution of Cultural Property in Central Australia." In A. Reading and T. Katriel (eds.), *Cultural Memories of Nonviolent Struggles: Powerful Times*. London: Springer, Palgrave Macmillan, pp. 91–110.
Collmann, J. 1988. "'I'm proper number one fighter, me': Aborigines, gender, and bureaucracy in Central Australia," *Gender and Society*, 2(1): pp. 9–23.
Coughlan, F. 1991. "Aboriginal town camps and Tangentyere council: The battle for self-determination in Alice Springs." MA Thesis, La Trobe University, Bundoora, Victoria. www.tangentyere.org.au/publications/research_reports/coughlan-aboriginal-town-camps-and-tangentyere-council.pdf
Courto, V. 2004. "Ethnographer Erhard Eylmann." In W.F. Veit (ed.), *The Struggle for Souls and Science: Constructing the Fifth Continent: German Missionaries and Scientists in Australia*, Occasional Paper, Northern Territory Government, Alice Springs, NT, pp. 143–151.
Cowlishaw, G. 1992. "Studying aborigines: Changing canons in anthropology and history," *Journal of Australian Studies*, 16(35): pp. 20–31.
Cowlishaw, G. 2015. "Friend or Foe? Anthropology's encounter with Aborigines." *Inside Story*. insidestory.org.au/friend-or-foe-pranthropologys-encounter-with-aborigines
Cribbin, J. 1984. *The Killing Times: The Coniston Massacre 1928*. Sydney: Fontana/Collins.
Crossley, N. 1994. *The Politics of Subjectivity: Between Foucault and Merleau-Ponty*. Avebury, Aldershot, England and Brookfield, VT: Avebury.
Curran, G. 2010. *Contemporary Ritual Practice in an Aboriginal Settlement: The Warlpiri Kurdiji Ceremony*, PhD Thesis, Australian National University, Canberra.
Curran, G. 2011. "The 'Expanding Domain' of Warlpiri Initiation Rituals." In Y. Musharbash and M. Barber (eds.), *Ethnography and the Production of Anthropological Knowledge: Essays in Honour of Nicolas Peterson*. Canberra: ANU Press, pp. 39–50.
Dallwitz, J., and Hughes, J. 2007. "Ara Irititja: Towards Culturally Appropriate IT Best Practice in Remote Indigenous Australia." In L.E. Dyson, M. Hendriks, and S. Grant (eds.), *Information Technology and Indigenous People*. Hershey, PA: IGI Global, pp. 146–158.
Das, V., Jackson, M., Kleinman, A., and Singh, B. (eds.). 2014. *The Ground Between: Anthropologists Engage Philosophy*, Durham, NC and London: Duke University Press.
Dastur, F. 2010. "Phenomenology and anthropology," *Philosophy Today*, 54: pp. 5–14.
Davies, E.H. 1932, "Aboriginal songs of Central and Southern Australia," *Oceania*, 2(4): pp. 454–467.

Davies, H. 1927, "Palæolithic music," *The Musical Times*, 68(1014): pp. 691–695.
Davies, J., and Maru, Y. 2011. "Supporting cross-cultural brokers is essential for employment among Aboriginal people in remote Australia," *The Rangeland Journal*, 33(4).
Davis, S. 1989, *Tribes and Territories: Aspects of Aboriginal Political Geography in the Northern Territory of Australia*. Melbourne: University of Melbourne Press.
Davis, S., and Prescott, J.R.V. 1992. *Aboriginal Frontiers and Boundaries in Australia*. Melbourne: University of Melbourne Press.
Deloria, P.J. 2006. "What is the middle ground, anyway?" *The William and Mary Quarterly*, 63(1), pp. 15–22.
Denby, D. 2005. "Herder: culture, anthropology and the Enlightenment," *History of the Human Sciences*, 18(1), pp. 55–76.
Dening, G. 1980. *Islands and Beaches: Discourse on a Silent Land: Marquesas, 1774–1880*. Melbourne: University of Melbourne Press.
Dening, G. 2004. *Beach Crossings: Voyaging across Times, Cultures and Self*, Carlton, Victoria: Melbourne University Publishing.
Desjarlais, R., and Throop, C.J. 2011. "Phenomenological approaches in anthropology," *Annual Review of Anthropology*, 40(1), pp. 87–102.
Deveson, P. 2012. "The ethnographic filmmaking of Ian Dunlop in a decade of change," *Humanities Research*, 18(1), p. 21.
Devlin-Glass, F. 2002. "The politics of the sacred in Cyber Country: Deconstructing the 'primitive,'" *Antipodes*, 16(2), pp. 145–150.
Devlin-Glass, F. 2005. "An atlas of the sacred: Hybridity, representability, and the myths of Yanyuwa Country," *Antipodes*, 19(2), pp. 127–140.
Dirks, N. 1993. "Colonial Histories and Native Informants: Biography of an Archive." In C.A. Breckenridge and P. van der Veer (eds.), *Orientalism and the Postcolonial Predicament: Perspectives on South Asia*. Philadelphia: University of Pennsylvania Press, pp. 279–313.
Dobson, V. 2013. *Anpernirrentye: Kin and Skin: Talking about Family in Arrernte*, Alice Springs, NT: IAD Press.
Dobson, V., and Henderson, J. 1994. *Eastern and Central Arrernte to English Dictionary*. Alice Springs, NT: IAD Press.
Donaldson, T. 1984, "Kids That Got Lost: Variation in the Words of Ngiyampaa Songs." In J. Kassler and J. Stubbington (eds.), *Problems and Solutions: Occasional Essays in Musicology presented to Alice M. Moyle*. Sydney: Hale and Iremonger, pp. 229–253.
Doyle, H. 1999. "Coniston Massacre." In G. Davidson, J. Hirst, and S. Macintyre (eds.), *The Oxford Companion to Australian History*. Melbourne: Oxford University Press, pp. 145–146.
Driver, F., and Jones, L. 2009. *Hidden Histories of Exploration*. London: Royal Holloway, University of London.

Dunlop, I. 1979. "Ethnographic film-making in Australia: The first seventy years (1898–1968)," *Aboriginal History*, 3: pp. 111–119.
Eades, D. 2013. *Aboriginal Ways of Using English*. Canberra, ACT: Aboriginal Studies Press.
Edwards, B.F.R. 2005. *Paper Talk: A History of Libraries, Print Culture, and Aboriginal Peoples in Canada Before 1960*. Lanham, MD: Scarecrow Press.
Edwards, E., Gosden, C., and Phillips, R. 2006. *Sensible Objects: Colonialism, Museums and Material Culture*. Oxford: Berg.
Edwards, R. 1927. *A Reso Tour to Central Australia* (Documentary Film), Australia, Development and Migration Commission.
Edwards, R., and Stewart, J. (eds.). 1980. *Preserving Indigenous Cultures: A New Role for Museums: Papers from a Regional Seminar, Adelaide Festival Centre, 10–15 September 1978*. Canberra: Australian Government Publishing Service.
Eickelkamp, U. 2010. "Children and youth in Aboriginal Australia: An overview of the literature," *Anthropological Forum*, 20(2): pp. 147–166.
Eickelkamp, U. 2014. "Formalizing the interpersonal in anthropological field research," *ClioŠ Psyche: Special Issue on Psychoanalytic Anthropology*, 20(4): pp. 412–417.
Elkin, A.P. 1935. "Anthropology in Australia, Past and Present." In G.W. Leeper (ed.), *Report of the Twenty-Second Meeting of the Australian and New Zealand Association for the Advancement of Science*. Melbourne: H.J. Green, Government Printer, pp. 196–207.
Elkin, A.P. 1970. *The Australian Aborigines: How to Understand Them*, 4th. ed. Sydney: Angus and Robertson.
Elkin, A.P. 1975. "Review of songs of Central Australia," *Oceania*, 45(3): pp. 245–247.
Elkin, A.P. 1977. *Aboriginal Men of High Degree*. St. Lucia: University of Queensland Press.
Elliott, B. 1977. "Jindyworobaks and Aborigines," *Australian Literary Studies*, 8: pp. 29–50.
Elliott, B. 1979. *The Jindyworobaks*. St. Lucia: University of Queensland Press.
Ellis, C.J. 1964. *Aboriginal Music Making: A Study of Central Australian Music*, Adelaide: Libraries Board of South Australia.
Ellis, C.J. 1985. *Aboriginal Music: Education for Living*. St. Lucia: University of Queensland Press.
Ellis, C.J., and Barwick, L.M. 1987. "Musical syntax and the problem of meaning in a central Australian songline," *Musicology Australia*, 10(1): pp. 41–57.
Ermann, M. 1999. "Editorial: Psychoanalysis in Germany," *International Forum of Psychoanalysis*, 8(2): pp. 57–58.
Eylmann, E. 1908. *Die Eingeborenen der Kolonie Südaustralien*, D. Reimer (E. Vohsen), 1908. archive.org/details/dieeingeborenen00eylmgoog
Eylmann, E. 2011. *A Further Translation of Selected Chapters of Dr. Erhard Eylmann's Die Eineborenen der Kolonie Sudaustralien (The Aborigines of the Colony*

of South Australia). Australian National University, Canberra: Intellectual Property Publications.

Fabian, J. 1983. *Time and the Other: How Anthropology Makes Its Object*. New York: Columbia University Press.

Fabian, J. 1990. *Power and Performance: Ethnographic Explorations through Proverbial Wisdom and Theater in Shaba, Zaire*. Madison: University of Wisconsin Press.

Fabian, J. 2008. *Ethnography as Commentary: Writing from the Virtual Archive*. Durham, NC and London: Duke University Press.

Feld, S., and Brenneis, D. 2004. "Doing anthropology in sound," *American Ethnologist*, 31(4): pp. 461–474.

Ferguson, C.A. 1987. "Literacy in a hunting-gathering society: The case of the Diyari," *Journal of Anthropological Research*, 43(3): pp. 223–237.

Fine-Dare, K.S. 2002. *Grave Injustice: The American Indian Repatriation Movement and Nagpra*. Lincoln: University of Nebraska Press.

Finlayson, J. 1998. "Sustaining Memories: The Status of Oral and Written Evidence in Native Title Claims." In B. Rigsby, J. Finlayson, and H.J. Bek (eds.), *Connections in Native Title: Genealogies, Kinship and Groups*. Research monograph (Australian National University Centre for Aboriginal Economic Policy Research), no. 13. Canberra: Centre for Aboriginal Economic Policy Research, Australian National University, pp. 85–98.

Finnane, K. 2010. "Kimber's McDouall Stuart: Reading between the lines," *Alice Springs News*, n.p.

Forrest, C. 2012. *International Law and the Protection of Cultural Heritage*. London: Routledge

Foster, R. 2009. "'Don't mention the war': Frontier violence and the language of concealment," *History Australia*, 6(3): pp. 68.5–68.7.

Freud, S. 1922. *Totem und Tabu: Einige Übereinstimmungen im Seelenleben der Wilden und der Neurotiker*. Verlag, Leipzig: Internationaler Psychoanalytischer.

Freud, S. 2014. *Civilization and Its Discontents*. Melbourne: Penguin Classics.

Furlan, A. 2008. "Indigenous Songs as 'Operational Structures of Transactional Life': A Study of Song Genres at Wadeye." In M. Hinkson and J. Beckett (eds.), *Appreciation of Difference: WEH Stanner and Aboriginal Australia*. Canberra: Aboriginal Studies Press, pp. 151–165.

Galt-Smith, B. 2001. "A Certain Trajectory: The Journey of Aboriginal Cultural Material in the Strehlow Collection." In *From Point to Pathway: the Heritage of Routes and Journeys*. Alice Springs, NT: Australia International Council on Monuments and Sites. www.aicomos.com/wp-content/uploads/A-certain-trajectory-the-journey-of-Aboriginal-cultural-material-in-the-Strehlow-Collection.pdf

Gammage, B. 2011. *The Biggest Estate on Earth: How Aborigines Made Australia*. Crows Nest, NSW: Allen and Unwin.

Gandhi, L. 1998. *Postcolonial Theory: A Critical Introduction*. St. Leonards, NSW: Allen and Unwin.

Garde, M. 2013. "The Forbidden Gaze: The 1948 Wubarr ceremony performed for the American-Australian Scientific Expedition to Arnhem Land." In *Exploring the Legacy of the 1948 Arnhem Land Expedition*. Canberra: ANU Press, pp. 404–421.

Gardner, H., and McConvell, P. 2015. *Southern Anthropology—A History of Fison and Howitt's Kamilaroi and Kurnai*. Hampshire: Palgrave Macmillan.

Geest, S.V.D. 2003. "Confidentiality and pseudonyms: A fieldwork dilemma from Ghana," *Anthropology Today*, 19(1): pp. 14–18.

Geismar, H. 2009. "Photographs and Foundations: Visualising the Past on Atchin and Vao." In H. Geismar and A. Herle (eds.), *Moving Images: John Layard, Fieldwork and Photography on Malakula since 1914*. Adelaide: Crawford House Publishing, pp. 259–292.

Geismar, H. 2015. "Anthropology and heritage regimes," *Annual Review of Anthropology*, 44(1): pp. 71–85.

Geismar, H., and Herle, A. 2009. *Moving Images: John Layard, Fieldwork and Photography on Malakula Since 1914*, Crawford House Publishing, Adelaide.

Gergen, M., and Gergen, K. 2002. "Ethnographic Representation as Relationship." In A.P. Bochner and C. Ellis (eds.), *Ethnographically Speaking: Autoethnography, Literature, and Aesthetics*. Walnut Creek, CA: AltaMira Press.

Gibson, J. 2007. "People, Place and Community Memory: Creating Digital Heritage Databases in Remote Aboriginal Communities." In Australian Society of Archivists, Canberra, ACT.

Gibson, J. 2008. "Unpacking the 'Indigenous' Knowledge Centre Concept." In *Australian Library and Information Association Biennial Conference*, ALIA, Alice Springs. conferences.alia.org.au/alia2008/papers/pdfs/117.pdf

Gibson, J. 2009. *Managing Indigenous Digital Data: An Exploration of the Our Story Database in Indigenous Libraries and Knowledge Centres in the Northern Territory*. Sydney: Sydney University of Technology. epress.lib.uts.edu.au/research/bitstream/handle/10453/19485/2009%20-%20Gibson.pdf?sequence=1

Gibson, J. 2013. "Addressing the Arrernte: FJ Gillen's 1896 Engwura speech," *Australian Aboriginal Studies*, 1: pp. 57–72.

Gibson, J. 2015a, "Central Australian songs: A history and reinterpretation of their distribution through the earliest recordings," *Oceania*, 85(2): pp. 165–182.

Gibson, J. 2015b. "John McDouall Stuart Remembered in Central Australia." In F. Cahir, A. Inglis, and S. Beggs (eds.), *Scots Under the Southern Cross*. Ballarat: Ballarat Heritage Press, pp. 41–52.

Gibson, J. 2017. "'Only the Best Is Good Enough for Eternity': Revisiting the Ethnography of T.G.H. Strehlow." In A. Kenny and N. Peterson (eds.), *The German Language Tradition of Ethnography in Australia*, Monographs in

Anthropology. Canberra: ANU Press, pp. 243–271, dx.doi.org/10.22459/GEA.09.2017.10

Gibson, J., and Batty, P. 2014. "Reconstructing the Spencer and Gillen Collection Online: Museums, Indigenous Perspectives and the Production of Cultural Knowledge in the Digital Age." In H. Meyer, C. Schmitt, A.-C. Shering, and S. Janssen (eds.), *Corpora ethnographica online Strategien der Digitalisierung kultureller Archive und ihrer Präsentation im Internet* Munster: Waxman, pp. 29–48.

Gibson, J., Lloyd, B., and Richmond, C. 2011. "Localisation of Indigenous Content: Libraries and Knowledge Centres and the Our Story Database in the Northern Territory." In J. Steyn, J. Van Belle, and E. Mansilla (eds.), *ICTs for Global Development and Sustainability: Practice and Applications*. Hershey, PA: IGI Global, pp. 151–175.

Gillen, F.J. 1968. *Gillen's Diary: The Camp Jottings of F.J. Gillen on the Spencer and Gillen Expedition across Australia, 1901–1902*. Adelaide: Libraries Board of South Australia.

Gillen, F.J. 2001. *"My Dear Spencer": The Letters of F.J. Gillen to Baldwin Spencer*. Carlton, Victoria: Hyland House Publishing Pty Limited.

Gingrich, A. 2005. "The German-Speaking Countries: Ruptures, Schools and Nontraditions: Reassessing the History of Sociocultural Anthropology in Germany." In F. Barth, R. Parkin, S. Silverman, and A. Gingrich (eds.), *One Discipline, Four ways: British, German, French, and American Anthropology*. Chicago: University of Chicago Press, pp. 76–153.

Glowczewski, B. 2005. "Lines and criss-crossings: Hyperlinks in Australian indigenous narratives," *Media International Australia*, 116, pp. 24–35.

Goody, J. 1987. *The Interface between the Written and the Oral*. Cambridge: Cambridge University Press.

Goody, J. 2010a. "Introduction." In *Myth, Ritual and the Oral*. New York: Cambridge University Press, pp. 1–12.

Goody, J. 2010b. "Writing and Oral Memory: The Importance of the 'Lecto-Oral.'" In *Myth, Ritual and the Oral*. Cambridge: Cambridge University Press, pp. 153–161.

Gosse, W.C., and Goyder, G.W. 1874. "Mr. W.C. Gosse's Explorations, 1873," *Proceedings of the Royal Geographical Society of London*, 19(1): pp. 51–53.

Gray, G.G. 2007. *A Cautious Silence: The Politics of Australian Anthropology*. Canberra: Aboriginal Studies Press.

Green, J. 2001. "Both Sides of the Bitumen: Ken Hale Remembering 1959." In J. Simpson, D. Nash, M. Laughren, P. Austin, and B. Alpher (eds.), *Forty Years On: Ken Hale and Australian languages*. Canberra: Australian National University, pp. 29–43.

Green, J. 2003. *Central Anmatyerr Picture Dictionary*. Alice Springs, NT: IAD Press.

Green, J. 2010. *Central and Eastern Anmatyerr to English Dictionary*. Alice Springs, NT: IAD Press.

Green, J. 2012. "The Altyerre Story—'Suffering Badly by Translation,'" *The Australian Journal of Anthropology*, 23(2): pp. 158–178.

Green, J. 2013. "Coming into Being: A Cluster of Cultural Keywords in Arandic Languages." Unpublished.

Green, J.A. 2014. *Drawn from the Ground: Sound, Sign and Inscription in Central Australian Sand Stories*. Cambridge: Cambridge University Press.

Griffiths, T. 1996. *Hunters and Collectors: The Antiquarian Imagination in Australia*. New York: Cambridge University Press.

Gruber, J.W. 1970. "Ethnographic salvage and the shaping of anthropology," *American Anthropologist*, 72(6): pp. 1289–1299.

Haddon, A.C., Rivers, W.H.R., Seligman, C.G., Myers, C.S., McDougal, W., Ray, S.H., and Wilkin, A. 1901. *Reports of the Cambridge Anthropological Expedition to Torres Straits*.

Hafner, D. 2010. "Viewing the past through Ethnographic Collections," *Museum History Journal*, 3(2): pp. 257–280.

Hale, K. 1984. "Remarks on Creativity in Aboriginal Verse." In J. Kassler and J. Stubington (eds.), *Problems and Solutions: Occasional Essays in Musicology Presented to Alice M. Moyle*. Sydney: Hale and Iremonger, pp. 254–262.

Halstead, N. 2001. "Ethnographic encounters. Positionings within and outside the insider frame," *Social Anthropology*, 9(3): pp. 307–321.

Hamilton, A. 1998. "Descended from Father, Belonging to Country: Rights to Land in the Australian Western Desert." In W.H. Edwards (ed.), *Traditional Aboriginal Society*. South Yarra: Macmillan Education, pp. 90–108.

Harney, B. 1946. *North of 23: Ramblings in Northern Australia*. Sydney: Australasian Publishing Co.

Harper, D. 2002. "Talking about pictures: A case for photo elicitation," *Visual Studies*, 17(1): pp. 13–26.

Harris, A. (ed.). 2014. *Circulating Cultures: Exchanges of Australian Indigenous Music, Dance and Media*. Canberra: The Australian National University.

Harrison, R., Byrne, S., and Clarke, A. (eds.). 2013. *Reassembling the Collection: Ethnographic Museums and Indigenous Agency*. Santa Fe, NM: School for Advanced Research Press.

Hartwig, M.C. 1965. *The Progress of White Settlement in the Alice Springs District and Its Effects upon the Aboriginal Inhabitants, 1860–1894*. Adelaide: University of Adelaide.

Hendry, J. 2005. *Reclaiming Culture: Indigenous People and Self-Representation*. Basingstoke: Palgrave Macmillan.

Hercus, L. 2009. "Some Area Names in the Far North-East of South Australia." In H.J. Koch and L.A. Hercus (eds.), *Aboriginal Placenames: Naming and Re-Naming the Australian Landscape*. Canberra: ANU Press.

Hercus, L., Hodges, F., and Simpson, J. (eds.). 2002. *The Land is a Map: Placenames of Indigenous Origin in Australia*. Canberra: Pandanus Books, Research School of Pacific and Asian Studies, The Australian National University.
Hersey, S., and Cohen, H. 2004. "Visualising Anthropology: Ethnography Documentary and the Films of T.G.H. Strehlow." In *Traditions in the Midst of Change: Proceedings of the Strehlow Conference 2002*. Alice Springs, NT: Strehlow Research Centre, pp. 177–183.
Hester, J.J. 1968. "Pioneer methods in salvage anthropology," *Anthropological Quarterly*, 41(3): pp. 132–146.
Hiatt, L.R. 1965. *Kinship and Conflict: A Study of an Aboriginal Community in Northern Arnhem Land*. Canberra: ANU Press.
Hiatt, L.R. 1996. *Arguments about Aborigines: Australia and the Evolution of Social Anthropology*. Melbourne: Cambridge University Press.
Hill, B. 2003. *Broken Song: T.G.H. Strehlow and Aboriginal Possession*. Milsons Point, NSW: Random House.
Hinkson, M. 2005. "The intercultural challenge of Stanner's first fieldwork," *Oceania*, 75(3): pp. 195–208.
Hinkson, M., and Beckett, J. 2008. *An Appreciation of Difference: WEH Stanner and Aboriginal Australia*. Canberra: Aboriginal Studies Press.
Hokari, M. 2002. "Reading oral histories from the pastoral frontier: A critical revision," *Journal of Australian Studies*, 26(72): pp. 21–28.
Hokari, M. 2005. "Gurindji Mode of Historical Practice." In L. Taylor, G. Ward, G. Henderson, R. Davis, and L. Wallis (eds.), *The Power of Knowledge, the Resonance of Tradition*. Canberra: Aboriginal Studies Press, pp. 214–222.
Holcombe, S. 2009. *Indigenous Ecological Knowledge and Natural Resources in the Northern Territory: Guidelines for Indigenous Ecological Knowledge Management*. Natural Resource Management Board (NT), Charles Darwin University Press.
Holquist, M. 2000. *Dialogism: Bakhtin and His World*. New York: Routledge.
Howard-Wagner, D., and Kelly, B. 2011. "Indigeneity, identity and mobility: Containing Aboriginal mobility in the Northern Territory: From 'protectionism' to 'interventionism,'" *Law/text/culture*, 15: pp. 102–233.
Hugo, D. 1997. "Acquisition of the Strehlow Collection by the Northern Territory Government—a Chronology." In D. Hugo (ed.), *Strehlow Research Centre Occasional Paper no. 1*. Alice Springs, NT: Strehlow Centre Board, pp. 127–136.
Hunt, J. (ed.). 2008. "Regionalism That Respects Localism: The Anmatjere Community Government Council and Beyond." In *Contested Governance: Culture, Power and Institutions in Indigenous Australia*. Canberra: ANU Press, pp. 283–309.
Hymes, D. 1972. *Reinventing Anthropology*. New York: Pantheon Books.
Hymes, D.H. 1981. *"In vain I tried to tell you": Essays in Native American Ethnopoetics*. Philadelphia: University of Pennsylvania Press.

Inglis, K.S. 2002. *The Stuart Case*. Melbourne: Black Inc.
Ingold, T. 2011. *Being Alive: Essays on Movement, Knowledge and Description*. UK: Taylor and Francis.
Jackson, J.B. 2007. "The paradoxical power of endangerment: Traditional native American dance and music in Eastern Oklahoma," *World Literature Today*, 81(5): pp. 37–41.
Jackson, J.B. 2010. "Boasian ethnography and contemporary intellectual property debates," *Proceedings of the American Philosophical Society*, 154(1): pp. 40–49.
Jackson, M. 1995. *At Home in the World*. Durham, NC: Duke University Press.
Jackson, M. 1996. "Introduction: Phenomenology, Radical Empiricism, and Anthropological Critique." In M. Jackson (ed.), *Things As They Are: New Directions in Phenomenological Anthropology*. Bloomington: Indiana University Press, pp. 1–50.
Jackson, M. 1998. *Minima Ethnographica: Intersubjectivity and the Anthropological Project*. Chicago: University of Chicago Press.
Jackson, M. 2003. "Broken song: T.G.H. Strehlow and Aboriginal possession [Book Review]," *Australian Aboriginal Studies*, 1: pp. 88–89.
Jackson, M. 2005. *Existential Anthropology: Events, Exigencies and Effects*. New York: Berghahn Books.
Jackson, M. 2006. "In the footsteps of Walter Benjamin," *Harvard Divinity School Bulletin*, 34(2): pp. 1–17.
Jackson, M. 2013. *Lifeworlds: Essays in Existential Anthropology*. Chicago: University of Chicago Press.
Jackson, M. 2015. "Afterword." In K. Ram and C. Houston (eds.), *Phenomenology in Anthropology: A Sense of Perspective*. Bloomington: Indiana University Press, pp. 293–303.
Jackson, M., and Piette, A. (eds). 2015. *What Is Existential Anthropology?* New York: Berghahn Books.
Jessiman, S.R. 2011. "The repatriation of the G'psgolox totem pole: A study of its context, process, and outcome," *International Journal of Cultural Property*, 18(3): pp. 365–391.
Johansen, B.E. 2004. "Back from the (nearly) dead: Reviving Indigenous languages across North America," *American Indian Quarterly*, 28(3/4): pp. 566–582.
Johnson, V. 1994. *The Art of Clifford Possum Tjapaltjarri*. East Roseville, NSW: Gordon and Breach Arts International.
Jones, P. 1987. "South Australian Anthropological History: The Board for Anthropological Research and Its Early Expeditions." In *Records of the South Australian Museum*, 20, pp. 71–92.
Jones, P. 1995a. "'Objects of Mystery and Concealment': A History of Tjurunga Collecting." In C. Anderson (ed.), *Politics of the Secret*, Oceania Monograph. Sydney: University of Sydney, pp. 67–96.

Jones, P. 1995b. "Norman B. Tindale: An obituary," *Records of the South Australian Museum*, 28(2): pp. 159–176.

Jones, P. 2002. "Strehlow, Theodor George Henry (Ted) (1908–1978)," *Australian Dictionary of Biography*. adb.anu.edu.au/biography/Strehlow-theodor-george-henry-ted-11792

Jones, P. 2004. "A Maverick and His Mentors." In M. Cawthorn (ed.), *Traditions in the Midst of Change: Communities, Cultures and the Strehlow Legacy in Central Australia*. Proceedings of the Strehlow Conference 2002. Alice Springs, NT: Strehlow Research Centre, pp. 36–41.

Jones, P. 2005. " 'Indispensable to Each Other': Spencer and Gillen or Gillen and Spencer?" Occasional Paper no. 4, Strehlow Research Centre, pp. 6–25.

Jones, P. 2011. *Images of the Interior: Seven Central Australian Photographers*. Adelaide: Wakefield Press.

Jones, P. 2012. *Smoke, Spears and Mirrors: Stuart's Aboriginal Encounters*. Adelaide: John McDouall Stuart Society, Inc.

Jones, P. 2015. "The Theatre of Contact: Aborigines and Exploring Expeditions." In M. Thomas (ed.), *Expedition to Empire: Exploratory Journeys and the Making of the Modern World*. Routledge Studies in Cultural History. New York: Taylor and Francis, pp. 88–107.

Jones, S., and Russell, L. 2012. "Archaeology, memory and oral tradition: An introduction," *International Journal of Historical Archaeology*, 16(2): pp. 267–283.

Jorgensen, D. 2010. "Simulating the sacred in Theodore Strehlow's songs of Central Australia," *The Bible and Critical Theory*, 6(2): pp. 22.2–22.10.

Kahn, M. 1990. "Stone-faced ancestors: The spatial anchoring of myth in Wamira, Papua New Guinea," *Ethnology*, 29(1): pp. 51–66.

Kahn, M. 1996. "Your Place and Mine: Sharing Emotional Landscapes in Wamira, Papua New Guinea." In S. Feld and K. Basso (eds.), *Senses of place*. School of American Research Advanced Seminar Series. Santa Fe, NM: School of American Research Press, pp. 167–196.

Kahunde, S. 2012. "Repatriating archival sound recordings to revive traditions: The role of the Klaus Wachsmann recordings in the revival of the Royal Music of Bunyoro-Kitara, Uganda," *Ethnomusicology Forum*, 21(2): pp. 197–219.

Kaiser, S. 2004. "The Stern Case." In M. Cawthorn (ed.), *Proceedings of the Strehlow Conference 2002*. Alice Springs: Northern Territory Government, pp. 66–76.

Kan, S. 2001. *Strangers to Relatives: The Adoption and Naming of Anthropologists in Native North America*. Lincoln: University of Nebraska Press.

Kapferer, B. 2007. "Anthropology and the dialectic of enlightenment: A discourse on the definition and ideals of a threatened discipline," *The Australian Journal of Anthropology*, 18(1): pp. 72–94.

Kasten, E., and de Graaf, T. 2013. *Sustaining Indigenous Knowledge: Learning Tools and Community Initiatives for Preserving Endangered Languages and*

Local Cultural Heritage. Norderstedt: Verlag der Kulturstiftung Sibirien | SEC Publications.

Kaus, D. 2008. "The management of restricted Aboriginal objects by the National Museum of Australia," *Recollections*, 3(1). recollections.nma.gov.au/issues/vol_3_no_1/notes_and_comments/the_management_of_restricted_aboriginal_objects#nav

Kearney, A. 2016. *Violence in Place, Cultural and Environmental Wounding*. New York: Routledge.

Kearney, A., Bradley, J., McKee, B., and Chandler, T. 2012. "Representing Indigenous cultural expressions through animation: The Yanyuwa animation project," *Animation Journal*, 20: pp. 4–29.

Keen, I. 1997. "The Western Desert vs. the Rest: Rethinking the Contrast." In F. Merlan, J. Morton, and A. Rumsey (eds.), *Scholar and Sceptic*. Canberra: Aboriginal Studies Press, pp. 65–94.

Kendon, A. 1988, *Sign Languages of Aboriginal Australia: Cultural, Semiotic and Communicative Perspectives*. Cambridge: Cambridge University Press.

Kenny, A. 2005. "A Sketch Portrait: Carl Strehlow's Editor Baron Moritz Von Leonhardi." In S. Mitchell and A. Kenny (eds.), *Collaboration and Language*, Occasional Paper, Strehlow Research Centre, Alice Springs, pp. 54–69.

Kenny, A. 2008. From Missionary to Frontier Scholar: An Introduction to Carl Strehlow's Masterpiece. PhD Thesis, University of Sydney.

Kenny, A. 2013. *The Aranda's Pepa: An Introduction to Carl Strehlow's Masterpiece Die Aranda-und Loritja-Stämme in Zentral-Australien (1907–1920)*. Canberra: ANU Press.

Kimber, R.G. 1991. "The End of the Bad Old Days: European Settlement in Central Australia, 1871–1894." Eric Johnston Lecture, State Library of the Northern Territory, Occasional Paper no. 25, pp. viii–24.

Kimber, R.G. 1998. "Gillen Time: The Creation of an Era." In S. Parry and T. Austin (eds.), *Connection and Disconnection: Encounters between Settlers and Indigenous People in the Northern Territory*. NT, Australia: Charles Darwin University Press, pp. 49–76. espace.cdu.edu.au/view/cdu:9213

Kimber, R.G. 2003. " 'Real True History': The Coniston Massacre" (Part Ten). *Alice Springs News*. www.alicespringsnews.com.au/1041.html

Kimber, R.G. 2004. "Iriakura, Kolbarinja and T.G.H. Strehlow." In M. Cawthorn (ed.), *Proceedings of the Strehlow Conference, September 18–20, 2002*. Alice Springs: Northern Territory Government, pp. 77–83.

Kirby, M. 1978, "Strehlow Festschrift: T.G.H. Strehlow and Aboriginal Customary Laws." www.michaelkirby.com.au/images/stories/speeches/1970s/vol3/1978/87-Strehlow_Festschrift_-_TGH_Strehlow_and_Aboriginal_Customary_Laws.pdf

Kirshenblatt-Gimblett, B. 1998. *Destination Culture: Tourism, Museums, and Heritage*. Berkeley: University of California Press.

Kirshenblatt-Gimblett, B. 2004. "The Museum—A Refuge for Utopian Thought." In J. Rüsen, M. Fehr, and A. Ramsbrock (eds.), *Die Unruhe der Kultur: Potentiale des Utopischen*, Velbrück Wissenschaft. www.nyu.edu/classes/bkg/web/museutopia.pdf

Koch, G. 2013. *We Have the Song, So We Have the Land: Song and Ceremony as Proof of Ownership in Aboriginal and Torres Strait Islander Land Claims.* Canberra: AIATSIS.

Koch, G., and Koch, H. 1993. *Kaytetye Country: An Aboriginal History of the Barrow Creek Area.* Alice Springs, NT: Institute for Aboriginal Development.

Koch, G., and Turpin, M. 2008. "The Language of Central Australian Aboriginal Songs." In C. Bowern, B. Evans, and L. Miceli (eds.), *Morphology and Language History: In Honour of Harold Koch.* Amsterdam/Philadelphia: John Benjamins Publishing, pp. 167–183.

Kolig, E. 2000. "Social causality, human agency and mythology: Some thoughts on history-consciousness and mythical sense among Australian Aborigines," *Anthropological Forum*, 10(1): pp. 9–30.

Konishi, S., Nugent, M., and Shellam, T. (eds). 2015. *Indigenous Intermediaries: New Perspectives on Exporation Archives* Canberra: ANU Press and Aboriginal History Inc.

Kral, I. 2000. The Socio-Historical Development of Literacy in Arrernte: A Case Study of the Introduction of Writing in an Aboriginal Language and the Implications for Current Vernacular Literacy Practices. MA thesis, Department of Linguistics and Applied Linguistics, University of Melbourne.

Kral, I. 2009. "Oral to literate traditions: Emerging literacies in remote Aboriginal Australia," *TESOL in Context*, 19(2): p. 34.

Kruger, A., and Waterford, G. 2007. *Alone on the Soaks: The Life and Times of Alec Kruger.* Alice Springs, NT: IAD Press.

Kuklick, H. 2012. "The Theory of Evolution and Cultural Anthropology." In A. Fasolo (ed.), *The Theory of Evolution and Its Impact.* New York: Springer Milan, pp. 83–102.

Langton, M., and David, B. 2003. "William Ricketts Sanctuary, Victoria (Australia) sculpting nature and culture in a primitivist theme park," *Journal of Material Culture*, 8(2): pp. 145–168.

Lassiter, L.E. 2001. "From 'reading over the shoulders of natives' to 'reading alongside natives,' Literally: Toward a collaborative and reciprocal ethnography," *Journal of Anthropological Research*, 57(2): pp. 137–149.

Lattas, A., and Morris, B. 2010. "Embedded anthropology and the intervention," *Arena Magazine*, 107: pp. 15–20.

Latz, P.K. 2014. *Blind Moses: Aranda Man of High Degree and Christian Evangelist / Peter Latz.* Alice Springs, NT: Author.

Laufer, B. 2001. " 'We were proper horsemen, us": Aboriginal women: Workers of the outback," *Studies in Western Australian History* (22): pp. 41–51.

Leo, D. 2008. "An Ark of Aboriginal Relics: The Collecting Practices of Dr. L.P. Winterbotham." In N. Peterson, L. Allen . . . and L. Hamby (eds.), *The Makers and Making of Indigenous Australian Museum Collections*. Carlton, Victoria: Melbourne University Publishing, pp. 76–110.

Lewis, D. 1976, "Route finding by desert Aborigines in Australia," *The Journal of Navigation*, 29(1): pp. 21–38.

Lonetree, A. 2012. *Decolonizing Museums: Representing Native America in National and Tribal Museums*. Chapel Hill: University of North Carolina Press.

Long, J. 1992. *The Go-Betweens: The Origins of the Patrol Officer Service in the Northern Territory*. State Library of the Northern Territory, Charles Darwin University Press.

Lovell, J. 2014. *When the Studio Left the Room: What do Wallace's Paintings and Stories of the Eastern Arrernte Homelands Reveal?* Melbourne: RMIT University.

Lydon, J. 2010. "Return: The photographic archive and technologies of Indigenous memory," *Photographies*, 3(2): pp. 173–187.

Lydon, J. 2014. *Calling the Shots: Indigenous Photographies*. Canberra: Aboriginal Studies Press.

Macintyre, S., and Clark, A. 2004. *The History Wars*. Melbourne: Melbourne University Publishing.

Madison, D.S. 2012. *Critical Ethnography: Method, Ethics, and Performance*, 2nd ed. Thousand Oaks, CA: Sage.

Mahood, K. 2012. "Kartiya are like Toyotas: White workers on Australia's cultural frontier," *Griffith Review*, 36: pp. 43–59.

Malaurie, J. 2003. *Ultima Thulé: Explorers and Natives of the Polar North*. New York: Norton.

Malbunka, M. 2004. "Accessing Family Information at the Strehlow Research Centre." In M. Cawthorn (ed.), *Traditions in the Midst of Change: Communities, Cultures and the Strehlow Legacy in Central Australia*. Alice Springs, NT: Strehlow Research Centre, pp. 13–15.

Manne, R. 2003. *Whitewash: On Keith Windschuttle's Fabrication of Aboriginal History*. Carlton, Victoria: Black, Inc.

Marcus, G.E. 1998. *Ethnography through Thick and Thin*. Princeton, NJ: Princeton University Press.

Marcus, J. 2001. *The Indomitable Miss Pink: A Life in Anthropology*. Sydney: University of NSW Press.

Marcuse, H. 1968. *Negations: Essays in Critical Theory*. London: Penguin.

Marmion, D., Obata, K., and Troy, J. 2014. *Community, Identity, Wellbeing: The Report of the Second National Indigenous Languages Survey*. Australian Institute of Aboriginal and Torres Strait Islander Studies, Canberra.

Martin, R. 2013. "The politics of the voice: Ethnographic fetishism and Australian literary studies," *Journal of the Association for the Study of Australian*

Literature, 13(2). www.nla.gov.au/openpublish/index.php/jasal/article/view Article/2646
Martinez, J. 2007. "When wages were clothes: dressing down Aboriginal workers in Australia's Northern Territory," *International Review of Social History*, 52(2): pp. 271–286.
McCarthy, C. 2016. *Museums and Maori: Heritage Professionals, Indigenous Collections, Current Practice*. New York: Routledge.
McCarthy, F.D. 1966. "Ethnographic Films on the Australian Aborigines." Report prepared at the request of UNESCO for presentation to the Sydney (Australia) Round Table meeting (July 25–29), UNESCO Archives, Paris. unesdoc.unesco.org/images/0014/001438/143802eb.pdf
McDonald, B. 1997. "Tradition as personal relationship," *The Journal of American Folklore*, 110(435): pp. 47–67.
McGrath, A. 1987. *Born in the Cattle: Aborigines in Cattle Country*. Sydney: Allen and Unwin.
McGrath, A. 1997. "The History of Pastoral Coexistence." Native Title Report to Human Rights and Equal Opportunity Commission. www.austlii.edu.au/au/other/IndigLRes/1997/4/2.html
McGregor, R. 2005. "Assimilation as Acculturation: A.P. Elkin on the Dynamics of Cultural Change." In T. Rowse (ed.), *Contesting Assimilation*. Perth: API Network, pp. 169–183.
McGregor, R. 2011. *Indifferent Inclusion: Aboriginal People and the Australian Nation*. Canberra: Aboriginal Studies Press.
McNally, W. 1981. *Aborigines, Artefacts, and Anguish*. Adelaide: Lutheran Publishing House.
Meggitt, M.J. 1962. *Desert People: A Study of the Walibiri Aborigines of Central Australia*. Sydney: Angus and Robertson.
Meggitt, M.J. 1966. *Gadjari among the Walbiri Aborigines of Central Australia*. Sydney: University of Sydney.
Memmott, P., Thomson, L., and Long, S. 2006. *Indigenous Mobility in Rural and Remote Australia*. Australian Housing and Urban Research Institute Queensland Research Centre. www.ahuri.edu.au/__data/assets/pdf_file/0011/2126/AHURI_Final_Report_No90_Indigenous_mobility_in_rural_and_remote_Australia.pdf
Merlan, F. 1986, "Australian Aboriginal conception beliefs revisited," *Man*, 21(3): pp. 474–493.
Merlan, F. 1991. "The limits of cultural constructionism: The case of Coronation Hill," *Oceania*, 61(4): pp. 341–352.
Merlan, F. 1998. *Caging the Rainbow: Places, Politics, and Aborigines in a North Australian Town*. Honolulu: University of Hawaii Press.
Merlan, F. 2005. "Explorations towards intercultural accounts of socio-cultural reproduction and change," *Oceania*, 75(3): pp. 167–182.

Merlan, F. 2006. "Beyond tradition," *The Asia Pacific Journal of Anthropology*, 7(1): pp. 85–104.

Merlan, F. 2007. "Indigeneity as Relational Identity: The Construction of Australian Land Rights." In O. Starn and M. de la Cadena (eds.), *Indigenous Experience Today*. New York: Wenner-Gren Foundation for Anthropological Research, pp. 125–150.

Merlan, F. 2013. "Theorizing relationality: A response to the Morphys," *American Anthropologist*, 115(4): pp. 637–638.

Michaels, E. 1985, "Constraints on knowledge in an economy of oral information," *Current Anthropology*, 26(4): pp. 505–510.

Mills, C.W. 2000. *The Sociological Imagination*. New York and Oxford: Oxford University Press.

Mitchell, S. 2012. "Opinion: Return Aboriginal sacred objects," *Australian Geographic*, Sept–Oct(110). www.australiangeographic.com.au/topics/history-culture/2012/12/opinion-return-aboriginal-sacred-objects

Montagu, A. 1974, *Coming into Being among the Australian Aborigines: A Study of the Procreative Beliefs of the Native Tribes of Australia*, 2nd ed. New York and London: Routledge and Kegan Paul.

Monteath, P. 2013. "Globalising German anthropology: Erhard Eylmann in Australia," *Itinerario*, 37 (Special Issue 1): pp. 29–42.

Monteath, P., and Munt, V. 2015. *Red Professor: The Cold War Life of Fred Rose*, Adelaide: Wakefield Press.

Moore, D. 2003. "TGH Strehlow and the linguistic landscape of Australia, 1930–60." Honors thesis, University of New England, Armidale.

Moore, D. 2008. "T.G.H. Strehlow and the linguistic landscape of Australia 1930–1960." In W. McGregor (ed.), *Encountering Aboriginal Languages: Studies in the History of Australian Linguistics*. Canberra: Pacific Linguistics Research School of Pacific and Asian Studies, the Australian National University, pp. 273–300.

Moore, D. 2016. "Altjira, Dream and God." In J.L. Cox and A. Possamai (eds.), *Religion and Non-Religion among Australian Aboriginal Peoples*. London: Routledge, pp. 85–108.

Morphy, F., and Morphy, H. 2013. "Anthropological theory and government policy in Australia's Northern Territory: The hegemony of the "Mainstream," *American Anthropologist*, 115(2): pp. 174–187.

Morphy, H. 1989, "On Representing Ancestral Beings." In H. Morphy (ed.), *Animals into Art*. London: Unwin Hyman, pp. 144–160.

Morphy, H. 1992. *Ancestral Connections: Art and an Aboriginal System of Knowledge*. Chicago: University of Chicago Press.

Morphy, H. 1996. "Empiricism to Metaphysics: In Defence of the Concept of Dreamtime." In T. Bonyhady and T. Griffiths (eds.), *Prehistory to Politics: John Mulvaney, the Humanities and the Public Intellectual*. Melbourne: University of Melbourne Press, pp. 163–189.

Morphy, H. 1997. "Gillen—Man of Science." In D.J. Mulvaney, H. Morphy, and A. Petch (eds.), *My Dear Spencer: The Letters of F.J. Gillen to Baldwin Spencer*, Melbourne: Hyland House.
Morphy, H. 2006. "Sites of Persuasion: Yinapungapu at the National Museum of Australia." In I. Karp, C.A. Kratz, L. Szwaja, and T. Ybarra-Frausto (eds.), *Museum Frictions: Public Cultures/Global Transformations*. Durham, NC: Duke University Press, pp. 469–496.
Morphy, H. 2009. "Re-reading Ronald Berndt: Exploring the depths of his Yolngu ethnography," *Anthropological Forum*, 19(1): pp. 73–97.
Morphy, H. 2010a. "Afterword." In S.H. Dudley (ed.), *Museum Materialities Objects, Engagements, Interpretations*. London and New York: Routledge, pp. 275–285.
Morphy, H. 2010b. "Scientific Knowledge and Rights in Skeletal Remains—Dilemmas in the Curation of "Other" People's Bones." In M. Pickering and P. Turnbull (eds.), *The Long Way Home: The Meaning and Values of Repatriation*. New York and Oxford: Berghahn Books, pp. 147–162.
Morphy, H. 2012. "Becoming a visual anthropologist," *Humanities Research, Canberra*, 18(1): p. 5.
Morrison, G. 2017. *Writing Home: Walking, Literature and Belonging in Australia's Red Centre*. Melbourne: Melbourne University Publishing.
Morton, J. 1993. "Romancing the stones," *Arena Magazine*, April/May (4): pp. 39–40.
Morton, J. 1994. *The Proposed Anmatjere Land Council: Its Historical Antecedents and an Estimation of Levels of Support*. Canberra: Aboriginal and Torres Strait Islander Commission.
Morton, J. 1995. "Secrets of the Arandas": T.G.H. Strehlow and the Course of Revelation." In C. Anderson (ed.), *Politics of the Secret*. Oceania Monograph. Sydney: University of Sydney, pp. 51–66.
Morton, J. 1997. "Arrernte (Aranda) Land tenure: An Evaluation of the Strehlow Model," Occasional Paper, no. 1. Alice Springs, NT: Strehlow Research Centre, pp. 107–126.
Morton, J. 2004. "Krippendorf's Lesson in the Centre: The Shaping of the Arrernte through T.G.H. Strehlow's 'Family Romance.'" In M. Cawthorn (ed.), *Traditions in the Midst of Change: Communities, Cultures and the Strehlow Legacy in Central Australia*. Alice Springs, NT: Strehlow Research Centre, pp. 42–47.
Morton, J. "The Strehlow Collection of Sacred Objects," *Central Land Council*. www.clc.org.au/articles/info/Strehlow
Moyle, A. 1959. "Sir Baldwin Spencer's Recordings of Australian Aboriginal Singing." In *Memoirs of the National Museum*. Melbourne: National Museum of Victoria, pp. 7–36.
Moyle, A.M. 1966. *Handlist of Field Collections of Recorded Music in Australia and the Torres Strait*. Canberra: Australian Institute of Aboriginal Studies, Canberra. trove.nla.gov.au/version/44842399
Moyle, R.M. 1986. *Alyawarra Music: Songs and Society in a Central Australian Community*. Canberra: Australian Institute of Aboriginal Studies.

Mulvaney, D.J. 1976. "'The Chain of Connection': The Material Evidence." In N. Peterson (ed.), *Tribes and Boundaries in Australia*. Canberra: AIAS, pp. 72–94.

Mulvaney, D.J. 1991. "Past regained, future lost: The Kow Swamp pleistone burials," *Antiquity*, 65(246): pp. 12–21.

Mulvaney, D.J. 2001. "Erlikilyika: Arrernte Ethnographer and Artist." In A.J. Anderson, I. Lilley, and S. O'Connor (eds.), *Histories of Old Ages: Essays in Honour of Rhys Jones*. Canberra: Pandanus Books, pp. 277–286.

Mulvaney, J. 2004. "'The Purpose of a Good Translation': T.G.H. Strehlow and the Oral History of Barrow Creek." In M. Cawthorn (ed.), *Strehlow Conference Proceedings: Traditions in the midst of change*. Alice Springs: Northern Territory Government, pp. 84–89.

Mulvaney, J., Petch, A., and Morphy., H. 2000. *From the Frontier: Outback Letters to Baldwin Spencer*. Sydney: Allen and Unwin.

Munn, N.D. 1970. "The Transformation of Subjects into Objects in Walbiri and Pitjantjatjara Myth." In R.M. Berndt (ed.), *Australian Aboriginal Anthropology: Modern Studies in the Social Anthropology of the Australian Aborigines*. Perth: University of Western Australia Press, pp. 141–163.

Munn, N.D. 1973. *Walbiri Iconography: Graphic Representation and Cultural Symbolism in a Central Australian Society*. Ithaca, NY: Cornell University Press.

Myers, F. 1980. "A broken code: Pintupi political theory and temporary social life," *Mankind*, 12(4): pp. 311–326.

Myers, F. 1982. "Always Ask: Resource Use and Land Ownership among Pintupi Aborigines of the Australian Western Desert." In E. Hunn and N. Williams (eds.), *Resource Managers: North American and Australian Hunter-Gatherers*, Boulder, CO: Westview Press for the American Association for the Advancement of Science, pp. 173–195.

Myers, F. 1991. *Pintupi Country, Pintupi Self: Sentiment, Place and Politics among Western Desert Aborigines*. Berkeley: University of California Press.

Myers, F. 1997. "Ways of Placemaking." In H. Morphy and K. Flint (eds.), *Culture, Landscape, and the Environment: The Linacre Lectures*. Oxford: Oxford University Press, pp. 73–110.

Myers, F. 2002. *Painting Culture: The Making of an Aboriginal High Art*. Durham, NC: Duke University Press.

Myers, F. 2006. "'Primitivism,' Anthropology and the Category of 'Primitive Art.'" In C. Tilley, W. Keane, S. Kuechler, M. Rowlands, and P. Spyer (eds.), *Handbook of Material Culture*. Thousand Oaks, CA: Sage, pp. 267–284.

Myers, F. 2010. "All around Australia and overseas: Christianity and Indigenous identities in Central Australia 1988," *The Australian Journal of Anthropology* 21(2010): 110–128.

Myers, F. 2014. "Paintings, publics, and protocols: The early paintings from Papunya," *Material Culture Review / Revue de la culture matérielle*, 79: pp. 78–91.

Nakata, M. 2007. *Disciplining the Savages, Savaging the Disciplines.* Canberra: Aboriginal Studies Press.

Nakata, M., Gardiner, G., Gibson, J., McKeough, J., Byrne, A., and Nakata, V. 2008. "Indigenous digital collections: An early look at the organisation and culture interface," *Australian Academic and Research Libraries*, 39(4): pp. 223–236.

Nash, D. 1982. "An Etymological Note on Warlpiri Kurdungurlu." In J. Heath, F. Merlan, and A. Rumsey (eds.), *Languages of Kinship in Aboriginal Australia*, Sydney: University of Sydney, pp. 141–159.

Nash, D. 1998. "Ethnocartography: Understanding Central Australian geographic literacy." Unpublished Draft.

Nash, S.E., and Colwell-Chanthaphonh, C. 2010. "Nagpra after two decades," *Museum Anthropology*, 33(2): pp. 99–104.

Nettelbeck, A., and Foster, R. 2007. *In the Name of the Law: William Willshire and the Policing of the Australian Frontier.* Adelaide: Wakefield Press.

News. 1937. "Police to probe native killing report," p. 2.

Nora, P. 1989. "Between memory and history: Les lieux de mémoire," *Representations* 26: pp. 7–24.

O'Byrne, D. 1993. *Strehlow Research Centre.* Alice Springs: Northern Territory Government.

Olson, D.R., and Torrance, N. 1991. *Literacy and Orality.* Cambridge: Cambridge University Press.

Ong, W. 1988. *Orality and Literacy: The Technologizing of the Word.* London: Routledge.

O'Reilly, K. 2009. *Key Concepts in Ethnography.* Los Angeles and London: Sage.

Ottosson, Å. 2016. *Making Aboriginal Men and Music in Central Australia.* London: Bloomsbury Academic.

Palmer, K. 1982. *Mental Maps and Lines of Enquiry.* Melbourne: Deakin University Press.

Palmer, S. 2013. "Making histories 'Ngapartji-ngapartji way': Exploring collaboration, exchange and intercultural histories in a colonised settler nation," *History Compass*, 11(2): pp. 117–132.

Paterson, L. 2010. "Print culture and the collective Māori consciousness," *Journal of New Zealand Literature*: 28: pp. 105–129.

Pawu-Kurlpurlurnu, W.J., Holmes, M., and Box, A. 2008. *Ngurra-Kurlu: A Way of Working with Warlpiri People.* Desert Knowledge CRC, Alice Springs. www.desertknowledgecrc.com.au/resource/DKCRC-Report-41-Ngurra-kurlu.pdf

Peers, L., Reinius, L.G., and Shannon, J. 2017. "Introduction: Repatriation and ritual, repatriation as ritual," *Museum Worlds*, 5(1): pp. 1–8.

Perkins, R. 2016. "Songs to live by: The Arrernte women's project is preserving vital songs and culture," *The Monthly.* www.themonthly.com.au/issue/2016/july/1467295200/rachel-perkins/songs-live

Peterson, N. 1976. *Tribes and Boundaries in Australia*. Canberra: Australian Institute of Aboriginal Studies.

Peterson, N. 2000. "An expanding Aboriginal domain: Mobility and the initiation journey," *Oceania*, 70(3): pp. 205–218.

Peterson, N. 2003. "The Changing Photographic Contract: Aborigines and Image Ethics." In N. Peterson and C. Pinny (eds.), *Photography's Other Histories*, Durham, NC: Duke University Press, pp. 119–145.

Peterson, N. 2004. "Myth of the 'Walkabout': Movement in the Aboriginal Domain." In J. Taylor and M. Bell (eds.), *Population Mobility and Indigenous Peoples in Australasia and North America* London: Routledge, pp. 223–238.

Peterson, N., Allen, L., and Hamby, L. 2008a, "Introduction." In N. Peterson, L. Allen, and L. Hamby (eds.), *The Makers and Making of Indigenous Australian Museum Collections*. Carlton, Victoria: Melbourne University Press, pp. 1–26.

Peterson, N., Allen, L., and Hamby, L. 2008b. *The Makers and Making of Indigenous Australian Museum Collections*. Carlton, Victoria: Melbourne University Publishing.

Peterson, N., and Long, J. 1986, *Australian Territorial Organization: A Band Perspective*. Sydney: University of Sydney.

Pink, O. 1933. "Spirit ancestors in a northern Aranda Horde Country," *Oceania*, IV(2): pp. 176–186.

Pink, O. 1936. "The landowners of the northern division of the Aranda tribe, Central Australia," *Oceania*, 6(3): pp. 275–305.

Platt, T., and Quisbert, P. 2007. "Knowing Silence and Merging Horizons: The Case of the Great Protosi Cover-Up." In *Ways of Knowing: New Approaches in the Anthropology of Learning and Experience*. Wiltshire: Berghahn Books.

Porteus, S.D. 1931. *The Psychology of a Primitive People: A Study of the Australian Aborigine*. London: Edward Arnold.

Povinelli, E.A. 2002. *The Cunning of Recognition: Indigenous Alterities and the Making of Australian Multiculturalism*. Durham, NC: Duke University Press.

Pratt, M.L. 1992. *Imperial Eyes: Travel Writing and Transculturation*. London: Routledge.

Prosser, J. 2011. "Visual Methodology: Toward a More Seeing Research." In N.K. Denzin and Y.S. Lincoln (eds.), *The SAGE Handbook of Qualitative Research*. London: Sage, pp. 479–495.

Purvis, A.V. 1940. "Heroes Unsung." Unpublished manuscript. Alice Springs, NT.

Radcliffe-Brown, A.R. 1918. "Notes on the social organization of Australian tribes," *Journal of the Royal Anthropological Institute of Great Britain and Ireland*, 48: pp. 222–253.

Radcliffe-Brown, A.R. 1930. "The social organization of Australian tribes," *Oceania*, 1(1): pp. 444–456.

Ram, K., and Houston, C. 2015. "Introduction: Phenomenology's Methodological Invitation." In M. Jackson, K. Ram, and C. Houston (eds.), *Phenomenology*

in Anthropology: A Sense of Perspective. Bloomington: Indiana University Press, pp. 1–28.
Ramsland, J., and Mooney, C. 2012. *Remembering Aboriginal Heroes: Struggle, Identity and the Media.* Melbourne: Brolga Publishing.
Read, P. 1983, "'A rape of a soul so profound': Some reflections on the dispersal policy in New South Wales," *Aboriginal History*, 7(1/2): pp. 23–33.
Read, P., and Read, J. (eds). 1993. *Long Time, Olden Time: Aboriginal Accounts of Northern Territory History.* [Electronic resource.] Penrith, NSW: Firmware Publishing.
Redmond, A. 2005. "Strange relatives: Mutualities and dependencies between Aborigines and pastoralists in the Northern Kimberley," *Oceania*, 75(3): pp. 234–246.
Rigsby, B. 1998. "Genealogies, Kinship and Local Group Organisation: Old Yintjingga (Port Stewart) in the Late 1920s." In B. Rigsby, J. Finlayson, and H.J. Bek (eds.), *Connections in Native Title: Genealogies, Kinship and Groups.* Research monograph no. 13. Canberra: Australian National University Centre for Aboriginal Economic Policy Research.
Rigsby, B., Finlayson, J., and Bek, H.J. 1998. *Connections in Native Title: Genealogies, Kinship and Groups.* Canberra: Australian National University Centre for Aboriginal Economic Policy Research.
Roberts, T. 2009. "The brutal truth: What happened in the Gulf Country," *The Monthly* (November): pp. 42–51.
Robinson, E. 2010. "Touching the void: Affective history and the impossible," *Rethinking History*, 14(4): pp. 503–520.
Robinson, R. 1956. *The Feathered Serpent: The Mythological Genesis and Recreative Ritual of the Aboriginal Tribes of the Northern Territory of Australia: The Kuppapoingo [and others].* . . . NSW: Edwards and Shaw.
Roennfeldt, D., and Western Arrarnta Communities. 2006. *Western Arrarnta Picture Dictionary.* Alice Springs, NT: Institute of Aboriginal Development Press,
Róheim, G. 1925. *Australian Totemism: A Psycho-Analytic Study in Anthropology,* London: Allen and Unwin.
Róheim, G. 1932. "Psychoanalysis of primitive cultural types," *International Journal of Psycho-Analysis*, 8.
Róheim, G. 1945. *The Eternal Ones of the Dream: A Psychoanalytic Interpretation of Australian Myth and Ritual.* New York: International Universities Press.
Róheim, G. 1974. *Children of the Desert: The Western Tribes of Central Australia.* Edited by W. Muensterberger. New York: Basic Books.
Róheim, G. 1988. *Children of the Desert II: Myths and Dreams of the Aborigines of Central Australia.* Edited by J. Morton and W. Muensterberger. Sydney: Oceania Publications.
Rolls, M. 2010. "Finding fault: Aborigines, anthropologists, popular writers and walkabout," *Australian Cultural History*, 28(2–3): pp. 179–200.
Rose, D.B. 1992. *Dingo Makes Us Human: Life and Land in an Australian Aboriginal Culture.* Melbourne: Cambridge University Press.

Rose, D.B. 1999. "Taking notice," *Worldviews: Global Religions, Culture and Ecology*, 3(1): pp. 97–103.
Rose, D.B. 2000. "To dance with time: A Victoria River Aboriginal study," *The Australian Journal of Anthropology*, 11(2): pp. 287–296.
Rose, D.B. 2004. *Reports from a Wild Country: Ethics for Decolonisation*. Sydney: UNSW Press.
Rose, D.B. 2005. "The Redemptive Frontier: A Long Road to Nowhere." In D.B. Rose and R. Davis (eds.), *Dislocating the Frontier: Essaying the Mystique of the Uutback*. Canberra: ANU Press, pp. 49–66.
Rowse, T. 1992. "Strehlow's strap: Functionalism and historicism in a colonial ethnography," *Journal of Australian Studies*, 16(35): pp. 88–103.
Rowse, T. 1998. *White Flour, White Power: From Rations to Citizenship in Central Australia*. New York: Cambridge University Press.
Rowse, T. 1999. "The Collector as Outsider—T.G.H. Strehlow as 'Public Intellectual.'" Occasional Paper, Strehlow Research Centre. Alice Springs: Northern Territory Government, pp. 61–120.
Rowse, T. 2012. "Strehlow Dams Coombs." In *Rethinking Social Justice: From "Peoples" to "Populations."* Canberra: Aboriginal Studies Press, pp. 45–61.
Roy, L. 2015. "Indigenous Cultural Heritage Preservation: A Review Essay with Ideas for the Future," *IFLA Journal*, 41(3): pp. 192–203.
Rubuntja, M. 2011. "Foreword." In R.G. Kimber (ed.), *Cultural Values Associated with Alice Springs Water*. Alice Springs: Northern Territory Department of Natural Resources, Environment and Sport. www.territorystories.nt.gov.au/handle/10070/235032
Rubuntja, W., and Green, J.A. 2002. *The Town Grew Up Dancing: The Life and Art of Wenten Rubuntja*. Alice Springs, NT: Jukurrpa Books.
Rumsey, A. 1999. "Comment on Mulvaney et al. 1997: 'My Dear Spencer' and review of it in *Oceania* by Diane Austin-Broos," *Oceania*, 70(2): pp. 177–178.
Sahlins, M. 1985. *Islands of History*. Chicago: University of Chicago Press.
Sahlins, M. 1995. *How "Natives" Think about Captain Cook, for Example*. Chicago: University of Chicago Press.
Sandall, R. 1972. *Coniston Muster* (Documentary Film). Australian Institute of Aboriginal Studies.
Sanders, W., and Holcombe, S. 2005. *Anmatjere: Representation in an Early Regional Structure*. Canberra: Centre for Aboriginal Economic Policy Research, Australian National University.
Sansom, B. 2006. "Looter of the dreamings: Xavier Herbert and the taking of Kaijek's new song story," *Oceania*, 76(1): pp. 83–104.
Scherer, P.A. 1993. *Sunset of an Era: The Heffernan's of Ti Tree*. Tanunda, SAPA: Scherer.
Schröder, W. 2004. "Erhard Eylmann: A pioneer of exploration and anthropology in Australia," *Anthropological Forum*, 14(1): pp. 43–51.

Schulz, D. 1992. "Sacred objects in tug-of-war: Ted Strehlow collection of Aboriginal artefacts is on sale," *The Bulletin*: pp. 60–61.
Scott, E., and Luby, E. 2007. "Maintaining relationships with native communities: The role of museum management and governance," *Museum Management and Curatorship*, 22(3): pp. 265–285.
Scott, J.C. 1990. *Domination and the Arts of Resistance: Hidden Transcripts*. New Haven, CT: Yale University Press.
Shakespeare, N. 2000. *Bruce Chatwin*. London: Vintage.
Shryock, A. 1997. *Nationalism and the Genealogical Imagination: Oral History and Textual Authority in Tribal Jordan*. Berkeley, CA: University of California Press.
Sider, G.M., and Smith, G.A. 1997. *Between History and Histories: The Making of Silences and Commemorations*. Toronto: University of Toronto Press.
Sinclair, C. 2013. "A series of riots in Ti Tree have been blamed on an invading Aboriginal group," *NT News/Centralian Advocate*.
Smith, B., and Hinkson, M. (eds). 2005. "Figuring the intercultural in Aboriginal Australia," *Oceania*, Special Issue, 75(3).
Smith, L.T. 1999. *Decolonizing Methodologies: Research and Indigenous Peoples*. Otago: Zed Books.
Smith, M. 2013. *The Archaeology of Australia's Deserts*. New York: Cambridge University Press.
Smith, R. 2009. "Stuff at the core of land rights claims: The Strehlow collection," *Journal of Northern Territory History*, 20: pp. 75–93.
Smith, R.J. 1990. "Hearing Voices, Joining the Chorus: Appropriating Someone Else's Fieldnotes." In R. Sanjek (ed.), *Fieldnotes: The Makings of Anthropology*. Ithaca, NY: Cornell University Press, pp. 356–370.
Spencer, B., and Gillen, F. 1899. *The Native Tribes of Central Australia*. New York: Dover Publications.
Spencer, S.B., and Gillen, F.J. 1927. *The Arunta: A Study of a Stone Age People*. London: Macmillan and Company Ltd.
Spencer, W.B. 1928. *Wanderings in Wild Australia*. London: MacMillan and Co.
Spencer, W.B. 2013. *Walter Baldwin Spencer's Diary from the Spencer and Gillen Expedition 1901–1902*. Edited by J. Gibson. Melbourne: Museum Victoria. spencerandgillen.net/files/Spencers%20Expedition%20Diary.pdf
Spencer, W.B., and Gillen, F.J. 1904. *The Northern Tribes of Central Australia*. London: MacMillan and Co.
Spierings, J. 1984. "The History of Ti Tree." In *Ti Tree Land Claim: Claim Book*. Alice Springs, NT: Central Land Council, pp. 1–52.
Spivak, G. 1988. "Can the Subaltern Speak?" In C. Nelson and L. Grossberg (eds.), *Marxism and the Interpretation of Culture*. Urbana: University of Illinois Press, pp. 271–313.
Stanley, N. (ed.). 2007a. *The Future of Indigenous Museums: Perspectives from the Southwest Pacific*. New York: Berghahn Books.

Stanley, N. 2007b. "Introduction: Indigeneity and Museum Practice in the Southwest Pacific." In N. Stanley (ed.), *The Future of Indigenous Museums: Perspectives from the Southwest Pacific*. New York: Berghahn Books, pp. 1–20.

Stanner, W.E.H. 1979. *White Man Got No Dreaming: Essays 1938–1973*. Canberra: Australian National University Press.

Stanton, J. 2011. "Ethnographic Museums and Collections: From the Past into the Future." In L. Paroissien and D. Griffin (eds.), *Understanding Museums: Australian museums and museology*. Canberra: National Museum of Australia. nma.gov.au/research/understanding-museums/JStanton_2011.html

Starn, O. 2004. *Ishi's Brain in Search of America's Last "Wild" Indian*. New York: Norton.

Starn, O. 2011. "Here Come the Anthros (Again): The Strange Marriage of Anthropology and Native America," *Cultural Anthropology*, 26(2): pp. 179–204.

Stevens, C. 1994. *White Man's Dreaming: Killalpaninna Mission, 1866–1915*. Melbourne: Oxford University Press.

Stocking, G.W. (ed.). 1983. *Observers Observed: Essays on Ethnographic Fieldwork*. Wisconsin: University of Wisconsin Press.

Stocking, G.W. 1989. *Romantic Motives: Essays on Anthropological Sensibility*. Wisconsin: University of Wisconsin Press.

Stocking, G.W. (ed.). 1993. *Colonial Situations: Essays on the Contextualization of Ethnographic Knowledge*. Madison: University of Wisconsin Press.

Stoler, A. 2006. "Colonial Archives and the Arts of Governance: On the Content in the Form." In *Archives, Documentation, and Institutions of Social Memory: Essays from the Sawyer Seminar*.

Stoler, A.L. 2010. *Along the Archival Grain: Epistemic Anxieties and Colonial Common Sense*. Princeton, NJ: Princeton University Press.

Strehlow, C. 1907a. *The Aranda and Loritja Tribes of Central Australia Part 1: Myths, Legends and Fables of the Aranada Tribe*. Edited by M.F. Von Leonhardi. Frankfurt Am Main: Municipal Ethnological Museum.

Strehlow, C. 1907b. *Die Aranda Und Loritja Stamme in Zentral Australien*, Hermannsburg. Unpublished.

Strehlow, J. 2011. *The Tale of Frieda Keysser: Frieda Keysser and Carl Strehlow: An Historical Biography*. Istanbul: Wild Cat Publishing.

Strehlow, T.G.H. 1932. *Book I: Field Diary (1) 1932*. Alice Springs, NT: Strehlow Research Centre.

Strehlow, T.G.H. 1933a. "Ankotarinja, an Aranda myth," *Oceania*, 4(2): pp. 187–200.

Strehlow, T.G.H. 1933b. *Book II: Field Diary (2) 1933–34*. Alice Springs, NT: Strehlow Research Centre.

Strehlow, T.G.H. 1937. *Personal Diary 3(a) (1937–1938)*. Alice Springs, NT: Strehlow Research Centre.

Strehlow, T.G.H. 1938. *An Aranda Grammar*. MA thesis, University of Adelaide, Adelaide.

Strehlow, T.G.H. 1942. "Aranda phonetics," *Oceania*, 12(3): pp. 255-302.
Strehlow, T.G.H. 1947. *Aranda Traditions* (2nd ed.). New York: Johnson Reprint.
Strehlow, T.G.H. 1948. *Book XIII, Legends and Chants collected at Hermannsburg Fed-March 1948*. Alice Springs, NT: Strehlow Research Centre.
Strehlow, T.G.H. 1949. *Book XV: Field Diary*. Alice Springs, NT: Strehlow Research Centre.
Strehlow, T.G.H. 1950a. *London Diary 1 (b)*. Alice Springs, NT: Strehlow Research Centre.
Strehlow, T.G.H. 1950b. "Agencies of Social Control in Central Australian Aboriginal Societies." Occasional Paper, Strehlow Research Centre. Alice Springs: Northern Territory Government, pp. 1-50.
Strehlow, T.G.H. 1952. *London Diary 3 (1951-1952)*. Alice Springs, NT: Strehlow Research Centre.
Strehlow, T.G.H. 1953a. *Book XVII: Field Diary (17) 1953*. Alice Springs, NT: Strehlow Research Centre.
Strehlow, T.G.H. 1953b. *Book XVIII: Field Diary and Myths 18 (1953)*. Strehlow Research Centre, Alice Springs. Unpublished.
Strehlow, T.G.H. 1955a. *Book XVIIII: Field Diary (19) 1955*. Alice Springs, NT: Strehlow Research Centre.
Strehlow, T.G.H. 1955b. *Book XXI: Field Diary (21) 1955*. Alice Springs, NT: Strehlow Research Centre.
Strehlow, Theodor George Henry. 1956. *Friendship with South-East Asia: A Cultural Approach*. Melbourne: Riall Bros.
Strehlow, T.G.H. 1956. *The Sustaining Ideals of Australian Aboriginal Societies*. Adelaide: Aboriginal Advancement League of South Australia.
Strehlow, T.G.H. 1958a. *Dark and White Australians*. Melbourne: Riall Bros.
Strehlow, T.G.H. 1958b. *Book XXII: Field Diary (22) 1958*. Alice Springs, NT: Strehlow Research Centre.
Strehlow, T.G.H. 1959. *The Land of Altjira*. Strehlow Research Centre. Unpublished manuscript.
Strehlow, T.G.H. 1961a. *Rex Battarbee: Artist and Founder of the Aboriginal Art Movement in Central Australia*. Sydney: Legend Press.
Strehlow, T.G.H. 1961b. *Nomads in No-Man's Land*. Adelaide: The Aborigines Advancement League.
Strehlow, T.G.H. 1962. *Book XXVIII. Field Diary 28 (1962)*. Alice Springs, NT: Strehlow Research Centre.
Strehlow, T.G.H. 1963. *Office Diary 2 (1963)*. Alice Springs, NT: Strehlow Research Centre.
Strehlow, T.G.H. 1964a. *Book XXXIII: Field Diary (33) 1964*. Alice Springs, NT: Strehlow Research Centre.
Strehlow, T.G.H. 1964. "The Art of Circle, Line, and Square." In R.M. Berndt (ed.), *Australian Aboriginal Art*. Sydney: Ure Smith, pp. 44-59.

Strehlow, T.G.H. 1964b. *Book XXXII: Field Diary (32) 1964*. Alice Springs, NT: Strehlow Research Centre.
Strehlow, T.G.H. 1964c. "Personal Monototemism in a Polytotemic Community." In M. Schuster, E. Haberland, and H. Straube (eds.), *Festschrift fur Ad. E. Jensen*. Munchen: Klaus Renner Verlag, pp. 723-754.
Strehlow, T.G.H. 1964d. *Assimilation Problems: The Aboriginal Viewpoint*. Adelaide: Aborigines Advancement League.
Strehlow, T.G.H. 1965a. *Book XXXIV: Field Diary (34) 1965*. Alice Springs, NT: Strehlow Research Centre.
Strehlow, T.G.H. 1965b. "William Ricketts and the Mount Dandenong Sanctuary." In *A Living Voice of the Living Bush*. Melbourne: The Forests Commission of Victoria.
Strehlow, T.G.H. 1965c. "Culture, Social Structure and Environment in Aboriginal Central Australia." In C.H. Berndt and R.M. Berndt (eds.), *Aboriginal Man in Australia*. Sydney: Angus and Robertson, pp. 121-145.
Strehlow, T.G.H. 1965d. *Book XXXVI: Field Diary (36) 1965*. Alice Springs, NT: Strehlow Research Centre.
Strehlow, T.G.H. 1966. "Relative relatives," *Australian Book Review*, 5(4): pp. 74-75.
Strehlow, T.G.H. 1967. *Comments on the Journals of John McDouall Stuart*. Adelaide: Libraries Board of South Australia.
Strehlow, T.G.H. 1968a. *Book XXVIII: Field Dairy (38) 1968*. Alice Springs, NT: Strehlow Research Centre.
Strehlow, T.G.H. 1968b. *Spencer 1901 Recordings*, Alice Springs. Unpublished manuscript.
Strehlow, T.G.H. 1969a. *Journey to Horseshoe Bend*. Sydney: Seal Books.
Strehlow, T.G.H. 1969b. "Landmark of anthropology," *Australian Book Review*, 8(8): p. 151.
Strehlow, T.G.H. 1969c. *Handbook to Central Australian Genealogies*. Adelaide: University of Adelaide.
Strehlow, T.G.H. 1970a. "Fortschritt ins Nichts [review]," *Journal of the Australasian Universities Modern Languages Association* (3): pp. 365-366.
Strehlow, T.G.H. 1970b. "Geography and the Totemic Landscape in Central Australia: A Functional Study." In R.M. Berndt (ed.), *Australian Aboriginal Anthropology: Modern Studies in the Social Anthropology of the Australian Aborigines*. Perth: University of Western Australia Press, pp. 93-140.
Strehlow T.G.H. 1971a. *Songs of Central Australia*. Sydney: Angus and Robertson.
Strehlow, T.G.H. 1971b. *Book XLII: Field Diary (42) 1971*. Alice Springs, NT: Strehlow Research Centre,
Strehlow, T.G.H. 1975. *The Alice Springs Aboriginal Land Rights: A Report Commissioned by the Northern Territory Country Liberal Party*. Unpublished report.
Strehlow, T.G.H. 1978a. "Central Australian man-making ceremonies with special reference to Hermannsburg, Northern Territory," *The Lutheran*, 12(7): pp. 150-155.

Strehlow, T.G.H. 1978b. *Central Australian Religion: Personal Monototemism in a Polytotemic Community*. Bedford Park: Australian Association for the Study of Religions.
Strehlow, T.G.H. 1978c. "In the beginning," *Journal of the Anthropological Society of South Australia*, 16(8): pp. 4–8.
Strehlow, T.G.H. 1999. "Aranda Regular and Irregular Marriages." In B. Galt-Smith (ed.), Occasional Paper, Strehlow Research Centre. Alice Springs: Northern Territory Government, pp. 1–45.
Strehlow, W. 1996. *Wüstentanz: Australien spirituell erleben durch Mythen, Sagen, Marchen und Gesange*, Strehlow Verlag, Allensbach am Bodensee.
Stuart, J.M. 1865. *The Journals of John McDouall Stuart* (2nd ed.). Edited by W. Hardman. London: Saunders, Otley and Co.
Stumpe, L.H. 2005. "Restitution or repatriation? The story of some New Zealand Māori human remains," *Journal of Museum Ethnography* (17): pp. 130–140.
Sturmer, J.R.V. 1981. *Talking with Aborigines*. Canberra: Australian Institute of Aboriginal Studies.
Sullivan, P. 2005. "Searching for the intercultural, searching for the culture," *Oceania*, 75(3): pp. 183–194.
Sullivan, P. 2006. "Introduction: Culture without cultures—The culture effect," *The Australian Journal of Anthropology*, 17(3): pp. 253–264.
Summers, J. 2000. "The Parliament of the Commonwealth of Australia and Indigenous Peoples 1901–1967," *Research Papers 2000-01*, 10. www.aph.gov.au/About_Parliament/Parliamentary_Departments/Parliamentary_Library/pubs/rp/rp0001/01RP10
Sutton, P. 1987. "Mystery and Change." In T. Donaldson, M.C. Ross, and S. Wild (eds.), *Songs of Aboriginal Australia*. Sydney: University of Sydney, pp. 77–92.
Sutton, P. 1988. "Myth as History, History as Myth." In I. Keen (ed.), *Being Black: Aboriginal Cultures in "Settled" Australia*. Canberra: Aboriginal Studies Press, pp. 251–268.
Sutton, P. 1995. *Country: Aboriginal Boundaries and Land Ownership in Australia*. Canberra: Aboriginal History.
Sutton, P. 1996. "The robustness of Aboriginal land tenure systems: Underlying and proximate customary titles," *Oceania*, 67(1): pp. 7–29.
Sutton, P. 1998. *Native Title and the Descent of Rights*. Perth: National Native Title Tribunal.
Sutton, P. 2002. "Unusual couples: Relationships and research on the knowledge frontier." www.aiatsis.gov.au/_files/events/wentworth/lectures/Suttton.pdf
Sutton, P. 2003. *Native Title in Australia: An Ethnographic Perspective*. Melbourne: Cambridge University Press.
Sutton, P. 2009a. *The Politics of Suffering: Indigenous Australia and the End of the Liberal Consensus*. Melbourne: Melbourne University Publishing.
Sutton, P. 2009b. "Melbourne's outback," *Dialogue*, 28(2): pp. 74–78.

Sutton, P. 2010. "Aboriginal spirituality in a new age," *Australian Journal of Anthropology*, 21(1): pp. 71–89.
Sweeney, D. 2006. "Taking Ethnographic Film Back." In *Being There: After*, ses. library.usyd.edu.au/bitstream/2123/2515/1/ADSA2006_Sweeney.pdf
Tamisari, F. 2006. "'Personal Acquaintance": Essential Individuality and the Possibilities of Encounters." In T. Lea, E. Kowal, and G. Cowlishaw (eds.), *Moving Anthropology: Critical Indigenous Studies*. NT, Australia: Charles Darwin University Press, pp. 17–36.
Tamisari, F. 2014. "'Sitting around the fire ashes.' An epistemology of personal acquaintance." In *Les actes de colloques en ligne du musée du quai Branly*, Musée du quai Branly (département de la recherche et de l'enseignement). actesbranly.revues.org/522
Taylor, A. 2013. "Caterpillar childhoods: Engaging the otherwise worlds of Central Australian Aboriginal children," *Global Studies of Childhood*, 3(4): pp. 366–379.
Tedlock, D. 1979. "The analogical tradition and the emergence of a dialogical anthropology," *Journal of Anthropological Research*, 35(4): pp. 387–400.
Tedlock, D. 1983. *The Spoken Word and the Work of Interpretation*. Philadelphia: University of Pennsylvania Press.
Tedlock, D., and Mannheim, B. 1995. *The Dialogic Emergence of Culture*. Urbana: University of Illinois Press.
Thieberger, N. 1995. *Paper and Talk: A Manual for Reconstituting Materials in Australian Indigenous Languages from Historical Sources*. Canberra: Aboriginal Studies Press.
Thomas, M. 2007. "Taking them back: Archival media in Arnhem land today," *Cultural Studies Review*, 13(2): pp. 20–37.
Thomas, N. 1999. *Possessions: Indigenous Art, Colonial Culture*. London: Thames and Hudson.
Thomas, N. 2000. "Epilogue." In M. O'Hanlon and R.L. Welsch (eds.), *Hunting the Gatherers: Ethnographic Collectors, Agents, and Agency in Melanesia, 1870s–1930s*. New York and Oxford: Berghahn Books, pp. 273–277.
Thorpe, K., and Galassi, M. 2014. "Rediscovering Indigenous languages: The role and impact of libraries and archives in cultural revitalisation," *Australian Academic and Research Libraries*, 45(2): pp. 81–100.
Tindale, N. 1931. *Expedition to Cockatoo Creek, Central Australia: Journal and field notes, Aug.–Sept. 1931*. Adelaide: South Australian Museum, Adelaide University.
Toren, C., and Pina-Cabral, J. de 2011. *The Challenge of Epistemology: Anthropological Perspectives*. New York: Berghahn Books.
Torrence, R., and Clarke, A. 2011. "Suitable for Decoration of Hals and Billiard Rooms": Finding Indigenous Agency in Historic Auction and Sale Catalogues." In S. Byrne, R. Torrence, R. Harrison, and A. Clarke (eds.), *Unpacking*

the Collection Networks of Material and Social Agency in the Museum. New York: Springer, pp. 29–53.

Treloyn, S., and Emberly, A. 2013. "Sustaining traditions: Ethnomusicological collections, access and sustainability in Australia," *Musicology Australia*, 35(2): pp. 159–177.

Trigger, D.S. 1992. *"Whitefella comin": Aboriginal Responses to Colonialism in Northern Australia*. Melbourne: Cambridge University Press.

Trouillot, M.-R. 1995. *Silencing the Past: Power and the Production of History*. Boston: Beacon Press.

Turnbull, P., and Pickering, M. (eds). 2010. *The Long Way Home: The Meaning and Values of Repatriation*. New York: Berghahn Books.

Turner, M.K. 2010. *Iwenhe Tyerrtye: What It Means to Be an Aboriginal Person*. Alice Springs, NT: IAD Press.

Turner, V.E. 1930. *The "Good fella missus."* Adelaide: United Aborigines Mission.

Turpin, M. 2002. "Body part terms in Kaytetye feeling expressions," *Pragmatics and Cognition*, 10(1/2): pp. 271–305.

Turpin, M. 2005. "Form and Meaning of Akwelye: A Kaytetye Women's Song Series from Central Australia." PhD dissertation. ses.library.usyd.edu.au:80/handle/2123/1334

Turpin, M. 2013. *Antarrengeny Awely: Alyawarr Women's Songs from Antarrengeny*. Alice Springs, NT: Batchelor Press.

Turpin, M. 2004. "Have you ever wondered why Arrernte is spelt the way it is?" *Central Land Council*. www.academia.edu/5208191/Have_you_ever_wondered_why_Arrernte_is_spelt_the_way_it_is

Turpin, M., and Green, J. 2011. "Trading in Terms: Linguistic Affiliation in Arandic Songs and Alternate Registers." In I. Mushin, R. Gardner, and M. Marvey (eds.), *Indigenous Language and Social Identity: Papers in Honour of Michael Walsh*. Canberra: Pacific Linguistics, pp. 297–318.

Turpin, M., Green, J., and Gibson, J. 2016. "Mustering up a Melody: An Anmatyerr Cattle Truck Song." In P. Austin, H. Koch, and J. Simpson (eds.), *Language, Land and Story in Australia: Essays in Honour of Luise Hercus*. London: The School of Oriental and African Studies, University of London, pp. 450–465.

Vallee, P. 2007. *God, Guns and Government on the Central Australian Frontier*. Canberra: Restoration.

van Toorn, P. 2006. *Writing Never Arrives Naked: Early Aboriginal Cultures of Writing in Australia*. Canberra: Aboriginal Studies Press.

Varutti, M. 2013. "Learning to Share Knowledge: Collaborative Projects in Taiwan." In V. Golding and W. Modest (eds.), *Museums and Communities: Curators, Collections and Collaboration*. London: Bloomsbury, pp. 59–78.

Veit, W.F. 2004. "Social Anthropology versus Cultural Anthropology: Baldwin Walter Spencer and Carl Friedrich Strehlow in Central Australia." In W.F. Veit (ed.), *The Struggle for Souls and Science: Constructing the Fifth Continent:*

German Missionaries and Scientists in Australia. Alice Springs: Northern Territory Government.

Veracini, L. 2011. "Introducing," *Settler Colonial Studies*, 1(1): pp. 1–12.

Verran, H., Christie, M., Anbins-King, B., Van Weeren, T., and Yunupingu, W. 2007. "Designing digital knowledge management tools with Aboriginal Australians," *Digital Creativity*, 18(3): pp. 129–142.

Voloder, L. 2008. "Autoethnographic challenges: Confronting self, field and home," *Australian Journal of Anthropology*, 19(1): pp. 27–40.

Wallace, K., and Lovell, J. 2009. *Listen Deeply, Let These Stories In.* Alice Springs, NT: IAD Press.

Walsh, F., Dobson, V., and Douglas, J. 2013. "Anpernirrentye: A framework for enhanced application of Indigenous ecological knowledge in natural resource management," *Ecology and Society*, 18(3).

Walsh, M. 1995. "'Tainted Evidence': Literacy and Traditional Knowledge in an Aboriginal Land Claim." In D. Eades (ed.), *Language in Evidence: Issues Confronting Aboriginal and Multicultural Australia*. Sydney: UNSW Press, pp. 97–124.

Warner, W.L. 1964. *A Black Civilization: A Social Study of an Australian Tribe.* New York: Harper and Row.

Watson, D. (ed.). 2017. *A Single Tree: Voices from the Bush.* Ringwood: Penguin Books Australia.

Watson, G. 1987. "Make me reflexive, but not yet: Strategies for managing essential reflexivity in ethnographic discourse," *Journal of Anthropological Research*, 43(1): pp. 29–41.

Webster, J.P., and John, T.A. 2010. "Preserving a space for cross-cultural collaborations: An account of insider/outsider issues," *Ethnography and Education* (2): pp. 175–191.

Weiner, J.F. 1999. "Culture in a sealed envelope: The concealment of Australian Aboriginal heritage and tradition in the Hindmarsh Island bridge affair," *Journal of the Royal Anthropological Institute*, 5: pp. 193–210.

The West Australian. 1937. "Fatal Spearing: Native to Stand Murder Trial," p. 17.

White, R. 2010. *The Middle Ground: Indians, Empires, and Republics in the Great Lakes Region, 1650–1815.* Leiden: Cambridge University Press.

Wild, S., and Jangala, T. 1990. "Central Australian Men's Love Song (yilpinji)." In R.M.W. Dixon and M. Duwell (eds.), *The Honey Ant Men's Love Song and Other Aboriginal Song Poems.* St. Lucia: University of Queensland Press, pp. 48–69.

Wilkins, D. 1989. "Mparntwe Arrernte (Aranda): Studies in the structure and semantics of grammar." www.researchgate.net/publication/291336710_Mparntwe_Arrernte_Aranda_Studies_in_the_structure_and_semantics_of_grammar

Wilkins, D. 1997. "Alternative Representations of Space: Arrernte Narratives in Sand." In M. Biemans and J. van de Weijer (eds.), *Proceedings of the CLS opening Academic Year 97/98.* Chicago: Chicago Linguistic Society.

Wilkins, D. 2001. "Glossary." In A. Petch, H. Morphy, and D.J. Mulvaney (eds.), *My Dear Spencer: The Letters of F. J. Gillen to Baldwin Spencer*. Flemington, Victoria: Hyland House Publishing Pty. Ltd., pp. 487–533.

Wilkins, D. 2002. "The Concept of Place among the Arrernte." In L. Hercus, F. Hodges, and J. Simpson (eds.), *The Land is a Map: Placenames of Indigenous Origin in Australia*. Canberra: Pandanus Books, Research School of Pacific and Asian Studies, The Australian National University.

Willis, P., and Cohen, H. 2001. *Catalogue of the Filmworks of TGH Strehlow, 1935–1962*. Sydney: University of Western Sydney and Strehlow Research Centre.

Willshire, W. 1884. *Police Report by Mounted Constable William Willshire to the Inspector of Police Port Augusta*. South Australian Police Historical Society.

Wilmot, H., and Morgan, R. 2010. "Written proof: The appropriation of genealogical records in contemporary Arrernte society," *Land, Rights, Laws: Issues of Native Title*, 4(5): pp. 1–12.

Wilson, B., and O'Brien, J. 2003. "'To infuse an universal terror': A reappraisal of the Coniston killings," *Aboriginal History*, 27.

Wirf, L., Campbell, A., and Rea, N. 2008. "Implications of gendered environmental knowledge in water allocation processes in central Australia," *Gender, Place, and Culture*, 15(5): pp. 505–518.

Wise, T. 1985. *The Self-Made Anthropologist: A Life of A.P. Elkin*. Sydney: Allen and Unwin.

Wolfe, P. 1991. "On being woken up: The dreamtime in anthropology and in Australian settler culture," *Comparative Studies in Society and History*, 33(2): pp. 197–224.

Wolfe, P. 1997. "Should the Subaltern Dream? 'Australian Aborigines' and the Problem of Ethnographic Ventriloquism." In S.C. Humphreys (ed.), *Cultures of Scholarship*. Ann Arbor: University of Michigan Press, pp. 57–96.

Wolfe, P. 1999. *Settler Colonialism and the Transformation of Anthropology*. London: Continuum.

Wolfe, P. 2006. "Settler colonialism and the elimination of the native," *Journal of Genocide Research*, 8(4): pp. 387–409.

Wootten, H. 1993. "The Commonwealth and Land Rights before Mabo: The Alice Springs dam and sacred sites," *Australian Quarterly*, 65(4): pp. 8–22.

Yanyuwa families, Bradley, J.J., and Cameron, N. 2003. *Forget about Flinders: A Yanyuwa Atlas of the South West Gulf of Carpentaria*. espace.library.uq.edu.au/view/UQ:40572

Young, E. 1987. "Resettlement and caring for the country: The Anmatyerre experience, *Aboriginal History*, 11(2): pp. 156–170.

Young, M. 2004. *Malinowski: Odyssey of an Anthropologist 1884–1920*. New Haven, CT: Yale University Press.

Index

Aboriginal and Torres Strait Islander Heritage Act, 216
Aboriginal Land Rights Act, 167
acts of remembrance, 197
Adorno, Theodor, 23, 240
agency, 2, 7–8, 99
Aileron Station, 34, 76, 119, 149
Akerman, Kim, 231
Akngeyetneme, Fred, 116
Akwerrperl, 28, 38, 120–123, 130
  objects, 224–225
  recording ceremonies of, 120–123, 152, 157
Albrecht, Paul, 140, 214
Alcoota Station, 27, 119, 124
alhernter (white people), 47, 130, 137, 140
Alice Springs, 10
Alyawarr, 114, 130, 134–135, 142
Alyelkelhayeka, Jim (Erlikilyika), 59
Amoonguna Aboriginal Settlement, 116, 129
Anderson, Chris, 15, 222
Anengkerr, 26, 28, 37, 130, 138, 168, 170, 173, 221; *see also* Dreaming
Angeles, Shaun, 1, 178–179, 216–217
Ankerr-areny, Friday Ngal, 134, 163, 221
Anmatjere Regional Council, 25

Anmatyerr, 9–10, 11, 57–58, 193
  cultural group, 1–2, 9–11, 33–36, 57–58, 193
  cultural transmission, 194, 229–234, 245
  employment, 36
  generational relationships and differences, 26, 37, 38, 40, 126, 151, 166, 174, 219, 232, 236, 245, 250
  historical practice, 17, 188, 193, 209, 251
  interactions with ethnographers, 57
  interactions with settler-colonists, 48–71
  mobility, 192, 194
  oral culture, 186–188
  perspectives on TGH Strehlow, 9–11, 129–153, 147–149, 151–153
  rights to the collection, 225
  singing, 123
  western education, 36, 185–186
Anna's Reservoir, 51
Anningie station, 167
Anningie tin mines, 164, 184
anpernerrenty, 33, 137
anthropology, 36, 243
  attitudes to, 29
  British tradition, 89
  German speaking tradition, 78, 86
  in land rights, 10, 36, 167, 243

anyenheng, 35, 84–85, 201; *see also* estates
Aranda Traditions, 93, 165
Arandic languages, 6, 34, 60
 distribution, 6, 99
 spoken by non-Indigenous peoples, 63, 141
Arawe-irreke (Rauwiraka), Nathanael, 77, 78, 178
archives, 7–9
Arleyekwarte, Tom Pengarte, 113, 117, 118, 149
Arrernte
 cultural group, 10
 interpreters and intermediaries, 59, 65–66, 70, 126
 language, 80
 Northern, 80
 perspectives on TGH Strehlow, 11, 116, 139, 151
 Western, 4, 78, 135, 138, 175
assimilation policies, 116, 124, 146
Atwel, 28, 170
Austin-Broos, Dianne, 13, 16, 203, 207
authenticity, 15, 91, 95, 108, 117, 118, 187, 215
Awengatherr, ceremony, 169

Barrett, Charles, 61, 63–64
Barrow Creek Telegraph Station, 58
 violence, 50, 103
Bastian, Adolf, 78
Battarbee, Rex, 82
Baudrillard, Jean, 231
Berndt, Ronald, 5, 83, 215
Bird, Tommy Mpetyan, 148
Black Hills, 102
Blackfellows' Bones, 52
Board for Anthropological Research, 109
 Cockatoo Creek Expedition, 64–65, 105
 Mt. Liebig Expedition, 80, 105

Boas, Franz, 4, 87
Bradley, John, 233
Breen, Gavan, 133
Bringhurst, Robert, 187
Bungalow, the, 111, 129, 132, 165

Cambridge Anthropological Expedition, 5
Campbell, Bruce, 119
Campbell, Donald Peltharr, 219
Campbell, Joseph, 87
Campbell, Thomas Draper, 80
Catholic Missions, 10, 13, 185; *see also* Santa Teresa Mission
Central Mount Stuart (Amakweng), 100
Ceremonial festivals
 Ajura, 109
 Werlatyatherre, 109, 111, 129, 145, 240
Ceremonial knowledge
 anxiety around, 232
 attenuated, 174–175
 and Christianity, 175
 as currency, 61, 64, 70
 shared, 60
 shared between generations, 151–153, 174, 176–177, 229–230
 traded with settler-colonists, 70
Ceremonies
 althart, 62–63, 178
 akernenty, 134, 166, 176
 change and continuity, 166
 honey ant (Yerramp), 114, 130, 134–135
Chisholm, Tony, 167
Christianity, 175–176, 206, 245, 252
 biblical texts, 186
Cleland, John Burton, 65, 80
Clifford, James, 73, 92
Cole, Peter, 178–179
collaborative ethnography, 37–38
collections, as productions, 9

Index

Coniston Station, 251
  shootings, 52, 66
Conway, Mort, 135
cultural heritage, 90, 183, 213–215
Cushing, Frank Hamilton, 73

Devitt, Jeanie, 148
dialogue, between researcher and researched, 8–9, 92, 156, 239
digital technology, 24–25, 235–236
Diyari, 75
Dow Dow, Mickey Akwerre, 65–66, 80, 94–95, 100
Dreaming, 3
  associated sacred objects, 221
  baby (arathap), 138–139
  conception, 201
  defining the, 29
  fish (irrpenng), 168
  history and, 29
  inherited, 200, 203
  native currant (ahakey), 206
  place animated by, 194
  sand goanna (arlewatyerr), 195–196
Dunlop, Ian, 108, 157

Elymann, Erhard, 57
equal wages, 124
estates (*see also* anyenheng)
  concept of, 35, 84–85, 101
  no longer being held by owners, 231
  songs travelling across, 171–173
  songs and ceremonies related to, 176–177
ethnography, 17
  personal accrual of knowledge, 92–93
Eurocentrism, 90

Fabian, Johannes, 24, 95, 122
films of ceremony
  reactions to, 27–28, 43, 162–164
  Strehlow's documentation of, 41

Firth, Raymond, 76, 83, 87
FitzHerbert, John Aloysius, 79
'following' ceremonial knowledge, 20, 29, 133–134, 171, 175
Frazer, James George, 89
Freud, Sigmund, 87
Frobenius Institute, 87
frontier violence, 50–54, 184, 189
Fry, Henry Kenneth, 80
Functionalism, 84–85

Galt-Smith, Brett, 222
Gason, M.C. Samuel, 51
Geismar, Haidy, 15, 140
gendered knowledge, 11–14
genealogies, 10, 199–209
Giese, Harry, 150
Gillen, Francis James, 5, 59–60, 73, 79, 85, 93, 99, 109, 112, 147, 235, 247
Green, Jennifer, 64
Gurindji, 251

Haasts Bluff Settlement, 114, 132
Haddon, Alfred Cort, 5
Hagan, Martin, 178–179
Haines, Jimmy Ngwarray, 62, 102, 159, 176, 194, 198, 202, 252
hand sign and gesture, 98
Hanson River, 49, 189, 190, 192, 194, 195, 196, 198
Hartwig, Mervyn, 50, 55, 204
Heffernan, Bill, 54, 62
Heffernan, Charlie (Artetyerwenguny), 119, 178, 185, 189, 200, 233, 242
Heffernan, Malcolm Pengart, 21, 183–185, 188–191, 199, 200, 204, 233, 234, 242, 252
Herder, Johann Gottfried, 86
Hermannsburg Mission, 4, 75, 78, 91, 132, 135, 145, 214
Hill, Barry, 74, 111

history, 17
  ethnography informing, 17
  oral history, 131
  relationship to Dreaming, 29
Hokari, Minoru, 17, 251
Honey ant (Yerramp), ceremony, 114, 130, 134–135

Ilewerr (Lake Lewis), 132, 172, 178, 185, 195
Ilkewartn, 145
Indigenous Knowledge Centre, 25
Indigenous/non-indigenous binary, 14, 15, 248
Ingkaparleparl, 184, 189–191, 194, 197
Ingkart, 131
  Strehlow as, 114, 125, 135–136
  Tindale using the concept of, 68–70
ingwa (night), songs, 124–125
initiation ceremony, 124, 176, 190–191, 195, 221, 236
Inkamala, Mark, 138
intercultural, 15–16, 185

Jackson, Michael D., 3, 14, 16, 32, 47–48, 136
Jay Creek Aboriginal Settlement, 97, 132
Jensen, Adolf Ellegard, 87
Jung, Carl, 87

Kahn, Miriam, 197
Kaltyirrpek, Paddy, 104–105, 148
Kaltyirrpek, Tommy, 104–105
Kemarr, Ned, 124–125, 142
Kemarr, Paddy, 29, 33, 38, 62, 102, 113, 132, 146, 161, 163, 164, 170, 173, 194–196, 197, 205, 221, 241
  challenging authority of archive, 197–198
  on defining the Anmatyerr, 11
  memory of Strehlow, 129
  singing with recordings, 173
  story of Nugget Morton, 53–54
Kenny, Anna, 13, 78, 87, 187
King Brown Snake (ikwelengk), songs, 142–143
knowledge, ethnography and the production of, 8–9, 24
Koop, A.E., 190, 198
Kramer, Ernest, 56, 65, 80, 95, 100, 222
  remembered by the Anmatyerr, 69
Kwekaty, Reilly, 120
kwertengerl, 119, 136, 143, 169, 202, 205, 225
  museums as, 225–229

Lassiter, Luke, 37
Layard, John, 140
literate culture, 185, 208, 250
Lock, Annie, 61–62
Ltarerlkek, Tom, 120, 125, 141, 145
Luritja, 78
Lutheran Mission, 4, 141
  association with the Anmatyerr, 26, 176
  literacy, 185–186
  trade in sacred objects, 221
Lynch, Huckitta, 51, 155, 168, 172, 175, 178, 178–179
Lywenge, Tom, 97, 100–102, 111, 117, 126, 221, 240, 252
  assisting with song translation, 102
  classificatory father to Strehlow, 104
  comments on trade of sacred objects, 103, 221
  refusing to relay story to Strehlow, 106

Macfie, Adam, 28, 227
Mahood, Kim, 115
Malinowski, Bronislaw, 78

Malpangk, Bob, 160, 202
mapping
  of Arandic language regions, 80
  of sites, 11, 118
Marcuse, Herbert, 91
McCoy, Billy, 116
Mclean, Mick Irinyili, 141
McMillan, Martin, 1, 12–13
McNamara, Ronnie, 51, 131–132, 141, 152, 168, 175–176, 178–179, 252
Melbourne Museum, 1, 59, 151, 192, 219, 226
merek-artwey, 136, 169, 200, 231
Merlan, Francesca, 167, 187, 244
Michaels, Eric, 13, 14
Moar, Thomas, 56
mobility, 124, 192
Morphy, Howard, 228, 237, 246
Morton, John, 136, 212
Moyle, Richard, 177
Mpetyan, Albie, 146, 163
Mpetyan, Archie, 134, 221
Mt Peake Station, 100–101, 103
Mulga Bore, 147
Murray, M.C. William George, 53, 61
museums, 214
  Anmatyerr understandings of, 68–69
  British Museum, 82, 214
  ethnographic collections, 211
  Indigenous control of collections, 213
  as kwertengerl (managers), 225–229
  for male objects, 215
  policies and practices, 224
  preservation, 223, 228
  repatriation, 212, 218, 219, 230, 235, 245
  role in cultural transmission, 230, 232, 248
  transformation of, 237
Myers, Fred, 29, 134, 227

Napperby Station, 102, 124, 132, 152, 171, 185, 207, 227
Native Affairs, 74, 81, 114–115
Native American Graves Protection and Repatriation Act, 219
Nelson, Ray Penangk, 147
Ngal, Kwetyaney, 159–161, 163, 165, 206
Ngal, Silas, 53, 69
Ngkwarlerlanem, 135
non-indigenous and Indigenous relationships, 31, 115
Northern Territory Library, 25

Ong, Walter, 187
oral culture, 186–188, 206, 208, 250

pastoralism, Anmatyerr relations with, 35, 175, 206, 230
Payne, Harold Mpetyan, 9, 125–126, 141–146, 169, 230, 245
Penangk, Eric, 28, 56, 149, 193, 194, 221–222, 231, 232
Petri, Helmut, 87
Petyarr, Jacob, 64
phenomenology, 17
photographs
  restrictions on taking, 116
  treated as sacred objects, 235
  used in elicitation, 42–43
Pine Hill Station, 56, 202
Pink, Olive Muriel, 95, 203
Pintupi, 133, 227
postcolonial studies, 15
Presely, Don Pengart, 141, 161, 166, 170–171, 174, 204
protectionism, 124
psychoanalysis, 87–88
Purvis, Dick, 125

Rain
  ceremony, 160, 163, 164, 166
  Dreaming, 159–160

Rayekwarr, Tom, 120, 125
relationality, 15, 248, 251
repatriation, 1, 212, 218, 219, 230, 235, 245
researcher/researched relationship, 9, 14, 23–24, 98
   Indigenous and non-Indigenous, 31
   Insider/outsider binary, 31
'Reso' Tour to Central Australia, 60–61, 109
restricted cultural knowledge, 11–12, 26, 36, 214, 245–247
   photography and, 116
Ricketts, William, 82, 114
Rltwamparwenguny, Sambo, 149
Roheim, Geza, 87
Rubuntja, Bob Penangke, 111–116, 117, 118, 126, 129, 133, 135, 136, 138, 149, 216, 240, 252
Rubuntja, Wenten, 138, 216
Ryan's Well, 119

sacred objects, trade in, 67, 68, 103, 221–222, 224–225
salvage ethnography, 5, 244
Santa Teresa Mission, 13, 25, 185, 233
Sapir, Edward, 5, 87
Scrutton, Tony Ngwarray, 26–27, 150, 156
secret/sacred, knowledge, 13–14, 69, 93, 106, 131, 147, 156, 177
self-determination, 124
settler primitivism, 82–83, 90, 96
Skull Creek, 50
song recordings, 41, 179
   value of, 179–181
songlines, 86, 101, 133, 169, 170, 171
songs
   althart, 177
   anmanty, 178
   contemporary knowledge of, 175
   dangerous, 245–246
   in everyday life, 180
   fish (irrpenng), 171, 173
   grey teal (pelyakw), 251
   to heal, 179
   ikwelengk, 142–144, 145
   ilpenty, 177
   initiation ceremony, 178
   mulga seed, 171, 174
   night, 125
   related to Angenty, 171
   relationship to place, 170
   to stop the wind, 123
   transcribing, 101, 145
Songs of Central Australia, 88–89, 93, 110, 159
South Australian Museum, 104, 222
Spencer, Walter Baldwin, 5, 52, 73, 78, 79, 85, 93, 99, 109, 112, 247
spiritual conception, 85, 106, 205
   inherited, 203
   listed on genealogies, 201
   site, 125, 204
   site of TGH Strehlow, 137–138
   tradition changing, 206–208
Stafford, Alice, 55
Stafford, Lesley Pwerrerl, 148, 178–179
Stafford, Randall, 55
Stanner, W.E.H., 95
Stirling Station, 103
Stoler, Anne, 7, 8
Stoll, Gary, 140, 145
Strehlow, Bertha, 97
Strehlow, Carl, 4, 75, 79
Strehlow, Frieda, 4, 75
Strehlow, Kathleen, 5, 215
Strehlow, T.G.H., 130, 204
   Aboriginal perspectives on, 11–12
   accrual of people's knowledge, 92–93, 122, 248
   accused of cultural theft, 150

associated with a historical period, 146, 177
associations with Christianity, 132
biography, 3–7, 73–76
ceremonial festivals, 106–111
concept of 'inner cycles,' 121, 152
conception of culture, 90–91
on conception sites, 204
contribution to anthropology, 82–86
contribution to linguistics, 80–81
denizen of the ceremonial ground, 114
'disowned' by people, 125
films made by, 108
focus on collecting texts, 88, 91, 214
focus on vulnerable repertoires, 177
genealogies or 'family trees,' 199–209
influence of German anthropology on, 86
language abilities, 141
mapping work, 11, 80, 118, 192
material culture collection, 104, 214
orthography of Arrernte, 26, 205
participant in ceremonies, 121–122, 137, 140
patrol officer, 184, 190, 204
personal conception site, 76, 137–138, 247
perspectives on TGH Strehlow, 147–149
plans for his collection, 213
protection of sites, 120
regional scope, 130, 159, 241
singing, 122, 144–145
subsection affiliation of, 76, 137, 139
thoughts on national identity, 82, 215
transcription of songs by, 101, 145
views on younger generations, 125–126, 142, 214
Strehlow collection
analysis of, 38–39, 40–45
Arrernte perspectives on, 216–217, 246
as a co-production, 239
interpreted by Anmatyerr men, 172
as testimony, 245
Strehlow Research Centre, 1, 7, 11, 13, 21, 25, 36, 147, 151, 155, 157, 160, 183, 228, 237
Aboriginal involvement with, 211–212, 222
access to genealogies, 200
Arrernte views on, 216
policies of repatriation, 211–213
as a restricted place, 13
Strehlow Research Centre Act 1988, 212, 218
Strehlow Research Foundation, 214, 215
Strong, Archibald, 79
Stuart, John McDouall, 49
Stuart, Rupert Max Kngwarraye, 97–98, 115, 126, 133
Sutton, Peter, 33, 56, 165, 228

The Golden Bough, 89
Thomas, Nicolas, 82
Thompson, Tommy, 134
Ti Tree Township, 25, 34, 61, 206
Tilmouth, Bobby, 169
Tilmouth, Ken, 9, 27, 52, 120–121, 122, 125, 141–146, 151, 156, 158, 170, 214, 226, 229, 240, 245, 252
conception site, 125
described by Strehlow, 213
on repatriation, 224–225
Tindale, Norman, 66–67, 95, 247
remembered by the Anmatyerr, 69
Tjalkabota, Moses, 77, 100

tradition, 188, 234
Turner, Margaret Kemarr, 33, 105

Uneynt, Tom, 119, 149, 150
Urarty (Jacky), 100–102
urrempel, 2, 133
  defining the, 133
  festival, 53, 109, 117, 121, 240, 247
  performance as exchange with settlers, 69–71

Virchow, Rudolph, 78

Wangkangurru, 141
Wapiti, 77
Warlapanpa, 158–160, 165

Warlpiri, 58, 136, 184
Werlaty, Mick Pengart, 12, 28, 120, 122, 124, 151, 214, 252
Wheeler, Tom Tjungala, 66
White, Sandy Penangk, 120, 122, 140
Williams, Tom, 133
women
  perspectives of, 12–13
  and restricted male knowledge, 43, 116, 132, 217–218
Woodgreen Station, 102

Yambah Station, 185
Yerramp, George Pengart, 120
Yerramp, George Rlwengapeltyey, 119, 149

www.ingramcontent.com/pod-product-compliance
Ingram Content Group UK Ltd.
Pitfield, Milton Keynes, MK11 3LW, UK
UKHW041916140426
5217IPUK00013B/174